Western Wind

Western wind, when will thou blow,
The small rain down can rain?
Christ! if my love were in my arms,
And I in my bed again!

Western

RANDOM HOUSE NEW YORK

Western Wind an introduction to poetry

John Frederick Nims
UNIVERSITY OF FLORIDA

 Published in the United States by Random House, Inc. and simultaneously in Canada by Random House of Canada Limited, Toronto.

Library of Congress Cataloging in Publication Data

Nims, John Frederick, 1913—
Western wind.
1. Poetry—History and criticism. I. Title.
PN1111.N5 809'.1 73-19764
ISBN 0-394-31231-7

Manufactured in the United States of America. Composed by Cherry Hill Composition, Pennsauken, N.J.

Cover by Jeheber & Peace.

Design by James M. Wall.

9876

PHOTO CREDITS

P. 43: Photo by Edwin J. Gross; p. 76: Wide World Photos; p. 136: Windsor Castle Royal Library; p. 173: Courtesy, The Art Institute of Chicago, Clarence Buckingham Collection; pp. 185 and 190: From *The Expression of the Emotions in Man and Animals,* by Charles Darwin. No. 2 of Plate V and No. 1 of Plate IV. University of Chicago Press © 1872; p. 198: American Museum of Natural History; p. 209: Black Star; p. 214: Marburg—Art Reference Bureau; p. 250: Oeffentliche Kunstsammlung Basel; p. 254: *The New York Times*; p. 281: The Bettmann Archive; p. 292: Alinari—Art Reference Bureau; p. 348: V. B. Scheffer/National Audubon Society; p. 351: The Metropolitan Museum of Art, Fletcher Fund, 1925; p. 358: From *Snow Crystals* by W. A. Bentley and W. H. Humphreys; p. 385: The New York Public Library, Picture Collection; p. 393: Courtesy, The Art Institute of Chicago; p. 410: Fogg Art Museum, Harvard; p. 414: University of Connecticut Photo; p. 416: British Museum; p. 429: Redrawn from *Leaves of Grass,* by Walt Whitman, © 1855; p. 440: British Museum.

Acknowledgments

Kingsley Amis, "A Note on Wyatt" from *A Case of Samples.* Copyright © 1956 by Kingsley Amis. Reprinted by permission of Curtis Brown Ltd.

A. R. Ammons, "Winter Scene" from *Selected Poems.* Copyright © 1968 by Cornell University. Reprinted by permission of Cornell University Press. 5 lines from "Raft" from *Expressions of Sea Level.* Copyright © 1963 by A. R. Ammons. Reprinted by permission of the Ohio State University Press.

Anonymous, "Brief Autumnal" from *Poems from the Greek Anthology,* translated by Dudley Fitts. Copyright 1938, 1941, © 1956 by New Directions Publishing Corporation. Reprinted by permission of New Directions Publishing Corporation.

Anonymous, "The Animal Runs, It Passes, It Dies," 17 lines from "Song for the Elephant Hunt," and "Slowly, Slowly" from *Primitive Song* by C. M. Bowra. Copyright © 1962 by C. M. Bowra. Reprinted by permission of The World Publishing Company and George Weidenfeld and Nicolson.

Anonymous, "There Was a Man of Double Deed" from *The Oxford Dictionary of Nursery Rhymes,* edited by Iona and Peter Opie, 1951. Reprinted by permission of The Clarendon Press.

Jean Arp, "What the Violins Sing in their Baconfat Bed," translated by John Frederick Nims. Copyright ©1974 by John Frederick Nims. Printed by permission of Viking Press, Inc., publisher of *Arp on Arp,* edited by Marcel Jean, translated by Joachim Neugroschel.

W. H. Auden, "Musée des Beaux Arts" from *Collected Shorter Poems 1927–1957.* Copyright 1940 and renewed 1968 by W. H. Auden. "Doom is Darker and Deeper" and "The Wanderer" from *Collected Shorter Poems 1927–1957.* Copyright 1934; renewed 1962 by W. H. Auden. "Moon Landing" from *Epistle to a Godson.* Copyright © 1969 by W. H. Auden. "The Shield of Achilles" from *Collected Shorter Poems 1927–1957.* Copyright 1952 by W. H. Auden. 18 lines from *The Age of Anxiety.* Reprinted by permission of Random House, Inc. and Faber and Faber Ltd.

Hilaire Belloc, "On His Books" from *Complete Verse.* Published by Gerald Duckworth & Co. Ltd. Reprinted by permission of A. D. Peters and Company.

John Berryman, "Sigh As It Ends" from *Berryman's Sonnets.* Copyright © 1952, 1967 by John Berryman. "He Resigns" from *Delusions, Etc.* Copyright © 1969, 1971 by John Berryman. "The Dream Songs 4, 22" from *The Dream Songs.* Copyright © 1959, 1962, 1963, 1964, 1966, 1967, 1968, 1969 by John Berryman. Reprinted by permission of Farrar, Straus & Giroux, Inc.

Elizabeth Bishop, "Sestina," "Filling Station," "The Fish," and "12 O'Clock News" from *Complete Poems.* Copyright © 1940, 1955, 1956, 1969, 1973 by Elizabeth Bishop. Reprinted by permission of Farrar, Straus & Giroux, Inc.

Richard Brautigan, "Gee, You're So Beautiful That It's Starting to Rain" from *The Pill Versus the Springhill Mine Disaster.* Copyright © 1968 by Richard Brautigan. Reprinted by permission of Seymour Lawrence/Delacorte Press.

Gwendolyn Brooks, "The Sonnet-Ballad" from *The World of Gwendolyn Brooks.* Copyright 1949 by Gwendolyn Brooks Blakey. "We Real Cool" from

The World of Gwendolyn Brooks. Copyright © 1959 by Gwendolyn Brooks. Reprinted by permission of Harper & Row, Publishers, Inc.

Gray Burr, "Eye" from *A Choice of Attitudes.* Copyright © 1969 by Gray Burr. Reprinted by permission of Wesleyan University Press.

Helen Chasin, "City Pigeons" from *Coming Close.* Copyright © 1968 by Yale University. Reprinted by permission of Yale University Press.

John Ciardi, "Most Like an Arch This Marriage" from *I Marry You: A Sheaf of Love Poems.* Published by Rutgers University Press, 1958. Reprinted by permission of the author.

John Clare, "Remember Dear Mary" from *The Later Poems of John Clare,* edited by E. Robinson and G. Summerfield. Published by Manchester University Press, 1964. Reprinted by permission of Manchester University Press.

Frances Cornford, "To a Fat Lady Seen from the Train" from *Collected Poems.* Published by Cresset Press, 1954. Reprinted by permission of Barrie & Jenkins Ltd.

Adelaide Crapsey, "The Warning" from *Verse.* Copyright 1922 by Algernon S. Crapsey and renewed 1950 by The Adelaide Crapsey Foundation. Reprinted by permission of Alfred A. Knopf, Inc.

Stephen Crane, "A Man Said to the Universe" and "Think as I Think" from *The Collected Poems of Stephen Crane.* Published by Random House, Inc. Reprinted by permission of Random House, Inc.

Robert Creeley, "Four" from *Pieces.* Copyright © 1969 by Robert Creeley. Reprinted by permission of Charles Scribner's Sons.

Saint John of the Cross, "The Dark Night" from *The Poems of Saint John of the Cross,* translated by John Frederick Nims. Copyright © 1959, 1968 by John Frederick Nims. Reprinted by permission of Grove Press, Inc.

J. V. Cunningham, 4 lines from "Doctor Drink" from *The Exclusions of a Rhyme: Poems and Epigrams.* Copyright © 1960 by J. V. Cunningham. Reprinted by permission of The Swallow Press.

E. E. Cummings, "me up at does" and 4 lines from "since feeling is first" from *Complete Poems 1913–1962.* Copyright © 1963 by Marion Morehouse Cummings. "wherelings whenlings," "anyone lived in a pretty how town," and 7 lines from "as freedom is a breakfastfood" from *Complete Poems 1913–1962.* Copyright 1940 by E. E. Cummings; renewed 1968 by Marion Morehouse Cummings. "if everything happens that can't be done" from *Complete Poems 1913–1962.* Copyright 1944 by E. E. Cummings; renewed 1972 by Nancy Andrews. "(im)c-a-t(mo)" from *Complete Poems 1913–1962.* Copyright 1950 by E. E. Cummings. "Chansons Innocentes, I" from *Complete Poems 1913–1962.* Copyright 1923, 1951 by E. E. Cummings. Reprinted by permission of Harcourt Brace Jovanovich, Inc.

Peter Davison, "The Firstling" from *The Breaking of the Day.* Copyright 1954, copyright © 1958 by Peter Davison. Reprinted by permission of Yale University Press.

Robert Desnos, "The Day It Was Night" (Un jour qu'il faisait nuit) from *Corps et Biens.* Reprinted by permission of Editions Gallimard. The translation in this book is by John Frederick Nims.

H. D., "Oread" from *Selected Poems.* Reprinted by permission of Norman Holmes Pearson, owner of the copyright.

James Dickey, "Adultery" from *Poems 1957–1967.* Copyright © 1966 by James Dickey. Reprinted by permission of Wesleyan University Press.

Emily Dickinson, "My Life had Stood—a Loaded Gun" and "After Great Pain a Formal Feeling Comes" from *The Complete Poems of Emily Dickinson,* edited by Thomas H. Johnson. Copyright © 1957 by Mary L. Hampson. "Wild Nights," "'Hope' Is the Thing with Feathers," and "A Narrow Fellow in the Grass" from *The Complete Poems of Emily Dickinson,* edited by Thomas H. Johnson. Published by Little, Brown and Company. Two lines of "My Life had Stood—a Loaded Gun" from *The Complete Poems of Emily Dickinson,* edited by Thomas H. Johnson. Copyright 1951, 1955 by The President and Fellows of Harvard College. Reprinted by the permission of the publishers and Trustees of Amherst College and Little, Brown and Company.

Reinhard Dohl, "Pattern Poem with an Elusive Intruder" from *An Anthology of Concrete Poetry,* edited by Emmett Williams. Copyright © 1967 by the Something Else Press. All rights reserved. Reprinted by permission of the publisher.

Ronald Duncan, "Written on a Girl's Table-Napkin at Wiesbaden" from *Unpopular Poems.* Reprinted by permission of David Higham Associates, Ltd.

Alan Dugan, "Tribute to Kafka for Someone Taken" from *Poems.* Copyright © 1961 by Alan Dugan. Reprinted by permission of Yale University Press.

T. S. Eliot, "Preludes," "New Hampshire," 9 lines from "Ash Wednesday," 2 lines from "Rhapsody on a Windy Night," 5 lines from "The Love Song of J. Alfred Prufrock," 4 lines from "Gerontion," 2 lines from "La Figlia che Piange," and 6 lines from "Burnt Norton" from *Collected Poems 1909–1962.* Copyright © 1963 by Harcourt Brace Jovanovich, Inc.; copyright © 1963, 1964 by T. S. Eliot. Reprinted by permission of Harcourt Brace Jovanovich, Inc. and Faber and Faber Ltd.

D. J. Enright, 12 lines from "The Typewriter Revolution" from *The Typewriter Revolution.* Copyright © 1971 by D. J. Enright; copyright © 1972 by Chatto and Windus as "An ew erra" from *Daughters of Earth.* Reprinted by permission of Library Press Incorporated and Chatto and Windus.

Dave Etter, "Romp" from *Go Read the River.* Copyright © 1966 by the University of Nebraska Press. Reprinted by permission of the author and the University of Nebraska Press.

Kenneth Fearing, "Love, 20¢ the First Quarter Mile" and "Yes, the Agency Can Handle That" from *New and Selected Poems.* Published by Indiana University Press, 1956. Reprinted by permission of Indiana University Press.

Edward Field, "Curse of the Cat Woman" from *Variety Photoplays.* Copyright © 1967 by Edward Field. Reprinted by permission of Grove Press, Inc.

Ian Hamilton Finlay, "Green Waters" from *An Anthology of Concrete Poetry.* Copyright © 1967 by the Something Else Press. All rights reserved. Reprinted by permission of the publisher.

Robert Fitzgerald, "Cobb Would Have Caught It" from *In The Rose of Time.* Copyright 1943 by Robert Fitzgerald. Reprinted by permission of New Directions Publishing Corporation.

Robert Frost, "Once by the Pacific" and "The Subverted Flower" from *The Poetry of Robert Frost,* edited by Edward Connery Lathem. Copyright 1928, copyright © 1969 by Holt, Rinehart and Winston, Inc; copyright 1942, copyright © 1956 by Robert Frost; copyright © 1970 by Lesley Frost Ballantine. 3 lines from "The Vantage Point" and 6 lines from "A Masque of Reason" from *The Poetry of Robert Frost,* edited by Edward Connery Lathem. Copyright 1923, 1934, copyright © 1969 by Holt, Rinehart and Winston, Inc; copyright 1945, 1951, copyright © 1962 by Robert Frost; copyright © 1973 by Lesley Frost Ballantine. "A Soldier," "Acquainted with the Night," 17 lines from "My Butterfly," "Dust of Snow," "Neither Out Far Nor In Deep," and " 'Out, Out—' " from *The Poetry of Robert Frost,* edited by Edward Connery Lathem. Copyright 1916, 1923, 1928, 1934, copyright © 1969 by Holt, Rinehart and Winston, Inc; copyright 1936, 1944, 1951, copyright © 1956 and 1962 by Robert Frost; copyright © 1964 by Lesley Frost Ballantine. Reprinted by permission of Holt, Rinehart and Winston, Inc.

Isabella Gardner, "Gimboling" from *West of Childhood.* Copyright © 1965 by Isabella Gardner Tate. Reprinted by permission of Houghton Mifflin Company.

Brewster Ghiselin, "Rattler, Alert" and 6 lines from "Waking" from *Against the Circle.* Copyright 1946 by E. P. Dutton & Co., Inc. Reprinted by permission of E. P. Dutton & Co., Inc.

Andrew Glaze, "Zeppelin" from *Damned Ugly Children.* Copyright © 1963, 1965, 1966 by Andrew Glaze. Reprinted by permission of Trident Press, a division of Simon & Schuster, Inc.

Eugen Gomringer, "Wind" from *Concrete Poetry,* edited by Mary Ellen Solt. Copyright © 1969 by Indiana University Press. Reprinted by permission of Indiana University Press.

Robert Graves, "The Face in the Mirror," "Spoils," "The Persian Version," "The Thieves," and "Counting the Beats" from *Collected Poems.* 4 lines from "Rocky Acres" from *Collected Poems.* Copyright © 1958, 1961 by Robert Graves. Published by Doubleday & Company. Reprinted by permission of Collins-Knowlton-Wing, Inc.

Ronald Gross, "Barbie-Doll Goes to College" from *Pop Poems.* Copyright © 1967 by Ronald Gross. Reprinted by permission of Simon & Schuster, Inc.

Arlo Guthrie, 2 lines from *The Motorcycle Song.* Copyright © 1967, 1969 by Appleseed Music Inc. All rights reserved. Used by permission.

Ramon Guthrie, 6 lines from "Scherzo for a Dirge" from *Asbestos Phoenix.* Copyright © 1968 by Ramon Guthrie. Reprinted by permission of Funk & Wagnalls Publishing Company, Inc.

Donald Hall, "Woolworth's" from *The Alligator Bride.* Copyright © 1968 by Donald Hall. Reprinted by permission of Harper & Row, Publishers, Inc.

Thomas Hardy, "The Ruined Maid" and 5 lines from "And There was a Great Calm" from *Collected Poems.* Copyright 1925 by Macmillan Publishing Co., Inc. Reprinted by permission of Macmillan Publishing Co., Inc. and The Macmillan Co. of Canada Ltd.

Jim Harrison, "Ghazal XXVI" from *Outlyer and Ghazals.* Copyright © 1969, 1971 by Jim Harrison. Reprinted by permission of Simon & Schuster, Inc.

John Hart, Two "B. C." cartoons. Reprinted by permission of John Hart and Field Enterprises, Inc.

Robert Hayden, "O Daedalus, Fly Away Home" from *Selected Poems.* Copyright © 1966 by Robert Hayden. Reprinted by permission of October House, Inc.

Anthony Hecht, "The End of the Weekend" from *The Hard Hours.* Copyright © 1959 by Anthony E. Hecht. Reprinted by permission of Atheneum Publishers. Originally appeared in *Hudson Review.*

Mary Thacher Higginson, "In Shining Groups" from *How to Know the Wild Flowers* by Mrs. William Starr Dana. Published by Dover Publications, Inc., 1963. (A revised version of a 1900 revision of a work published by Scribner's in 1893.) Reprinted by permission of Dover Publications, Inc.

John Hollander, "Swan and Shadow" from *Types of Shape*. Copyright © 1966 by John Hollander. Reprinted by permission of Atheneum Publishers. Originally appeared in *Poetry*.

M. Carl Holman, "Notes for a Movie Script" from *American Negro Poetry*, edited by Arna Bontemps. Published by Hill and Wang, 1963. Reprinted by permission of the author.

A. D. Hope, "The Lingam and the Yoni" from *Collected Poems 1930–1965*. Copyright © 1963, 1966 by A. D. Hope. All rights reserved. 2 lines from "Totentanz: The Coquette" from *Collected Poems*. Copyright © 1960 by A. D. Hope. Reprinted by permission of The Viking Press, Inc.

Lawrence Hope, "Youth" from *Selected Love Lyrics*. Reprinted by permission of William Heinemann Ltd.

Richard Howard, 6 lines from "Private Drive" from *Damages*. Copyright © 1967 by Richard Howard. Reprinted by permission of Wesleyan University Press.

A. E. Housman, "I To My Perils" from *The Collected Poems of A. E. Housman*. Copyright © 1964 by Robert E. Symons. "I Hoed and Trenched and Weeded," "With Rue My Heart Is Laden," "Loitering With a Vacant Eye," "Along the Field as We Came By," and 6 lines from "The True Lover" from "A Shropshire Lad" (Authorized Edition) from *The Collected Poems of A. E. Housman*. Copyright 1939, 1940, © 1965 by Holt, Rinehart and Winston, Inc; copyright © 1967, 1968 by Robert E. Symons. "The Oracles" from *The Collected Poems of A. E. Housman*. Copyright 1922 by Holt, Rinehart and Winston, Inc.; copyright 1950 by Barclays Bank Ltd. Reprinted by permission of Holt, Rinehart and Winston, Inc., The Society of Authors as the literary representative of the Estate of A. E. Housman, and Jonathan Cape Ltd.

Langston Hughes, "Dream Variations" from *Selected Poems*. Copyright 1926 by Alfred A. Knopf, Inc.; renewed 1954 by Langston Hughes. Reprinted by permission of the publisher.

H. E. Huntley, illustration, "Spiral Pattern in the Sunflower" from *The Divine Proportion*. Published by Dover Publications, Inc., 1970. Reprinted by permission of Dover Publications, Inc.

David Ignatow, "Simultaneously" from *Figures of the Human*. Copyright © 1962 by David Ignatow. Reprinted by permission of Wesleyan University Press.

Randall Jarrell, "The Knight, Death, and the Devil" from *The Complete Poems*. Copyright 1951 by Randall Jarrell, copyright © 1969 by Mrs. Randall Jarrell. Reprinted by permission of Farrar, Straus & Giroux, Inc.

Robinson Jeffers, "The Purse-Seine" from *Selected Poetry of Robinson Jeffers*. Copyright 1937 and renewed 1965 by Donnan Jeffers and Garth Jeffers. Reprinted by permission of Random House, Inc.

Ted Joans, "The .38" from *Black Pow-Wow*. Copyright © 1964, 1969 by Ted Joans. Reprinted by permission of the author's representative, Gunther Stuhlmann.

Allen Katzman, "The Rhododendron Plant" from *The Immaculate*. Copyright © 1970 by Allen Katzman. Reprinted by permission of Doubleday & Company, Inc.

X. J. Kennedy, "B Negative" from *Nude Descending a Staircase*. Copyright © 1960 by X. J. Kennedy. "Loose Woman" from *Growing Into Love*. Copyright © 1969 by X. J. Kennedy. Reprinted by permission of Doubleday & Company, Inc.

Hugh Kingsmill, extract from "What, Still Alive at Twenty-Two" from *The Table of Truth.* Published by Jarrold, London.

Kenneth Koch, 8 lines from "Ko, or A Season On Earth" from *Ko, or A Season On Earth.* Copyright © 1959 by Kenneth Koch. Reprinted by permission of Grove Press, Inc.

Maxine Kumin, "The Hermit Wakes to Bird Sounds" from *Up Country.* Copyright © 1972 by Maxine Kumin. Reprinted by permission of Harper & Row, Publishers, Inc. Originally appeared in *The New Yorker.*

R. D. Laing, 27 lines from "Jill" from *Knots.* Copyright © 1970 by The R. D. Laing Trust. Reprinted by permission of Pantheon Books/A Division of Random House, Inc., Tavistock Publications Limited, and the author.

D. H. Lawrence, "To Women, As Far as I'm Concerned," "Piano," "The Piano," "Mystic," and 2 lines from "Letter from Town, on a Grey Morning in March" from *The Complete Poems of D. H. Lawrence,* edited by Vivian de Sola Pinto and F. Warren Roberts. Copyright © 1964, 1971 by Angelo Ravagli & C. M. Weekley, Executors of the Estate of Frieda Lawrence Ravagli. Reprinted by permission of The Viking Press.

Denise Levertov, 6 lines from "A Sequence" from *Jacob's Ladder.* Copyright © 1961 by Denise Levertov Goodman. 3 lines from "The Take Off" and 3 lines from "Another Journey" from *With Eyes At the Back of our Heads.* Copyright © 1959 by Denise Levertov Goodman. Reprinted by permission of New Directions Publishing Corporation.

Federico García Lorca, "Sleepwalkers' Ballad" from *Sappho to Valéry: Poems in Translation,* by John Frederick Nims. Published by Rutgers University Press, 1971. Reprinted by permission of Rutgers University Press. Original Spanish version copyright 1955 by New Directions Publishing Corporation. By permission of New Directions Publishing Corporation, Agents for the Estate of Federico García Lorca.

Lucilius, "On Apis the Prizefighter" from *Poems from the Greek Anthology,* translated by Dudley Fitts. Copyright 1938, 1941, © 1956 by New Directions Corporation. Reprinted by permission of New Directions Publishing Corporation.

Robert Lowell, "Skunk Hour" from *Life Studies.* Copyright © 1958 by Robert Lowell. Reprinted by permission of Farrar, Straus & Giroux, Inc.

Thomas Lux, "My Grandmother's Funeral" from *Memory's Handgrenade.* Copyright © 1972 by Thomas Lux. Reprinted by permission of the author and Pym-Randall Press.

Archibald Macleish, "You, Andrew Marvell" and "Eleven" from *The Collected Poems of Archibald Macleish.* Copyright © 1962 by Archibald Macleish. Reprinted by permission of Houghton Mifflin Company.

Walter de la Mare, "The Listeners" from *The Complete Poems of Walter de la Mare,* 1970. Reprinted by permission of The Literary Trustees of Walter de la Mare and The Society of Authors as their representative.

Hansjorg Mayer, "Oil" from *Concrete Poetry,* edited by Mary Ellen Solt. Copyright © 1969 by Indiana University Press. Reprinted by permission of the publishers.

Rod McKuen, 10 lines from "A Cat Named Sloopy" from *Listen to the Warm.* Reprinted by permission of Random House, Inc.

William Meredith, "Effort at Speech" from *Earth Walk: New and Selected Poems*. Copyright © 1969 by William Meredith. Reprinted by permission of Alfred A. Knopf, Inc. Originally appeared in *The New Yorker*.

James Merrill, "An Urban Convalescence" from *Water Street*. Copyright © 1962 by James Merrill. Reprinted by permission of Atheneum Publishers.

W. S. Merwin, extracts from "December Among the Vanished" and "Provision" from *The Lice*. Copyright © 1965 by W. S. Merwin. Extract from "Midnight in Early Spring" from *The Carrier of Ladders*. Copyright © 1970 by W. S. Merwin. Extracts from "The Nails" and "Route With No Number" from *The Moving Target*. Copyright © 1963 by W. S. Merwin. Reprinted by permission of Atheneum Publishers. Extract from "The Native" from *The Drunk In the Furnace*. Copyright © 1959 by W. S. Merwin. Published by Macmillan Publishing Company. Reprinted by permission of Harold Ober Associates.

Edna St. Vincent Millay, 4 lines from "Sonnet XLV" from *Collected Poems*. Copyright 1923, 1951 by Edna St. Vincent Millay and Norma Millay Ellis. Published by Harper & Row, Publishers, Inc. Reprinted by permission of Norma Millay Ellis.

Marianne Moore, "A Carriage from Sweden" from *Collected Poems*. Copyright 1944 and renewed 1972 by Marianne Moore. Reprinted by permission of Macmillan Publishing Co. Inc.

Christian Morgenstern, "Fish's Nightsong" from *Gallows Songs*, translated by Snodgrass and Segal. Published by the University of Michigan Press. Reprinted by permission of the University of Michigan Press.

Eugenio Montale, "The Eel," translated by John Frederick Nims from *Selected Poems* by Eugenio Montale. Copyright © 1965 by New Directions Publishing Corporation. Reprinted by permission of New Directions Publishing Corporation.

Ogden Nash, "Very Like A Whale" from *Verses from 1929 On*. Copyright 1934 by Curtis Publishing Company. Reprinted by permission of Little, Brown and Company.

Ladislav Novák, "Gloria" from *An Anthology of Concrete Poetry*, edited by Emmett Williams. Copyright © 1967 by the Something Else Press. All rights reserved. Reprinted by permission of the publisher.

Howard Nemerov, "Money," 7 lines from "Landscape with Figures," 4 lines from "Creation of Anguish," and 2 lines from "For Robert Frost" from *The Blue Swallows*. Copyright © 1967 by Howard Nemerov. "A Primer of the Daily Round" from *New and Selected Poems*. Copyright © 1960 by University of Chicago Press. Reprinted by permission of University of Chicago Press and Margot Johnson.

Frank O'Hara, one line from "Music," 3 lines from "Poem," and 3 lines from "Romanze or the Music Students" from *The Collected Poems of Frank O'Hara*. Reprinted by permission of Alfred A. Knopf, Inc.

Wilfred Owen, "Arms and the Boy" and "Anthem for Doomed Youth" from *Collected Poems*. Copyright 1946, © 1963 by Chatto & Windus, Ltd. Reprinted by permission of New Directions Publishing Corporation, the Executors of the Estate of Harold Owen, and Chatto & Windus, Ltd.

Robert Pack, "The Pack Rat" from *Nothing but Light*. Published by Rutgers University Press, 1972. Reprinted by permission of Rutgers University Press.

Nicanor Parra, 7 lines from "The Viper," translated by W. S. Merwin, from

Poems & Antipoems. Copyright © 1967 by Nicanor Parra. Reprinted by permission of New Directions Publishing Corporation.

Paul Pascal, "Tact" from *Jiggery-Pokery, A Compendium of Double-Dactyls,* edited by Anthony Hecht and John Hollander. Copyright © 1966 by Anthony Hecht and John Hollander. Reprinted by permission of Atheneum Publishers.

Kenneth Patchen, "Moon, Sun, Sleep, Birds, Live" and "O All Down within the pretty Meadow" from *Collected Poems.* Copyright 1942, © 1967, 1968 by New Directions Publishing Corporation; copyright 1946 by Kenneth Patchen. Reprinted by permission of New Directions Publishing Corporation.

John Peck, "A Quarrel" from *Shagbark.* Published by Bobbs-Merrill, 1972. First appeared in *Quarterly Review of Literature,* vol. XVIII, Nos. 1-2, 1972. Reprinted by permission of *Quarterly Review of Literature.*

Wilder Penfield and Theodore Rasmussen, illustration from *The Cerebral Cortex of Man.* Reprinted by permission of Macmillan Publishing Co., Inc.

Sylvia Plath, "Mushrooms," 5 lines from "Hardcastle Crags," and 3 lines from "Metaphors" from *The Colossus and Other Poems.* Copyright © 1960 by Sylvia Plath. Reprinted by permission of Alfred A. Knopf, Inc. and Olwyn Hughes. Stanzas 9 & 12 from "Daddy" from *Ariel.* Copyright © 1963 by Ted Hughes. Reprinted by permission of Harper & Row, Publishers, Inc. and Olwyn Hughes.

Pluvkaq, "I Wonder Why" from *Primitive Song* by C. M. Bowra. Copyright © 1962 by C. M. Bowra. Reprinted by permission of The World Publishing Company.

Ezra Pound, "In a Station of the Metro," "Alba (Langue d'Oc)," "Alba (When the nightingale . . .)," and "The Return" from *Personae.* Copyright 1926 by Ezra Pound. Extract from "Canto LXXX" from *The Cantos.* Copyright 1948 by Ezra Pound. Reprinted by permission of New Directions Publishing Corporation.

Jacques Prévert, "The Message" from *Paroles.* Copyright 1949 by Editions Gallimard. Reprinted by permission of Editions Gallimard. The translation in this text is by John Frederick Nims.

Dudley Randall, "Blackberry Sweet" from *The New Black Poetry,* edited by C. Major. Copyright © 1969 by International Publishers Co., Inc. Reprinted by permission of International Publishers Co., Inc.

John Crowe Ransom," Good Ships" and "Bells for John Whiteside's Daughter" from *Selected Poems.* Copyright 1924 by Alfred A. Knopf, Inc.; renewed 1952 by John Crowe Ransom. "Blue Girls" from *Selected Poems.* Copyright 1927 by Alfred A. Knopf, Inc.; renewed 1955 by John Crowe Ransom. 4 lines from "Winter Remembered" from *Selected Poems,* Third Edition, Revised and Enlarged. Reprinted by permission of Alfred A. Knopf, Inc.

Ishmael Reed, "beware, do not read this poem" from *Soulscript,* edited by June Jordan. Reprinted by permission of the author.

Charles Reznikoff, "The House-Wreckers" and "About an Excavation" from *By the Waters of Manhattan.* Copyright 1927 by Charles Reznikoff. "Domestic Scenes, 2" from *Testimony.* Copyright © 1965 by Charles Reznikoff. Reprinted by permission of New Directions Publishing Corporation and *San Francisco Review.*

Rainer Maria Rilke, "The Merry-Go-Round" from *Selected Poems,* translated by C. F. MacIntyre. Reprinted by permission of University of California Press.

Edward Arlington Robinson, "The Mill" and "The Dark Hills" from *Collected Poems.* Copyright 1920 by Edward Arlington Robinson; renewed

1948 by Ruth Nivison. Reprinted by permission of Macmillan Publishing Co., Inc.

Theodore Roethke, "My Papa's Waltz" from *Collected Poems of Theodore Roethke*. Copyright 1942 by Hearst Magazines, Inc. "The Geranium" from *Collected Poems of Theodore Roethke*. Copyright © 1963 by Beatrice Roethke. Reprinted by permission of Doubleday & Company, Inc.

Dante Gabriel Rossetti, "The Woodspurge" from *The Poetical Works of Dante Gabriel Rossetti*. Published by Little, Brown and Company. Reprinted by permission of Little, Brown and Company.

Muriel Rukeyser, "Effort at Speech Between Two People," from *Theory of Flight*. Copyright 1935 by Yale University Press; copyright © 1960 by Muriel Rukeyser. Reprinted by permission of International Famous Agency.

Carl Sandburg, "A Fence" from *Chicago Poems*. Copyright 1916 by Holt, Rinehart and Winston, Inc.; copyright 1944 by Carl Sandburg. 22 lines from "They Have Yarns" from *The People Yes*. Copyright 1936 by Harcourt Brace Jovanovich, Inc.; renewed 1964 by Carl Sandburg. Reprinted by permission of Harcourt Brace Jovanovich, Inc.

Sappho, "There's a Man, I Really Believe" from *Sappho to Valéry, Poems in Translation*, by John Frederick Nims. Published by Rutgers University Press, 1971. Reprinted by permission of Rutgers University Press.

Charles Schultz, "Peanuts" cartoon. Copyright © 1971 by United Feature Syndicate, Inc. Reprinted by permission of United Feature Syndicate, Inc.

E. William Seaman, "Higgledy-piggledy Ludwig van Beethoven" from *Jiggery-Pokery, A Compendium of Double-Dactyls*, edited by Anthony Hecht and John Hollander. Copyright © 1966 by Anthony Hecht and John Hollander. Reprinted by permission of Atheneum Publishers.

Pete Seeger, from "Where Have All the Flowers Gone?" Copyright © 1961 by Fall River Music Inc. Used by permission of Fall River Music, Inc.

Robert Service, "Inspiration" and stanzas 3 & 4 from "The Outlaw" from *The Best of Robert Service*. Copyright 1907, 1909, 1912 by Dodd, Mead & Company, Inc; copyright 1916, 1921, 1949, 1951, 1952, 1953 by Dodd, Mead & Company, Inc; copyright 1940 by Robert Service. Reprinted by permission of Dodd, Mead & Company, Inc.

Karl Shapiro, "A Cut Flower" from *Selected Poems*. Copyright © 1968 by Karl Shapiro. Reprinted by permission of Random House, Inc. "Girls Working in Banks" from June 1972 *Esquire Magazine*. Copyright © 1972 by Esquire, Inc. Reprinted by permission of *Esquire Magazine*.

Louis Simpson, "Summer Storm" from *The Arrivistes*. Copyright 1949 by Louis Simpson. 4 lines from "Hot Night on Water Street" from *A Dream of Governors*. Copyright © 1957 by Louis Simpson. Reprinted by permission of Wesleyan University Press.

L. E. Sissman, extract from "In and Out: A Home Away From Home, 1947" from *Dying: An Introduction*. Copyright © 1961 by L. E. Sissman. Reprinted by permission of Atlantic-Little, Brown and Co.

Stevie Smith, "Our Bog Is Dood" from *The Best Beast*. Copyright © 1966 by Stevie Smith. Published by Longman Group Ltd., 1969. Reprinted by permission of Longman Group Ltd. and Alfred A. Knopf, Inc.

W. D. Snodgrass, "Leaving the Motel" from *After Experience*. Copyright © 1966 by W. D. Snodgrass. Reprinted by permission of Harper & Row, Publishers, Inc.

Gary Snyder, "Marin-An," "Oil," and extract from "Four Poems for Robin" from *The Back Country*. Copyright © 1968 by Gary Snyder. "Some Good Things to Be Said for the Iron Age" from *Regarding Wave*. Copyright © 1970 by Gary Snyder. 10 lines from "Bubbs Creek Haircut" from *Six Sections from Mountains and Rivers without End*. Copyright © 1970 by Gary Snyder. Reprinted by permission of New Directions Publishing Corporation and the author.

Mary Ellen Solt, "Lilacs" from *Flowers in Concrete*, Indiana University, 1966. Copyright © 1966 by Mary Ellen Solt. Reprinted by permission of Mary Ellen Solt.

Stephen Spender, 4 lines from "The Landscape Near an Airdrome" from *Selected Poems*. Reprinted by permission of Random House, Inc.

William Stafford, 5 lines from "A Memorial Day" from *Allegiances*. Copyright © 1966 by William Stafford. "Traveling Through the Dark" from *Traveling Through the Dark*. Copyright © 1960 by William Stafford. Reprinted by permission of Harper & Row Publishers, Inc.

Wallace Stevens, "Autumn Refrain" from *The Collected Poems of Wallace Stevens*. Copyright 1936 by Wallace Stevens; renewed 1964 by Holley Stevens. "Sunday Morning," "Life is Motion," "Disillusionment of Ten O'clock," "The Emperor of Ice-Cream," 6 lines from "Connoisseur of Chaos," and 3 lines from "Le Monocle de Mon Oncle" from *The Collected Poems of Wallace Stevens*. Copyright 1923 and renewed 1951 by Wallace Stevens. Reprinted by permission of Alfred A. Knopf, Inc.

Mark Strand, "The Tunnel" from *Reasons for Moving*. Copyright © 1964 by Mark Strand. Reprinted by permission of Atheneum Publishers. Originally appeared in *Partisan Review*.

J. M. Synge, "A Question" from *The Plays and Poems of J. M. Synge*. Published by Methuen & Co. Ltd. Reprinted by permission of Associated Book Publishers Ltd.

May Swenson, "The Blindman" from *Half Sun Half Sleep*. Copyright © 1965 by May Swenson. 4 lines from "A City Garden in April" from *Half Sun Half Sleep*. Copyright © 1967 by May Swenson. 12 lines from "Robert Frost at Breadloaf: His Hand Against a Tree" from *A Cage of Spines*. Copyright © 1958 by May Swenson. "Cat and the Weather" from *To Mix with Time*. Copyright © 1963 by May Swenson. Reprinted by permission of Charles Scribner's Sons and the author.

Allen Tate, "The Mediterranean" from *The Swimmers and Other Selected Poems*. Copyright © 1970 by Allen Tate. Reprinted by permission of The Swallow Press.

James Tate, "Miss Cho Composes in the Cafeteria" from *The Lost Pilot*. Copyright © 1967 by Yale University. Reprinted by permission of Yale University Press.

Rod Taylor, "The Death of Lester Brown, House Painter" and "Dakota: October, 1822 Hunkpapa Warrior" from *Florida East Coast Champion*. Copyright © 1972 by Rod Taylor. Reprinted by permission of Straight Arrow Books.

Dylan Thomas, "The Hand That Signed the Paper," "Do Not Go Gentle Into That Good Night," "In My Craft or Sullen Art," and extract from "Fern Hill" from *The Poems of Dylan Thomas*. Copyright 1939, 1946 by New Directions Publishing Corporation; copyright 1952 by Dylan Thomas. Reprinted by permission of New Directions Publishing Corporation and J. M. Dent & Sons Ltd.

John Thompson, "Adultery at the Plaza" from *The Talking Girl*. Copyright © 1968 by John Thompson. Reprinted by permission of the author and Pym-Randall Press.

John Updike, "Player Piano" from *The Carpentered Hen and Other Tame Creatures*. Copyright 1954 by John Updike. Originally appeared in *The New Yorker*. Reprinted by permission of Harper & Row, Publishers, Inc. 4 lines from "The Origin of Laughter" and 9 lines from "The Dance of the Solids" from *Midpoint and Other Poems*. Reprinted by permission of Alfred A. Knopf, Inc.

Peter Viereck, "The Lyricism of the Weak" from *New and Selected Poems*. Copyright © 1967 by Peter Viereck. Reprinted by permission of The Bobbs-Merrill Company, Inc.

François Villon, "Ballade to His Mistress" from "The Testament" from *Poems of François Villon*, translated by Norman Cameron. Reprinted by permission of Alan S. Hodge and Jonathan Cape Limited.

R. G. Vliet, "Games, Hard Press and Bruise" from *Events and Celebrations*. Copyright © 1960 by R. G. Vliet. Reprinted by permission of The Viking Press, Inc.

Andrei Voznesensky, "I am Goya" from *Antiworlds and the Fifth Ace*, edited by Patricia Blake & Max Hayward. Copyright © 1966, 1967 by Basic Books, Inc. Reprinted by permission of Basic Books, Inc.

John Wain, 4 lines from "A Boisterous Poem about Poetry" from *Weep before God*. Reprinted by permission of Macmillan, London and Basingstoke and Curtis Brown Ltd.

Keith Waldrop, 3 lines from "Graven Images" from *A Windmill Near Calvary*, 1968. Reprinted by permission of The University of Michigan Press.

Alice Walker, 9 lines of section iii in the poem "Love" from *Once*. Copyright © 1968 by Alice Walker. Reprinted by permission of Harcourt Brace Jovanovich, Inc.

Donald Watson, illustration from *The Oxford Book of Birds*. Copyright © 1964 by Oxford University Press. Reprinted by permission of The Clarendon Press.

Philip Whalen, "Plus Ça Change . . ." from *Like I Say*. Copyright © 1960 by Philip Whalen. Reprinted by permission of Corinth Books Inc.

Richard Wilbur, "Playboy" from *Walking to Sleep*. Copyright © 1968 by Richard Wilbur. "Junk" from *Advice to a Prophet & Other Poems*. Copyright © 1961 by Richard Wilbur. 4 lines from "The Death of a Toad" from *Ceremony and Other Poems*. Reprinted by permission of Harcourt Brace Jovanovich, Inc.

Emmett Williams, "Like Attracts Like" from *An Anthology of Concrete Poetry*, edited by Emmett Williams. Copyright © 1967 by the Something Else Press. All rights reserved. Reprinted by permission of the publisher.

Miller Williams, 7 lines from "Let me tell you" from *The Only World There Is*. Copyright © 1968, 1969, 1970, 1971 by Miller Williams. "Sale" from *So Long at the Fair*. Published by E. P. Dutton & Co., Inc., 1968. Reprinted by permission of E. P. Dutton & Co., Inc.

William Carlos Williams, "The Dance" from *Collected Later Poems*. Copyright 1944 by William Carlos Williams. "The Descent" from *Pictures from Brueghel*. Copyright 1948 by William Carlos Williams. "Iris," 2 lines from "Mounted as an Amazon," the last stanza from "To A Woodpecker," and 6 lines from "Asphodel, That Greeny Flower" from *Pictures from Brueghel*. Copyright 1955, © 1962 by William Carlos Williams. "Smell" and "Nantucket" from *Collected Poems*. Copyright 1938 by New Directions Publishing Corporation. Reprinted by permission of New Directions Publishing Corporation.

L. Woiwode, "A Deserted Barn." Copyright © 1969 by The New Yorker Magazine, Inc. Reprinted by permission of The New Yorker Magazine, Inc.

James Wright, 5 lines from "From a Bus Window in Central Ohio" from *The Branch will not Break*. "Speak" from *Shall We Gather at the River*. Copyright © 1968 by James Wright. Originally appeared in *The New Yorker*. 3 lines from "A Poem Written Under an Archway" from *Shall We Gather at the River*. Copyright © 1961, 1963 by James Wright. "A Song for the Middle of the Night" from *The Green Wall*. Reprinted by permission of Wesleyan University Press and the author.

William Butler Yeats, "A Last Confession" from *Collected Poems*. Copyright 1933 by Macmillan Publishing Co., Inc.; renewed 1961 by Bertha Georgie Yeats. "An Irish Airman Foresees His Death" from *Collected Poems*. Copyright 1919 by Macmillan Publishing Co., Inc.; renewed 1947 by Bertha Georgie Yeats. "No Second Troy" and "Friends" from *Collected Poems*. Copyright 1912 by Macmillan Publishing Co., Inc.; renewed by Bertha Georgie Yeats. "The Statues" from *Collected Poems*. Copyright 1940 by Bertha Georgie Yeats; renewed 1968 by Bertha Georgie Yeats, Michael Butler Yeats and Anne Yeats. "The Second Coming" from *Collected Poems*. Copyright 1924 by Macmillan Publishing Co., Inc.; renewed 1952 by Bertha Georgie Yeats. "The Lake Isle of Innisfree" and "The Lover Mourns for the Loss of Love" from *Collected Poems*. Copyright 1906 by Macmillan Publishing Co., Inc., renewed by William Butler Yeats. 6 lines from "The Tower," "Sailing to Byzantium," and "Leda and the Swan" from *Collected Poems*. Copyright 1928 by Macmillan Publishing Co., Inc.; renewed 1956 by Bertha Georgie Yeats. 3 lines from "He Remembers Forgotten Beauty" from *Collected Poems*. Copyright 1906 by Macmillan Publishing Co., Inc.; renewed 1934 by William Butler Yeats. 2 lines from "The Folly of Being Comforted" and 5 lines from "Adam's Curse" from *Collected Poems*. 11 lines from "Under Ben Bulben, VI" from *Collected Poems*. Copyright 1940 by Bertha Georgie Yeats; renewed 1968 by Bertha Georgie Yeats, Michael Butler Yeats and Anne Yeats. "The Lamentation of the Old Pensioner" (1925 version) from *Collected Poems*. Copyright 1906 by Macmillan Publishing Co., Inc.; renewed 1934 by William Butler Yeats. "The Lamentation of the Old Pensioner" (1890 version) from *Poems*. Reprinted by permission of M. B. Yeats. "Among School Children" from *Collected Poems*. Copyright 1928 by Macmillan Publishing Co., Inc.; renewed 1956 by Georgie Yeats. The fifth stanza of an early version of "Among School Children" from *Yeats at Work* by Curtis Bradford. The material in this text is arranged by John Frederick Nims from the Yeats manuscript as given in *Yeats at Work* by Curtis Bradford. Published by Southern Illinois Press, 1965. Reprinted by permission of Macmillan Publishing Co., Inc., The Macmillan Co. of Canada Ltd., and A. P. Watt & Son Ltd.

preface

Why another introduction to poetry?

Why yet another when there is already a choice among many, the best so good that one can hardly hope to write a better one?

But, if not better, he can hope to write a different one. It seemed to me that one approach, the most natural of all, has not been given its due: the approach that sees poetry as not just part of the curriculum, as not just a matter of arbitrary rules and the say-so of critics, but as the natural expression of our humanity. Imagery, sound-symbolism, rhythm—these are not merely classroom terms designed to harass and perplex the young. They are living functions of our physiology. All the elements of poetry (I am not speaking now of "verse") are wholly natural.

Nor is poetry merely something that happens at 10:00 MWF for three hours' credit. It is inseparable from the rest of our life and from the nature of the universe. It is related, for example, to the other arts, perhaps most obviously to music and painting. An introductory book on poetry without a single musical note or a single picture is too restrictive. Poetry is also related to the sciences: the nature of rhythm, for example, is as much a matter of scientific observation as the nature of light. Since poetry is an expression of our human experience, there is no aspect of that experience which is not relevant to it.

This relevance may take us into matters that seem more "technical" than are handled in the usual introduction to poetry. But it is time to disinfect the word "technical" of its unfavorable connotations. Whenever we are talking about anything we are really interested in—the movements of a pass receiver, the way to repair a motorbike or make bread—we are talking about technique, which means nothing more than the "way to do" something.

Some introductions to poetry gloss over the difficulties naturally present. They seem to assume that the average student is what the young themselves might call a "dum-dum"—an empty-eyed gawker who slouches about mumbling "Far out" and "Like wow, man." The writer has not found this alleged stupidity to be a fact: the typical college student cares about the basic realities of his experience and is more than willing to think about them, often with surprising originality. His ability to cope with problems should not be underrated; nor should he be insulted with oversimplicity. In a way our introduction to poetry is a vote of confidence in the young.

If poetry cannot be cut off from the rest of our experience, neither can it be limited, any more than humanity itself can, only to our own time and our own language. The poems in this book are from many different human "now's"—from the now of Sappho and Shakespeare as well as from the now of Pete Seeger and Gwendolyn Brooks. A few poems are from other languages—though here we are forced to rely on the necessarily second-best of the translator. But though the selection is wide-ranging, the emphasis is on modern poetry, and, among modern poems, on the contemporary. Not that the contemporary world of poetry is any more "real" than the world that Shakespeare lived in. But it is more available: the world the modern student moves most easily in, since it is the world of his concerns and interests. Once at home with the poetry of that world, he can step over into the poetry of other centuries—which he will find in every human way very much like his own.

The experience that has gone into the making of this book comes not only from several decades in the classroom, but also from a practitioner's knowledge of the problems of writing. Not only through his own writing, but through work with many poets, young and not so young, on campuses and at writers' conferences. Close work with their problems has shown that what matters above everything else is the concrete example. Year after year, wherever writers gather, no piece of advice is heard more often than "Show, don't tell!" Good writers *show* us a world. In critical writing too the advice applies. It is far more important to show what a poem is than to talk and talk about it; more important to show examples of metaphor than to define it. The definition is a sort of mental shadow without individual features; the example is the reality itself. This book is richer in examples, mostly contemporary, than other introductions known to the author. Even the title, *Western Wind*, is an example: it reminds us what poetry is by alluding to its embodiment in one of the best known quatrains in our language.

The author has tried to avoid lugging in the usual baggage of classroom paraphernalia. The exercises provided at the ends of chapters are designed not so much to test the knowledge of facts as to lure the student into thinking creatively. More fundamental questions than those given will suggest themselves to every instructor, who will have his favorite way of asking the basic questions: Paraphrase this, Scan that, Compare such and such with such and such. He is of course free to do as little or as much as he likes with the exercises given.

There are chiefly two ways of handling courses thought of as "introductions to poetry." There is the rather brief treatment of poetry sometimes found as a part of freshman English. There is also the semester-long course in which the teacher may find a mixed group from all levels, often including upperclassmen. This book can be used with either kind of program. For the more elementary course, the first sixteen chapters provide discussion and examples of the basic elements of poetry: imagery, emotion, diction, sound, and rhythm. If additional poems are desired, as in the "anthologies" given in some introductions, they can be taken from the seven additional chapters—which go more deeply into the nature of poetry, for more advanced classes or for classes with more time at their disposal. The flexibility of this design also allows for the differences one finds in individual classes or in individual students, either of which may be happier doing more or less than the typical class or the typical individual.

I am grateful to the several Random House editors who worked with me on this project: to David Dushkin, who first encouraged it; to James Smith, who saw the manuscript grow to a monster three times its present size; and especially to Helen Litton, whose intelligent concern for structure and detail helped gentle it into a more reasonable form.

J. F. N.

contents

I the senses

V the rhythms

VI the mind

postscript

before we begin

Sometimes we feel like jumping a fence for the fun of jumping, or we burst into song for the fun of singing, or we string words together just for the fun of saying them. What we do "for fun" we do for the sheer pleasure of doing it, without having any other purpose in mind. Fun is an expression of the exuberance we feel at being alive, an overflow of the spirit of play that characterizes so much human activity, though it may be less evident in adults than in children, less common in our time than in earlier and simpler ages. When we *imagine* anything, we are playing with images, combining them as they have never been combined before, perhaps not even in nature itself. Out of such playing with images came primitive ritual and the mythologies of early religion. Out of our playing with rocks and herbs and the mystery of fire came early science. Out of our playing with hollow reeds or tightened sinews or the beat of bone on deerskin came early music; musicians still "play" on their pianos or guitars. And out of our playing with words, with their sounds and shapes and rhythms and the images they conjured, came early poetry, so wonderful that in all parts of the world it seemed a kind of magic.

To some of us today, poetry may seem an artificial refinement of natural speech. But in the literature of every country poetry comes before prose does. It is closer than prose to the origins of language. One can even say it is more natural: more primitive, more basic, a more total expression of the muscular, sensuous, emotional, rhythmical nature of the human animal. The ancient Greeks, childlike for all their sophistication, considered the poet an "athlete of the word." In the universities of a truly humane society, they might have felt, poetry would belong at least as much to departments of physical education as to departments of literary criticism.

But what *is* poetry? That is the question this book is setting out to answer. Whatever it is, it is so closely related to the other activities of our life that we will find ourselves dealing with many curious questions about man and his world. Some of them are:

If a baby were born with no senses, would it know it exists?
How can we see sounds and hear colors?
Why do cats dislike getting their feet wet?
Why did the thought of a line of poetry make A. E. Housman stop shaving?
When do singers get a sore throat listening to other singers?
Why does the pitch get higher if we play a 33⅓ rpm record at 78 rpm?
Why do charms against the devil fail to work in translation?
Why do French dogs say "ouâ-ouâ" instead of "bow-wow"?
What kind of rhyme is like a blue note in music?
What American President wrote a treatise on the nature of rhythm in poetry?
Why do metronomes have a poor sense of rhythm?
Why did Picasso say, "Man invented the alarm clock"?

Poetry—like so much we are closest to and know best—is not easy to define. We can begin by saying what it is not. Poetry is not the same as *verse*. Verse is any singsong with rhythm and rhyme, as in

> Thirty days hath September,
> April, June, and November. . . .

The word *verse* refers only to the shape an expression takes, not to its content or quality.

Poetry *may* be in verse, and often does use some kind of verse-like structure. Many poets, for example, have been attracted by the shape of the sonnet, which arranges rhythms and rhymes in a definite formation. But the sonnet in itself is only a verse-form; a sonnet may be poetry or it may not. Poetry is not poetry *because* it is in verse; to the shape of verse it has to add qualities of imagination and emotion and of language itself. Such qualities, not easy to describe briefly, are what this book is about.

Much about verse (as opposed to poetry) is arbitrary, just as the rules of a game are arbitrary. The limerick, for example, has five lines of a certain length, with the third and fourth shorter than the others, the longer lines having one rhyme, the shorter ones another. There is nothing in nature that says a limerick should have this form, just as there is nothing in nature that says we should have four balls and three strikes in baseball, or four downs to make ten yards in football.

But though verse is arbitrary, poetry is not. Everything in poetry is an expression of what is natural: it is the way it is because we are the way we are.

The whole approach of this book will be based upon this certainty: the nature of poetry follows from the nature of man. Our six main divisions are organized as man himself is. Human experience begins when the senses give us

I. IMAGES of ourself or the world outside. These images arouse
II. EMOTIONS, which (with their images) we express in
III. WORDS, which are physically produced and have
IV. SOUND, which comes riding the air on waves of
V. RHYTHM. The whole process, from the beginning, is fostered and overseen by an organizing
VI. MIND, acting now with the common sense of our everyday life, now with the uncommon sense of dreams or visions.

In a good poem the elements work together as a unit, just as our own combination of body and mind works together. But if we were studying body-and-mind as medical students do, we would soon realize that it is impossible to consider all parts of it at once. The way to deal with a complicated subject is to look at it part by part. In medical school we would expect separate lectures on the heart, the stomach, the lungs, and so forth, even though we realize no organ can function apart from the others. And so with poetry: we have to talk separately about the elements that make it up—such as imagery, diction, rhythm—even though we know they cannot exist in isolation.

Although poetry is not bound by such arbitrary rules as games are, it does fall under the influence of certain natural laws, like those that govern mountain climbing. Mountain climbers are not subject to anything as formal as the three-strike rule in baseball, but they cannot forget that they have only so many arms and legs, that some kinds of rock crumble and some do not, and that the law of gravitation can exact more severe penalties than any man-made rulebook. Poetry may not have rules and regulations, but, as we shall see, its play is limited to the possibilities of our existence. It has to make sense in terms of man and his destiny.

In such a study as this, specific examples are more persuasive than definitions. It is helpful to give the definition of a metaphor; it is even more helpful to give enough examples so that—as in life itself—we can come to our own conclusions about what it is.

We can also learn about things by observing what they are not. Just as cruelty can teach us to value kindness, so a bad line or bad stanza can teach us to appreciate a good one. Some of our bad examples are so clumsy we may find ourselves laughing at them. Nothing wrong with that: a sense of humor is a sense of proportion. It is also a sense of delight—delight in noting that life has its incongruities and absurdities and that we can live in spite of them. Only a fool, said the French poet Paul Valéry, thinks a man cannot joke and be serious.

Our attitude to poetry—as to any subject—should be a questioning one. We might think of nearly every sentence in this book as ending with a ghostly question mark. Is this statement—we should ask ourselves—really true? We can decide only by considering the evidence we have: the poems we have read, the poems we are reading, and what we know of our own human nature.

Although we will have to make some general statements about poetry, we can find exceptions to nearly all of them. A recent cartoon showed a professor of mathematics who had written 2+2=4 on the blackboard. He was beginning his lecture with a "However. . . ." Readers may come across sentences in this book that they would like to see followed by a "However. . . ." They are certainly free to supply their own. This is a book to live with and be alive with; being alive is often a process of disagreement.

As individual human beings we differ greatly. In a time of increasing standardization, when more and more things and more and more people are being referred to by number instead of by name, it is important to cherish these differences. It seems to be a part of the general sameness of our culture that we are expected to give indiscriminate approval to accepted values. If we say we like poetry, it is assumed we like all poetry. But why should we? It is only human to have what Robert Frost called "passionate preferences." Not all readers are going to like all the poems in this book; nor should they expect to. Nor are these chapters like a tape to be fed into a computer, every millimeter of which is to be processed in exactly the same way. Human attention, like everything human, has its rhythms: now we concentrate, now we relax, pretty much as our interests dictate. Individual teachers and individual classes, as well as individual students, will have their preferences. There is no reason they should read every poem or every chapter with equal interest. Some groups may prefer to skim or skip certain sections so that they can concentrate on others that are more to their liking. Some may prefer to read, here and there, only the poems, which are always more important than what is being said about them. We should not be misled into thinking that the poems are here only to illustrate something about poetry. Any poem might be cited to illustrate many other points besides the one being made in the text that accompanies it. (A special index at the back of the book will indicate some of the possibilities.) Over and above their relevance to any context, however, is the importance the poems have in themselves.

If we confined ourselves to poetry that belonged to the always changing world of "now," this could be a much shorter book than it is. A few years ago we would not have needed many introductory remarks to understand the lyrics of the Beatles. We would hardly have needed a book at all; we could have learned what we needed to know by going around with a transistor plugged into one ear. But the trouble with the "now" poetry of a season or two is that it fades with the season—whereas poetry, in a phrase of Ezra Pound, ought to be "news that stays news." What Emily Dickinson had to say a hundred years ago is as fresh today as when she said it. So is much of what Shakespeare said nearly 400 years ago. Many of the lines of Sappho, from about 2600 years ago, are as vivid as news flashes.

If most of the world's great poetry is a product of the past—which is the sum of all our now's—it is only for statistical reasons: more human beings lived in those many centuries than are alive today. In discussing such a body of poetry, we can save time by resorting to what look like technical terms. These may put off some readers, who forget that they themselves make extensive use of such terms in speaking of their own interests. Referring to a midline pause in a poem as a "caesura" is no more pedantic than referring to split T's or tight ends or topspin or a chipshot or fuel-injection. Such technical terms are nothing but convenient shortcuts.

Finally, with poetry we have to return to the reading habits of a more primitive age than our own. Poetry has no use for the kind of speed-reading techniques we are encouraged to practice with informational materials. In speed reading, we are told not to fixate on any one word, not to backtrack over what we have already read, and not to subvocalize, by half pronouncing or by moving our lips. But in reading poetry we have to dwell on the words to savor their implications and relationships; we have to glance back and reread whenever we have a mind to; and we have to feel the words alive in our mouths, even if we move our lips to do so. A poem, unlike a newspaper, is not meant to be read once and thrown away. We may have to read it several times to feel we know it—and then (as with a favorite record) return to it as many times as we want for further pleasure. In a world increasingly sophisticated, poetry is one of the few ways in which we can still afford to be primitive.

I
the senses

Where Experience Starts 1 the image

The Role of the Senses

Our first contact with reality begins with what we call an **image**—a piece of news from the external world or from our own bodies which is brought into the light of consciousness through one of the senses. It may come through the eye as color, through the ear as sound, through the tongue as taste, or through one of the other senses as another kind of physical information. When we remember with any vividness, we remember in images. It is difficult to reason without using them; our dreams are almost wholly made up of them.

We can think of images as differing from ideas or thoughts in that images are always made up of sense data: they deal in such impressions as color or sound or taste or smell or temperature or the feeling of physical contact. Ideas and thoughts may involve images, but they do not necessarily do so. We can think "Charity is a virtue" or "Exercise is good for the health" without having impressions of color, sound, smell, etc. But if we wanted to convince anyone else of the truth of these ideas, we could not make a very convincing case without using the imagery of specific examples.

Images are so important to the way mind and body work together that they are believed to have influenced even the origin of language. Emerson, in *Nature*, puts it this way:

> Every word which is used to express a moral or intellectual fact, if traced to its root, is found to be borrowed from some material appearance. *Right* means *straight; wrong* means *twisted. Spirit* primarily means *wind; trans-*

gression, the crossing of a *line*; *supercilious,* the *raising of the eyebrow.* We say the *heart* to express emotion, the *head* to denote thought. . . .[1]

However that may be, it is certainly true that poets (like children, like primitive tribesmen, like all of us when we dream) naturally think in images. "I no sooner have an idea," said Goethe, "than it turns into an image." But it *was* an image even before it was an idea, because that is how the mind—or the inseparable mind-body combination—naturally works. Juliet, thinking of the family feud that threatens her love for Romeo, wonders, "What 's in a name?" Immediately an image wells up: "That which we call a rose/By any other name would smell as sweet." Juliet knew the smell and feel and color of a flower long before she speculated about problems of nomenclature. About three-fourths of our brain area is given over to processing data produced by sight and hearing and smell. Poets use imagery because it makes up so much of the human experience. We can hardly imagine anything we value or despise that does not come home to us in terms of sensation.

If a child could be born with no senses whatsoever—with no feeling even of warmth—it would have no way of knowing it existed. If we know that we are, and if we know that what we call the outside world seems to exist, from the page at our fingertip to the farthest reach of the newest telescope, we know it only through the senses. Even imagination is dependent upon them for the elements it rearranges in fantasy.

How the senses work is largely mysterious. The eye gives us information about light rays, but nobody understands how the cells of the retina react photochemically to the rays, or how these chemical reactions turn into electrical impulses along the optic nerve, or how these impulses are perceived by sight-centers in the brain not as flickers of electricity but as "sundance gold" or "Capri blue" or "apple green." All we know is that some kind of stimulus to the cells in the eye (or in the ear or fingertip or any other part of the body) triggers a reaction, creating a current that travels along the nerve circuits. Like a telephoned series of *click click click,* which is essentially the same for all the senses, the current is somehow turned by the brain into perceptions of tulips or tennis courts or another's hand warm in our own as moonlight plays on the lake and a loon laughs in the distance, the air tangy with pine. Or of blood warm on the skin, a voice choking in the throat, the smell of foreign foliage as a young man falls in a war he never wanted. The images of poetry are based on the fantastic realities of body and mind.

An "image" is anything presented to the consciousness as a bodily sensation. We call such images **concrete** (from the Latin word for *solid*), as opposed to ideas that may be **abstract** (Latin, *withdrawn*)—stripped, that is, of physical detail. Such words as "violet," "pizza," "sunlight," "surf," and "blond" are concrete; such words as "entity,"

[1] From Section IV, "Language," of Ralph Waldo Emerson's *Nature.*

"nutrition," "meteorology," "recurrence," and "blondness" are abstract.

"Western Wind" is a little poem that was found, with its music, in an early sixteenth-century manuscript.

> Westron wynde when wyll thow blow
> the smalle rayne downe can rayne
> Chryst yf my love wer in my armys
> and I yn my bed agayne
>
> *Anonymous (c. 1500)*

Or, more comfortably in modern spelling:

> Western wind, when will thou blow,
> The small rain down can rain?
> Christ! if my love were in my arms,
> And I in my bed again!

A boy misses his girl (or a girl her boy); he wishes spring would come so he could see her again. The prose meaning of the poem—its ideas—might look like this:

> Characteristic of the coming of spring in Europe is the fact that prevailing winds are from the west; with them comes a marked increase of rainfall, though the spring rains tend to be gentle. I look forward with impatience to its coming, because at that time circumstances will be such that I will be reunited with the person I love and be given an opportunity to express that love in the normal human way.

For the anonymous poet the experience is all *one*, and all sensuous, as in reality. Spring means the wind and the rain on his cheek, so real that he addresses the wind as if it were alive—as it might seem alive to a child or to a simple tribesman untouched by civilization. He imagines the reunion, too, in its physical reality. The poem does not come just from a mind; it comes from a mind in, and very aware of, a body. Aware of two bodies. Aware of the world. It sounds—though from long ago—like a real voice speaking. If we do not believe the voice in a poem, nothing else matters: the poet has left a credibility gap we will never bridge. Whatever else a poem may be, unless it seems a real voice in a real body in a real world, it is not likely to affect us deeply.

Our preference for sense detail has been embedded in the human psyche for some 700,000 years or so. It surfaces most vividly in the free-floating world of dreams and hallucinations, in the poetry of people farthest from the schooling of civilization, and in the thoughts of children before they too, at about the age of thirteen, give up their poetically concrete way of experiencing for the abstractions of adulthood. The child of MacLeish's poem is still living in the richly sensuous anti-think world of the body.

ELEVEN

And summer mornings the mute child, rebellious,
Stupid, hating the words, the meanings, hating
The Think now, Think, the Oh but Think! would leave
On tiptoe the three chairs on the verandah
And crossing tree by tree the empty lawn
Push back the shed door and upon the sill
Stand pressing out the sunlight from his eyes
And enter and with outstretched fingers feel
The grindstone and behind it the bare wall
And turn and in the corner on the cool 10
Hard earth sit listening. And one by one,
Out of the dazzled shadow in the room,
The shapes would gather, the brown plowshare, spades,
Mattocks, the polished helves of picks, a scythe
Hung from the rafters, shovels, slender tines
Glinting across the curve of sickles—shapes
Older than men were, the wise tools, the iron
Friendly with earth. And sit there, quiet, breathing
The harsh dry smell of withered bulbs, the faint
Odor of dung, the silence. And outside 20
Beyond the half-shut door the blind leaves
And the corn moving. And at noon would come,
Up from the garden, his hard crooked hands
Gentle with earth, his knees still earth-stained, smelling
Of sun, of summer, the old gardener, like
A priest, like an interpreter, and bend
Over his baskets.
And they would not speak:
They would say nothing. And the child would sit there
Happy as though he had no name, as though 30
He had been no one: like a leaf, a stem,
Like a root growing—

Archibald MacLeish (b. 1892)

The Gabon Pygmies, like all who belong to the childhood of the human race, live in an equally sensuous universe.

FROM SONG FOR THE ELEPHANT HUNT

(African)

In the frightened forest the tree sleeps, the leaves are dead,
The monkeys have closed their eyes, hanging from branches on high.
The antelopes slip past with silent steps,
Eat the fresh grass, prick their ears attentively,
Lift their heads and listen frightened.
The cicada is silent and stops his grinding song.
Elephant-hunter, take your bow!
Elephant-hunter, take your bow!

In the forest lashed by the great rain,
Father elephant walks heavily, *baou, baou,* 10

Careless, without fear, sure of his strength,
Father elephant, whom no one can vanquish;
Among the trees which he breaks he stops and starts again.
He eats, roars, overturns trees and seeks his mate.
Father elephant, you have been heard from afar.
Elephant-hunter, take your bow!
Elephant-hunter, take your bow!

"The poet," said García Lorca, "is a professor of the five bodily senses." We could easily assemble an anthology of poems devoted to each of the five.

For sight:

EYE

Only the eye can drink
From a lake a mile away
Or climb ten mountains in
Less time than it takes to say,

Land on the moon, the stars;
Fall, rise, hurdle, sprint;
Put a lid on the world
Or narrow it to a squint.

Lover of light, whose lies
Deceive us, doctors say, 10
Let physics chew surmise.
Dine out on the crusty day

And drink the sun's gold wine,
Devouring all that seems.
From color, form, and depth
Concoct your optic dreams

And give them to the mind
As its best evidence.
Then only, thought may grind
A harder sharper lens. 20

Gray Burr (b. 1919)

For hearing and taste:

SOME GOOD THINGS TO BE SAID FOR THE IRON AGE

A ringing tire iron
        dropped on the pavement

Whang of a saw
brusht on limbs

                the taste
                of rust.

Gary Snyder (b. 1930)

For taste:

MYSTIC

They call all experience of the senses *mystic*, when the experience is
considered.
So an apple becomes *mystic* when I taste in it
the summer and the snows, the wild welter of earth
and the insistence of the sun.
All of which things I can surely taste in a good apple.
Though some apples taste preponderantly of water, wet and sour
and some of too much sun, brackish sweet
like lagoon-water, that has been too much sunned.

If I say I taste these things in an apple, I am called *mystic*, which means a liar. 10
The only way to eat an apple is to hog it down like a pig
and taste nothing
that is *real*.

But if I eat an apple, I like to eat it with all my senses awake.
Hogging it down like a pig I call the feeding of corpses.

D. H. Lawrence (1885–1930)

For smell:

SMELL!

Oh strong ridged and deeply hollowed
nose of mine! what will you not be smelling?
What tactless asses we are, you and I, boney nose,
always indiscriminate, always unashamed,
and now it is the souring flowers of the bedraggled
poplars: a festering pulp on the wet earth
beneath them. With what deep thirst
we quicken our desires
to that rank odor of a passing springtime!
Can you not be decent? Can you not reserve your ardors 10
for something less unlovely? What girl will care
for us, do you think, if we continue in these ways?
Must you taste everything? Must you know everything?
Must you have a part in everything?

William Carlos Williams (1883–1963)

For touch:

Games, hard press and bruise of the flesh,
boys banging one another, break and breathless
brush past arms, brash flagsnatcher!
push, press, pound, pummel and pop

bodies, hearts thick in the birdchests,
ache, squeeze, topple and tum-
ble tornshirted and kindercrazy, scramble and scratch
in the grass, bump bone and shoulder scratch,
smack, slap, swat, greenkneed, raw,
nosewhacked breath faster and cold, 10
shove! and then rip-out-ragged, knuckle, ankle,
stomach sucked tight on the run, balls
hugged up, trip, but though thump overhead
overheels, crumple safe at base, spit, rise,
spout snot and tearstreakers, bloodyhot rage,
rampage, weep, holler, clobber them, clout,
snort triumph! trample, gag, and rout:
not flags of sex even can brag such sport.

R. G. Vliet (b. 1929)

Few poems limit themselves to one or two senses; most range as our minds do, using whatever sense gives the most relevant information. Nor are the senses limited to five: we can feel what our muscles are doing, can keep our balance, can sense a hot stove in a dark room, can feel pain and other bodily intimations. The mechanisms that give us our "body image" or self-awareness are called proprioceptive; in health they operate so smoothly we are not aware they exist.

One of the most celebrated of proprioceptive poems is by Sappho, who wrote some very modern poems in the sixth century B.C. In it, she tells how it feels to see someone sitting casually next to the person she is in love with. She lets us share the whole force of her passion by detailing, almost without comment, her physical symptoms.

There's a man, I really believe, compares with
any god in heaven above! To sit there
knee to knee so close to you, hear your voice, your
  cozy low laughter,
close to *you*—enough in the very thought to
put my heart at once in a palpitation.
I, come face to face with you even briefly,
  stand in a stupor:
tongue a lump, unable to lift; elusive
little flames play over the skin and smolder 10
under. Eyes go blind in a flash; and ears hear
  only their own din.
Head to toe I'm cold with a sudden moisture;
knees are faint; my cheeks, in an instant, drain to
green as grass. I think to myself, the end? I'm
  really going under?
Well, endure is all I can do, reduced to . . . .

Sappho (fl. c. 600 B.C.)

If one lets his senses range through T. S. Eliot's urban impressions, he will find all of them engaged in the experience.

PRELUDES

I

The winter evening settles down
With smell of steaks in passageways.
Six o'clock.
The burnt-out ends of smoky days.
And now a gusty shower wraps
The grimy scraps
Of withered leaves about your feet
And newspapers from vacant lots;
The showers beat
On broken blinds and chimney-pots, 10
And at the corner of the street
A lonely cab-horse steams and stamps.
And then the lighting of the lamps.

II

The morning comes to consciousness
Of faint stale smells of beer
From the sawdust-trampled street
With all its muddy feet that press
To early coffee-stands.
With the other masquerades
That time resumes, 20
One thinks of all the hands
That are raising dingy shades
In a thousand furnished rooms.

III

You tossed a blanket from the bed,
You lay upon your back, and waited;
You dozed, and watched the night revealing
The thousand sordid images
Of which your soul was constituted;
They flickered against the ceiling.
And when all the world came back 30
And the light crept up between the shutters
And you heard the sparrows in the gutters,
You had such a vision of the street
As the street hardly understands;
Sitting along the bed's edge, where
You curled the papers from your hair,
Or clasped the yellow soles of feet
In the palms of both soiled hands.

IV

His soul stretched tight across the skies
That fade behind a city block, 40

Or trampled by insistent feet
At four and five and six o'clock;
And short square fingers stuffing pipes,
And evening newspapers, and eyes
Assured of certain certainties,
The conscience of a blackened street
Impatient to assume the world.

I am moved by fancies that are curled
Around these images, and cling:
The notion of some infinitely gentle 50
Infinitely suffering thing.

Wipe your hand across your mouth, and laugh;
The worlds revolve like ancient women
Gathering fuel in vacant lots.

T. S. Eliot (1888–1965)

Operating with imagery is more than a preference of the mind; it is an actual necessity. When one is sense-deprived, left alone in darkness and silence, he begins to hallucinate. We find something like this hallucination in the poetry of John Keats, who said, "O for a life of Sensations rather than of Thoughts!" His "Ode to a Nightingale," which begins with proprioceptive sensations, whirls away on images of sight, sound, touch, taste, and smell, escaping into pure imagination in spite of the interference of "the dull brain." The fifth stanza is an example of compensatory dreaming: unable to see what flowers—imaginary flowers—are around him, Keats proceeds to identify them by their imaginary smells.

ODE TO A NIGHTINGALE

1

My heart aches, and a drowsy numbness pains
  My sense, as though of hemlock I had drunk,
Or emptied some dull opiate to the drains
  One minute past, and Lethe-wards had sunk:
'Tis not through envy of thy happy lot,
  But being too happy in thine happiness,—
    That thou, light-winged Dryad of the trees,
        In some melodious plot
  Of beechen green, and shadows numberless,
    Singest of summer in full-throated ease. 10

2

O, for a draught of vintage! that hath been
  Cool'd a long age in the deep-delved earth,

---

[4] **Lethe:** *A river in the underworld whose waters caused the drinker to forget his past*
[7] **Dryad:** *a wood-nymph*

Tasting of Flora and the country green,
Dance, and Provençal song, and sunburnt mirth!
O for a beaker full of the warm South,
Full of the true, the blushful Hippocrene,
With beaded bubbles winking at the brim,
And purple-stained mouth;
That I might drink, and leave the world unseen,
And with thee fade away into the forest dim: 20

3

Fade far away, dissolve, and quite forget
What thou among the leaves hast never known,
The weariness, the fever, and the fret
Here, where men sit and hear each other groan;
Where palsy shakes a few, sad, last gray hairs,
Where youth grows pale, and spectre-thin, and dies;
Where but to think is to be full of sorrow
And leaden-eyed despairs,
Where Beauty cannot keep her lustrous eyes,
Or new Love pine at them beyond to-morrow. 30

4

Away! away! for I will fly to thee,
Not charioted by Bacchus and his pards,
But on the viewless wings of Poesy,
Though the dull brain perplexes and retards:
Already with thee! tender is the night,
And haply the Queen-Moon is on her throne,
Cluster'd around by all her starry Fays;
But here there is no light,
Save what from heaven is with the breezes blown
Through verdurous glooms and winding mossy ways. 40

5

I cannot see what flowers are at my feet,
Nor what soft incense hangs upon the boughs,
But, in embalmed darkness, guess each sweet
Wherewith the seasonable month endows
The grass, the thicket, and the fruit-tree wild;
White hawthorn, and the pastoral eglantine;
Fast fading violets cover'd up in leaves;
And mid-May's eldest child,
The coming musk-rose, full of dewy wine,
The murmurous haunt of flies on summer eves. 50

---

[13] **Flora:** *goddess of flowers*
[14] **Provençal:** *of Provence, in the south of France*
[16] **Hippocrene:** *a spring sacred to the Muses*
[32] **pards:** *leopards*
[37] **Fays:** *fairies*

6

Darkling I listen; and, for many a time
I have been half in love with easeful Death,
Call'd him soft names in many a mused rhyme,
To take into the air my quiet breath;
Now more than ever seems it rich to die,
To cease upon the midnight with no pain,
While thou art pouring forth thy soul abroad
In such an ecstasy!
Still wouldst thou sing, and I have ears in vain—
To thy high requiem become a sod. 60

7

Thou wast not born for death, immortal Bird!
No hungry generations tread thee down;
The voice I hear this passing night was heard
In ancient days by emperor and clown:
Perhaps the self-same song that found a path
Through the sad heart of Ruth, when, sick for home,
She stood in tears amid the alien corn;
The same that oft-times hath
Charm'd magic casements, opening on the foam
Of perilous seas, in faery lands forlorn. 70

8

Forlorn! the very word is like a bell
To toll me back from thee to my sole self!
Adieu! the fancy cannot cheat so well
As she is fam'd to do, deceiving elf.
Adieu! adieu! thy plaintive anthem fades
Past the near meadows, over the still stream,
Up the hill-side; and now 'tis buried deep
In the next valley-glades:
Was it a vision, or a waking dream?
Fled is that music:—Do I wake or sleep? 80

John Keats (1795–1821)

Sir Philip Sidney, the Elizabethan who died young of a war wound, felt the need of a definite image when complaining that the woman he loved was unappreciative. He found it in the moon, as pale and dull and unhappy as he felt himself to be. Sidney is not really talking to the moon; he is using it only as a kind of communications satellite off which to rebound his own moods.

---

[51] **darkling:** *in the dark*

[66] **Ruth:** *see the Book of Ruth, in the Old Testament*

WITH HOW SAD STEPS, O MOON

With how sad steps, O moon, thou climb'st the skies,
  How silently, and with how wan a face.
  What, may it be that even in heavenly place
That busy archer his sharp arrows tries?
Sure, if that long-with-love-acquainted eyes
  Can judge of love, thou feel'st a lover's case;
  I read it in thy looks; thy languisht grace,
To me that feel the like, thy state descries.

Then, even of fellowship, O moon, tell me
  Is constant love deemed there but want of wit? 10
Are beauties there as proud as here they be?
  Do they above love to be loved, and yet
Those lovers scorn whom that love doth possess?
Do they call virtue there ungratefulness?

Sir Philip Sidney (1554–1586)

Poets in all ages have turned ideas into images, as the ancient Greek poet did when he lamented that a lady who had turned him down in youth and middle age was still rejecting him.

BRIEF AUTUMNAL

Green grape, and you refused me.
  Ripe grape, and you sent me packing.
    Must you deny me a bite of your raisin?

Anonymous (date uncertain)
(Translated by Dudley Fitts)

The Specific Image

Our senses note only particulars. We never see color, we see particular colors; we never just touch, we touch something. For a long time philosophers have been saying that being exists only in individual things. "The individual," says Jung, "is the only reality." E. E. Cummings puts it more catchily: "There's nothing as something as one." *Humanity* does not exist as a thing we can see; but *this* person does, *that* person does. This human preference for the particular is shown in many primitive languages, which may have no word for "tree" but which may have many such words as "oak," "pine," "maple," "elm," etc. Poets, like primitives and children, prefer the specific image. Ezra Pound, who urged writers to go in fear of abstractions, and who believed "It is better to present one image in a lifetime than to produce voluminous works," has given us some memorable images.

---

[9] **of fellowship:** *as a friend in the same situation*

[14] **call virtue . . . ungratefulness:** *call ungratefulness a virtue*

IN A STATION OF THE METRO

The apparition of these faces in the crowd;
  Petals on a wet, black bough.

Ezra Pound (1885–1972)

ALBA

As cool as the pale wet leaves of lily-of-the-valley
  She lay beside me in the dawn.

Ezra Pound

So have others in our century.

The house-wreckers have left the door and a staircase,
now leading to the empty room of night.

Charles Reznikoff (b. 1894)

About an excavation
a flock of bright red lanterns
has settled.

Charles Reznikoff

The way to read such poems as these and the two that follow is to let them run through the mind, stirring up what associations they will.

DISILLUSIONMENT OF TEN O'CLOCK

The houses are haunted
By white night-gowns.
None are green,
Or purple with green rings,
Or green with yellow rings,
Or yellow with blue rings.
None of them are strange,
With socks of lace
And beaded ceintures.
People are not going 10
To dream of baboons and periwinkles.
Only, here and there, an old sailor,
Drunk and asleep in his boots,
Catches tigers
In red weather.

Wallace Stevens (1879–1955)

---

[9] **ceintures:** *belts (French)*

MARIN-AN

sun breaks over the eucalyptus
grove below the wet pasture,
water's about hot,
I sit in the open window
& roll a smoke.

distant dogs bark, a pair of
cawing crows; the twang
of a pygmy nuthatch high in a pine—
from behind the cypress windrow
the mare moves up, grazing. 10

a soft continuous roar
comes out of the far valley
of the six-lane highway—thousands
and thousands of cars
driving men to work.

Gary Snyder

One could say that the first poem means that most people live colorless lives, with no gaudy individual gestures. One could say that the second means that a simple savoring of existence is better than joining the nine-to-five rat race. But both poems (like life itself) give only sense detail for us to interpret; neither openly professes a meaning or a moral. Neither does the poem that follows.

THE END OF THE WEEKEND

A dying firelight slides along the quirt
Of the cast-iron cowboy where he leans
Against my father's books. The lariat
Whirls into darkness. My girl, in skin-tight jeans,
Fingers a page of Captain Marryat,
Inviting insolent shadows to her shirt.

We rise together to the second floor.
Outside, across the lake, an endless wind
Whips at the headstones of the dead and wails
In the trees for all who have and have not sinned. 10
She rubs against me and I feel her nails.
Although we are alone, I lock the door.

The eventual shapes of all our formless prayers,
This dark, this cabin of loose imaginings,
Wind, lake, lip, everything awaits
The slow unloosening of her underthings.
And then the noise. Something is dropped. It grates
Against the attic beams.
I climb the stairs,

Armed with a belt. 20
A long magnesium strip
Of moonlight from the dormer cuts a path

Among the shattered skeletons of mice.
A great black presence beats its wings in wrath.
Above the boneyard burn its golden eyes.
Some small grey fur is pulsing in its grip.

Anthony Hecht (b. 1923)

The author presents his evidence—tells what happens—without comment.

Film makers often use imagery in a similar way.

In Claude Autant-Lara's *Le Diable au corps*, when the lovers embrace each other the camera leaves the bed and stands still in front of the fire, with its symbolic flames, while the music swells out, transforming and exalting an episode that could not have been handled visually. Later in the film, when the girl is dead and the man, in despair, mopes about the scene of his love, the camera makes exactly the same movement round the bed—this time empty—and finishes on the same grate—this time full of ashes.

There is a famous sequence at the end of Lewis Milestone's *All Quiet on the Western Front* in which the hero, Paul, a German soldier, is shot by a French sniper. The sniper is shown carefully aiming his rifle but all we see of Paul is his hand stretching out to try and touch a butterfly that has come to rest. We recognize it as Paul's hand because we already know he is a butterfly collector, and, because of the sniper, watch it stretching farther in anxious suspense. Then there is a shot, the hand jerks, slowly drops, and lies still. Paul's death is as vivid as if we had seen a full picture of him dying. . . .[1]

The fire, the bed, the ashes, the butterfly, the hand—these are the kind of images the poet also uses. A good way to check on the *visual* imagery in a poem is to ask: What kind of camerawork would it take to present this image? Could it be filmed at all?

NOTES FOR A MOVIE SCRIPT

Fade in the sound of summer music,
Picture a hand plunging through her hair,
Next his socked feet and her scuffed dance slippers
Close, as they kiss on the rug-stripped stair.

Catch now the taxi from the station,
Capture her shoulders' sudden sag;
Switch to him silent in the barracks
While the room roars at the corporal's gag.

Let the drums dwindle in the distance,
Pile the green sea above the land; 10
While she prepares a single breakfast,
Reading the V mail in her hand.

[1] R. Stephenson and Jean R. Debrix, *The Cinema as Art* (Baltimore: Penguin, 1965), pp. 205, 207.

---

[12] **V mail:** *"victory mail"—a photographic mail system used by the armed forces in World War II*

Ride a cold moonbeam to the pillbox,
Sidle the camera to his feet
Sprawled just outside in the gummy grasses,
Swollen like nightmare and not neat.

Now doorbell nudges the lazy morning:
She stills the sweeper for a while,
Twitches her dress, swings the screendoor open,
Cut—with no music—on her smile. 20

M. Carl Holman (b. 1919)

For examples of a technique like that of cinema we can go to some of the oldest poems in English, the folk ballads, which move, through graphic scenes generally without transition, from emotional highpoint to emotional highpoint.

SIR PATRICK SPENS

The king sits in Dumferling toune,
  Drinking the blude-reid wine:
"O whar will I get guid sailor,
  To sail this schip of mine?"

Up and spak an eldern knicht,
  Sat at the kings richt kne:
"Sir Patrick Spens is the best sailor,
  That sails upon the se."

The king has written a braid letter,
  And signd it wi' his hand; 10
And sent it to Sir Patrick Spens,
  Was walking on the sand.

The first line that Sir Patrick red,
  A loud lauch lauched he:
The next line that Sir Patrick red,
  The teir blinded his ee.

"O wha is this has don this deid,
  This ill deid don to me;
To send me out this time o' the yeir,
  To sail upon the se? 20

"Mak haste, mak haste, my mirry men all,
  Our guid schip sails the morne."
"O say na sae, my master deir,
  For I feir a deadlie storme.

---

[9] **braid:** *broad, long*
[14] **lauch:** *laugh*
[16] **ee:** *eye*
[17] **wha:** *who*
[23] **na sae:** *not so*

"Late, late yestreen I saw the new moone
  Wi' the auld moone in hir arme;
And I feir, I feir, my deir master,
  That we will cum to harme."

O our Scots nobles wer richt laith
  To weet their cork-heild shoone; 30
Bot lang owre a' the play wer playd,
  Thair hats they swam aboone.

O lang, lang, may thair ladies sit
  Wi' thair fans into their hand,
Or eir they se Sir Patrick Spens
  Cum sailing to the land.

O lang, lang, may the ladies stand,
  Wi' thair gold kems in their hair,
Waiting for thair ain deir lords,
  For they'll se thame na mair. 40

Haf owre, haf owre to Aberdour,
  It's fiftie fadom deip,
And thair lies guid Sir Patrick Spens,
  Wi' the Scots lords at his feit.

Anonymous (date uncertain)

One can imagine the action here filmed as a short art-movie, following the order of the stanzas. The scenario for the first three might run as follows:

1. Shot of king, surrounded by councillors. King's fingers move nervously on stem of wine goblet. He glances at window; storm outside. Tossing branches, fast-moving clouds, etc. King asks his question.
2. Camera goes from face to face of councillors. They look toward window. Gradually all look toward old knight. He answers. Reluctantly?
3. Shot of king's hand, signing letter with great flourish. Shot of Sir Patrick Spens, walking by surf. Stormy background. Small medieval ships drawn up on shore. His men nearby. He is handed the letter.

---

[25] **yestreen:** *yesterday evening*
[26] **auld:** *old*
[29] **richt laith:** *right loth*
[30] **weet . . . shoone:** *wet . . . shoes*
[31] **Bot lang owre a':** *but long before all*
[32] **swam aboon:** *floated above*
[35] **Or eir:** *before ever*
[38] **kems:** *combs*
[40] **na mair:** *no more*
[41] **Haf owre:** *half way over*

Exercises and Diversions

A. Since snakes do not have the same sensory equipment as we have, special problems come up for the poet who tries to get into the consciousness of a snake. How successfully is it done here?

RATTLER, ALERT

Slowly he sways that head that cannot hear,
Two-jeweled cone of horn the yellow of rust,
Pooled on the current of his listening fear.
His length is on the tympanum of earth,
And by his tendril tongue's tasting the air
He sips, perhaps, a secret of his race
Or feels for the known vibrations, heat, or trace
Of smoother satin than the hillwind's thrust
Through grass: the aspirate of my half-held breath,
The crushing of my weight upon the dust, 10
My foamless heart, the bloodleap at my wrist.

Brewster Ghiselin (b. 1903)

Rattlesnakes, which are deaf, are very sensitive to vibrations of the earth, their "tympanum" or eardrum. Their flickering tongues are "chemoreceptive," providing them with a chemical analysis of the environment. They also have infrared temperature-differential receptors to help locate warm-blooded prey. These are the scientific facts. How does the poet present them?

After several lines of "he . . . his" (referring to the snake), we suddenly get the "my" of the observer in the last three lines. What proprioceptive clues are there to the observer's emotional state?

Most of the lines end with a *th* sound or an *s* sound or an *st* sound. Could this use of sound be meaningful?

B. There is no point in trying to "speed read" a poem. Most have to be read slowly, with attention paid to the weight and suggestions of the words. Read and reread "The End of the Weekend" until you feel you understand the situation. Ask yourself such questions as these:

1. Does it matter that the firelight is "dying"?
2. Why is the girl "inviting" shadows? Why are they "insolent"?
3. Why are the imaginings "loose"?
4. Is there any special reason, in the poem, for the girl to be reading a book by Captain Marryat, a naval officer who wrote adventurous sea stories?
5. If they are alone, why does the man lock the door?
6. What does the image of the "great black presence" have to do with the love affair? What effect, if any, did it probably have on the lovers?

C.

O that 'twere possible
After long grief and pain
To find the arms of my true love
Round me once again!

Tennyson, in this excerpt from "Maud," is saying about the same thing as the author of "Western Wind." Most readers would probably feel that he is saying it less memorably. Would you agree? Find as many *specific* reasons as you can for the superiority of whichever version you prefer.

D. 1. What concrete images can you think of that might be used in a poem to stand for the essence of the following abstractions: exercise, diversion, nutriment, wretchedness, situation, velocity, attraction, immateriality, dryness, spiciness, agitation, deception, insufficiency, authority, success?

2. While walking, driving, or idling, make a list of ten objects that come to your attention. What abstractions (qualities, conditions, processes, etc.) could each stand for if mentioned in a poem?
3. Complete the scenario of "Sir Patrick Spens," using, where effective, concrete details not mentioned in the text but suggested by it. What other poems in this chapter would lend themselves to cinematic treatment?
4. Keeping as close to the original as you can, rewrite "Marin-An" so that the images imply—*without ever stating*—that it would be better to work at a regular job than to lounge around the house enjoying oneself.
5. The poem below (some would feel) is too abstract. What images could have been used to make the same point? Rewrite his poem, using your images—perhaps in the manner of "Marin-An" or another poem in this chapter. (For the present, write freely, disregarding "rules" about form, rhythm, etc.)

To spend uncounted years of pain,
Again, again, and yet again,
In working out in heart and brain
  The problem of our being here;
To gather facts from far and near,
Upon the mind to hold them clear,
And, knowing more may yet appear,
Unto one's latest breath to fear
The premature result to draw—
Is this the object, end and law, 10
  And purpose of our being here?

Arthur Hugh Clough (1819–1861)

E. A poem that directly expresses the emotion of its real or imagined speaker is called a **lyric**. It tends to be brief and in some way songlike—originally, a lyric was a poem sung to the music of a lyre. (We still speak of the "lyrics" of popular songs.) "Western Wind" is a perfect example of the lyric cry: the direct outpouring of the love and longing felt by the speaker. When lyric feeling chooses to express itself more self-consciously, at more length, in a more elaborate form, it is often called an **ode**, as in Keats' "Ode to a Nightingale" (p. 11).

If Keats *had* expressed the feelings of his ode in a four-line lyric, what kind of thing might he have said? If the author of "Western Wind" *had* written a six-stanza ode to his absent love, what might have been the substance of each of the six stanzas?

What's It Like? 2 simile and metaphor

The poet's preference for thinking in images, as we have seen, is not merely a literary mannerism; it is based on the way our body and mind put us in touch with the universe.

In the next four chapters we are going to consider how all of us—including the poets—compare and relate the images that come into our minds. To begin with, we organize them according to resemblances. A thought-pattern we use many times a day takes such forms as, "What is she really like?" "What's it like, being in college?" "What's it *like*?" Our effort to understand anything starts by relating it to something better known which it resembles. In 1971 two of our astronauts, working in moondust which they had never seen before, could use nothing but *like's* to describe it:

"When you put your scoop in, it smoothes it out—just like plaster."
"I was going to say—like cement."

The mind itself operates by finding likenesses. When a new piece of information is fed into the brain, it is whirled around the circuits until it finds its place with similar things. Otherwise we would not only learn nothing; we would not even long survive in a world full of hazards we have to identify.

Poets are only being like other people in wondering what things are like. "To what shall I compare thee, dear bridegroom?" asks Sappho. "Shall I compare thee," Shakespeare wonders, "to a summer's day?" The Song of Songs from the Bible delights in telling what things are like: "As the lily among thorns, so is my love among the daughters. As the apple tree among the trees of the wood, so is my beloved among the sons." The best known of the Psalms begins, "The Lord is my shepherd."

This need to compare is psychological and emotional. To describe the nature of moondust, the astronauts had to relate it to something familiar. But poets are not merely trying to convey information; they feel pleasure and give us pleasure in discovering resemblances that no one had noticed before. *It's true,* we feel, when coming on a good comparison, *It's true, but I never realized it!*

The meaning of Robinson Jeffers' "The Purse-Seine" is solemn enough, but there is something exciting and even beautiful in the way he relates his two sets of images. The discovery of any surprising likeness is one more clue to the fact that there seems to be an order—however deep and mysterious—in the universe.

THE PURSE-SEINE

Our sardine fishermen work at night in the dark of the moon; daylight or moonlight
They could not tell where to spread the net, unable to see the phosphorescence of the shoals of fish.
They work northward from Monterey, coasting Santa Cruz; off New Year's Point or off Pigeon Point
The look-out man will see some lakes of milk-color light on the sea's night-purple; he points, and the helmsman
Turns the dark prow, the motor-boat circles the gleaming shoal and drifts out her seine-net. They close the circle 10
And purse the bottom of the net, then with great labor haul it in.

I cannot tell you
How beautiful the scene is, and a little terrible, then, when the crowded fish
Know they are caught, and wildly beat from one wall to the other of their closing destiny the phosphorescent
Water to a pool of flame, each beautiful slender body sheeted with flame, like a live rocket
A comet's tail wake of clear yellow flame; while outside the narrowing
Floats and cordage of the net great sea-lions come up to watch, sighing in the dark; the vast walls of night 20
Stand erect to the stars.

Lately I was looking from a night mountain-top
On a wide city, the colored splendor, galaxies of light: how could I help but recall the seine-net
Gathering the luminous fish? I cannot tell you how beautiful the city appeared, and a little terrible.
I thought, We have geared the machines and locked all together into interdependence; we have built the great cities; now
There is no escape. We have gathered vast populations incapable of free survival, insulated 30
From the strong earth, each person in himself helpless, on all dependent. The circle is closed, and the net
Is being hauled in. They hardly feel the cords drawing, yet they shine already. The inevitable mass-disasters

Will not come in our time nor in our children's, but we and our children
Must watch the net draw narrower, government take all powers—or
  revolution, and the new government
Take more than all, add to kept bodies kept souls—or anarchy, the
  mass-disasters.
                    These things are 40
  Progress;
Do you marvel our verse is troubled or frowning, while it keeps its reason?
  Or it lets go, lets the mood flow
In the manner of the recent young men into mere hysteria, splintered
  gleams, cracked laughter. But they are quite wrong.
There is no reason for amazement: surely one always knew that cultures
  decay, and life's end is death.

Robinson Jeffers (1887–1962)

The discovery of likeness is often expressed by the figures of speech called **simile** and **metaphor.** There may be readers who think that "figures of speech" are artificial or fancy ways of saying what an honest man could say simply. But the important figures of speech are not merely tricks of rhetoric; they are names for natural operations of the mind. If a law were passed tomorrow that no one should use metaphorical expressions, people might indeed talk less than now, but their minds would continue to work in metaphor. Language itself is nothing but "figure of speech": we use a word when we mean a thing.

"Simile" is the Latin word for *like*; we use simile when we say one thing is *like* another. "Metaphor" is from the Greek word for *transfer*; in using it we transfer to one thing the name of something else we associate with it, as when we say that the heart of a cruel man is a stone or that a grumpy man is a bear. The obvious difference between simile and metaphor is that the first, by means of a word such as "like," "as," "as if," "than," compares two terms or images ("I feel like a wreck"); the second omits the linking word and seems to identify the two more wholeheartedly ("I'm a wreck!"). But often when we speak in metaphor we are really thinking in simile. When we say "That swimmer is a fish in the water" or "That boxer is a bull in the ring," we probably feel a *like* in our own thought: there is no question of a real fish or real bull being involved. Metaphor, since unqualified, is stronger than simile; since it is more concentrated, it hits with greater impact. The two terms cover different intensities of the same process, as the surrealist leader André Breton recognized when he said, "The most exalting word is the word LIKE, whether it is pronounced or implied."

In the essay quoted from in Chapter One, Emerson gives a number of examples of time-tested metaphors. Each could be made a simile by inserting a "like" between the two terms related.

> An enraged man is a lion, a cunning man is a fox, a firm man is a rock, a learned man is a torch.

We can see how language developed out of metaphor by noting the fossil metaphors it still contains: the *leg* of a table, the *mouth* of a river, the *teeth* of the wind. Nearly all slang is metaphor: "It's a drag"; "Let's split."

When we say, "A is like B" or "A is B," we are trying to show, in a fresh and vivid way, something about the nature of A. A good figure jolts us out of accustomed ruts of thinking and surprises us into a pleasant shock of recognition. Good metaphors, James Dickey reminds us, are adventurous. When John Clare writes:

> In gentle waves the river heaves
> That sways like boats the lily-leaves . . . .

we may feel that the floating leaves are so much like little boats that the point is hardly worth expressing. We may think that the head of a seal and a poodle in the water are so much alike that Robert Lowell is not being at his adventurous best in writing:

> A seal swims like a poodle through the sheet
> of blinding salt . . . .

Brewster Ghiselin, in comparing his killer whales to birds, is being bolder—and eerier:

> Slant of their fins asway like a wing speeding
> And heads rising blunt like a feeding swallow's
> They circle . . . .

On the other hand, the two things compared may be so far apart that we fail to see the point. "The sky's like an old tomato can." Surrealist images, often constructed gadgets rather than discoveries, are sometimes of this sort. Some are good, some bad (more about surrealist techniques later). Nothing, however, is easier than to be "original" in one's metaphors; what is hard is to be original and also true to experience. One can *say* anything is like anything else; there are no two things in the world, said Cicero, that cannot somehow be compared.

When a writer is using an "A is like B" formula to make a connection between two images, the B should be better known, more familiar, than the A, since the B is telling us something about the A. The greatest writers prefer very common, "unpoetic" objects for their B's, as Dante does when he compares a winged monster, resting his forepaws on the brink of a cliff, to a *scow* on a riverbank, or when he says that people passing in the moonlight squint, in order to recognize each other, like an *old tailor threading his needle*, or that the mind rests in the truth it has been seeking like an *animal in its den*; or as Villon does when he says that the teeth of a starving man stand out from his shrunken gums like those of a *rake*, or that the body of a hanged man on which the birds feed is more pecked at than a *thimble*. Many readers, coming on the metaphors that Maxine Kumin uses for early-morning birdsong, will find themselves reading with a smile of pleasant surprise. Birds are supposed to make pretty sounds. But these birds are compared to machines—and cranky, out-of-kilter machines at that. (Metaphors need not follow any one formula: speaking of "the typewriter bird" is another way of saying, "The bird is [like] a typewriter.")

THE HERMIT WAKES TO BIRD SOUNDS

He startles awake. His eyes are full of white light.
In a minute the sun will ooze into the sky.
Meanwhile, all the machines of morning start up.

The typewriter bird is at it again.
Her style is full of endearing hesitations.
The words, when they come, do so in
the staccato rush of a deceitful loveletter.

The sewing machine bird returns to the doddering elm.
Like Penelope, she rips out yesterday's stitches
only to glide up and down, front and back 10
reentering the same needle holes.

The bird who presides at the wellhouse primes the pump.
Two gurgles, a pause, four squeaks of the handle
and time after time a promise of water
can be heard falling back in the pipe's throat.

Far off the logging birds saw into heartwood
with rusty blades, and the grouse cranks up
his eternally unstartable Model T
and the oilcan bird comes with his liquid pock pock

to attend to the flinty clanks of the disparate parts 20
and as the old bleached sun slips into position
slowly the teasing inept malfunctioning
one-of-a-kind machines fall silent.

Maxine Kumin (b. 1925)

The B is also likely to be the more concrete of the two terms, as in John Donne's

Let falsehood like a *discord* anger you . . . .

or

If they are good it would be seen;
Good is as visible as *green* . . . .

In some comparisons, A is indeed like B in one respect, but B can imply other qualities so discordant that we feel the difference more strongly than the likeness:

Her even teeth, whiter than new [born] lambs,
When they with tender cries pursue their dams . . . .
Sir Charles Sedley

Thy teeth in white do Leda's swan exceed . . . .
Thomas Carew

Teeth and lambs are both white, but otherwise are ridiculously unlike. Teeth leaping around in the mouth? Feathery teeth?

The sheep more eager bite the grass
Where moisture gleams like drops of glass . . . .
John Clare

Edible glass?

CAUTION! HAZARDOUS READING! PROCEED WITH CARE!

On this page and similar pages throughout the book are selected examples, given as a kind of sensitivity training to sharpen the awareness of simile, metaphor, etc., when such figures do occur. They are not always present in poetry ("Western Wind" has none). They are never likely to occur as densely as they do on this page. A poem can have too many figures as well as too few.

[God] hangs in shades the orange bright,
Like golden lamps in a green night. — *Andrew Marvell*

The rushes whistle, sedges rustle,
The grass is buzzing round like bees. . . . — *John Clare*

Deep in the sun-searched growths the dragon-fly
Hangs like a blue thread loosened from the sky. . . . — *Dante Gabriel Rossetti*

The lamps, just lit, began to outloom
Like dandelion-globes in the gloom. . . . — *Thomas Hardy*

You tell me the lambs have come, they lie like daisies
white in the grass. . . . — *D. H. Lawrence*

[The blue bird] runs in the snow like a bit of blue metal . . .
You acid-blue metallic bird . . .
You copper-sulphate blue bird! — *D. H. Lawrence*

And then Llewellyn leapt and fled
Like one with hornets in his hair. . . . — *Edwin Arlington Robinson*

the goldfinches
leap up about my
feet like angry
dandelions — *Yvor Winters*

She rides her hips as
it were a horse — *William Carlos Williams*

Sun on their naked shoulders
Like a sparkling hand. . . . — *Kenneth Patchen*

We walk a great deal when the weather allows,
The women in shoes that look like baked potatoes. . . . — *Hollis Summers*

It was cold . . .
A ragman passed with his horses, their breaths
Blooming like white peonies. . . . — *Donald Hall*

Swift footsteps mount the stair; the door flies wide;
She sweeps in, brilliant as a breaking wave. . . . — *A. D. Hope*

The moon is blazing like a sign for beer. — *Louis Simpson*

My woman has a heart like a stone cast in the sea . . .
Put your arms around me like the circle 'round the sun. . . . — *Blues song*

. . . a sow
Displaying a valentine rump. . . . — *Adrien Stoutenburg*

. . . A light rain, as tranquil as an apple. . . . — *Anne Sexton*

Thomas Hardy has this to say of a growing family:

> And infant shapes might soon abound;
> Their shining heads would dot us round
> Like mushroom balls in grassy ground....

Even more dubious than Thomas Hardy's mushroom-headed babies is Elizabeth Barrett Browning's vision of the breasts of a nursing mother, luminously a-throb.

> ... mother's breasts
> Which, round the new-made creatures hanging there,
> Throb luminous and harmonious like pure spheres....

There is a possibility of such distraction arising in one of the most famous of the Imagist poems:

OREAD

Whirl up, sea—
whirl your pointed pines,
splash your great pines
on our rocks,
hurl your green over us,
cover us with your pools of fir.

H. D. (Hilda Doolittle, 1886–1961)

Waves may look like pine trees. But do pine trees splash? And would not a swimmer feel uncomfortable, thinking of all those needles? The textures of sea and pine trees are so different that our sense of touch may take over, and if it does the visual resemblance is not enough.

Sometimes a simile or metaphor will determine the structure of an entire poem, as we saw with "The Purse-Seine."

MOST LIKE AN ARCH THIS MARRIAGE

Most like an arch—an entrance which upholds
and shores the stone-crush up the air like lace.
Mass made idea, and idea held in place.
A lock in time. Inside half-heaven unfolds.

Most like an arch—two weaknesses that lean
into a strength. Two fallings become firm.
Two joined abeyances become a term
naming the fact that teaches fact to mean.

Not quite that? Not much less. World as it is,
what's strong and separate falters. All I do 10
at piling stone on stone apart from you
is roofless around nothing. Till we kiss

I am no more than upright and unset.
It is by falling in and in we make

the all-bearing point, for one another's sake,
in faultless failing, raised by our own weight.

John Ciardi (b. 1916)

MY LIFE HAD STOOD—A LOADED GUN

My Life had stood—a Loaded Gun—
In Corners—till a Day
The Owner passed—identified—
And carried Me away—

And now We roam the Sovereign Woods—
And now We hunt the Doe—
And every time I speak for Him
The Mountains straight reply—

And do I smile, such cordial light
Upon the Valley glow— 10
It is as a Vesuvian face
Had let its pleasure through—

And when at Night—Our good Day done—
I guard My Master's Head—
'Tis better than the Eider-Duck's
Deep Pillow—to have shared—

To foe of His—I'm deadly foe—
None stir the second time—
On whom I lay a Yellow Eye—
Or an emphatic Thumb— 20

Though I than He—may longer live
He longer must—than I—
For I have but the power to kill,
Without—the power to die—

Emily Dickinson (1830–1886)

In the above, the figures of speech are explicit. Merely to imply a metaphor can also be effective: to say that A is like B without ever naming B, but giving clues to B's identity.

. . . I looked, and Stella spied,
Who, hard by, made a window send forth light . . . *Sir Philip Sidney*

Stella's beauty is like a candle, a lamp, or some other source of light. Metaphors are also implied in:

Let ditch-bred wealth henceforth forget to wag
Her base, though golden, tail. . . . *Francis Quarles*

After all a poem is meant to be lived in
to be gone in and out of
and to learn from. . . . *Ramon Guthrie*

. . . When I next speak
Love buries itself in me, up to the hilt. . . . *James Merrill*

On Wednesday nights, the children rinsed and stacked,
The wives, their husbands closeted with *Time*. . . . *X. J. Kennedy*

Richard Brautigan implies one metaphor in the title of the poem that follows, but his poem develops a different one: Marcia's beauty is a subject as worthy of study as those taught in high school.

GEE, YOU'RE SO BEAUTIFUL THAT IT'S STARTING TO RAIN

Oh, Marcia,
I want your long blonde beauty
to be taught in high school,
so kids will learn that God
lives like music in the skin
and sounds like a sunshine harpsichord.
I want high school report cards
to look like this:

Playing with Gentle Glass Things
A 10

Computer Magic
A

Writing Letters to Those You Love
A

Finding out about Fish
A

Marcia's Long Blonde Beauty
A+!

Richard Brautigan (b. 1935)

In "No Second Troy" Yeats has written about a woman whose beauty and intensity are likely to bring trouble to the world: he implies she is like Helen of Troy.

NO SECOND TROY

Why should I blame her that she filled my days
With misery, or that she would of late
Have taught to ignorant men most violent ways,
Or hurled the little streets upon the great,
Had they but courage equal to desire?
What could have made her peaceful with a mind
That nobleness made simple as a fire,
With beauty like a tightened bow, a kind
That is not natural in an age like this,
Being high and solitary and most stern? 10

> Why, what could she have done, being what she is?
> Was there another Troy for her to burn?
>
> *W. B. Yeats (1865–1939)*

Besides the implied image, the poem has two others of an especially powerful sort. In some "A is like B" images, certain overtones of the B make the comparison ridiculous. Images in "No Second Troy" do just the opposite: besides being like A, the B is charged with other suggestions that throw light on A. The woman has a mind "that nobleness made simple as a fire." Fire is simple, yes; but, like all basic symbols, it is ambivalent. It is beautiful, vivid, life-giving; it is also ominous and destructive, as the woman is. Her nobility may be simple, but—watch out! Her beauty is "like a tightened bow," its lines gracefully and dynamically curved. But a tightened bow is also threatening, like a pointed revolver. The apparently simple images carry what we could call a *supercharge.*

Images can be weak because the tone or suggestion of one part is at odds with the effect intended, as in

> Once more at dawn I drive
> The weary cattle of my soul to the mudhole of your eyes.

"Mudhole" is right with "cattle"; with "your eyes," however, it is hardly apt.

Another common weakness is what is called a *mixed metaphor*—that is, a metaphor made up of components that do not go together. "Skating on thin ice" and "being in hot water" are sensible enough metaphors (though trite) for hazardous actions and embarrassing predicaments. But if a person says, "People who skate on thin ice are likely to find themselves in hot water," he is mixing a metaphor and, unless he intends to be funny, is writing awkwardly. Mixed metaphors are like double exposures in photography. Some may be deliberate, some may accidentally result in a good picture. Most are plain failures, with results comic, ugly, or merely blurred.

John Ciardi, in describing the fields just after a spring thaw, begins, "The paper fields . . . ." "Paper," then, is his metaphor. He continues the line, ". . . lay crumpled by the road." If the fields are paper, they have to do something paperlike; they have to be "crumpled." A less skillful writer might have said, "The paper fields lie shattered by the road," forgetting that paper cannot shatter. Pablo Neruda, as translated by W. S. Merwin, writes:

> The clouds travel like white handkerchiefs of goodbye . . . .

and then continues the image with:

> The wind, travelling, waving them in its hands . . . .

Suppose he had written:

metaphor

. . . She dressed her mind
As others do their bodies, and refined
That better part with care, and still did wear
More jewels in her manners than her ear. . . . *William Cartwright*

Forbear, thou great good husband, little ant,
A little respite from thy flood of sweat;
Thou, thine own horse and cart, under this plant
Thy spacious tent. . . . *Robert Herrick*

Our hearts are paper, beauty is the pen
Which writes our loves, and blots 'em out again. . . . *Sir Charles Sedley*

Love melts the rigor which the rocks have bred;
A flint will break upon a feather-bed. . . . *John Cleveland*

A stately frontispiece of poor
Adorns without the open door;
Nor less the rooms within commends
Daily new furniture of friends. . . . *Andrew Marvell*

Where bird with painted oars did ne'er
Row through the trackless ocean of the air. *Abraham Cowley*

A bird . . .
And he unrolled his feathers
And rowed him softer home—

Than oars divide the ocean
Too silver for a seam. *Emily Dickinson*

Her nimble tongue, love's lesser lightning, played
Within my mouth, and to my thoughts conveyed
Swift orders that I should prepare to throw
The all-dissolving thunderbolt below. . . . *The Earl of Rochester*

The haughty thistle o'er all danger towers,
In every place the very wasp of flowers. *John Clare*

She held out
Her deck of smiles, I cut, and she dealt. . . . *Randall Jarrell*

Boys are the cash of war. Whoever said
we're not free-spenders doesn't know our likes. *John Ciardi*

. . . If you can beg the
money for it, dial God, and if a
creed answers, hang up. *John Ciardi*

. . . You slip in
Noisy knives of why. *Richard Hugo*

The clouds travel like white handkerchiefs of goodbye;
The wind is balancing them like a juggler....

The image would have been ridiculous: handkerchiefs are hard to balance. Sylvia Plath gives a particularly sustained example of imagery in her "Hardcastle Crags":

Flintlike, her feet struck
Such a racket of echoes from the steely street,
... that she heard the quick air ignite
Its tinder and shake

A firework of echoes....

She begins with "flintlike," the street is "steely," the air a "tinder" that can "ignite" a "firework." Four stanzas later she is "a pinch of flame." In the last stanza there is "Enough to snuff the quick of her small heat out." Beginning as flint, she ends the poem as "mere quartz grit."

Sometimes an image is sustained throughout a poem, as when a dead soldier is seen as a fallen lance.

A SOLDIER

He is that fallen lance that lies as hurled,
That lies unlifted now, come dew, come rust,
But still lies pointed as it plowed the dust.
If we who sight along it round the world,
See nothing worthy to have been its mark,
It is because like men we look too near,
Forgetting that as fitted to the sphere,
Our missiles always make too short an arc.
They fall, they rip the grass, they intersect
The curve of earth, and striking, break their own; 10
They make us cringe for metal-point on stone.
But this we know, the obstacle that checked
And tripped the body, shot the spirit on
Further than target ever showed or shone.

Robert Frost (1874–1963)

Unity of image can act as a powerful cohesive force. The poem would have been less strongly structured if it had begun:

He is that fallen lance that lies as hurled;
He is a bright wing blasted from the sky;
A ship that sank in sight of port; a sigh
Breathed heavenward; glory's flag forever furled...

Frost's poem is based on a metaphor; the following one, on a simile. Again, the basic figure—old people are like birds—makes sense on *both* levels (that of people and that of birds) all through the poem.

CITY PIGEONS

Old people are like birds:
the same words flock to the mind's eye
in speaking of them.
They perch in public places,
scratch for the world's crumbs, seek
its shiny trifles—
easily ruffled
are quick to realight, alert
and nodding,
cheeky occupants of plazas, 10
monuments' companions, supplicants
in lime-specked groves
to dirty mysteries.

Helen Chasin (b. 1938)

On the other hand, images may be sustained at too great a cost, as they are in this anonymous little verse:

God took our flower—our little Nell.
He thought He too would like a smell.

Images are not felt as mixed when the poet makes a clean break with one before going on to another, as Burns does when he writes:

O my love's like a red, red rose
That's newly sprung in June;
O my love's like the melody
That's sweetly played in tune ....

If he had written:

O my love's like a red, red rose
That sings a merry tune ....

it would be mixed. But, as with a dissolve in the movies, when one scene fades out and another appears, no confusion is felt. Unfortunately, there is no such dissolve in Henry Vaughan's lines:

Here like two balls of new fallen snow
Her breasts, love's native pillows, grow....

Breasts can be pillows. Or—less pleasantly—they can be snowballs. They cannot reasonably be both at the same time.

Analogy

Any resemblance, in form or function, between unlike objects can be called analogy. More specifically, **analogy** is a kind of metaphor that reasons: since A is like B in some respects, it is possible to suppose

ANALOGY

And why take ye thought for raiment? Consider the lilies of the field, how they grow; they toil not, neither do they spin: and yet I say unto you, That even Solomon in all his glory was not arrayed like one of these.

Matthew, 6

Old wood inflamed, doth yield the bravest fire,
When younger doth in smoke his virtue spend. . . . *Sir Philip Sidney*

Yet him for this my love no whit disdaineth;
Suns of the world may stain, when heaven's sun staineth.

William Shakespeare

No more be grieved at that which thou hast done:
Roses have thorns, and silver fountains mud;
Clouds and eclipses stain both moon and sun,
And loathsome canker lives in sweetest bud.
All men make faults. . . . *William Shakespeare*

Thin airy things extend themselves in space,
 Things solid take up little place. . . . *Abraham Cowley*

But 'tis too much on so despised a theme:
No man would dabble in a dirty stream. . . . *The Earl of Rochester*

Nothing in progression can rest on its original plan. We may as well think of rocking a grown man in the cradle of an infant. *Edmund Burke*

The worthless cipher when alone
Is in himself much less than one,
But placed behind more cunning men
Exalts each figure up to ten,
And when two thoughtless noughts have blundered,
The knave before becomes a hundred.

So, by the aid of worthless fools,
The man who knows to use his tools. . . . *Matthew Prior*

Try as he will, no man breaks wholly loose
 From his first love, no matter who she be.
Oh, was there ever sailor free to choose,
 That didn't settle somewhere near the sea? *Rudyard Kipling*

I want
to do with you what spring does with the cherry trees. *Pablo Neruda*

The genuine justifies the genuine:
A false coin dropped on a stone farmhouse floor
Is heard as false: but every coiner knows
This cannot happen on the boardroom carpet. . . . *John Wain*

that other resemblances follow. The poet's mind—like the subconscious mind of the dreamer and the prelogical mind of the child—is more moved by similarities and parallels than by stricter forms of logic; analogy seems to be the poet's favorite form of reasoning. When Sir Philip Sidney writes:

> Thus noble gold down to the bottom goes,
> When worthless cork aloft doth floating lie....

he means that since certain values in life are good as gold and others cheap and lightweight as cork, perhaps these values behave like gold and cork in the current of life: the best may sink from sight, the worst stay conspicuously on top.

THE LOWEST TREES HAVE TOPS

The lowest trees have tops, the ant her gall,
The fly her spleen, the little sparks their heat;
The slender hairs cast shadows, though but small;
And bees have stings, although they be not great.
  Seas have their source, and so have shallow springs,
  And love is love, in beggars as in kings.

Where rivers smoothest run, deep are the fords;
The dial stirs, yet none perceives it move;
The firmest faith is in the fewest words;
The turtles cannot sing, and yet they love. 10
  True hearts have eyes and ears, no tongues to speak;
  They hear, and see, and sigh, and then they break.

Sir Edward Dyer (1534–1607)

Dyer's argument is that there are certain features or qualities possessed just as surely by humble things as by great ones: small trees have tops just as tall ones have. So too with love, he analogizes—a humble man can love. The second stanza says that things which possess certain qualities may be quiet about possessing them. True lovers are not those who talk the most.

Abraham Cowley has written a playfully analogical argument for the naturalness of drinking.

DRINKING

The thirsty Earth soaks up the Rain,
And drinks, and gapes for drink again.
The Plants suck in the Earth, and are
With constant drinking fresh and fair.

---

8 **dial:** *sundial*
10 **turtles:** *turtledoves, which are proverbially affectionate*

The Sea itself, which one would think
Should have but little need of Drink,
Drinks ten thousand Rivers up,
So fill'd that they or'eflow the Cup.
The busie Sun (and one would guess
By's drunken fiery face no less)
Drinks up the Sea, and when h'as done,
The Moon and Stars drink up the Sun.
They drink and dance by their own light,
They drink and revel all the night.
Nothing in Nature's Sober found,
But an eternal Health goes round.
Fill up the Bowl then, fill it high,
Fill all the Glasses there, for why
Should every creature drink but *I*,
Why, Man of Morals, tell me why?

Abraham Cowley (1618–1667)

One might, however, turn the tables on Cowley by pointing out that what his poem proves is that we should drink nothing but water.

Allusion

Another recognition of similarity is **allusion,** which follows an "it-reminds-me-of" pattern. An allusion is an incomplete reference to something that those who share our knowledge or background will understand. In conversation we often use such allusions as "There he goes acting like Bill!" or "I hope this evening won't be like the last one." To an outsider, the meaning of such an allusion would be obscure. Poets, naturally at home with poetry, sometimes quote from or allude to other writers (as Picasso likes to "quote" from other painters). When Robert Frost, writing about the accidental death of a farm boy, calls his poem " 'Out, Out—,' " he assumes we will remember Macbeth's famous remarks on life and death,

Out, out, brief candle!
Life's but a walking shadow. . . .

and that his poem will pick up an added pathos from the memory. When Alexander Pope writes his "Intended for Sir Isaac Newton," he trusts we will all hear the allusion to the first chapter of Genesis.

INTENDED FOR SIR ISAAC NEWTON

Nature and Nature's laws lay hid in Night:
God said, *Let Newton be!* and all was Light.

Alexander Pope (1688–1744)

Coming across a description of a sleeping girl in a poem by L. E. Sissman, some readers will immediately remember three lines that Wordsworth wrote in his "Composed Upon Westminster Bridge" (p. 77):

> This city now doth, like a garment, wear
> The beauty of the morning; silent, bare,
> Ships, towers, domes, theaters, and temples lie. . . .

They will be amused at what use the poet, with the help of a pun or two, has made of them:

> This Sally now does like a garment wear
> The beauty of the evening; silent, bare,
> Hips, shoulders, arms, tresses, and temples lie. . . .

Exercises and Diversions

A. Ponder the similes and metaphors in the following quotations. Do any of them work out well?

1. Fair under these [her lips] doth stately grow
   The handle of this pleasant work,
   The neck. . . . — *Sir Philip Sidney*
2. O honied sighs, which from that breast do rise,
   Whose pants do make unspilling cream to flow. . . . — *Sir Philip Sidney*
3. Money is like muck, not good except it be spread. — *Sir Francis Bacon*
4. Slow time, with woollen feet make thy soft pace,
   And leave no tracks in the snow of her pure face. . . . — *Richard Lovelace*
5. Fain would I kiss my Julia's dainty leg,
   Which is as white and hairless as an egg. — *Robert Herrick*
6. Sweet marmalade of kisses newly gathered. . . . — *Margaret Cavendish*
7. Sweet maidens with tanned faces,
   And bosoms fit to broil. . . . — *John Clare*
8. Silently one by one, in the infinite meadows of heaven,
   Blossom the lovely stars, the forget-me-nots of the angels. . . .
   Henry Wadsworth Longfellow
9. And sometimes it is raining
   And the little drops scuttle
   Like the feet of angels on the roof. . . . — *Kenneth Patchen*
10. . . . Up the path that's pinpricked with
    yellow fallen crumbs of pollen. . . . — *Denise Levertov*
11. The water sweeps past in flood,
    dragging a whole tree by the hair. . . . — *Denise Levertov*
12. a gentle quiet filling the house like
    a glass of water. . . . — *Ron Loewinsohn*

B. 1. How are metaphors used in the following passage?
("Cat's-paws" are movements of the wind as shown on the surface of water.)

> I watched his face swept by cat's-paws
> when we found the camp tumbledown,
> and back of cabins drunken Chryslers,
> Hudsons even—old elephants—fallen
> on alder swords through their ribs. . . . *William Stafford*

2. To describe the nature of a quarrel, John Peck has recourse to metaphor, first telling what the quarrel was not like, then telling what it was like. Until we begin to think in images and to feel the emotions they arouse, this may seem a difficult poem. Try visualizing the images, especially the rowing scene; see what emotions they stir up. Now, explain the nature of the quarrel in "everyday English."

A QUARREL

It was no polished blade,
Nor the bright accidental blood,
Nor even rock split clean
By the green wedge
Of saxifrage—

But more like March wind, heady
And chill,
With sculls rehearsing for their race,
Their crews hunched into place,
One of them poised and still, 10
Oars at the ready,
Until another warily
Pulls even with it—
then together
They lunge out suddenly in step,
Stroke and then feather,
Accurate flash and dip
Down their barked cadences.

John Peck (b. 1941)

C. 1. In attacking the notion, held by some linguists, that there is no such thing as "good English," and that the only standard is what people say, Theodore M. Bernstein, in *The Careful Writer*, uses three analogies: there are more bad fiddlers than good, yet no one hesitates to say there is such a thing as good violin playing; there are more golfers who shoot in the nineties than in the seventies, yet we know there is a right way to play golf; there are more awkward do-it-yourself carpenters than competent professionals, yet we know there are right and wrong ways of doing carpentry work. "In language alone," he concludes, "are the bunglers blessed." Do his analogies constitute good metaphoric reasoning?

In the cartoon on p. 40, the use of metaphor has led to a failure of communication. Has the poet chosen his metaphors badly? Or has the bird misin-

2.

B.C. **By Johnny Hart**

By permission of John Hart and Field Enterprises, Inc.

terpreted them? Through malice? Through stupidity? (The lazy mind hates metaphor, says Diana in George Meredith's *Diana of the Crossways.*)

D. 1. Make up five deliberately mixed metaphors.

2. Marianne Moore found a simple, true, and original comparison in her ". . . the elephants with their *fog-colored* skin. . . ." Can you think of a comparison, at once simple, true, and original, to fill in the blank ". . . the lions with their ________-colored skin . . ."? Replace "lions" with "zebras," "giraffes," "polar bears," "toads," and then fill in the blanks.

3. Sylvia Plath found a simple, true, and original simile for pears in the orchard in her "The pears fatten like little buddhas." With what verb and what simile would you fill in the blanks in "The bananas ________ like ________"? What if the fruit were peaches, grapes, coconuts, strawberries?

The Broken Coin 3
the use of symbol

In the preceding chapter we saw that a typical metaphor has an "A-is-B" pattern, as in "life is a dream." (Even though we express this as "the dream of life" or "this dream-life we live," we are still relying on our basic equation.) In such a pattern, the focus is on the A; we are being told more about the nature of life than about the nature of dreams.

We also saw that in metaphor the B is likely to be better known, more concrete, more of a sense-image than the A: the nature of a dream is more readily grasped than the nature of life.

The **symbol**, an image that stands for more than it denotes literally, is like metaphor in that it transfers meaning from one thing to another. But with symbol the current of interest is reversed: our concern is directed from the first term to the second. The A is better known, more concrete, more of a sense-image than what should be the B—which is often an abstraction the user does not even identify. If the poet mentions a rose, but is really thinking of the nature of beauty, then he is using *rose* as a symbol of beauty. If he mentions that he is halfway along a road, but is really thinking that he is in his middle thirties, then he is using *road* as a symbol of his life-span. If he uses his *rose* and *road* symbols well, he need not refer to beauty or life at all; we will know that he has something more in mind than a real rose or a real road. If we think of the metaphoric process as "A-is-B," we might think of the symbolic one as "A-is-X," with the X usually unidentified.

Symbolic images generally are physical objects: a hill, a well, a river. They symbolize such abstractions as spiritual ascent, vitality, time. If we look back at the passage of Emerson quoted for its examples of metaphor (p. 24), we can see that if we reverse the A's and B's, turning what were the A's into abstractions, we have a series of symbols. A lion can be a symbol for anger; a fox, for cunning; a rock for firmness; a torch, for learning. Light is a symbol for knowledge; darkness for ignorance. "Who looks upon a river in a meditative hour," wonders Emerson, "and is not reminded of the flux of all things?" A river, that is, can be a symbol for time or change.

In García Lorca's "Sleepwalkers' Ballad" (p. 401), a young man, dying of gunshot wounds, comes to see for the last time the woman he loves. To her father he says:

> "Friend, what I want is to trade
> this horse of mine for your house,
> this saddle of mine for your mirror,
> this knife of mine for your blanket."

None of this is meant literally; the young man would not have inserted in a Córdoba newspaper a want ad reading: "Will trade horse, saddle, knife for house, mirror, blanket." The objects mentioned are symbols of two ways of life; the dying man means, "I wish I could settle down and marry your daughter."

The use of such symbols, like that of other poetic "devices," is based on the way the mind really works. Our senses are affected by something. They send their electrical message to the brain, which interprets it as an image, a symbol of the original object that moved them. We express the image by using a word which is a symbol for that symbol. When we say anything we have already built symbol on symbol.

A baby begins to think symbolically early in its development, associating the opening of a door with food-mother-warmth. Later, the adult dreams in symbols. For man in the uncivilized state, almost everything is symbolic, stands for something else. The most meaningful symbols are such natural ones as fire, water, air, and earth. Although these symbols are few in number, they have been significant to man for the hundreds of thousands of years he has existed. "No genius," says Jung, "has ever sat down with a pen or a brush in his hand and said, 'Now I am going to invent a symbol.' "

Not a natural symbol, that is. There are symbols that we do make up. Most words are invented symbols; so are flags, crosses, traffic signs, valentine hearts, and the like.

Howard Nemerov gives us an introductory lecture, with illustrations, on the symbolism of a coin.

MONEY
an introductory lecture

> This morning we shall spend a few minutes
> Upon the study of symbolism, which is basic
> To the nature of money. I show you this nickel.
> Icons and cryptograms are written all over
> The nickel: one side shows a hunchbacked bison
> Bending his head and curling his tail to accommodate
> The circular nature of money. Over him arches
> UNITED STATES OF AMERICA, and, squinched in

Between that and his rump, E PLURIBUS UNUM,
A Roman reminiscence that appears to mean 10
An indeterminately large number of things
All of which are the same. Under the bison
A straight line giving him a ground to stand on
Reads FIVE CENTS. And on the other side of our nickel
There is the profile of a man with long hair
And a couple of feathers in the hair; we know
Somehow that he is an American Indian, and
He wears the number nineteen-thirty-six.
Right in front of his eyes the word LIBERTY, bent
To conform with the curve of the rim, appears 20
To be falling out of the sky Y first; the Indian
Keeps his eyes downcast and does not notice this;
To notice it, indeed, would be shortsighted of him.
So much for the iconography of one of our nickels,
Which is now becoming a rarity and something of
A collectors' item: for as a matter of fact
There is almost nothing you can buy with a nickel,
The representative American Indian was destroyed
A hundred years or so ago, and his descendants'
Relations with liberty are maintained with reservations, 30
Or primitive concentration camps; while the bison,
Except for a few examples kept in cages,
Is now extinct. Something like that, I think,
Is what Keats must have meant in his celebrated
Ode on a Grecian Urn. 
Notice, in conclusion,
A number of circumstances sometimes overlooked
Even by experts: (*a*) Indian and bison,
Confined to obverse and reverse of the coin,
Can never see each other; (*b*) they are looking 40
In opposite directions, the bison past
The Indian's feathers, the Indian past
The bison's tail; (*c*) they are upside down
To one another; (*d*) the bison has a human face
Somewhat resembling that of Jupiter Ammon. 
I hope that our studies today will have shown you
Something of the import of symbolism
With respect to the understanding of what is symbolized.

Howard Nemerov (b. 1920)

It helps to remember that the Greek word *symbolon* means something *put together*—originally a coin (or potsherd) broken into two pieces, one of which was given to each of the parties in a legal agreement as identification. This half coin became a *symbol*: it hinted that something more was needed to complete its meaning.

A poem ascribed to Plato uses the apple symbolically. To toss an apple in someone's direction meant to make a "pass" at this person; it was a way of saying, "I want your love." But the apple in Plato's poem means even more: it stands for the brevity of natural life and beauty. The poem is saying, as so many have said, "Now is the time for making love; man does not have forever."

THE APPLE

I've tossed an apple at you; if you can love me,
take it. Give me your girlhood in exchange.
If you think what I hope you won't, though,
take it, look at it:
consider how briefly its beauty is going to last.

Plato (late fifth and early fourth century B.C.*)*

It is not always easy to distinguish between symbol and metaphor. Most readers would probably feel that Plato's poem is symbolic because it does preserve the "A-is-X" pattern. A is for apple—a real apple. But we are not told precisely what the apple stands for, though the words "love" and "beauty" are clues. But Plato has more in mind than the beauty of the apple. To some readers, Jeffers' "The Purse-Seine" (p. 23) might seem a symbolic poem, but since both the A and B are concrete and explicit, it is not really using symbol. Jeffers could have made it symbolic by describing only the sardine-fishing, but in such a way that we knew he had more than fishing in mind. Helen Chasin's "City Pigeons" (p. 34) also uses simile rather than symbol, since she is talking about both A and B. It could have been made symbolic if she had described only pigeons, but in such a way that we began to feel the human overtones, and to suspect that she was talking about more than birds.

One of our problems is to know a symbol when we see one. Freud, twitted because his cigars looked like Freudian symbols, replied tartly that sometimes a cigar was just a cigar. Sometimes the images in a poem are just themselves. An apple is an apple; a rose is a rose. They are impoverished, not enriched, by being seen as symbols. When the poet says "bed" in "Western Wind," we can be pretty sure he means an actual bed. One could read the poem symbolically and decide the lines mean: "When will the breath of the Spirit descend on me with life-giving grace, so that I may rest in the security of true belief with what I love the most—my virtue?" Common sense tells us such a reading is improbable.

Common sense also tells us that the corkscrew mentioned in the poem below is a symbolic one that will never be put to literal use.

WRITTEN ON A GIRL'S TABLE-NAPKIN AT WIESBADEN

If he were to walk into this cafe
I doubt if you'd notice him
Nor know how long he sat there alone
Stirring his coffee, perhaps smoking one cigarette after another

As though waiting for somebody
But without an appointment,

Nor would you notice that he was gone.
If he walked beside you, you would quicken your step.
And if he spoke to you with his slow eyes
You would look away and order another cocktail. 10

You would mistake his gentleness for effeminacy.
You would call his kindness, weakness.
You would have no time for him.
So why not take off that crucifix round your neck
And hang a corkscrew there?

Ronald Duncan (b. 1914)

Angry at being neglected by a girl he thinks lacking in understanding and sympathy, the speaker feels that the symbolism of the crucifix she is wearing does not really fit in with her character. A more appropriate symbol, he suggests, would be a corkscrew—a twisted thing associated with cocktail lounges.

When physical objects do not quite seem to make sense on a literal level, we may find they are serving as symbols. This seems to be happening with the rather odd exchange of property in the poem that follows.

HOPE

I gave to Hope a watch of mine: but he
An anchor gave to me.
Then an old prayer-book I did present:
And he an optic sent.
With that I gave a vial full of tears:
But he a few green ears.
Ah loiterer! I'll no more, no more I'll bring:
I did expect a ring.

George Herbert (1593–1633)

Even if we assumed that "Hope" was not a symbolic figure for the virtue of that name, but an actual person named, say, Wilbur P. Hope, junk-shop owner, it is difficult to imagine such an exchange taking place. The third transaction is particularly bizarre—but so is this whole way of doing business. None of this, we soon suspect, is meant literally. The watch means, "It's time!" The anchor, a traditional symbol of faith, means, "Hold on a while." The old prayer book, "But I've been devout for a long time!" The "optic" or telescope, "Look beyond." The vial, "I've suffered and longed!" The green ears, "Some day the time will be ripe." The ring, "But I want fulfillment, complete joy—like that of a marriage."

A. D. Hope addresses one of his poems to the lingam and yoni, Hindu symbols of male and female sexuality. Here they represent a typical he and she who fall in love, only to be burdened by the usual obligations.

THE LINGAM AND THE YONI

The Lingam and the Yoni
Are walking hand in glove,
O are you listening, honey?
I hear my honey-love.

The He and She our movers
What is it they discuss?
Is it the talk of Lovers?
And do they speak of us?

I hear their high palaver—
O tell me what they say! 10
The talk goes on for ever
So deep in love are they;

So deep in thought, debating
The suburb and the street;
Time-payment calculating
Upon the bedroom suite.

But ours is long division
By love's arithmetic,
Until they make provision
To buy a box of brick, 20

A box that makes her prisoner,
That he must slave to win
To do the Lingam honour,
To keep the Yoni in.

The mortgage on tomorrow?
The hemorrhage of rent?
Against the heart they borrow
At five or six per cent.

The heart has bought fulfilment
Which yet their mouths defer 30
Until the last instalment
Upon the furniture.

No Lingam for her money
Can make up youth's arrears:
His layby on the Yoni
Will not be paid in years.

And they, who keep this tally,
They count what they destroy;
While, in its secret valley
Withers the herb of joy. 40

A. D. Hope (b. 1907)

Images are not always as explicit as in the two preceding poems.

LULLY, LULLEY, LULLY, LULLEY

Lully, lulley, lully, lulley,
The fawcon hath born my mak away.

He bare hym up, he bare hym down;
He bare hym in to an orchard browne.

In that orchard ther was an halle,
That was hangid with purpill and pall.

And in that hall ther was a bedde;
Hit was hangid with gold so redde.

And yn that bed ther lythe a knyght,
His wowndes bledyng day and nyght. 10

By that bedes side kneleth a may,
& she wepeth both nyght and day.

& by that bedes side ther stondeth a ston,
Corpus Christi wretyn ther on.

Anonymous (early sixteenth century)

Much of the appeal of these lines, which are at least as old as "Western Wind," lies in their mystery. We feel that something significant is going on, but are not quite sure what. The symbolic situation could stand for many things in the drama of life and death.

Symbolic poems are not less satisfactory when we cannot provide the symbols with an exact meaning. In fact, it often seems the most compelling symbols direct us to an area of speculation rather than to any single object.

THE SICK ROSE

O Rose, thou art sick!
The invisible worm
That flies in the night,
In the howling storm,

Has found out thy bed
Of crimson joy:
And his dark secret love
Does thy life destroy.

William Blake (1757–1827)

The rose, traditionally a symbol of love and beauty, is here something that has life and is in a bed of vivid joy. The worm is a source of corruption, is secret, works in the dark, is associated with a violent dis-

---

2 **fawcon:** *falcon*
mak: *mate*
6 **pall:** *rich cloth*
11 **may:** *maiden*
14 **Corpus Christi:** *body of Christ*

order in nature. Many kinds of beauty and love are threatened by many kinds of destructive secret forces. The poem is more powerful in not compelling us to fix on any one of the possibilities; we are free to range among them, feeling the force of now one, now another. A symbol that has to explain itself, that feels apologetic about its presence, is not a healthy symbol.

Robert Frost can be a tricky writer, faking out a hasty reader in poem after poem. Frost himself said he never wrote a nature poem. Instead, he got a great deal of fun—to use a favorite word of his—out of saying one thing and meaning another.

ACQUAINTED WITH THE NIGHT

I have been one acquainted with the night.
I have walked out in rain—and back in rain.
I have outwalked the furthest city light.

I have looked down the saddest city lane.
I have passed by the watchman on his beat
And dropped my eyes, unwilling to explain.

I have stood still and stopped the sound of feet
When far away an interrupted cry
Came over houses from another street,

But not to call me back or say good-by; 10
And further still at an unearthly height
One luminary clock against the sky

Proclaimed the time was neither wrong nor right.
I have been one acquainted with the night.

Robert Frost

Good symbols always seem real; unless they are convincing in themselves we probably do not care what they stand for. Frost knew about walks in the city at night. Everything about his poem is authentic—and yet suggestions, like widening ripples, fade off into remoteness and mystery. The poem would be poorer if it simply said: "I have known the dark side of life, the loneliness and misery and violence and oppression, the inability of all of our standards to give any ultimately satisfying answer."

The poet who works in symbols is likely to give more care to the vividness of his images than to the abstractions they stand for. Images can sometimes be so real that we are not at first aware they are symbols, though something a little strange about them may lead us to feel, perhaps only half consciously, that more is going on than we are aware of. If one came to the poem below with no knowledge about the author, he might take it for a literal love-poem: a girl steals away from her house secretly at night, makes her way through the darkness of a sleeping town, meets her lover in a cedar grove by a castle-wall, and is made so ecstatically happy that she almost loses consciousness.

THE DARK NIGHT

Once in the dark of night
when love burned bright with yearning, I arose
(O windfall of delight!)
and how I left none knows—
dead to the world my house, in dull repose;

in the dark, where all goes right,
by means of a secret ladder, other clothes
(O windfall of delight!)
in the dark, and hid from those—
dead to the world my house, in dull repose. 10

There in the lucky dark,
none to observe me; darkness far and wide;
no sign for me to mark,
no other light, no guide
except for my heart—the fire, the fire inside!

That led me on
true as the very noon is—truer too!—
to where there waited one
I knew—how well I knew!—
in a place where no one was in view. 20

O dark of night, my guide!
night dearer than anything all your dawns discover!
O night drawing side to side
the loved and lover—
she that the lover loves, lost in the lover!

On blossoms of my breast
kept for his pleasure garden, his alone,
the lover was sunk in rest;
I cherished him—my own—
there in air from plumes of the cedar blown. 30

Air from the castle wall,
as my hand in his hair moved lovingly at play,
let cool fingers fall
and it seared me where they lay!
All senses in oblivion drift away.

I stayed there, quite forgot me,
my forehead on the lover I reclined.
Earth ended. I was not-me,
left all my care behind
among the lilies falling and out of mind. 40

Saint John of the Cross (1549–1591)

But the poet, one of the greatest of Spanish mystics, is writing about the love between God and the human soul. Günter Grass, the contemporary German novelist, has said, "I don't know about God. I couldn't write about God in detail. The only things I know are what I see, hear, feel and smell." If a man can know anything about God, Saint John probably knew it—but he also knew that one writes a poem in images of what he sees, hears, feels, smells.

THING-POEMS

Sometimes a poem that seems to be a description of an object will offer a basis for a symbolic reading. Such poems—as written by Rilke, for example—have been called *Dinggedichte* or "thing-poems."

THE MERRY-GO-ROUND
Jardin du Luxembourg

Under the roof and the roof's shadow turns
this train of painted horses for a while
in this bright land that lingers
before it perishes. In what brave style
they prance—though some pull wagons.
And there burns
a wicked lion red with anger . . .

and now and then a big white elephant.

Even a stag runs here, as in the wood,
save that he bears a saddle where, upright, 10
a little girl in blue sits, buckled tight.

And on the lion whitely rides a young
boy who clings with little sweaty hands,
the while the lion shows his teeth and tongue.

And now and then a big white elephant.

And on the horses swiftly going by
are shining girls who have outgrown this play;
in the middle of the flight they let their eyes
glance here and there and near and far away—

and now and then a big white elephant. 20

And all this hurries toward the end, so fast,
whirling futilely, evermore the same.
A flash of red, of green, of gray, goes past,
and then a little scarce-begun profile.
And oftentimes a blissful dazzling smile
vanishes in this blind and breathless game.

Rainer Maria Rilke (1875–1926)
(Translated by C. F. MacIntyre)

While vividly realistic, the details hint at something beyond themselves —at life itself or some aspect of it.

"No ideas," William Carlos Williams liked to say, "but in things." His "Nantucket" is a thing-poem, though at first it may seem as objective as a well-made Kodachrome.

NANTUCKET

Flowers through the window
lavender and yellow

changed by white curtains—
Smell of cleanliness—

Sunshine of late afternoon—
On the glass tray

a glass pitcher, the tumbler
turned down, by which

a key is lying—And the
immaculate white bed 10

William Carlos Williams

Karl Shapiro's poem, while professing merely to describe, is also telling us something about the nature of banks and the kind of civilization in which they are important.

GIRLS WORKING IN BANKS

Girls working in banks wear bouffant hair and shed
In their passage over the rather magnificent floors
Tiny shreds of perforated paper, like body flakes.
They walk through rows of youngish vice-presidents
With faraway looks, who dandle pencils and tend to ignore
The little tigerish lights flashing on their telephones.
When the girls return to their stations behind a friendly grid
They give out money neatly or graciously take it,
For not far from them the great interior glow of a vault
Built out of beaten dimes, stands open, shines, 10
Beaming security without ostentation.
If you glance inside it there's nothing to be seen
But burnished drawers and polished steel elbows
Of the great machine of the door. It's a speckless world
With nobody inside it, like the best room in the gallery
Awaiting the picture which is still in a crate.
The girls change places frequently, moving their own addresses
From Open to Closed, Next Counter, or they walk away
With surprising freedom behind a wall or rise up on escalators
Past aging and well-groomed guards whose pistols seem 20
Almost apologetic as they watch people
Bending over Formica stand-up desks writing
With ballpoint pens attached to rosary chains,
After which the people select a queue in which they stand
Pious, abashed at the papery transactions,
And eventually walk with the subtlest sense of relief
Out of revolving doors into the glorious anonymous streets.

Karl Shapiro (b. 1913)

Marianne Moore has written a number of poems that go deeper than the descriptions they seem to be. She admires a country cart because, in a world of increasingly shoddy productions, it is lovingly and honestly made.

A CARRIAGE FROM SWEDEN

They say there is a sweeter air
  where it was made, than we have here;
  a Hamlet's castle atmosphere.
At all events there is in Brooklyn
something that makes me feel at home.

No one may see this put-away
  museum-piece, this country cart
  that inner happiness made art;
and yet, in this city of freckled
integrity it is a vein 10

of resined straightness from north-wind
  hardened Sweden's once-opposed-to-
  compromise archipelago
of rocks. Washington and Gustavus
Adolphus, forgive our decay.

Seats, dashboard and sides of smooth gourd-
  rind texture, a flowered step, swan-
  dart brake, and swirling crustacean-
tailed equine amphibious creatures
that garnish the axletree! What 20

a fine thing! What unannoying
  romance! And how beautiful, she
  with the natural stoop of the
snowy egret, gray-eyed and straight-haired,
for whom it should come to the door—

of whom it reminds me. The split
  pine fair hair, steady gannet-clear
  eyes and the pine-needled-path deer-
swift step; that is Sweden, land of the
free and the soil for a spruce tree— 30

vertical though a seedling—all
  needles: from a green trunk, green shelf
  on shelf fanning out by itself.
The deft white-stockinged dance in thick-soled
shoes! Denmark's sanctuaried Jews!

The puzzle-jugs and hand-spun rugs,
  the root-legged kracken shaped like dogs,
  the hanging buttons and the frogs
that edge the Sunday jackets! Sweden,

---

[37] **kracken:** *sea-monsters*

you have a runner called the Deer, who 40

when he's won a race, likes to run
  more; you have the sun-right gable-
  ends due east and west, the table
spread as for a banquet; and the put-
in twin vest-pleats with a fish-fin

effect when you need none. Sweden,
  what makes the people dress that way
  and those who see you wish to stay?
The runner, not too tired to run more
at the end of the race? And that 50

cart, dolphin-graceful? A Dalen
  lighthouse, self-lit?—responsive and
  responsible. I understand;
it's not pine-needle-paths that give spring
when they're run on, it's a Sweden

of moated white castles—the bed
  of white flowers densely grown in an S
  meaning Sweden and stalwartness,
skill, and a surface that says
Made in Sweden: carts are my trade. 60

Marianne Moore (1887–1972)

---

[51] In 1912 Nils Gustaf Dalén (1869–1937) won the Nobel Prize in physics for contributions he made in coastal lighting. Among his inventions was a device that would start up an acetylene flame at twilight and extinguish it at dawn.

Exercises and Diversions

A. **SOFT SNOW**

I walked abroad in a snowy day:
I asked the soft snow with me to play:
She played and she melted in all her prime,
And the winter called it a dreadful crime.

William Blake

1. How do we know that William Blake's "Soft Snow" does not mean literally what it says? What precisely directs us to a symbolic reading?
2. On first impression, to what does the symbolism seem to refer?
3. If you knew that Blake had originally written,

   Ah, that sweet love should be thought a crime!

   instead of his revised last line, would you change your interpretation?
4. Did his revision improve the poem as a poem? As a symbolic poem?

B. "Lully, Lulley, Lully, Lulley" has been given an historical interpretation. One scholar believes that the weeping lady is Catherine of Aragon, lamenting the loss of her husband Henry VIII to Anne Boleyn, whose heraldic emblem was a white falcon.

1. Do the details of the poem seem to support such a reading?
2. Does it make the symbolism richer or poorer?

C. Would you agree with the following explication of William Carlos Williams' "Nantucket"? Or do you think the critic, Guy T. Wise, is "reading things into" the poem?

> Dr. Williams has written a sharp attack on the New England ethos and its prevailing Puritanism in this deceptively simple little poem. There is nothing vital, nothing natural in the world he shows us—except the flowers, and notice that they are *outside* the room, their actual color "changed" by the veil of curtains they are seen through. There is a "smell of cleanliness"—but we all know what cleanliness is next to, and Dr. Williams knows we know. The sunshine is "late afternoon" sunshine—tired and weak, as sunshine goes. The tray and the pitcher are both glass—a colorless and monotonous little still-life: glass has no character of its own, but simply reflects or shows that of other things. The tumbler, now. Is it fanciful to propose that although Dr. Williams means a drinking-glass, he would like us to think also, by contrast, of the colorful tumblers, or acrobats, of the circus world, so unlike the staid New Englanders? The tumbler, anyway, is turned down. The expression implies a refusal; the very image in itself is negative. One cannot fill a downturned tumbler—folly to try. Next to the tumbler is a key, obvious symbol of exclusion. There is unmistakable irony in the heavy "And" of the last sentence. The bed is not only dead white, it is "immaculate," which suggests a hypocritical spirituality hardly appropriate to a hotel-room bed. *(Insights)*

D. 1. To what extent are the following poems symbolic?

THE RHODODENDRON PLANT

We bought it
with

leaves made of
plastic

needing no earth or
water.

Will last as long as
we last.

Like the man said
who sold it, 10

only the beauty is
real.

Allen Katzman (b. 1937)

WOOLWORTH'S

My whole life has led me here.

Daisies made out of resin,
hairnets and submarines,
sandwiches, diaries, green
garden chairs,
and a thousand boxes of cough drops.

Three hundred years ago I was hedging
and ditching in Devon.

I lacked freedom of worship,
and freedom to trade molasses 10
for rum, for slaves, for molasses.

"I will sail to Massachusetts
to build the Kingdom
of Heaven on Earth!"

The side of a hill
swung open.
It was Woolworth's!

I followed this vision to Boston.

Donald Hall (b. 1928)

2. **A FENCE**

Now the stone house on the lake front is finished and the workmen are beginning the fence.
The palings are made of iron bars with steel points that can stab the life out of any man who falls on them.
As a fence, it is a masterpiece, and will shut off the rabble and all vagabonds and hungry men and all wandering children looking for a place to play.
Passing through the bars and over the steel points will go nothing except Death and the Rain and Tomorrow.

Carl Sandburg (1878–1967)

Is it true that this fence, which begins as a real one, becomes more symbolic in every line? Do you think the personifications of the last line (indicated by the capital letters) make the symbolism too insistent?

E. Write a poem, in any form, that describes a simple object or situation so that it picks up symbolic overtones as the poem progresses.

Ways of Seeing with some figures of speech 4

Among the processes—all of which are related to imagery—that we have to look at now, some would seem to be exotic specimens: allegory, personification, synesthesia, synecdoche, metonymy. Those with the strangest names are the ones that occur most often in ordinary speech.

Allegory

The line between metaphor and symbol is not as distinct as that separating mathematical concepts; one cannot always say with assurance where one ends and the other begins. Nor is it clear exactly where symbol gives way to **allegory,** which can be defined as a narrative in which characters and events stand for ideas and actions on another level. Such fables as those of Aesop are a simple form of allegory; they seem to be telling us about animals but are really telling us about human behavior. Such parables as those in the Bible are often allegories; they seem to be telling us about the shepherd and his sheep or the bridegroom and his bride when they are really telling us about God and man. Most allegory has a narrative framework, either a short incident or a long story.

A mountain may be a symbol of salvation, a traveler may be a symbol of man in this life. But if the traveler takes as much as one step toward the mountain, it seems that he and the mountain become allegorical figures, because a story has now begun. Even a landscape can be called allegorical if a continuity is found in the symbolism used to describe it—if everything mentioned, that is, stands for something else.

In other ages, when people thought that everything happening in our world corresponded to something in a spiritual world, it was easy to see things allegorically. Today we rarely have this kind of double vision. The modern objection to allegory is to its artificiality. It is easy enough to see that natural objects like rivers and mountains can serve as symbols for a cluster of associations, but when we force such objects, and human characters as well, into a continuous narrative in which they "really mean" something else, it seems we are regimenting them into an unnatural order in which things can no longer be themselves. What is felt to be the main difference between symbolism and allegory is that the symbolic detail is a real thing which suggests other things—as we know a real thing can do. But the allegorical detail exists primarily to stand for something else; the emphasis is more on the abstraction it stands for than on the image itself.

Allegories tend to be long; in a book like this we can consider only such miniature allegories as the sonnet below, which Sir Thomas Wyatt translated from Petrarch. The ship itself is not very real; it exists only to stand for love and its troubles. The cargo is forgetfulness (for which there is not much market in the real world); the oars are desperate thoughts; the wind is the lover's gust of sighs; the rain, the lover's tears. Any one of these similes or metaphors might work in itself; the attempt to coordinate so many may seem oppressively contrived.

MY GALLEY CHARGÈD WITH FORGETFULNESS

My galley chargèd with forgetfulness
Through sharp seas in winter nights doth pass
'Tween rock and rock, and eke mine enemy, Alas!
That is my lord, steereth with cruelness;
And every oar a thought in readiness
As though that death were light in such a case;
An endless wind doth tear the sail apace
Of forced sighs and trusty fearfulness.
A rain of tears, a cloud of dark disdain
Hath done the wearèd cords great hinderance, 10
Wreathed with error and eke with ignorance.
The stars be hid that led me to this pain;
Drownèd is reason that should me comfort,
And I remain despairing of the port.

Sir Thomas Wyatt (1503–1542)

Kingsley Amis is playing on Wyatt's poem, not without seriousness, when he describes a modern girl.

A NOTE ON WYATT

See her come bearing down, a tidy craft!
Gaily her topsails bulge, her sidelights burn!

---

[1] **chargèd:** *loaded, cargoed* [3] **eke:** *also, moreover*

There's jigging in her rigging fore and aft,
And beauty's self, not name, limned on her stern.

See at her head the Jolly Roger flutters!
"God, is she fully manned? If she's one short . . ."
Cadet, bargee, longshoreman, shellback mutters;
Drowned is reason that should me comfort.

But habit, like a cork, rides the dark flood,
And, like a cork, keeps her in walls of glass; 10
Faint legacies of brine tingle my blood,
The tide-wind's fading echoes, as I pass.

Now, jolly ship, sign on a jolly crew:
God bless you, dear, and all who sail in you.

Kingsley Amis (b. 1922)

Details are handled allegorically. What saves the poem is the feeling that Amis is having fun with a rather burdensome convention.

Wyatt leaves no doubt that his ship poem is allegorical. We would be mistaken, however, if we read his "They Flee From Me" as if it were (although in puritanical times it has been so read, in the belief that it was improper for a real girl to show up barefoot and in a loose gown in the poet's bedroom).

THEY FLEE FROM ME

They flee from me that sometime did me seek
With naked foot stalking in my chamber.
I have seen them gentle, tame and meek
That now are wild and do not remember
That sometime they put themself in danger
To take bread at my hand, and now they range
Busily seeking with a continual change.

Thankèd be fortune, it hath been otherwise
Twenty times better, but once in special,
In thin array, after a pleasant guise, 10
When her loose gown from her shoulders did fall
And she me caught in her arms long and small,
Therewith all sweetly did me kiss,
And softly said, "Dear heart, how like you this?"

It was no dream; I lay broad waking.
But all is turnèd through my gentleness
Into a strange fashion of forsaking;
And I have leave to go of her goodness,
And she also to use newfangleness.
But since that I so kindly am servèd, 20
I would fain know what she hath deservèd.

Sir Thomas Wyatt

---

[19] **newfangleness:** *desire for change*
[20] **kindly:** *according to [her and my] nature (also the modern meaning)*

Wyatt is complaining, as men will, about the fickleness of women—real women, not allegorical statues. A few decades after Wyatt, Sir Philip Sidney warned his readers that when he named a girl he meant a *girl*:

> You that with allegory's curious frame
> Of other's children changelings use to make,
> With me those pains, for God's sake, do not take . . .
> When I say "Stella", I do mean the same . . . .

His word "curious" ("elaborate" or "worked over") sums up the objection to allegory.

Some of the poems we have read earlier have allegorical elements. George Herbert's "Hope" (p. 45), though made up of symbols, is an allegory if we see the exchange of presents as an incident. Some might even consider "The Dark Night" of Saint John of the Cross (p. 49) an allegorical adventure, since the poet uses one level of reality to stand for events on another level. Others would say that the words put so much stress on the earthly symbols and so little on what they symbolize that it would be wrong to call the poem allegorical.

Confusion between symbol and allegory is sometimes possible. To offer any sure-fire solution would be to falsify the problem.

For the use of allegory in art, see Dürer's "The Knight, Death, and the Devil" (p. 173), which shows the Christian knight—or simply the good man—ignoring such spooks and phantoms as death and the devil as he journeys through life toward the castle of salvation.

Personification

In the childhood of the individual, in the childhood of the race, in the mind of the dreamer, we find extensive use of **personification.** The child may pet or punish his toy wagon for being good or bad. Early human societies show a tendency toward animism or psychism, toward attributing life to lifeless things. Even in our civilized society the adult reduced to primitive rage breaks his golf club or kicks his flat tire. We speak of "friendly" colors or "timid" arguments or "yawning" chasms or chemical "reactions." We project our moods onto landscapes or onto the weather. Robert Burns, when unhappy, wondered how nature could go on being its happy self.

> Ye banks and braes o' bonnie Doon,
> How can ye bloom so fresh and fair?
> How can ye chant, ye little birds,
> And I so weary, full o' care . . . .

T. S. Eliot called April the "cruellest" month. Projecting the qualities of living things onto the nonliving is what Ruskin called the "pathetic fallacy." When used mechanically or sentimentally, it can be ridiculous or maudlin. Used sensitively, it can be vigorous: seeing a tree in a windstorm, one might imagine tree and storm as wrestling antagonists. Today we have our own personifications: "Football is king . . ."; "Med-

There had been years of Passion—scorching, cold,
And much Despair, and Anger heaving high,
Care whitely watching, Sorrows manifold,
Among the young, among the weak and old,
And the pensive Spirit of Pity whispered, "Why?" . . . *Thomas Hardy*

it was almost dark when the wind
breathless from playing
with water
  came over and stopped
resting in the bare trees and dry grass
  and weeds. . . . *A. R. Ammons*

. . . my gaze follows hers
Out to the giant recumbent
Hills in their sullen haze
Brooding some brutal thought. . . . *Howard Nemerov*

The old snow gets up and moves taking its
Birds with it. . . . *W. S. Merwin*

At one moment a few old leaves come in
frightened
and lie down together and stop moving. . . . *W. S. Merwin*

. . . Near the gate
A lone iris was panting, purple-tongued. . . . *James Merrill*

Cribs loaded with roughage huddle together
Before the north clouds.
The wind tiptoes between poplars.
The silver maple leaves squint
Toward the ground. . . . *James Wright*

Around each of us, houses breathe.
Electricity gathers in wires
and phones crouch, preparing
to deliver poisonous messages. . . . *Vern Rutsala*

You can hear the silverware
catching its eager breath
inside the sleeping drawer.
It is waiting to elope. . . . *William Matthews*

ical science tells us . . ."; "Industry demands . . . ." Poets are still transferring their souls into plants, or even into barns.

A CUT FLOWER

I stand on slenderness all fresh and fair,
I feel root-firmness in the earth far down,
I catch in the wind and loose my scent for bees
That sack my throat for kisses and suck love.
What is the wind that brings thy body over?
Wind, I am beautiful and sick. I long
For rain that strikes and bites like cold and hurts.
Be angry, rain, for dew is kind to me
When I am cool from sleep and take my bath.

Who softens the sweet earth about my feet, 10
Touches my face so often and brings water?
Where does she go, taller than any sunflower
Over the grass like birds? Has she a root?
These are great animals that kneel to us,
Sent by the sun perhaps to help us grow.
I have seen death. The colors went away,
The petals grasped at nothing and curled tight.
Then the whole head fell off and left the sky.

She tended me and held me by my stalk.
Yesterday I was well, and then the gleam, 20
The thing sharper than frost cut me in half.
I fainted and was lifted high. I feel
Waist-deep in rain. My face is dry and drawn.
My beauty leaks into the glass like rain.
When first I opened to the sun I thought
My colors would be parched. Where are my bees?
Must I die now? Is this a part of life?

Karl Shapiro

A DESERTED BARN

I am a deserted barn—
my cattle robbed from me,
My horses gone,
Light leaking in my sides, sun piercing my tin roof
Where it's torn.
I am a deserted barn.

Dung's still in my gutter.
It shrinks each year as side planks shrink,
Letting in more of the elements,
and flies. 10

Worried by termites, dung beetles,
Maggots, and rats,
Visited by pigeons and hawks,

No longer able to say what shall enter,
or what shall not,
I am a deserted barn.

I stand in Michigan,
A gray shape at the edge of a cedar swamp.
Starlings come to my peak,
Dirty, and perch there; 20
swallows light on bent
Lightning rods whose blue
Globes have gone to

A tenant's son and his .22.
My door is torn.
It sags from rusted rails it once rolled upon,
Waiting for a wind to lift it loose;
Then a bigger wind will take out
My back wall.

But winter is what I fear, 30
when swallows and hawks
Abandon me, when insects and rodents retreat,
When starlings, like the last of bad thoughts, go off,
And nothing is left to fill me
Except reflections—
reflections, at noon,
From the cold cloak of snow, and
Reflections, at night, from the reflected light of the moon.

L. Woiwode (b. 1941)

Primitive man likes to make up stories that use personification. These stories, which might explain how the world began or where the sun goes when it sets, we call myths. **Mythology** is a natural product of the symbolizing mind; poets, when not making up myths of their own, are still commenting on the ancient ones. Yeats tells us how, at a time when he thought the world was in need of guidance from above, his imagination "began to play with Leda and the Swan for metaphor." But, as he was writing, "bird and lady took such possession of the scene that all politics went out of it." He concentrated on the imagined experience itself, which, for poetry, may be more important than any "ideas" expressed. What would it really be like, he wondered, for a girl to be loved by Zeus in the form of a swan?

LEDA AND THE SWAN

A sudden blow: the great wings beating still
Above the staggering girl, her thighs caressed
By the dark webs, her nape caught in his bill,
He holds her helpless breast upon his breast.

How can those terrified vague fingers push
The feathered glory from her loosening thighs?

And how can body, laid in that white rush,
But feel the strange heart beating where it lies?

A shudder in the loins engenders there
The broken wall, the burning roof and tower 10
And Agamemnon dead.
Being so caught up,
So mastered by the brute blood of the air,
Did she put on his knowledge with his power
Before the indifferent beak could let her drop?

W. B. Yeats

A poet may merely refer to an ancient myth.

DIRCE

Stand close around, ye Stygian set,
With Dirce in one boat conveyed!
Or Charon, seeing, may forget
That he is old and she a shade.

Walter Savage Landor (1775–1864)

Landor's quietly written poem is about a girl so beautiful that even when dead and a mere "shade" she might have brought out the potential rapist in Charon, old as he is.

Synesthesia

One kind of analogy that works with intersense relationships is called **synesthesia** (*sensing in common*): the perception or interpretation of one sense in terms of another. The process itself has been seen as regressive; early man had a less compartmentalized sensorium than we have. His sense data tended to overlap, as they still do in young children. But not only in children: Sir Isaac Newton associated colors with musical notes—red with C, orange with D, etc. There are reports of musicians who see vivid colors when they compose or conduct. Sense centers in the brain, when stimulated, can apparently arouse associated centers. There is a basis in the nature of our minds for synesthesia, which we frequently use in speech without being aware we are doing so. Words like "sweet," "sour," and "bitter" are taste words, but we speak of a sweet smile, a sour note, a bitter sight. Although "stink" is a smell word, we apply it to anything that affects us unpleasantly. "Loud" is a sound word, yet we speak of a loud necktie. We feel blue; we listen to cold words; we see dull colors; we drink dry martinis (which taste smooth). Wine experts would be lost without synesthesia: a glance at one of the standard guides reveals that the following words are all used of various vintages: hard, soft, light, heavy, smooth,

Synesthesia

Thou wert eye-music and no single part,
But beauty's concert. . . . *Aurelian Townshend*

And the hapless soldier's sigh
Runs in blood down palace walls. *William Blake*

To the bugle, every color is red. *Emily Dickinson*

Every street lamp that I pass
Beats like a fatalistic drum. . . . *T. S. Eliot*

And Cortez rode up, reining tautly in—
Firmly as coffee grips the taste—and away!— *Hart Crane*

When we were children words were colored
(Harlot and murder were dark purple). . . . *Louis MacNeice*

So fading from the branches the snow sang
With a strange perfume, a melodious twang. . . . *Edith Sitwell*

Baskets of ripe fruit in air
The bird's song seem. . . . *Edith Sitwell*

Cathedral evening, tinkle of candles
On the frosted air. . . . *Kenneth Patchen*

A crow's long scratch of sound
begins this valley's day. . . . *John Ciardi*

. . . the sun blared like a brass. . . . *Gray Burr*

[Of daffodils]
Yellow telephones
in a row in the garden
are ringing
shrill with light. . . . *May Swenson*

The darkness that flows from the sirens passes the windows. . . .
W. S. Merwin

. . . voices of dogs were lit on the hills. . . . *W. S. Merwin*

It's funny early spring weather, mild and washy
the color of a head cold. *James Schuyler*

A woman so skinny I could smell her bones
hugged me because I'd turned away from sin. . . . *Miller Williams*

Coming back in Autumn
the air loud with the colors of Saturday afternoon football. . . . *Adrian Henri*

In the summer rain,
The leaves of the plum tree
Are the colors of the chill breeze.
Saimaro (translated from the Japanese by P. H. Blyth)

rough, dry, spotty, fat, round, green, flinty, strong, sturdy, velvety, satiny, firm, sunny, harsh. Speech itself, which turns all of our experiences into sound, has been considered a kind of synesthesia.

THE BLINDMAN

The blindman placed
a tulip on his tongue for purple's taste.
Cheek to grass, his green

was rough excitement's sheen
of little whips.
In water to his lips

he named the sea blue and white,
the basin of his tears and fallen beads of sight.
He said: This scarf is red;

I feel the vectors to its thread (10)
that dance down from the sun. I know
the seven fragrances of the rainbow.

I have caressed
the orange hair of flames. Pressed
to my ear,

a pomegranate lets me hear
crimson's flute.
Trumpets tell me yellow. Only ebony is mute.

May Swenson (b. 1919)

Synecdoche, Metonymy

Synecdoche is a way of perceiving, thinking, speaking. In its commonest form, it singles out a part of a thing for special notice, as when we say, "A *sail!*" meaning a whole ship, or "All *hands* on deck," or "Let's count *noses*." (Or it may use a broader term for a narrower one—as when we see a policeman coming and say, "Here comes the law!") Without synecdoche, the mind itself might have trouble operating. From the great welter of sensations fed into our brain every instant, our attention focuses on some as standing for larger configurations—that is, we see "a part for the whole." A cave man coming suddenly upon his enemy, perhaps a more primitive type with snarling teeth bared, might later report to his cave wife, "Guess who I saw today! The Fang!" Like so many "rhetorical devices," synecdoche was nearer and dearer to primitive people than to us—for them, the part *was* the whole. This is a common assumption of magic all over the world. Get any part of a person—a lock of his hair, a fingernail, or even learn his real name (Rumpelstiltskin!)—and that person is subject to your magic power.

SYNECDOCHE, METONYMY

O 'tis not Spanish, but 'tis heaven she speaks! — *Richard Crashaw*

Hark! she is called, the parting hour is come.
Take thy Farewell, poor world! heaven must go home. . . . — *Richard Crashaw*

I should have been a pair of ragged claws
Scuttling across the floors of silent seas. — *T. S. Eliot*

[Of students on a school bus]
When a cough came from the compound interest problem,
And a sneeze from the third chapter of the Civicsbook. . . . — *John Ciardi*

Once at the Plaza. . . .
I heard three hundred-thousand-dollar bills
Talking at breakfast. One was male and two were female. . . . — *Randall Jarrell*

At the newsstand in the lobby, a cigar
Was talking: "Since I've been in this town
I've seen one likely woman, and a car
As she was crossing Main Street knocked her down." — *Louis Simpson*

Here and there the snowball fights began
As boys shaped white invective to be hurled — *Gray Burr*

Great pain was in the world before we came.
The shriek had learned to answer to the claw
Before we came; the gasp, the sigh, the groan,
Did not need our invention. . . . — *Howard Nemerov*

After I saw, as on my balcony
I stirred the afternoon into my tea. . . . — *Donald Hall*

And riding the trolley homeward this afternoon
With the errands in my lap. . . . — *Eleanor Ross Taylor*

I have a castle
Three stars high . . .
I have an apple-tree
Two birds thick . . .
Fetch me a coverlet
Four leaves thin . . .
In a pasture wide as sleep. . . . — *Julia Randall*

We listen while a dustpan eats
the scattered pieces of a quarrel. . . . — *Vern Rutsala*

men with wall street in their brief cases. . . . — *Víctor Hernández Cruz*

We often talk in synecdoche: "She was all eyes," or "Look at nosey!" or "Here comes big mouth," or "He's really a brain." According to *Sports Illustrated*, a tennis player with a formidable reach is currently called "The Arm." "That's life!" is a synecdoche; we see the one incident or situation as standing for the nature of existence. Any symbolic poem is a synecdoche.

Metonymy is so close it overlaps. If our cave man had run into a hostile but more advanced type of enemy, he might have been especially impressed by something the stranger was carrying: a sharp rock fastened with deerhide thongs to a stout stick, for instance. If he had had a second escape, he might have reported later, "I saw The Axe today!" A metonymy—the caveman is referring to one thing by using the name of something associated with it. Children use metonymy when they call a dog a "bowwow," from the associated sound. We use it when we say things like "Are there going to be any big names at the party?" or "His backhand [that is, the ball hit by his backhand] just nicked the line," or "I've been reading Shakespeare," or "I ate the whole plate" (even though the plate is still on the table), or "I drank two bottles." The last is that old favorite—container for thing contained. (James Thurber once thought up its opposite: "Get away from me or I'll hit you with the milk!") Metonymy is used by James Shirley when, instead of saying that kings die as surely as poor farmers do, he says:

> Scepter and crown
> Must tumble down,
> And in the dust be equal made
> With the poor crooked scythe and spade.

Exercises and Diversions

A. Identify, in the excerpts that follow, examples of personification, synesthesia, synecdoche, and metonymy. (Be on the lookout also for symbols.)

1. The brown enormous odor [of pigs] he lived by
   was too close, with its breathing and thick hair. . . . *Elizabeth Bishop*

2. March cleared
   His throat announcing significant snow.
   The blossoms . . . wore
   Snow for fragrance. . . . *Hollis Summers*

3. At midsummer before dawn an orange light
   Like a great weight. . . . *W. S. Merwin*

4. The yellow fog that rubs its back upon the window-panes,
   The yellow smoke that rubs its muzzle on the window-panes
   Licked its tongue into the corners of the evening. . . . *T. S. Eliot*

5. Blues grabbed me at midnight, didn't turn me loose till day.
   I didn't have no mama to drive those blues away. *Blues song*

6. A good golfer uses an iron on the third hole, not a wood.

7. And gowns the color of the thunder's reverberation. . . . *Edith Sitwell*

8. The moon drops one or two feathers into a field.
   The dark wheat listens. *James Wright*

9. But this sober grey darkness and pale light was happily broken through by the orange of the pealing of Mitton bells. *Gerard Manley Hopkins*

10. To see a world in a grain of sand
    And a heaven in a wild flower,
    Hold infinity in the palm of your hand
    And eternity in an hour. *William Blake*

11. Children of a future age,
    Reading this indignant page,
    Know that in a former time,
    Love, sweet love, was thought a crime. *William Blake*

12. Old families last not three oaks. *Sir Thomas Browne*

13. A fool there was and he made his prayer
    (Even as you and I)
    To a rag and a bone and a hank of hair
    (We called her the woman who did not care)
    But the fool he called her his lady fair—
    (Even as you and I!) *Rudyard Kipling*

B. A difference between symbol and allegory (to oversimplify) is that with symbol the attention is directed to the sense image itself (rose, worm, storm, etc.); what it stands for is left to the imagination. With allegory, the attention is directed to what the sense image stands for (beauty, evil, etc.); the reality of the image itself may be neglected.

1. If this is true, how could Wyatt's sonnet "My Galley Chargèd with Forgetfulness" be rewritten so that his allegorical ship becomes a symbolic one?
2. How could Blake's "The Sick Rose" be made into a miniature allegory?

C. In "Good Ships" two attractive young people meet at a party, but nothing comes of the encounter. The poet seems to feel that it is sad that convention smothers the possibilities of romance.

GOOD SHIPS

Fleet ships encountering on the high seas
Who speak, and then unto the vast diverge,
Two hailed each other, poised on the loud surge
Of one of Mrs. Grundy's Tuesday teas,
Nor trimmed one sail to baffle the driving breeze.
A macaroon absorbed all her emotion;
His hue was ruddy but an effect of ocean;
They exchanged the nautical technicalities.

It was only a nothing or so until they parted.
Away they went, most certainly bound for port, 10
So seaworthy one felt they could not sink;

---

[4] **Mrs. Grundy:** *a symbol for conventional behavior.*

Still there was a tremor shook them, I should think,
Beautiful timbers fit for storm and sport
And unto miserly merchant hulks converted.

John Crowe Ransom (b. 1888)

1. Is the ship imagery allegorical? Metaphoric? Symbolic?
2. Can all three overlap?
3. Does the "macaroon" stand for anything?
4. Instead of "ruddy" in line 7, the poet originally wrote "ashy." Which word fits in better with the sea imagery and the situation?

D. Landor's "Dirce" might be updated as follows:

That Dursey! She's *soooooooo* beautiful!
Look, if she ever dies, and
(like they say)
Ol' Charon gets to pole her over the Styx River,
Listen, all you cats lucky enough to catch the same scow
(Styx River Ferry Line Special Now Departing at Wharf 15! All Aboard Please!)
Kind of snuggle round her, see,
'Cause if ol' Charon once gloms on to her,
WOW!
Ghost or not,
That dirty ol' man's gonna jump her!
She's *soooooooo* beautiful!

What are the advantages and disadvantages of the new version?

E. Does the following poem depend on synesthesia for its effect? If not, on what figure of speech or way of thinking does it depend?

WINTER SCENE

There is now not a single
leaf on the cherry tree:

except when the jay
plummets in, lights, and,

in pure clarity, squalls:
then every branch

quivers and
breaks out in blue leaves.

A. R. Ammons (b. 1926)

F. Make up several examples of personification. Of synesthesia. Of synecdoche. Of metonymy.

Binocular Vision 5

"antipoetry," paradox, irony

Up to now we have been concerned with sense perception, the source of human awareness; with how our mind deals with the images the senses provide, with how it relates and compares them, condensing some into symbols, narrowing its focus onto parts of others. In this chapter we will consider how our mind—and the poet's—handles the conflicting evidence that its images sometimes present.

Dante mentions that Providence has written the word for *man* ("omo") in the bone structure of the human face. This fancy may no longer strike us with wonder, but perhaps Nature is trying to tell us something by the way she positions our eyes: everything we see, we see from two points of view.

Antipoetry

The world we perceive is made up of data both good and bad, with a wide range of the pleasant and unpleasant between the two extremes. If we look back over poems we have read, we find a number of sense details that are not conventionally appealing. William Carlos Williams and his nose were aware of

> . . . the souring flowers of the bedraggled
> poplars: a festering pulp on the wet earth . . . .

T. S. Eliot mentions "faint stale smells of beer" and

> . . . the yellow soles of feet
> In the palms of both soiled hands.

One false view of the poet is that his mission is to give us "beauty" by seeing only the good, the noble, the inspiring in reality. What he shows us is likely to be a more meaningful world than the unselective senses give, but not a "nicer" world, not a censored distortion of reality. He avoids images that are conventionally pretty and, for that reason, overused in middling poems of the past. Often his best work is made up of materials previously overlooked and therefore as fresh and unspoiled as experience itself is. The more consciously "poetic" (in the conventional sense) the materials out of which a poem is made, the poorer the poem is likely to be. Shakespeare goes out of his way to be unpretty in what may be the best winter poem in English.

WINTER

When icicles hang by the wall,
And Dick the shepherd blows his nail,
And Tom bears logs into the hall,
And milk comes frozen home in pail;
When blood is nipped and ways be foul,
Then nightly sings the staring owl,
To-whit to-who, a merry note,
While greasy Joan doth keel the pot.

When all aloud the wind doth blow,
And coughing drowns the parson's saw, 10
And birds sit brooding in the snow,
And Marion's nose looks red and raw;
When roasted crabs hiss in the bowl,
Then nightly sings the staring owl,
To-whit to-who, a merry note,
While greasy Joan doth keel the pot.

William Shakespeare (1564–1616)

Not a Christmas-card touch: no decorations, candles, carols. Yet out of this unpromising material Shakespeare has made a poem that gives a feeling of the energy and exhilaration of winter, of the challenge and vitality and sheer fun of it, such as no pretty poem could ever do.

WINTER FAIRYLAND IN VERMONT
(after Shakespeare)

When icicles by silver eaves
Proclaim old Winter's jolly reign,
When woodfires gleam like golden sheaves,
And Frost is blazoning the pane,
When lanes are fairylands in white,
And downy owls bejewel the night,

---

8 **keel:** *cool by stirring*
10 **saw:** *platitude*
13 **crabs:** *crabapples*

Joan baking, in a flowery blouse,
Sends rich aroma through the house.

When breezes carol merrily,
And herald angels tread the snows, 10
Wee chickadees are fluffs o' glee
And Marion's cheek a blushing rose.
When bowls of popcorn twinkle bright
And downy owls bejewel the night,
Joan baking, in a flowery blouse,
Sends rich aroma through the house.

Francis P. Osgood (b. 1910)

No gloomy birds or chapped noses here; everything is directed toward greeting-card charm. But if the roughness has gone out of the poem, so has the life, the convincing vitality.

The poet who sees only those details that flatter our fondest hopes has one eye closed to reality. But no more so than the poet who sees only what is ugly or shocking:

When icicles like frozen spit
Are drooling from the roof's mustache,
When roads are white as chicken sheds,
And pimpled skin's a scabby rash . . . .

Seeing everything as foul and joyless has become a more fashionable extreme—more warranted, some believe, by the world we live in. Yet dark glasses falsify as surely as rose-colored ones.

LIFE IS MOTION

In Oklahoma,
Bonnie and Josie,
Dressed in calico,
Danced around a stump.
They cried,
"Ohoyaho,
Ohoo" . . .
Celebrating the marriage
Of flesh and air.

Wallace Stevens

This unpretentious little piece is only saying that it's great to be alive, great to have real bodies of flesh in the real air of the world. The setting is far from glamorous; the girls have ordinary names, wear plain clothes, have only a stump to dance around.

Elizabeth Bishop goes beyond the plain to the gorgeously dirty.

FILLING STATION

Oh, but it is dirty!
—this little filling station,
oil-soaked, oil-permeated
to a disturbing, over-all
black translucency.
Be careful with that match!

Father wears a dirty,
oil-soaked monkey suit
that cuts him under the arms,
and several quick and saucy 10
and greasy sons assist him
(it's a family filling station),
all quite thoroughly dirty.

Do they live in the station?
It has a cement porch
behind the pumps, and on it
a set of crushed and grease-
impregnated wickerwork;
on the wicker sofa
a dirty dog, quite comfy. 20

Some comic books provide
the only note of color—
of certain color. They lie
upon a big dim doily
draping a taboret
(part of the set), beside
a big hirsute begonia.

Why the extraneous plant?
Why the taboret?
Why, oh why, the doily? 30
(Embroidered in daisy stitch
with marguerites, I think,
and heavy with gray crochet.)

Somebody embroidered the doily.
Somebody waters the plant,
or oils it, maybe. Somebody
arranges the rows of cans
so that they softly say:
ESSO—SO—SO—SO
to high-strung automobiles. 40
Somebody loves us all.

Elizabeth Bishop (b. 1911)

---

25 **taboret:** *stool*

Walt Whitman once registered his preference for the worn, the ragged, the ordinary, instead of the conventionally beautiful, by jotting down a "series of comparisons" he may have intended to use in a poem.

BEAUTY

series of comparisons

not the beautiful youth with features of bloom & brightness
but the bronzed old farmer & father
not the soldiers trim in handsome uniforms marching off to sprightly music with measured step
but the remnant returning thinned out,
not the beautiful flag with stainless white, spangled with silver & gold
But the old rag just adhering to the staff, in tatters—the remnant of many battle-fields
not the beautiful girl or the elegant lady with ? complexion,
But the mechanic's wife at work or the mother of many children, middle-aged or old 10
Not the vaunted scenery of the tourist, picturesque,
But the plain landscape, the bleak sea shore, or the barren plain, with the common sky & sun,—or at night the moon & stars.

Walt Whitman (1819–1892)

But Whitman, like the other poets we have been reading, did not swing to the easy extreme of the repulsive.

The contemporary Chilean poet Nicanor Parra uses the term "antipoems" for poetry in which "there is humor, irony, sarcasm . . . the author is making fun of himself and so of humanity." His antipoetry is not opposed to poetry as antimatter is to matter; instead of swinging to an extreme of ugliness, it swings away from a rapt and humorless fixation on accepted beauty back toward the human center from which we see the world. Parra's "The Viper," translated by W. S. Merwin, tells us that some love affairs are anything but lovely. It begins:

For years I was doomed to worship a contemptible woman,
Sacrifice myself for her, endure endless humiliations and sneers,
Work night and day to feed her and clothe her,
Perform several crimes, commit several misdemeanors,
Practice petty burglary by moonlight,
Forge compromising documents,
For fear of a scornful glance from her bewitching eyes.

Such "antipoems" are not new or modern. Poets have always been aware that some of our most exciting experiences, if seen honestly, present us with contradictory data and arouse mixed feelings.

LOVE, 20¢ THE FIRST QUARTER MILE

All right, I may have lied to you, and about you, and made a few pronouncements a bit too sweeping, perhaps, and possibly forgotten to tag the bases here or there,

And damned your extravagance, and maligned your tastes, and libeled your relatives, and slandered a few of your friends,
O.K.,
Nevertheless, come back.

Come home. I will agree to forget the statements that you issued so copiously to the neighbors and the press,
And you will forget that figment of your imagination, the blonde from Detroit; 10
I will agree that your lady friend who lives above us is not crazy, bats, nutty as they come, but on the contrary rather bright,
And you will concede that poor old Steinberg is neither a drunk, nor a swindler, but simply a guy, on the eccentric side, trying to get along.
(Are you listening, you bitch, and have you got this straight?)

Because I forgive you, yes, for everything,
I forgive you for being beautiful and generous and wise,
I forgive you, to put it simply, for being alive, and pardon you, in short, for being you. 20

Because tonight you are in my hair and eyes,
And every street light that our taxi passes shows me you again, still you,
And because tonight all other nights are black, all other hours are cold and far away, and now, this minute, the stars are very near and bright.

Come back. We will have a celebration to end all celebrations.
We will invite the undertaker who lives beneath us, and a couple of the boys from the office, and some other friends,
And Steinberg, who is off the wagon, by the way, and that insane woman who lives upstairs, and a few reporters, if anything should break.

Kenneth Fearing (1902–1961)

For one of the most famous "antipoems," we can go to Shakespeare:

SONNET 130

My mistress' eyes are nothing like the sun;
Coral is far more red than her lips' red;
If snow be white, why then her breasts are dun;
If hairs be wires, black wires grow on her head.
I have seen roses damasked, red and white,
But no such roses see I in her cheeks;
And in some perfumes is there more delight
Than in the breath that from my mistress reeks.
I love to hear her speak, yet well I know
That music hath a far more pleasing sound. 10
I grant I never saw a goddess go;
My mistress when she walks treads on the ground:
And yet, by heaven! I think my love as rare
As any she, belied with false compare.

William Shakespeare

---

5 **damasked:** *of mingled colors* 8 **reeks:** *is exhaled*

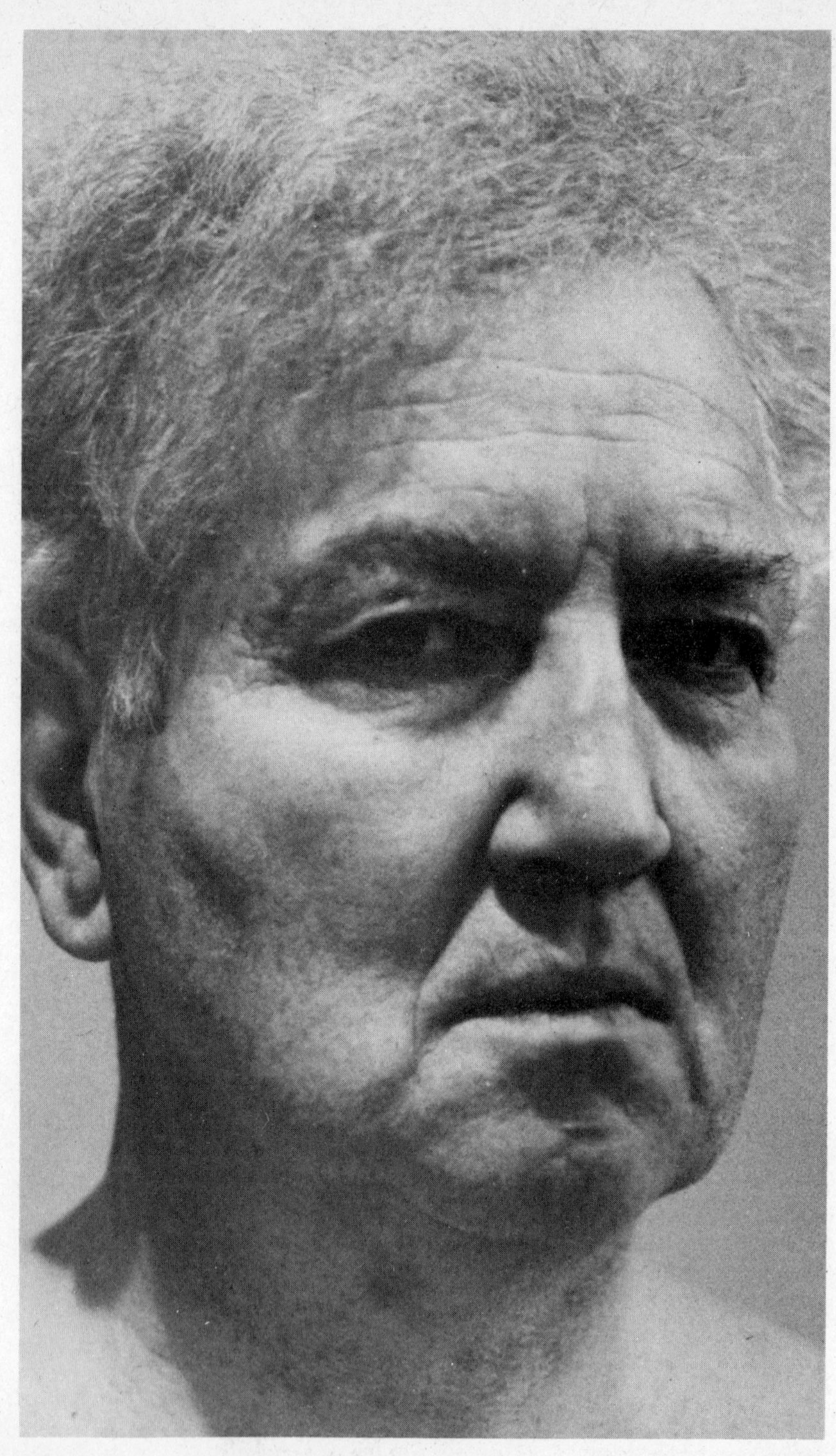

Robert Graves

Refusing to be taken in by the clichés of second-rate poetry, Shakespeare looks objectively at the woman he is in love with, and tells us only the exciting truth about her.

Robert Graves (whose picture we see opposite) can look objectively even at his own face in the mirror, but his realistic scrutiny does not interfere with romantic enthusiasm.

THE FACE IN THE MIRROR

Grey haunted eyes, absent-mindedly glaring
From wide, uneven orbits; one brow drooping
Somewhat over the eye
Because of a missile fragment still inhering,
Skin deep, as a foolish record of old-world fighting.

Crookedly broken nose—low tackling caused it;
Cheeks, furrowed; coarse grey hair, flying frenetic;
Forehead, wrinkled and high;
Jowls, prominent; ears, large; jaw, pugilistic;
Teeth, few; lips, full and ruddy; mouth, ascetic. 10

I pause with razor poised, scowling derision
At the mirrored man whose beard needs my attention,
And once more ask him why
He still stands ready, with a boy's presumption,
To court the queen in her high silk pavilion.

Robert Graves (b. 1895)

"Antipoems" are not automatically better than other poems. They do come to us with a guarantee of authenticity, but the authentic need not be, in itself, interesting or moving. Boring people are no less boring because they really exist. Wordsworth and Swift have both written poems about the morning. Wordsworth is solemn, even reverent. Swift, more in the manner of the antipoet, mentions, not without humor, things that are scandalous or ugly. He gives us a different poem but not necessarily a better one.

COMPOSED UPON WESTMINSTER BRIDGE
September 3, 1802

Earth has not anything to show more fair:
Dull would he be of soul who could pass by
A sight so touching in its majesty:
This City now doth, like a garment, wear
The beauty of the morning; silent, bare,
Ships, towers, domes, theatres, and temples lie
Open unto the fields, and to the sky;
All bright and glittering in the smokeless air.
Never did sun more beautifully steep
In his first splendour, valley, rock, or hill; 10
Ne'er saw I, never felt, a calm so deep!

The river glideth at his own sweet will:
Dear God! the very houses seem asleep;
And all that mighty heart is lying still!

William Wordsworth (1770–1850)

A DESCRIPTION OF THE MORNING

Now hardly here and there a Hackney-Coach
Appearing, show'd the Ruddy Morns Approach.
Now Betty from her Masters Bed had flown,
And softly stole to discompose her own.
The Slipshod Prentice from his Masters Door,
Had par'd the Dirt, and Sprinkled round the Floor.
Now Moll had whirl'd her Mop with dext'rous Airs,
Prepar'd to Scrub the Entry and the Stairs.
The Youth with Broomy Stumps began to trace
The Kennel-Edge, where Wheels had worn the Place. 10
The Smallcoal-Man was heard with Cadence deep,
'Till drown'd in Shriller Notes of Chimney-Sweep.
Duns at his Lordships Gate began to meet,
And Brickdust Moll had Scream'd through half a Street.
The Turnkey now his Flock returning sees,
Duly let out a Nights to Steal for Fees.
The watchful Bailiffs take their silent Stands,
And School-Boys lag with Satchels in their Hands.

Jonathan Swift (1667–1745)

Paradox

Our minds operate on balanced opposites (we even say a malfunctioning mind is "unbalanced"). If our instincts of love and death, of love and aggression are in conflict, that inner tension corresponds with what we find outside. "The sad truth is that man's real life consists of a complex of inexorable opposites—," said Jung, "day and night, birth and death, happiness and misery, good and evil . . . if it were not so, existence would come to an end." Creation and destruction seem to work curiously together.

The way in which the fundamental dualities of life coexist is represented by the Oriental symbol for the Yin and Yang, the opposed forces that make up our existence. The symbol is not merely a neatly halved circle of two colors. The dualities interact and interpenetrate, so that the semicircle of one curves into the semicircle of the other. In the midst of each colored area is a small circle of its opposite: in everything beautiful, there is something ugly; in everything true, something false; in every-

[10] **Kennel:** *channel, gutter*

thing male, something female. Poetry has said this in many ways. Shelley wrote:

> Our sincerest laughter
> With some pain is fraught;
> Our sweetest songs are those that tell of saddest thought.

His admirer, Francis Thompson, echoed him:

> She left me marvelling why my soul
> Was sad that she was glad;
> At all the sadness in the sweet,
> The sweetness in the sad . . . .

Paradox was a fact of life long before it was a literary figure. In its Greek form, the word meant *not what you would expect to be true.* We say a person is a paradox when we cannot reconcile his apparently contradictory tendencies. We say, "It wasn't like him to do that" or "I wasn't myself last night." No one can miss the fact that the nature of man is deeply contradictory. Alexander Pope, who had in mind Pascal's remarks on the "greatness and misery" of man, developed the theme in this excerpt from "An Essay on Man":

> Placed on this isthmus of a middle state,
> A being darkly wise, and rudely great:
> With too much knowledge for the Sceptic side,
> With too much weakness for the Stoic's pride,
> He hangs between; in doubt to act, or rest,
> In doubt to deem himself a God, or Beast;
> In doubt his Mind or Body to prefer,
> Born but to die, and reasoning but to err;
> Alike in ignorance, his reason such,
> Whether he thinks too little, or too much: 10
> Chaos of Thought and Passion, all confused;
> Still by himself abused, or disabused;
> Created half to rise, and half to fall;
> Great lord of all things, yet a prey to all;
> Sole judge of Truth, in endless Error hurled:
> The glory, jest, and riddle of the world!

Paradox, like everything else, can be abused, used mechanically or patly as a stylistic decoration. Some might think that a poet like W. S. Merwin dulls the effect of paradox by an overuse of it, but each of the examples that follow may be strong and effective in its own poem.

> I come back to where I have never been . . . .
>
> It was never there and already it's vanishing . . . .
>
> The old wind vanished and vanished but was still there . . .
>
> The extinct animals are still looking for home . . . .
>
> What I live for I can seldom believe in . . . .

Paradox has been found even in Wordsworth's apparently naïve

"Composed Upon Westminster Bridge" (p. 77)—paradoxical in that the poet attributes to the man-made city such beauty as we expect to find only in the things of nature.

Awareness of paradox is often expressed by means of **oxymoron,** which might be translated from the Greek as *cleverly stupid* or paraphrased as *absurd on purpose.* It links, in one syntactical unit, words that seem to cancel each other out: "honest thief," "saintly devil," "beautifully ugly," "terrible beauty," "boring excitement," "dull fun," "militant pacifist," "lucky disaster," "frigid kiss," "fight shy," "hurry slowly." "Superette" (for a little supermarket) is a kind of one-word oxymoron; so is the much older "bittersweet."

Irony

Irony directs our attention, in any of several ways, to a relation of opposites. The most familiar form of irony is the statement that means its contrary, as when, in the middle of an icy downpour, we comment, "Lovely weather!" Or "More good news!" on looking at the evening headlines. Sometimes the one to whom irony is directed does not know that the words have a double meaning, or the speaker himself may not be aware that they have. When Othello is confronted by an armed posse, he greets them with quiet irony:

> Keep up your bright swords, for the dew will rust them.

He is ironic in professing concern for the prettiness of their weapons; ironic too in implying that their swords are more likely to be stained by dew than by blood.

There is another kind of irony in Romeo's saying,

> If I may trust the flattering truth of sleep,
> My dreams presage some joyful news at hand....

because we know that at any moment he is going to receive the report that Juliet is dead.

Macbeth, after committing murder, looks at his bloody hand and thinks:

> Will all great Neptune's ocean wash this blood
> Clean from my hand? No, this my hand will rather
> The multitudinous seas incarnadine,
> Making the green, one red.

He knows the truth of his situation. Lady Macbeth does not: It is ironic when she enters almost immediately with the remark:

> A little water clears us of this deed....

We say that situations in life are ironic when there is some striking illustration of the way in which qualities, events, etc., contain something of their opposite—when a result, for example, is the contrary of what was intended. If one has just been given his driver's license, has

OXYMORON

Behold how goodly my fair love doth lie
In proud humility. . . . — *Edmund Spenser*

A dungeon horrible, on all sides round
As one great furnace flamed; yet from those flames
No light, but rather darkness visible. . . . — *John Milton*

Yet still he fills affection's eye,
Obscurely wise, and coarsely kind. . . . — *Samuel Johnson*

. . . in numbers warmly pure, and sweetly strong. . . . — *William Collins*

A terrible beauty is born. — *W. B. Yeats*

He stumbled, tumbled, fumbled to and fro
And had but broken knees for hire
And horrible splendor of desire. . . . — *W. B. Yeats*

. . . a soft tumult
of thy hair. . . . — *James Joyce*

My father moved through dooms of love
through sames of am through haves of give,
singing each morning out of each night
my father moved through depths of height — *E. E. Cummings*

. . . the giant hush
Was changed to soft explosion as the sage
Broke down to powdered ash. . . . — *Yvor Winters*

Great hairy seeds . . .
Break in the night with soft
Explosions into bloom. — *Stanley J. Kunitz*

I eye the statue with an awed contempt. . . . — *Robert Lowell*

. . . darkly auspicious as
The ace of spades. — *Richard Wilbur*

The lines blaze with a constant light, displayed
As in the maple's cold and fiery shade. . . . — *Howard Nemerov*

. . . the blank marble gaze
Brilliantly blind. . . . — *James Merrill*

Robert Frost
who said either we write
out of a strong weakness (poets
love oxymoronic forms). . . . — *Richard Howard*

just been congratulated by his instructor, and, when driving off, goes into reverse by mistake and backs up over someone, it is especially satisfactory—as irony!—if the person who was run over is the instructor himself. Such irony seems to imply pattern or design of some mischievous sort, as if a supreme jokester were planning the scenario of our lives. A writer who has made a study of the worst disasters of the twentieth century warns us to avoid any ship, plane, or building which is publicized as being especially safe.

Thomas Hardy was a poet fascinated by irony. In poem after poem he seems on the lookout for the little circle of the Yin in the asymmetrical half-circle of the Yang. One of the best known of his ironic poems is about the hypocritical discrepancy, in Victorian England, between the way virtue was extolled and its opposite rewarded. Amelia, a girl from the country, has been "ruined" (seduced) by a rich man who is keeping her in style; her very ruin has gained her a place in society.

THE RUINED MAID

"O 'Melia, my dear, this does everything crown!
Who could have supposed I should meet you in Town?
And whence such fair garments, such prosperi-ty?"—
"O didn't you know I'd been ruined?" said she.

—"You left us in tatters, without shoes or socks,
Tired of digging potatoes, and spudding up docks;
And now you've gay bracelets and bright feathers three!"—
"Yes: that's how we dress when we're ruined," said she.

—"At home in the barton you said 'thee' and 'thou,'
And 'thik oon,' and 'theäs oon,' and 't'other'; but now 10
Your talking quite fits 'ee for high compa-ny!"—
"Some polish is gained with one's ruin," said she.

—"Your hands were like paws then, your face blue and bleak
But now I'm bewitched by your delicate cheek,
And your little gloves fit as on any la-dy!"—
"We never do work when we're ruined," said she.

—"You used to call home-life a hag-ridden dream,
And you'd sigh, and you'd sock; but at present you seem
To know not of megrims or melancho-ly!"—
"True. One's pretty lively when ruined," said she. 20

—"I wish I had feathers, a fine sweeping gown,
And a delicate face, and could strut about Town!"—
"My dear—a raw country girl, such as you be,
Cannot quite expect that. You ain't ruined," said she.

Thomas Hardy (1840–1928)

---

[6] **spudding up docks:** *digging up weeds*
[9] **barton:** *farmyard*
[10] **thik oon . . . theas oon:** *that one . . . this one*
[18] **sock:** *sigh*
[19] **megrims:** *headache, depression*

The ironic view of life has been a favorite with many twentieth-century poets, perhaps because the events of our time have brought home to us the conviction that there is no simple way of looking at things.

In speech, we can make any statement ironic by the tone in which we utter it, the facial expression we assume, the gestures we dramatize it with. The poet's problem is to make his irony clear without any of the aids we have in speech. He has only words on the page to work with. He needs our intelligent collaboration; we have to be more wide awake than usual when reading a poet given to irony. In the following lines, Ramon Guthrie is writing about a political figure posing for press photographers. Most of us will feel that the apparent innocence of the last two lines is really tongue-in-cheek, really ironic, and that the statement is all the more cutting for seeming naïve.

He poses for press photographers
with bowed head, thumb holding his right eyelid shut,
auricular performing the same service for the left,
his three other fingers poised against his forehead.
It takes a very pious man to pray that fervently
with flash-light bulbs exploding all around him . . . .

Exercises and Diversions

A. The great example of irony in literature is the story of Oedipus as told by Sophocles in his play *Oedipus Rex.* The very steps Oedipus takes to avoid killing his father Laius make the crime inevitable. Sophocles has his hero say many things that we know have a different meaning than the speaker is aware of. He pronounces, for example, a solemn curse on the killer and says he will investigate the case as thoroughly as if the murdered man had been his father.

Does the following poem have the same kind of "dramatic irony"? The Hunkpapa were a tribe of the Dakota (or Sioux), the most impressive and prosperous of the American Indians. The year 1822 would have been a happy one for them; much of the rest of the century was not.

DAKOTA: OCTOBER, 1822
HUNKPAPA WARRIOR

New air has come around us.
It is cold enough to make us know we are different
from the things we touch. Before dark, we ride
along the high places or go deep in the long
grass at the edge of our people
and watch for enemies.
We are the strongest tribe of the Sioux. Buffalo
are plentiful, our women beautiful. Life
is good.
What bad thing can be done against us?

Rod Taylor (b. 1947)

1. Is the time of year symbolic or otherwise significant in the poem?
2. Is the time of day?

B. What elements of "antipoetry" are there in T. S. Eliot's "Preludes" (p. 10)?

C. 1. In what other poems that we have read are oppositions played off against each other?

2. Would you consider Yeats' phrase "a terrible beauty" a true oxymoron? How are the "beautiful" and the "terrible" related in Jeffers' "The Purse-Seine" (p. 23)?
3. The Elizabethan poet Thomas Bastard published a collection called *Chrestoleros* in 1598. Two of his sonnets, in lines like these, attack what today we would call the armaments race and pollution:

> Besides contentions to us natural
> And to our age, besides all wickedness
> So rife, so ripe, so reaching over all,
> And murdering malice raging in excess,
> We have invented engines to shed blood
> Such as no age did ever know before,
> Like as God thundereth from the airy cloud,
> Lightning forth death out of death's house of store. . . .
>
> Our fathers did but use the world before,
> And having used did leave the same to us. 10
> We spill whatever resteth of their store.
> What can our heirs inherit but our curse?
> For we have sucked the sweet and sap away,
> And sowed consumption in the fruitful ground.
> The woods and forests clad in rich array
> With nakedness and baldness we confound. . . .

What is "ironic" about these lines today?

D. 1. One of the poems of divine love of St. John of the Cross has the refrain: "I die because I do not die" (*muero porque no muero*). What do you suppose he means by his paradox?

2. There is a story of a clergyman who begins a prayer with: "Paradoxical as it may seem to Thee, O Lord. . . ." Is he orthodox about the nature of paradox?
3. T. S. Eliot's Gerontion (in the poem of that name) is disheartened by the inextricability of good and evil in man:

> Think
> Neither fear nor courage saves us. Unnatural vices
> Are fathered by our heroism. Virtues
> Are forced upon us by our impudent crimes.

How could this passage be made concrete? Think of some "vices" that are encouraged by our "heroism," and some "virtues" that result from our "crimes."

E. How many of the following are true paradoxes?

1. Hope is a good breakfast, but it is a bad supper. *Sir Francis Bacon*

2. But I have had a dreary dream,
   Beyond the Isle of Sky;
   I saw a dead man win a fight,
   And I think that man was I. *Ballad of Chevy Chase*

3. Greatly his foes he dreads, but more his friends;
   He hurts me most who lavishly commends. *Charles Churchill*

4. He who praises everybody praises nobody. *Samuel Johnson*

5. You ought certainly to forgive them as a christian, but never to admit them in your sight, or allow their names to be mentioned in your hearing. *Jane Austen*

6. While Adam slept, Eve from his side arose:
   Strange his first sleep should be his last repose. *Anonymous*

7. The greatest of faults, I should say, is to be conscious of none. *Thomas Carlyle*

8. No people do so much harm as those who go about doing good.
   Bishop Mandell Creighton

9. It has long been an axiom of mine that little things are infinitely the most important. *Sir Arthur Conan Doyle*

10. Tennyson was not Tennysonian. *Henry James*

11. A. A violent order is disorder; and
    B. A great disorder is an order. These
    Two things are one. *Wallace Stevens*

12. If time matters, and of course it does, take a plane;
    If time is even more important, go by ship. *Hollis Summers*

F. Write a short poem or a paragraph in which the chief effect you intend (beauty, sordidness, strength, weakness, etc.) is combined with elements of its opposite.

With Naked Foot the withheld image 6

Understatement

If each of the thousands of images pouring in from the senses had an equal claim on our attention, the mind, unable to handle that dazzling overload, would be destroyed. Fortunately, we have mechanisms to keep from consciousness all but the most significant details.

Poets too, though they may think in images, work selectively; they give us only so much of what could be a confusing abundance—often give us synecdoches, for example, instead of totalities. They know too how silence sometimes speaks louder than words, and how an image can be most vividly present to us when it is not mentioned at all.

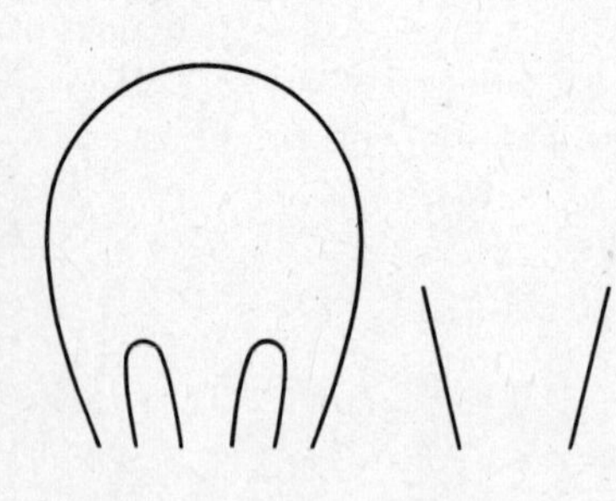

It is true also that we like to complete meanings for ourselves. A poem that starts us out on a process of discovery involves us more pleasurably than one in which the poet tells us all. For most people, the drawing on this page is more interesting in its incomplete form than if the missing lines were filled in and the label "Washerwoman with Bucket" affixed beneath. Children who have exciting news to tell are acting like poets when they dash up to us with a "Guess what?"

In 480 B.C., a few hundred Greek soldiers found themselves in the narrow pass at Thermopylae, between the mountains and the sea, facing an overwhelmingly larger Persian army. As the foreign troops came on, advance units were surprised to see the Spartans stretched out casually along the shore combing their long hair. A. E. Housman, in "The Oracles," describes the scene:

The King with half the East at heel is marched from lands of morning;
Their fighters drink the rivers up, their shafts benight the air.
And he that stands will die for nought, and home there's no returning.
The Spartans on the sea-wet rock sat down and combed their hair.

The first three lines are somewhat pompous and overwritten. They suggest the awe one is supposed to feel before the army of a king so great that he is referred to simply as "*the* King." The last line is different in tone; Housman uses only a detail or two to stir our feelings.

The poet Simonides, writing soon after the battle, was even more terse:

ON THE SPARTAN DEAD AT THERMOPYLAE

Go tell at Sparta, thou who passest by,
That here obedient to her laws we lie.

Simonides (556?–468 B.C.)

This poet was enough of a "professor of the five senses" to recognize one of the times he need not invoke them. Only too many of those he was talking to would have their own memories of a son or a father dead, their own knowledge of what a spear or sword can do to the human flesh one loves. Such images may be more effective when not mentioned at all. Every good writer, poet or not, knows this: Never tell a reader what will leap to his mind without your telling.

What we might call the **withheld image** can be as powerful as the presented one. It is difficult to imagine that "Western Wind" would have been better if it had been explicit, as current fiction often is, about the bedtime activities of the lovers.

We have seen the use of the withheld image in Wyatt's "They Flee From Me" (p. 58), in which the poet remembers girls "with naked foot" stalking in his chamber. Most of us have no difficulty in completing the girl's figure; we know too that the moment Wyatt mentions was probably not the climax of the evening.

The most famous example of the withheld image is in the love scene in which Paolo and Francesca, the adulterous lovers, pause to tell Dante about the day that spelled their ruin:

One day, for pleasure, we were reading about Lancelot, how love compelled him; we were all alone, unsuspected, unsuspecting. Our eyes met often over the reading, and often our faces went suddenly pale—and then in a single moment we were overcome. When we read how the smiling lips that Lancelot longed for were kissed by so great a lover, this one here, who will never leave me, kissed me all trembling on the mouth—

And then the withheld image. Instead of giving us the love scene, Dante merely adds:

That was the end of our reading for the day.

The movie camera might show their fingers relaxing on the book, then the book itself slipping to the floor.

The question of what to withhold may come up most urgently with themes of sex and violence, always among the great concerns of literature.

LORD RANDAL

"O where hae ye been, Lord Randal, my son?
O where hae ye been, my handsome young man?"
"I hae been to the wild wood; mother, make my bed soon,
For I'm weary wi' hunting, and fain wald lie down."

"Where gat ye your dinner, Lord Randal, my son?
Where gat ye your dinner, my handsome young man?"
"I din'd wi' my true-love; mother, make my bed soon,
For I'm weary wi' hunting, and fain wald lie down."

"What gat ye to your dinner, Lord Randal, my son?
What gat ye to your dinner, my handsome young man?" 10
"I gat eels boil'd in broo; mother, make my bed soon,
For I'm weary wi' hunting, and fain wald lie down."

"What became of your bloodhounds, Lord Randal, my son?
What became of your bloodhounds, my handsome young man?"
"O they swell'd and they died; mother, make my bed soon,
For I'm weary wi' hunting, and fain wald lie down."

"O I fear ye are poison'd, Lord Randal, my son!
I fear ye are poison'd, my handsome young man!"
"O yes! I am poison'd; mother, make my bed soon, 20
For I'm sick at the heart, and I fain wald lie down."

Anonymous (date uncertain)

Here, the main images are all withheld. Lord Randal has been meeting his "true-love," and yet there is no love scene. He has just been poisoned, and yet there is no poisoning scene. He is now dying, and yet there is no death scene.

No one would hold that crucial images should always be withheld, love scenes and deathbed scenes never presented. "Lord Randal" shows that powerful effects can be achieved by holding something back—not only certain images but certain facts, the meaning of which we piece together only gradually. Lord Randal might have entered,

---

1 **hae:** *have*
4 **fain wald:** *would like to*
5 **gat:** *got*
11 **broo:** *broth, juice*

crying, "Mother, I'm poisoned!" but his later revelations would have been less gripping than they now are. The poet might have shown the young man swelling and dying; it is probably better he did not. Both sex and violence are such highly charged subjects that any lack of sureness in describing them may set off the safety valve of laughter.

The story of Hippolytus and Phaedra has been told by both Euripides and Seneca. Hippolytus, a victim of sex, comes to a violent end. Entangled in the reins of his chariot, he is dragged over rugged ground to his death. Euripides, in referring to the body of Hippolytus, withholds the gorier details: he speaks of "his dear head battered on the rocks" and "his body bruised." Seneca, however, who lived in a sensation-loving age rather like our own, knows no such restraint. For him the body is like a dripping jigsaw puzzle, laid out to be reassembled. His chorus says:

> The scattered pieces of his torn body set in order, you his father, and fit back in place the odd assortment. His strong right hand should go here, and his left over there. I can recognize parts of his left side. But how many pieces are still missing!

The desolate father adds:

> What is this shapeless, ugly piece, with many a gash on every side? I do not know what part of you it is—but *some* part. Here, work it in, maybe not in its right place, but anywhere it sort of fits. Is this his *face?*

These are images that might better have been withheld—whether or not they correspond to an observed reality.

Sometimes, it is true, a bare account of brutal events may be gripping, as in this incident which the poet, himself a lawyer, found in court records of the nineteenth century.

DOMESTIC SCENES, 2

Late at night, their sow rooted open the door of their cabin,
and husband and wife
quarreled over driving her out.
His wife knocked him down with an iron shovel.
He started for his breeches and said,
"If I had my knife, I'd cut your throat,"
and she ran out at the door.
He shut the door after her
and propped it closed with a stick of wood.

When she was found, she was lying on her face, 10
frozen to death. The weather was extremely cold
and where she lay
the snow was about eighteen inches deep.

When she left the cabin, she was barefoot
and had very little clothing. The way she took
led through briers

and there were drops of blood on the snow—
where the briers had torn her legs from the knees down—
and bits of clothing that had been torn off;
at one place 20
she had struck her ankle against the end of a log
and it had bled freely.

Charles Reznikoff

Other poets, in dealing with such horrors, have preferred a different strategy. They give only such clues as will enable us to discover the central event, detective-fashion.

THE MILL

The miller's wife had waited long,
  The tea was cold, the fire was dead;
And there might yet be nothing wrong
  In how he went and what he said:
"There are no millers any more,"
  Was all that she had heard him say;
And he had lingered at the door
  So long that it seemed yesterday.

Sick with a fear that had no form
  She knew that she was there at last; 10
And in the mill there was a warm
  And mealy fragrance of the past.
What else there was would only seem
  To say again what he had meant;
And what was hanging from a beam
  Would not have heeded where she went.

And if she thought it followed her,
  She may have reasoned in the dark
That one way of the few there were
  Would hide her and would leave no mark: 20
Black water, smooth above the weir
  Like starry velvet in the night,
Though ruffled once, would soon appear
  The same as ever to the sight.

Edwin Arlington Robinson (1869–1935)

When we realize, without being told directly, that the lines are about a double suicide, the shock will be greater—as if we had stumbled on the bodies in real life.

A contemporary poet has presented an unsolved killing so that many details—the motive, the killer's identity, etc.—are withheld from us, just as they often are in crimes that make the headlines and puzzle the authorities.

LOOSE WOMAN

Someone who well knew how she'd toss her chin
Passing the firehouse oglers, at their taunt,
Let it be flung up higher than she'd want,
Just held fast by a little hinge of skin.
Two boys come from the river kicked a thatch
Of underbrush and stopped. One wrecked a pair
Of sneakers blundering into her hair
And that day made a different sort of catch.

Her next-best talent, setting tongues to buzz,
Lasts longer than her best. It still occurs 10
To wonder had she been our fault or hers
And had she loved him. Who the bastard was,
Though long they asked and notebooked round about
And turned up not a few who would have known
That white inch where her neck met shoulderbone,
Was one thing more we never did find out.

X. J. Kennedy (b. 1929)

Here are three recent poems—all by good poets—about making love in rooms temporarily engaged for the purpose. In none of the three is there any description of the love-making.

LEAVING THE MOTEL

Outside, the last kids holler
Near the pool: they'll stay the night.
Pick up the towels; fold your collar
Out of sight.

Check: is the second bed
Unrumpled, as agreed?
Landlords have to think ahead
In case of need,

Too. Keep things straight: don't take
The matches, the wrong keyrings— 10
We've nowhere we could keep a keepsake—
Ashtrays, combs, things

That sooner or later others
Would accidentally find.
Check: take nothing of one another's
And leave behind

Your license number only,
Which they won't care to trace;
We've paid. Still, should such things get lonely,
Leave in their vase 20

An aspirin to preserve
Our lilacs, the wayside flowers

We've gathered and must leave to serve
A few more hours;

That's all. We can't tell when
We'll come back, can't press claims;
We would no doubt have other rooms then,
Or other names.

W. D. Snodgrass (b. 1926)

ADULTERY

We have all been in rooms
We cannot die in, and they are odd places, and sad.
Often Indians are standing eagle-armed on hills

In the sunrise   open wide to the Great Spirit
Or gliding in canoes   or cattle are browsing on the walls
Far away   gazing down with the eyes of our children

Not far away   or there are men driving
The last railspike, which has turned
Gold in their hands. Gigantic forepleasure lives

Among such scenes, and we are alone with it   10
At last. There is always some weeping
Between us   and someone is always checking

A wrist watch by the bed to see how much
Longer we have left. Nothing can come
Of this   nothing can come

Of us: of me with my grim techniques
Or you who have sealed your womb
With a ring of convulsive rubber:

Although we come together,
Nothing will come of us. But we would not give   20
It up, for death is beaten

By praying Indians   by distant cows   historical
Hammers   by hazardous meetings that bridge
A continent. One could never die here

Never die   never die
While crying. My lover, my dear one
I will see you next week
When I'm in town. I will call you
If I can. Please get hold of   please don't
Oh God, Please don't any more I can't bear . . . Listen: 30

We have done it again   we are
Still living. Sit up and smile,
God bless you. Guilt is magical.

James Dickey (b. 1923)

ADULTERY AT THE PLAZA

Charged to mist by spring and midnight luxuries of space
Melt away fourteen floors down and miles past your white face
Maps of white lights, the Mall, the Zoo, dissolve in mist as we kiss
Standing on stone high in a cold and light-filled abyss.
This is what magic means. Cold energies of air
Chill your bare arms to snow, the mist is like ice in your hair,
But cells of air in your blood burn as the cold drinks revived
Old dreams from books abused, come true now, underived.
Lighted and at rest our rented room, our rented bed
Lie behind us like a mirror. "Look at the lamps," you said, 10
"Why are there seven lamps?" and touched your hair, as women do,
With your white gloves on. It is a mirror we can walk into,
And all New York out there at midnight shines from its dark stone,
Shines with the small cold lights of all that the rich own.
Furs and arctic crystals, hot beasts in frost, in your hair cold crests
Of mist the night puts there, in my hands how warm, how warm your breasts.
And drawing off your gloves you walked as one remembering
Or waiting, one who waits for what her memories will bring,
Stiff black silk, black leather, nylon, the black plume of your hair,
To the eight-foot double mirrors, the balcony, and "There, 20
Look there. I always knew, always, if I were a good girl,
Someday . . . ." We saw the round white rink of the skaters whirl
Spinning ice on ice far down in the long darkening park
And too much like a dream, and the balcony in the dark
Was too high, too much like a dream, if that is what magic means.
"Cold. The balcony's too cold." Far above us leans
With streaked frozen shoulders, frozen grin, his cast eyes frozen wide,
Out of his stone and darkness who sees you at my side;
We laugh and kiss, the gargoyle laughs. And when I drink
The ice cubes fetch up hard with a hard wet hurting clink 30
And that is comic, our laughter is comic. But there is a stone word,
"Quiet," it said. Ka-vy-et. "Down dere. It iss apsurd
Diss noiss at mitnight." And it was all foretold to this moment,
When the old voice we were bound to know speaks once and is silent.
Now only the mist waits miles out there in the night.
What is wrong you told us, but now tell us what is right,
Oh Mittel Europa, rich and far away from home and old,
Since you have spoken, speak to us now for we are cold
And far from home. What we have become, tell us, you know,
For I see now the ghosts of ourselves as we were a year ago 40
When we feared our eyes would meet but they did not in all that crowd,
And I would be kind, I would say now if it were allowed
To speak to the ghosts of a year ago, "Do not be afraid,
For I have come to you from the place where everything is made,
Or unmade, to be honest; children," so I should have said,
"A year from now you shall rise together from a rented bed,
You shall stand together above my city, see my lights unclear
Burning in the mist; so it shall all be in one year,
And you will remember together the ghosts that you are today,
And see the skaters whirling . . . . " What does the old voice say, 50
"Child, and you, poor child, hear, I haff come to tell you. . . . "

Something in an old expensive language that must be true:
"Many false hours are rising now far away over the sea,
And our tower, children, moves in time and moves with this dream city,
And you are bad, bad children. Lights are going out everywhere,
When morning comes you will only know that what was there is not there,
A year from now, poor children, only I know where you will be,
But I will send ghosts to you, your two ghosts, and you will see
That ghosts cannot speak kind words. I withdraw now my cold powers.
The skaters are gone home. All is dark. I leave you these hours." 60

John Thompson (b. 1918)

In all three of these poems the situation is viewed with mixed emotions. Often the wise writer, instead of making any judgment of his own, will give the reader a basis for making one if he cares to.

There are many kinds of love, many kinds of sex, and many kinds of poems about each. Campion's pretty song—even prettier with the music he wrote for it—is playful.

IT FELL ON A SUMMER'S DAY

It fell on a summer's day
While sweet Bessie sleeping lay
In her bower, on her bed,
Light with curtains shadowèd,
Jamey came; she him spies,
Opening half her heavy eyes.

Jamey stole in through the door;
She lay slumbering as before;
Softly to her he drew near;
She heard him, yet would not hear. 10
Bessie vowed not to speak;
He resolved that dump to break.

First a soft kiss he doth take;
She lay still, and would not wake.
Then his hands learned to woo;
She dreampt not what he would do,
But still slept, while he smiled
To see love by sleep beguiled.

Jamey then began to play;
Bessie as one buried lay, 20
Gladly still through this sleight
Deceived in her own deceit.
And since this trance began,
She sleeps every afternoon.

Thomas Campion (1567–1620)

---

[12] **dump:** *reverie* [21] **sleight:** *trick*

Very different is Richard Wilbur's poem of spectator sex and adolescent fantasy.

PLAYBOY

High on his stockroom ladder like a dunce
The stock-boy sits, and studies like a sage
The subject matter of one glossy page,
As lost in curves as Archimedes once.

Sometimes, without a glance, he feeds himself.
The left hand, like a mother-bird in flight,
Brings him a sandwich for a sidelong bite,
And then returns it to a dusty shelf.

What so engrosses him? The wild décor
Of this pink-papered alcove into which 10
A naked girl has stumbled, with its rich
Welter of pelts and pillows on the floor,

Amidst which, kneeling in a supple pose,
She lifts a goblet in her farther hand,
As if about to toast a flower-stand
Above which hovers an exploding rose

Fired from a long-necked crystal vase that rests
Upon a tasseled and vermilion cloth
One taste of which would shrivel up a moth?
Or is he pondering her perfect breasts? 20

Nothing escapes him of her body's grace
Or of her floodlit skin, so sleek and warm
And yet so strangely like a uniform,
But what now grips his fancy is her face,

And how the cunning picture holds her still
At just that smiling instant when her soul,
Grown sweetly faint, and swept beyond control,
Consents to his inexorable will.

Richard Wilbur (b. 1921)

"A Last Confession," in which the speaker is an old woman, is a kind of spiritualization of the sexual theme. The love of soul for naked soul, she says, will be more exciting and lasting than the love of body for body.

A LAST CONFESSION

What lively lad most pleasured me
Of all that with me lay?
I answer that I gave my soul
And loved in misery,
But had great pleasure with a lad
That I loved bodily.

Flinging from his arms I laughed
To think his passion such
He fancied that I gave a soul
Did but our bodies touch, 10
And laughed upon his breast to think
Beast gave beast as much.

I gave what other women gave
That stepped out of their clothes,
But when this soul, its body off,
Naked to naked goes,
He it has found shall find therein
What none other knows,

And give his own and take his own
And rule in his own right; 20
And though it loved in misery
Close and cling so tight,
There's not a bird of day that dare
Extinguish that delight.

W. B. Yeats

The withheld image is part of a good writer's overall strategy. Unskillful writers inflate their style so as to give their material more substance than it has, just as the puffer, or swellfish, gulps in water when panicked so as to appear larger and more formidable than it is. An old anecdote has a preacher writing in the margin of a sermon these directions to himself: "Argument weak here. Shout and pound pulpit." Weak writers rely on language that shouts and pounds. They like "unleashed titantic angers, throbbing and surging; awesome, specter-haunted anguish stalking the blood-soaked realm!"

More mature writers prefer to understate, to say less than they might rather than more, so that the meaning can explode *within the reader,* not just within the words on the page.

In "Michael," Wordsworth ends an account of the heartbreak of an old man by telling how he used to go out to the stone sheepfold he had been working on:

... many and many a day he thither went
And never lifted up a single stone.

Wordsworth does not have to tell why the man did not lift a stone; the meaning is more powerful if it bursts on us. A lesser poet might have said something like

... many and many a day he thither went
To pour forth tears of anguish and despair.

Frost concludes his story of the accidental death of a farm boy (p. 325) by having the doctor listening to his heartbeat:

Little—less—nothing! and that ended it.
No more to build on there. And they, since they
Were not the one dead, turned to their affairs.

When we realize what hopes the parents must have had for the boy's future, the "No more to build on there" is deeply moving. We might have remained unaffected if we had been told how the parent's horror-stricken eyes were fathomless pools of grief and anguish as they saw their brightest hopes trodden underfoot by callous Fate. The last line and a half is so understated it sounds cold, and yet Frost himself found the poem too moving to read in public. If the parents "turned to their affairs"—which would include not only milking the cows but getting in touch with the undertaker—we know with how heavy a heart they did so.

A form of understatement we all use is called **litotes.** It asserts a truth by denying its opposite. We say, "Not bad!" of a good cup of coffee, or "She's no Miss America!" of a plain girl. E. E. Cummings concludes a lyric with a litotes based on grammar:

> we are for each other: then
> laugh, leaning back in my arms
> for life's not a paragraph
>
> and death i think is no parenthesis

He gives what may be the supreme litotes of all time in his poem on the death of a politician he did not like. If he had not died, says Cummings,

> somebody might hardly never not have been unsorry, perhaps

Overstatement

There is a place too for the kind of overstatement called **hyperbole.** We frequently say things like "the best evening I ever had" or "the nicest dress I ever saw" or "I never heard such a lie!" Without hyperbole, some teen-agers—to use a hyperbole—could hardly get through a sentence. Slang relies on it: "He's the most!" "That music is too much!" A magazine writer calls it the chronic P.R. malady—we all know that in advertising everything is the best of its kind.

Hyperbole is not so much a way of writing as a way of seeing—the wildest hyperbole may be expressed in simple words. Perhaps it is an especially American way of seeing; the tall tales of frontier days are based on it. In "The People, Yes," Carl Sandburg gives a series of American hyperboles:

> They have yarns
> Of a skyscraper so tall they had to put hinges
> On the two top stories so to let the moon go by,
> Of one corn crop in Missouri when the roots
> Went so deep and drew off so much water
> The Mississippi riverbed that year was dry,
> Of pancakes so thin they had only one side,
> Of "a fog so thick we shingled the barn and six feet out on the fog,"
> Of Pecos Pete straddling a cyclone in Texas and riding it to the west
> coast where "it rained out under him,"

Of the man who drove a swarm of bees across the Rocky Mountains and the Desert "and didn't lose a bee,"
Of a mountain railroad curve where the engineer in his cab can touch the caboose and spit in the conductor's eye,
Of the boy who climbed a cornstalk growing so fast he would have starved to death if they hadn't shot biscuits up to him,
Of the old man's whiskers: "When the wind was with him his whiskers arrived a day before he did," ...
Of the man so tall he must climb a ladder to shave himself,
Of the runt so teeny-weeny it takes two men and a boy to see him ...
Of pigs so thin the farmer had to tie knots in their tails to keep them from crawling through the cracks in their pens ...

A householder's rueful humor is expressed in Hollis Summers'

April always finds us raking mountains
Of soggy leaves that burn more pokily
Than daisies turn to coal....

But such figures need not have comic intentions. The Earl of Rochester begins his love poem "The Mistress" with

An age in her embraces passed
  Would seem a winter's day....

Hyperboles are not lies; only the very naïve would take literally a poem like the following:

A QUESTION

I asked if I got sick and died, would you
With my black funeral go walking too,
If you'd stand close to hear them talk or pray
While I'm let down in that steep bank of clay.

And, No, you said, for if you saw a crew
Of living idiots pressing round that new
Oak coffin—they alive, I dead beneath
That board—you'd rave and rend them with your teeth.

John Millington Synge (1871–1909)

All the speaker means is that she would be highly indignant. Robert Graves, in making the concluding statement of "Spoils," is not necessarily ignorant of the properties of matter or of the techniques of safe-cracking.

SPOILS

When all is over and you march for home,
The spoils of war are easily disposed of:
Standards, weapons of combat, helmets, drums
May decorate a staircase or a study,
While lesser gleanings of the battlefield—
Coins, watches, wedding-rings, gold teeth and such—
Are sold anonymously for solid cash.

The spoils of love present a different case,
When all is over and you march for home:
That lock of hair, these letters and the portrait   10
May not be publicly displayed; nor sold;
Nor burned; nor returned (the heart being obstinate)—
Yet never dare entrust them to a safe
For fear they burn a hole through two-foot steel.

Robert Graves

His conclusion, mistaken as it might seem to a metallurgist, makes perfect sense in terms of the nature of emotion, whose effect cannot be insulated by any physical substance: love letters can continue to sear us, and the writer, wherever we keep them.

Exercises and Diversions

A. How much the poet should withhold is his own decision. He may want to tantalize us into "exploratory behavior." Difficulty is part of the fun in guessing games and detective stories; we are willing to spend time examining anything that gets our interest. (Some obscure poems never do—they are merely boring.) The poem that follows has been called "a famous puzzle-piece."

THE EMPEROR OF ICE-CREAM

Call the roller of big cigars,
The muscular one, and bid him whip
In kitchen cups concupiscent curds.
Let the wenches dawdle in such dress
As they are used to wear, and let the boys
Bring flowers in last month's newspapers.
Let be be finale of seem.
The only emperor is the emperor of ice-cream.

Take from the dresser of deal,
Lacking the three glass knobs, that sheet   10
On which she embroidered fantails once
And spread it so as to cover her face.
If her horny feet protrude, they come
To show how cold she is, and dumb.
Let the lamp affix its beam.
The only emperor is the emperor of ice-cream.

Wallace Stevens

The setting is a house in which preparations are being made for the final ceremonies for the dead.

1. (lines 1–2) Is there an element of irony, of play-of-opposites, in that the man making ice cream is the type he is?
2. (line 3) Why the highfalutin diction (not used elsewhere in the poem) and the gooey lushness of sound?

3. (lines 4–6) Why are the "wenches" described as "dawdling" in their everyday dresses? Why is it mentioned that the florists use last month's newspaper?
4. (line 7) Recall what a "finale" is. Some might paraphrase the line as meaning: Whatever seems to be true of life and death, whatever one likes to think about them, what we see in this house is the reality; ice cream and the horny feet of the dead are facts of our existence. Would you prefer to paraphrase it differently? How?
5. (line 8) Is the ice cream, which is real enough, also a symbol? If so, of what? Of the sweetness of life? Of the coldness of death? Of both combined?
6. (line 8) Is the emperor the "muscular one"? Or is the emperor the ruling principle that the ice cream represents? Or both?
7. (lines 9–16) Why does the diction change in the second stanza?
8. (line 10) Why does the poet bother to mention that the dresser has three missing knobs? Are they symbolic? (Trust your common sense.)
9. (lines 10–12) Is it ironic that the sheet she embroidered now covers the woman's face? "Fantails" can refer to either goldfish or pigeons. Stevens tells us he meant pigeons. Would the goldfish image have been as good? Are the pigeons (or goldfish) symbolic?
10. (line 13) Is it impolite or "not nice" of Stevens to mention that the dead woman has "horny feet"? With what tone does he seem to say this? Of fastidiousness? Of contempt? Or—?
11. (line 15) Is the lamp—what lamp?—to be affixed so that it focuses on the feet? Or on what?
12. After asking oneself such questions, should one still feel that the poem is a puzzle, with too much withheld to make an interpretation possible?

B. 1. At one time Stevens picked "The Emperor of Ice-Cream" as his favorite poem, giving what might seem paradoxical reasons. He said that it wore "a deliberately commonplace costume" and yet had "something of the essential gaudiness of poetry." Point out how—and why—the commonplace and the gaudy coexist in the poem.

C. 1. In the poems by Snodgrass, Dickey, and Thompson, there is little or no mention of the physical event for which the lovers came to their rented rooms. Other things are mentioned: matches, ashtrays, flowers, pictures, gargoyles, etc. If you listed the objects in each poem, would each list have a different character, appropriate to *its* poem? How many of the objects have emotional connotations? Without forcing a symbolic meaning decide which of the objects are genuinely symbolic.

2. Look around your own room until you find ten objects that might be of emotional value if you were writing about an important visit. If so minded, you might try writing a poem about such a visit, using the objects to suggest your feelings.

D. One can imagine an unliterary person giving a realistic account of a visit to the house of Stevens' poem, an account that would tally in all respects with the details which Stevens mentions. "I stopped in at poor Mrs. Foote's last night. What a scene! Smoke all over! There was this big guy in the kitchen, wearing a bowling shirt that said ROMA ICE CREAM PARLOR. . . ."

Write such an account in your own way, through the eyes of an imaginary visitor. Or describe the situation in a poem written in the manner of Charles Reznikoff's "Domestic Scenes."

II the emotions

The Color of Thought

7 the emotions in poetry

Up to now (to repeat an outline given earlier) we have been concerned with the source of human awareness, sense perception: with how our mind deals with the images the senses provide; with how it relates and compares them, condensing some into symbols, narrowing its focus onto parts of others; with how it handles conflicting evidence; and with how it presents, or chooses not to present, all this in poetry.

This chapter and the next will be about emotion, the reaction of the mind-body combination to the objects or situations that sense images make it aware of. Emotion, like imagery, is conditioned by our physiological history; we can no more feel a disembodied emotion than perceive a disembodied image.

Why do cats dislike getting their feet wet? Darwin, fascinated by the behavior of animals, thought he knew. About 3000 B.C. the Egyptians domesticated the native wildcat to serve as a guard animal. As cats slowly spread over the world they retained the racial preferences of the almost waterless land of their ancestors.

Darwin also tried to account for human facial expressions as inherited from our ancestors. When we express scorn or rage by sneering, we curl back our lip to bare the once large canine teeth, although it has been a long time since man, in his endless armaments race, has considered his dental weaponry of much account.

Psychologists believe that the mind also inherits predispositions. Certain images affect us more powerfully than any experience of our own would seem to account for. Scientists like Jung, poets like Yeats believe that such images have an inherited potential: we are moved by them because of their significance for man throughout his history. These reactions have been encoded in the nervous system itself, in the biochemistries of memory. **Archetypal image** is the term Jung has used for those patternings whose unconscious charge can stir and disturb us. Birth, love, guilt, death, rebirth are examples of such archetypal themes. So are sibling rivalry, the need for or envy of a father figure or earth mother, the quest for some kind of Grail, ideas of heaven or hell. We can think of images that affect us as if from long ago: the sun, darkness, the sea, mountains, trees, caves, shelter, storms, war—all of the basic realities that helped determine our happiness or misery, our survival or extinction, throughout the long history of mankind.

Certain passages of poetry touch us as if there were indeed such memories.

> The son of morn in weary night's decline,
> The lost traveller's dream under the hill.

It is not necessary to know what Blake meant to find his lines strangely haunting. Almost every word is rich with emotions that go back as far as the memory of man.

Emotional experience. This, more than anything else, is what poetry gives us. And this is what we value as much as anything in life and what we are willing to go to almost any extreme for. Our lives—if fully human—are afloat on seas of emotion; we live there more richly than we live in any geographical world.

The poet, unlike the philosopher, is not primarily a thinker. "The poet who 'thinks,'" T. S. Eliot reminds us, "is merely the poet who can express the emotional equivalent of thought."

We all know an emotion when we feel one. We know that strong emotion has a marked and instant physical effect on us. It influences our heartbeat, our breathing, the distribution of our blood flow (we flush or grow pale), our visceral activities, our glandular secretions, the temperature and electrical conductivity of our skin. Emotion affects all of our internal rhythms—and the rhythm of our poetry. Its physiological aspects could hardly be better illustrated than in the poem of Sappho we have read (p. 9); she is almost paralyzed with fear and love. If this seems to be a poetic flight of fancy we might recall that emotion releases adrenalin into the bloodstream, and that an excess of adrenalin, instead of assisting muscular activity, interferes with the reconversion of lactic acid to the needed glycogen, so that, under great emotional stress, we become muscularly handicapped. Sappho is right in feeling she may faint. A greatly increased heartbeat (*tachycardia*) will result in reduced circulation, since the heart then operates less efficiently as a pump; and as the brain gets less blood one becomes dizzy and may lose consciousness. Sappho did not know all this, but she did know what she was feeling, what her body image had become, and she did know that poets report in images.

It is no wonder that poetry, which is physical and emotional, affects sensitive readers in a physical way. William James, the psychologist, was susceptible: "In listening to poetry . . . we are often surprised at the cutaneous shiver which like a sudden wave flows over us, and at the heart-swelling and the lachrymal effusion that unexpectedly catch us at intervals. . . ." Emily Dickinson judged poetry by its physical effect: "If I read a book [and] it makes my whole body so cold no fire ever can warm me I know *that* is poetry. If I feel physically as if the top of my head were taken off, I know *that* is poetry. These are the only way I know it. . . ." So did A. E. Housman: "Experience has taught me, when I am shaving of a morning, to keep watch over my thoughts, because, if a line of poetry strays into my memory, my skin bristles so that the razor ceases to act. . . ." Though our emotions are so many and so complex that we could hardly classify them, they all develop from the two ways that babies feel: either they are satisfied, or they are not. If not, they evidence their dissatisfaction. Later on, the primordial states will subdivide: dissatisfaction will show itself as anger or as fear, satisfaction as love or pride. As the child grows older, the possibilities will become infinite, all of them going back to the two originals: something attracts us, something repels us.

We can visualize the emotions as a color wheel (p. 108) like the ones we see in art-supply shops, a wheel in which selected colors are arranged, like spokes, according to their prismatic or "spectral" order. We make more colors by adding white to get "tints," black to get "shades." If we start blending the colors themselves there is no end to the number we can make, just as there is no end to the number or complexity of our emotions.

Colors opposite each other on *their* wheel are complementary: mixed together, they cancel each other out, give us black or a neutral shade of gray. But when emotions are mixed, as they usually are, each can remain distinct. When we feel a passionate love and hate for the same person, the blend is anything but gray.

Catullus found he could love someone he did not even like.

75

Now my mind's been brought to such extremes—and it's your fault,
  Lesbia!—been so doomed by its devotion to you,
I couldn't like you again, if you turned truest of women;
  Yet couldn't fall out of love, not for the worst you could do.

Catullus (84?–54? B.C.)

He even begins one of his most famous little poems with *"Odi et amo"* (I hate and I love). It might be translated:

85

Her that I love, I hate! *How's that, do you know?* they wonder.
  Know? What's *know?* I feel. Ask any crucified man.

Catullus

Emotion, Catullus is also saying, is not easily subject to intellectual analysis or control.

Map of the Emotions

1626.
ruest Descriptions latest Discoueries & best Obseruations y^t haue beene made by English or Strangers.
EARTH
A Figure of the Sphaeare
M. Thomas Candish
Oliverus vander Noort
AIRE
Are to be sold in popes head Alle by Geo: Humble
The Eclipse of the Moone
Awe
Loyalty
Idolatry
Adoration
Reverence
Respect
Forgivingness
Mercifulness
Affection
Attraction
Gratitude
Admiration
Vainglory
Arrogance
Overconfidence
Love
Self-pity
Sympathy
Compunction
pity
Understanding
Possessiveness
Greed
Determination
Courage
Daring
Rashness
Defiance
Fieriness
Presumption
Desire
Lust
Infatuation
Longing
pride
Self-confidence
Self-display
spiration
Ambition
Self-Love
Striving
Consolation
Relief
Euphoria
Nonchalance
Gladness
Mirth
Elation
Exhilaration
thusiasm
Buoyancy
Hope
Alertness
Curiosity
Arousal
Gloating
Joy
Serenity
Triumph
Exaltation
onfidence
Optimism
Surprise
Shock
Contentment
Satisfaction
Gratification
pleasure
Ecstasy
Bliss
Fascination
Mania
Anticipation
Expectation
wonder
Obsession
Vacillation
Suspense
Confusion
Concern
Happiness
Fulfillment
Delight
Astonishment
wonder

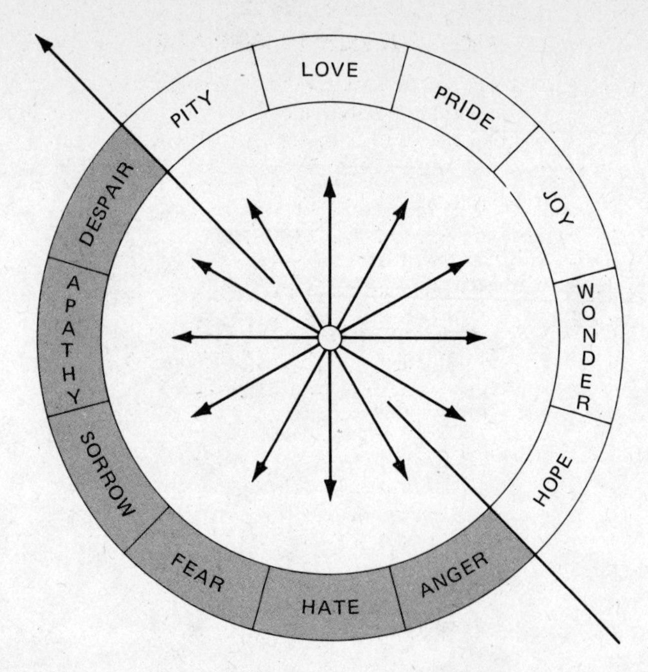

We do not have to believe in the ideas of a poem to share its experience: a pacifist can enjoy Homer; an atheist, Dante. But we do have to believe in its emotions. If the poem seems to fake anything here, it is not likely to involve us.

Classifying poems according to their predominant passion has no value in itself. But it will remind us that poetry has the entire wheel to range around, and that a poem that seems to be in one emotional key will be harmonically or dissonantly related to many others.

No one needs to tell us that there are many kinds and gradations of LOVE.

WILD NIGHTS

Wild Nights—Wild Nights!
Were I with thee
Wild Nights should be
Our luxury!

Futile—the Winds—
To a Heart in port—
Done with the Compass—
Done with the Chart!

Rowing in Eden—
Ah, the Sea! 10
Might I but moor—Tonight—
In Thee!

Emily Dickinson

THE NATIVITY OF OUR LORD

Where is this stupendous stranger,
  Swains of Solyma, advise,
Lead me to my Master's manger,
  Show me where my Saviour lies?

O Most Mighty! O MOST HOLY!
  Far beyond the seraph's thought,
Art thou then so mean and lowly
  As unheeded prophets taught?

O the magnitude of meekness!
  Worth from worth immortal sprung; 10
O the strength of infant weakness,
  If eternal is so young!

If so young and thus eternal,
  Michael tune the shepherd's reed,
Where the scenes are ever vernal,
  And the loves be love indeed!

See the God blasphemed and doubted
  In the schools of Greece and Rome;
See the pow'rs of darkness routed,
  Taken at their utmost gloom. 20

Nature's decorations glisten
  Far above their usual trim;
Birds on box and laurel listen,
  As so near the cherubs hymn.

Boreas now no longer winters
  On the desolated coast;
Oaks no more are riv'n in splinters
  By the whirlwind and his host.

Spinks and ouzels sing sublimely,
  "We too have a Saviour born;" 30
Whither blossoms burst untimely
  On the blest Mosaic thorn.

God all-bounteous, all-creative,
  Whom no ills from good dissuade,
Is incarnate, and a native
  Of the very world he made.

Christopher Smart (1722–1771)

Shelley gives an ironic treatment of the kind of PRIDE we might prefer to call arrogance.

---

[2] **Swains of Solyma:** *shepherds of Jerusalem*
[25] **Boreas:** *the north wind*
[29] **Spinks:** *finches*
ouzels: *blackbirds*

OZYMANDIAS

I met a traveller from an antique land
Who said: Two vast and trunkless legs of stone
Stand in the desert. Near them, on the sand,
Half sunk, a shattered visage lies, whose frown,
And wrinkled lip, and sneer of cold command,
Tell that its sculptor well those passions read
Which yet survive, stamped on these lifeless things,
The hand that mocked them and the heart that fed;
And on the pedestal these words appear:
"My name is Ozymandias, king of kings: 10
Look on my works, ye Mighty, and despair!"
Nothing beside remains. Round the decay
Of that colossal wreck, boundless and bare,
The lone and level sands stretch far away.

Percy Bysshe Shelley (1792–1822)

Pride has a favorable meaning too: the sense of human dignity in an individual. Auden has written about a contemporary world in which men have "lost their pride" or can be made to lose it. This depersonalized totalitarian world, hideous with the crime that accompanies poverty and urban demoralization, is contrasted with the more humane world of Homer. (In the *Iliad,* Book xviii, the sea goddess Thetis asks the crippled armorer Hephaestus to make new armor for her son Achilles.)

THE SHIELD OF ACHILLES

She looked over his shoulder
  For vines and olive trees,
Marble well-governed cities
  And ships upon untamed seas,
But there on the shining metal
  His hands had put instead
An artificial wilderness
  And a sky like lead.

A plain without a feature, bare and brown,
  No blade of grass, no sign of neighbourhood, 10
Nothing to eat and nowhere to sit down,
  Yet, congregated on its blankness, stood
  An unintelligible multitude,
A million eyes, a million boots in line,
Without expression, waiting for a sign.

Out of the air a voice without a face
  Proved by statistics that some cause was just
In tones as dry and level as the place:
  No one was cheered and nothing was discussed;
  Column by column in a cloud of dust 20
They marched away enduring a belief
Whose logic brought them, somewhere else, to grief.

She looked over his shoulder
  For ritual pieties,
White flower-garlanded heifers,
  Libation and sacrifice,
But there on the shining metal
  Where the altar should have been,
She saw by his flickering forge-light
  Quite another scene. 30

Barbed wire enclosed an arbitrary spot
  Where bored officials lounged (one cracked a joke)
And sentries sweated, for the day was hot:
  A crowd of ordinary decent folk
  Watched from without and neither moved nor spoke
As three pale figures were led forth and bound
To three posts driven upright in the ground.

The mass and majesty of this world, all
  That carries weight and always weighs the same
Lay in the hands of others; they were small 40
  And could not hope for help and no help came:
  What their foes liked to do was done, their shame
Was all the worst could wish; they lost their pride
And died as men before their bodies died.

She looked over his shoulder
  For athletes at their games,
Men and women in a dance
  Moving their sweet limbs
Quick, quick, to music,
  But there on the shining shield 50
His hands had set no dancing-floor
  But a weed-choked field.

A ragged urchin, aimless and alone,
  Loitered about that vacancy, a bird
Flew up to safety from his well-aimed stone:
  That girls are raped, that two boys knife a third,
  Were axioms to him, who'd never heard
Of any world where promises were kept,
Or one could weep because another wept.

The thin-lipped armourer, 60
  Hephaestos hobbled away,
Thetis of the shining breasts
  Cried out in dismay
At what the god had wrought
  To please her son, the strong
Iron-hearted man-slaying Achilles
  Who would not live long.

W. H. Auden (1907–1973)

In such a world as that, it would seem that poems about JOY would become increasingly difficult to write.

Pity the planet, all joy gone
from this sweet volcanic cone....

So Robert Lowell has lamented. But poets like E. E. Cummings, Dylan Thomas, and Theodore Roethke have thought of themselves as joyful poets. Yeats, in spite of his terrifying visions of an apocalyptic Second Coming (p. 269), found no scarcity of joy in his life:

FRIENDS

Now must I these three praise—
Three women that have wrought
What joy is in my days:
One because no thought,
Nor those unpassing cares,
No, not in these fifteen
Many-times-troubled years,
Could ever come between
Mind and delighted mind;
And one because her hand 10
Had strength that could unbind
What none can understand,
What none can have and thrive,
Youth's dreamy load, till she
So changed me that I live
Labouring in ecstasy.
And what of her that took
All till my youth was gone
With scarce a pitying look?
How could I praise that one? 20
When day begins to break
I count my good and bad,
Being wakeful for her sake,
Remembering what she had,
What eagle look still shows,
While up from my heart's root
So great a sweetness flows
I shake from head to foot.

W. B. Yeats

WONDER, or interest, or curiosity, is that excited state in which exploratory activity leads perhaps to fear, perhaps to love, perhaps to yet another emotion.

THE TYGER

Tyger, Tyger, burning bright,
In the forests of the night,
What immortal hand or eye
Could frame thy fearful symmetry?

In what distant deeps or skies
Burnt the fire of thine eyes?

On what wings dare he aspire?
What the hand dare seize the fire?

And what shoulder, & what art,
Could twist the sinews of thy heart? 10
And when thy heart began to beat,
What dread hand? & what dread feet?

What the hammer? what the chain?
In what furnace was thy brain?
What the anvil? What dread grasp
Dare its deadly terrors clasp?

When the stars threw down their spears
And watered heaven with their tears,
Did he smile his work to see?
Did he who made the Lamb make thee? 20

Tyger, Tyger, burning bright,
In the forests of the night,
What immortal hand or eye
Dare frame thy fearful symmetry?

William Blake

Elizabeth Bishop's contemplation of her "tremendous fish" takes her through a range of wondering emotions.

THE FISH

I caught a tremendous fish
and held him beside the boat
half out of water, with my hook
fast in a corner of his mouth.
He didn't fight.
He hadn't fought at all.
He hung a grunting weight,
battered and venerable
and homely. Here and there
his brown skin hung in strips 10
like ancient wallpaper,
and its pattern of darker brown
was like wallpaper:
shapes like full-blown roses
stained and lost through age.
He was speckled with barnacles,
fine rosettes of lime,
and infested
with tiny white sea-lice,
and underneath two or three 20
rags of green weed hung down.
While his gills were breathing in
the terrible oxygen
—the frightening gills,
fresh and crisp with blood,

that can cut so badly—
I thought of the coarse white flesh
packed in like feathers,
the big bones and the little bones,
the dramatic reds and blacks 30
of his shiny entrails,
and the pink swim-bladder
like a big peony.
I looked into his eyes
which were far larger than mine
but shallower, and yellowed,
the irises backed and packed
with tarnished tinfoil
seen through the lenses
of old scratched isinglass. 40
They shifted a little, but not
to return my stare.
—It was more like the tipping
of an object toward the light.
I admired his sullen face,
the mechanism of his jaw,
and then I saw
that from his lower lip
—if you could call it a lip—
grim, wet, and weaponlike, 50
hung five old pieces of fish-line,
or four and a wire leader
with the swivel still attached,
with all their five big hooks
grown firmly in his mouth.
A green line, frayed at the end
where he broke it, two heavier lines,
and a fine black thread
still crimped from the strain and snap
when it broke and he got away. 60
Like medals with their ribbons
frayed and wavering,
a five-haired beard of wisdom
trailing from his aching jaw.
I stared and stared
and victory filled up
the little rented boat,
from the pool of bilge
where oil had spread a rainbow
around the rusted engine 70
to the bailer rusted orange,
the sun-cracked thwarts,
the oarlocks on their strings,
the gunnels—until everything
was rainbow, rainbow, rainbow!
And I let the fish go.

Elizabeth Bishop

In the following poem, HOPE is our theme.

"HOPE" IS THE THING WITH FEATHERS

"Hope" is the thing with feathers—
That perches in the soul—
And sings the tune without the words—
And never stops—at all—

And sweetest—in the Gale—is heard—
And sore must be the storm—
That could abash the little Bird
That kept so many warm—

I've heard it in the chillest land—
And on the strangest Sea— 10
Yet, never, in Extremity,
It asked a crumb—of Me.

Emily Dickinson

A cold ANGER at the dictatorial power whose decisions can be catastrophic for mankind energizes a poem that refers to a tyrant only by a contemptuous synecdoche, "the hand."

THE HAND THAT SIGNED THE PAPER

The hand that signed the paper felled a city;
Five sovereign fingers taxed the breath
Doubled the globe of dead and halved a country;
These five kings did a king to death.

The mighty hand leads to a sloping shoulder,
The finger joints are cramped with chalk;
A goose's quill has put an end to murder
That put an end to talk.

The hand that signed the treaty bred a fever,
And famine grew, and locusts came; 10
Great is the hand that holds dominion over
Man by a scribbled name.

The five kings count the dead but do not soften
The crusted wound nor stroke the brow;
A hand rules pity as a hand rules heaven;
Hands have no tears to flow.

Dylan Thomas (1914–1953)

Poetry, it should be clear by now, does not confine itself to the nobler and more inspiring emotions. Yeats almost bragged, in his old age, that "lust and rage" were the prime sources of his inspiration. "Hatred," writes John Wain, "can be ink in a poet's pen." Walter

Savage Landor lives up to his middle name in the lines he wrote on an old and dying poet:

ALAS! 'TIS VERY SAD TO HEAR

Alas! 'tis very sad to hear,
You and your Muse's end draws near:
I only wish, if this be true,
To lie a little way from you.
The grave is cold enough for me
Without you and your poetry.

Walter Savage Landor

HATE poetry, more or less witty, goes back at least to the ancient Greeks.

EPITAPH OF NEARCHOS

Rest lightly O Earth upon this wretched Nearchos
That the dogs may have no trouble in dragging him out.

Ammianus (second century A.D.)
(Translated by Dudley Fitts)

One of the most impressive poems of self-hate, of disgust or revulsion, is a sonnet of Shakespeare.

SONNET 129

The expense of spirit in a waste of shame
Is lust in action; and, till action, lust
Is perjured, murderous, bloody, full of blame,
Savage, extreme, rude, cruel, not to trust;
Enjoyed no sooner but despisèd straight;
Past reason hunted, and, no sooner had,
Past reason hated as a swallowed bait
On purpose laid to make the taker mad;
Mad in pursuit, and in possession so;
Had, having, and in quest to have, extreme; 10
A bliss in proof, and proved, a very woe,
Before, a joy proposed; behind, a dream.
All this the world well knows, yet none knows well
To shun the heaven that leads men to this hell.

William Shakespeare

A FEAR like that of dreams is one of the emotions Keats evokes in his "ballad."

LA BELLE DAME SANS MERCI
A Ballad

I

O what can ail thee, knight-at-arms,
Alone and palely loitering?

The sedge has wither'd from the lake,
And no birds sing.

II

O what can ail thee, knight-at-arms!
So haggard and so woe-begone?
The squirrel's granary is full,
And the harvest's done.

III

I see a lily on thy brow,
With anguish moist and fever dew, 10
And on thy cheeks a fading rose
Fast withereth too.

IV

I met a lady in the meads,
Full beautiful—a faery's child,
Her hair was long, her foot was light,
And her eyes were wild.

V

I made a garland for her head,
And bracelets too, and fragrant zone;
She look'd at me as she did love,
And made sweet moan. 20

VI

I set her on my pacing steed,
And nothing else saw all day long,
For sidelong would she bend, and sing
A faery's song.

VII

She found me roots of relish sweet,
And honey wild, and manna dew,
And sure in language strange she said—
"I love thee true".

VIII

She took me to her elfin grot,
And there she wept, and sigh'd full sore, 30
And there I shut her wild wild eyes
With kisses four.

IX

And there she lulled me asleep,
And there I dream'd—Ah! woe betide!
The latest dream I ever dream'd
On the cold hill side.

X

I saw pale kings and princes too,
Pale warriors, death-pale were they all;
They cried—"La Belle Dame sans Merci
Hath thee in thrall!" 40

---

[18] **zone:** *belt*

XI

I saw their starved lips in the gloam,
  With horrid warning gaped wide,
And I awoke and found me here,
  On the cold hill's side.

XII

And this is why I sojourn here,
  Alone and palely loitering,
Though the sedge is wither'd from the lake,
  And no birds sing.

John Keats

A poem of more cosmic fear and awe uses space imagery like that of the telephotography of the astronauts.

LUCIFER IN STARLIGHT

ON a starred night Prince Lucifer uprose.
Tired of his dark dominion swung the fiend
Above the rolling ball in cloud part screened,
Where sinners hugged their spectre of repose.
Poor prey to his hot fit of pride were those.
And now upon his western wing he leaned,
Now his huge bulk o'er Afric's sands careened,
Now the black planet shadowed Arctic snows.
Soaring through wider zones that pricked his scars
With memory of the old revolt from Awe, 10
He reached a middle height, and at the stars,
Which are the brain of heaven, he looked, and sank.
Around the ancient track marched, rank on rank,
The army of unalterable law.

George Meredith (1828–1909)

Rossetti's sufferer in "The Woodspurge," his eyes unable to move from a little patch of ground, dramatizes a paralysis of SORROW, in which a trivial detail burns itself into his memory forever. Even the rhyme is paralyzed—a broken record on which the needle cannot get out of its one worn groove.

THE WOODSPURGE

The wind flapped loose, the wind was still,
Shaken out dead from tree and hill:
I had walked on at the wind's will,—
I sat now, for the wind was still.

---

[41] **gloam:** *twilight*

Between my knees my forehead was,—
My lips, drawn in, said not Alas!
My hair was over in the grass,
My naked ears heard the day pass,

My eyes, wide open, had the run
Of some ten weeds to fix upon; 10
Among those few, out of the sun,
The woodspurge flowered, three cups in one.

From perfect grief there need not be
Wisdom or even memory:
One thing then learnt remains to me,—
The woodspurge has a cup of three.

Dante Gabriel Rossetti (1828–1882)

In this and the following poem grief is almost frozen into APATHY, into what a psychologist calls that "stupefaction, amounting to loss of consciousness, which may occur as the result of violent emotional shock." Almost the death of the nervous system.

AFTER GREAT PAIN, A FORMAL FEELING COMES

After great pain, a formal feeling comes—
The Nerves sit ceremonious, like Tombs—
The stiff Heart questions was it He, that bore,
And Yesterday, or Centuries before?

The Feet, mechanical, go round—
Of Ground, or Air, or Ought—
A Wooden way
Regardless grown,
A Quartz contentment, like a stone—

This is the Hour of Lead— 10
Remembered, if outlived,
As Freezing persons, recollect the Snow—
First—Chill—then Stupor—then the letting go—

Emily Dickinson

Tennyson's "Tears, Idle Tears," though it mentions DESPAIR, is so rich in music and poignant melancholy that it seems less hopeless than other poems we have read.

TEARS, IDLE TEARS

Tears, idle tears, I know not what they mean,
Tears from the depth of some divine despair
Rise in the heart, and gather to the eyes,
In looking on the happy Autumn-fields,
And thinking of the days that are no more.

Fresh as the first beam glittering on a sail,
That brings our friends up from the underworld,
Sad as the last which reddens over one
That sinks with all we love below the verge;
So sad, so fresh, the days that are no more. 10

Ah, sad and strange as in dark summer dawns
The earliest pipe of half-awaken'd birds
To dying ears, when unto dying eyes
The casement slowly grows a glimmering square;
So sad, so strange, the days that are no more.

Dear as remember'd kisses after death,
And sweet as those by hopeless fancy feign'd
On lips that are for others; deep as love,
Deep as first love, and wild with all regret;
O Death in Life, the days that are no more. 20

Alfred Lord Tennyson (1809–1892)

Pete Seeger's song, part of which follows, arouses other emotions besides PITY, but the angrier ones are only implied. The main feeling seems to be in the sorrow and pity of the refrain.

FROM **WHERE HAVE ALL THE FLOWERS GONE?**

Where have all the flowers gone?
Long time passing.
Where have all the flowers gone?
Long time ago.
Where have all the flowers gone?
Young girls picked them, every one.
When will they ever learn,
O when will they ever learn?

Where have all the young girls gone?
Long time passing. 10
Where have all the young girls gone?
Long time ago.
Where have all the young girls gone?
Gone to young men, every one.
When will they ever learn,
O when will they ever learn?

Where have all the young men gone?
Long time passing.
Where have all the young men gone?
Long time ago. 20
Where have all the young men gone?
Gone for soldiers, every one.
When will they ever learn,
O when will they ever learn? . . .

Pete Seeger (b. 1919)

Wilfred Owen (p. 216), one of the greatest of the poets who have handled the theme of war, said in the Preface to his poems:

> My subject is War, and the pity of War.
> The Poetry is in the Pity.

With pity, we come full-circle back to love at the top of our emotion wheel.

Exercises and Diversions

A. In "The Shield of Achilles" (p. 110), Auden shows the horror of a contemporary world by contrasting it with an ancient world of naturalness, order, "ritual pieties," and the dance. Many of his details are taken from the eighteenth book of the *Iliad*, but there the artwork on the shield is not as sweetly innocent as that which Thetis hopes for in Auden's poem. The world of Homer is less idealized: Hephaestus depicts a murder trial and a city at war, in which appear the figures of Discord, Tumult, and Fate, whose cloak is soaked red with human blood. In the peaceful countryside there is a gory scene of a lion gorging on a dead bull.

1. Do you think Auden handles his contrast well by showing the ancient world as entirely idyllic and the contemporary one as entirely hideous?
2. Is it ironic that Achilles, the representative of the ancient world, is himself "iron-hearted," "man-slaying," and doomed to an early death?
3. In scenes of the modern world, what effective use is made of the withheld image? What is *not* shown?
4. What effective synecdoches or metonymies occur? Why is "boots" (l. 14) a better word than "shoes"?
5. Auden's idea might be expressed (oversimply) as: the conditions of contemporary life do not permit man to develop his full human potential as well as older civilizations did. Show the steps by which the poet turns this idea into images.
6. Why would the contemporary civilization Auden shows be hostile to poetry? What details indicate that all emotion has been stifled?
7. Some readers will feel a Biblical allusion in the number of the victims of modern tyranny (l. 36). Others may feel that when Auden says that his "multitude" is "waiting for a sign" (l. 15), he is referring to the twelfth chapter of Saint Matthew, in which some of the scribes and Pharisees tell Christ they would like to see "a sign" (a miracle). Would the allusion—if it is there—seem ironic?
8. In Homer, there is no "sacrifice," no "flower-garlanded heifers," no "altar" (fourth stanza). All are found in Keats' "Ode on a Grecian Urn":

   > Who are these coming to the sacrifice?
   > To what green altar, O mysterious priest,
   > Lead'st thou that heifer lowing at the skies,
   > And all her silken flanks with garlands dressed?

   Would you guess that Auden is making a deliberate allusion to the Keats poem? Or is this an involuntary echo? A mere coincidence?
9. The urchin (l. 53) is described as "aimless," but his stone is "well-aimed." In

a freshman writing class would this be called "clumsy repetition," or is it intentional?

10. Other words seem to be used with special effect, so that we almost do a double take with them. With derivation (see dictionary) and connotations in mind, weigh the use of "artificial" (l. 7), "feature" (l. 9), "neighbourhood" (l. 10), "congregated" (l. 12), "unintelligible" (l. 13), "cheered" (l. 19), "enduring" (l. 21), "arbitrary" (l. 31), "vacancy" (l. 54), "axioms" (l. 57).
11. What is the effect of the unusually high percentage of monosyllabic words in the sixth stanza?
12. Why is Hephaestus described as "thin-lipped" (l. 60)? The usual epithet for Thetis is *ἀργυρόπεζα* ("silver-footed"). Why, in line 62, did not Auden write "Thetis of the silver feet"?
13. When stanzas are used in a poem, they are generally the same throughout. One can see at a glance that two kinds of stanzas are used here. Why is the shift appropriate in this poem?
14. What is the inner logic of the stanzas? Do the second and third stanzas, for example, relate to the first? The fifth and sixth to the fourth?
15. The addition of one more stanza would make the structure symmetrical. Where should it be? Can you see any reason for its absence? (Heroic project for literary aspirants: try writing the "missing" stanza so it fits in with the others in all respects.)

B. 1. Look back over the poems we have read. Does it seem true that poets are not primarily thinkers? Do you find any poems that are remarkable for the power and originality of their *ideas*?

2. Poems not written as allegories can sometimes be read allegorically. Could MacLeish's "Eleven" (p. 6) be read as a poem about the poetic process, in that the child, hating the "Think now, Think . . . ," leaves the world of thought to get back to the world of sensation, imagination, and feeling?
3. Tennyson's "Tears, Idle Tears" takes on a peculiar coloring in its context. It occurs as a song in "The Princess" (1847), named after the progressive Princess Ida, who anticipated many of the ideas of the women's liberation movement. Wanting women to give up all "the tricks which make us toys of men," she founds an all-women's college. Any men found on the campus are to be executed. The unsentimental princess treats the song with some contempt, since it seems to be reactionary in praising the good old days, or, as she says, it "moans about the retrospect." It seems to her to be proestablishment because it fails to point out the injustices of the past.

   Does the poem seem to you to have political or social overtones?
4. All of us have personal images (of things, of people, of places, of seasons, etc.) that affect us deeply, perhaps because they condense memories and associations from childhood. Think of examples in your own mind. If you were writing poetry, how could you make use of these images so that others could be made to feel their power? Write a poem or prose paragraph around one or more of these personal images.

True Color and False

8

emotion and sentimentality

First, a brief detour.

There is no reason to worry about this bird. It has not been injured or "taken apart." If one is interested in birds, one likes to be able to tell one from another—a catbird from a mockingbird, a great racket-tail drongo from a blue-faced booby. The diagram shows where points of difference lie.

There are people who think that knowledge destroys their spontaneous reaction to anything beautiful. They are seldom right; gen-

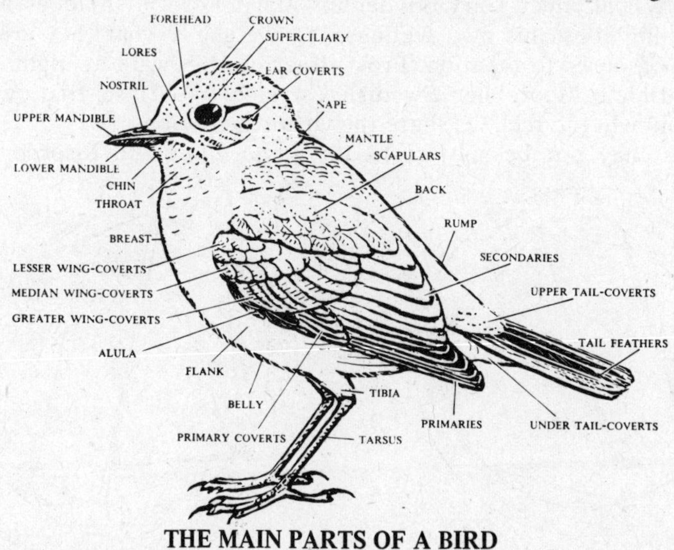

THE MAIN PARTS OF A BIRD

erally, the more we know, the more we see to appreciate. There are people who think that to analyze a poem or, as they like to say, to "tear it apart," is to destroy it. But one no more destroys a poem by means of analysis than one destroys birds or flowers or anything else by means of a diagram. The words of the poem lie on the page (or vibrate in the air, if they are spoken), radiating their energies as long as the language itself lasts—much like a piece of radium. One can trap these radiations and subject them to any kind of analysis that will reveal their nature. But the poem, the source of the energy, will not be affected. In this chapter and elsewhere there will be diagrams and analyses. They do not represent poems any more than the diagram (p. 123) represents a bird. But they may help to make a point or two.

The preceding chapter reminds us that poetry covers the whole range of our emotional life, and that ignoble feelings may provide as rich a source of material as noble ones. Most poems pulsate with an interplay of many emotions. Here are some diagrams that show how emotion crackles and arcs from point to point in certain representative poems until almost the whole wheel of feeling has come aglow.

These diagrams may be worth a glance as indicating how emotions interact and vitalize one another, and how certain poems have characteristic vibrancies that differ from those of other poems. But our feelings are not simple. Reducing them to a single line is like trying to give some notion of a symphony by pecking out its melodies, with one finger, on the piano. Real emotions are chords of feeling.

Our remarks on emotion bring us back to where we began our discussion of poetry: back to the role of the senses and to the fact that the poet is, as García Lorca said, a "professor of the five bodily senses." It is through the image that poetry can best convey emotion—either through the image of the object that arouses it, or through the image of its physical effect. Gary Snyder in "Marin-An" (p. 16) does not tell us anything about his own feelings, but we guess what they are from what he chooses to mention. Frost describes his walk at night (p. 48) and Marianne Moore her Swedish carriage (p. 52) so that, without being told what to feel, we share the writer's emotions.

Poems may not be subject to the same emotional disorders that

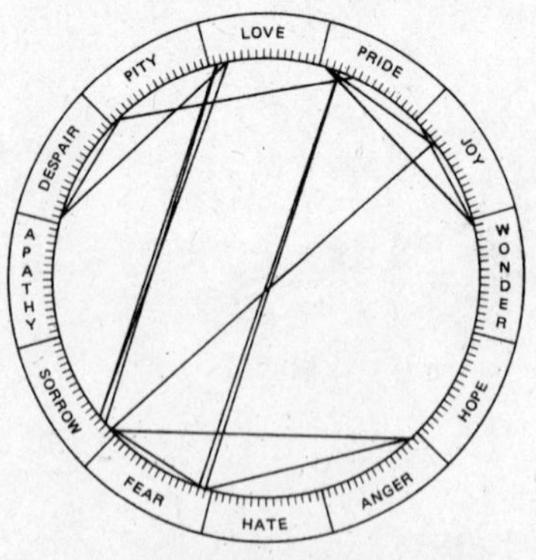

"Sir Patrick Spens"
(p. 18)

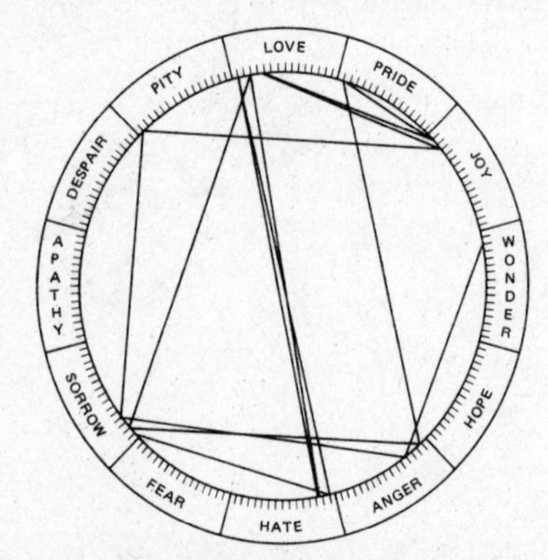

Sir Thomas Wyatt, "They Flee From Me"
(p. 58)

bring their readers to the psychoanalyst's couch, but they suffer from their own kinds of unbalance. These fall into the general classes of the "too little" and the "too much." Some poems fail to involve us because they seem to feel no passion and arouse none in us: frigid poems. Perhaps they substitute intellect or wit for passion; they may be nothing more than exercises in ingenuity. James Russell Lowell felt this in the work of Edgar Allan Poe,

> Who has written some things quite the best of their kind,
> But the heart somehow seems all squeezed out by the mind.

Some of the greatest poetry in English is to be found among the sonnets of Shakespeare. Yet a few of these leave us cold because we feel that Shakespeare wrote them coldly. "Sonnet 46" begins:

> Mine eye and heart are at a mortal war,
> How to divide the conquest of thy sight;
> Mine eye my heart thy picture's sight would bar,
> My heart mine eye the freedom of that right . . . .

He goes on to develop the argument between heart and eye as to which is most in love, but the question has little human interest. "Sonnet 113," also on the heart-eye theme, comes home to us as true and moving: when we are away from someone we love, our emotions can so affect our vision that we think we see the person everywhere.

SONNET 113

> Since I left you, mine eye is in my mind;
> And that which governs me to go about
> Doth part his function and is partly blind,
> Seems seeing, but effectually is out;
> For it no form delivers to the heart
> Of bird, of flower, or shape, which it doth latch.
> Of his quick objects hath the mind no part,

---

[3] **part:** *divide*

[6] **latch:** *grasp*

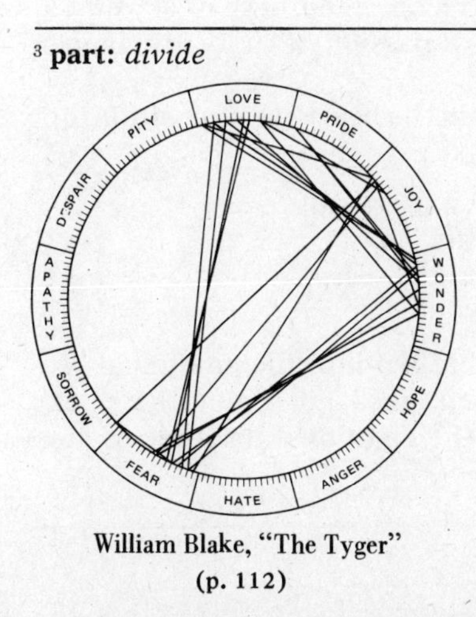

William Blake, "The Tyger"
(p. 112)

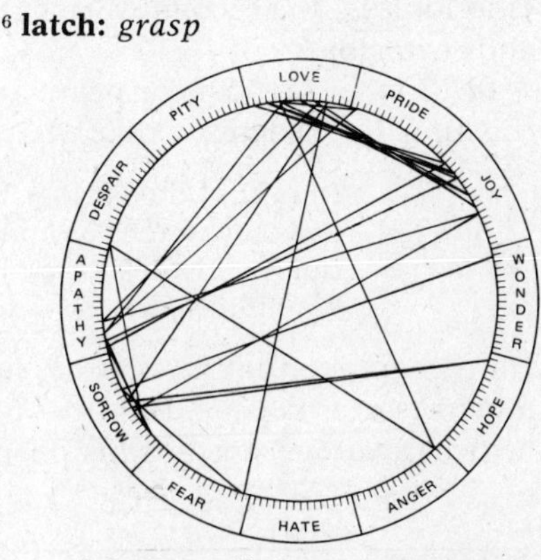

John Keats, "Ode to a Nightingale"
(p. 11)

Nor his own vision holds what it doth catch;
For if it see the rud'st or gentlest sight,
The most sweet favor or deformed'st creature, 10
The mountain, or the sea, the day, or night,
The crow, or dove, it shapes them to your feature.
Incapable of more, replete with you,
My most true mind thus maketh mine eye untrue.

William Shakespeare

A more emotional poem, still on the same theme, is "Sonnet 137." Involved in a sordid entanglement with a woman he knows is promiscuous, he wonders how his gaze can be so attracted to her that his heart is swept along with it. Though infatuated, the speaker can make use of savage sexual metaphors, as in lines 6 and 10.

SONNET 137

Thou blind fool, Love, what dost thou to mine eyes,
That they behold and see not what they see?
They know what beauty is, see where it lies,
Yet what the best is, take the worst to be.
If eyes, corrupt by overpartial looks,
Be anchored in the bay where all men ride,
Why of eyes' falsehood hast thou forgèd hooks,
Whereto the judgment of my heart is tied?
Why should my heart think that a several plot
Which my heart knows the wide world's common place? 10
Or mine eyes, seeing this, say this is not,
To put fair truth upon so foul a face?
In things right true my heart and eyes have erred,
And to this false plague are they now transferred.

William Shakespeare

The three sonnets show a gradation of feeling: the first is clever but emotionless; the second warmer; the third passionate in its love, anger, and revulsion.

In "Sonnet 141" Shakespeare again treats the heart-eye opposition, but this time he recognizes that what he feels is excessive:

In faith, I do not love thee with mine eyes,
For they in thee a thousand errors note;
But 'tis my heart that loves what they despise,
Who in despite of view is pleased to dote . . .

He recognizes, that is, that his heart has fallen into the emotional too-muchness of doting. But the poem itself does not dote; the poet's critical awareness keeps his poem from the emotional disorder of "too

---

[9] **several plot:** *private ground*

muchness," to which run-of-the-mill poetry has long been susceptible. The commonest kind of such "too muchness" is **sentimentality**—emotion in excess of its object, emotion gone out of control and taking over, as cancer cells take over in the body. Sentiment itself—opinion colored by feeling—is generally a good thing: Lincoln's Gettysburg Address expresses noble sentiments. Sentimentality is the disease to which it is subject.

That our grief for even the most worthy of objects can be excessive is the warning given in a folk ballad that probably goes back many centuries.

THE UNQUIET GRAVE

"The wind doth blow today, my love,
  And a few small drops of rain;
I never had but one truelove,
  In cold grave she was lain.

"I'll do as much for my truelove
  As any young man may;
I'll sit and mourn all at her grave
  For a twelvemonth, and a day."

The twelvemonth and a day being up,
  The dead began to speak, 10
"Oh who sits weeping on my grave,
  And will not let me sleep?"

" 'Tis I, my love, sits on your grave
  And will not let you sleep,
For I crave one kiss of your clay-cold lips
  And that is all I seek."

"You crave one kiss of my clay-cold lips,
  But my breath smells earthy strong;
If you have one kiss of my clay-cold lips
  Your time will not be long: 20

" 'Tis down in yonder garden green,
  Love, where we used to walk,
The finest flower that ere was seen
  Is withered to a stalk.

"The stalk is withered dry, my love,
  So will our hearts decay;
So make yourself content, my love,
  Till God calls you away."

Anonymous (date uncertain)

Excessive grief, which can turn into sentimental brooding, is a vexation to the dead.

Apathy and despair can be sentimental. If one enjoys wallowing in his own miseries, they become forms of self-pity. Love can be sentimental when the lover is "in love with love"—when he cares more about tending his own emotional hothouse than about the well-being of the person he loves. Or it can be sentimental when the object of his feelings—an animal, perhaps—deserves less than the fullness of human love.

Emotion is healthy when it is of the kind and in the amount that its object deserves: when what we love is really lovable, when what we fear is really fearful. It might seem better to love anything, to feel joy in anything, than to love nothing and feel no joy. But is it? In a play of Marlowe's, there is a character who sends a pot of poisoned rice pudding to a community of nuns. When they all fall sick and die, he exclaims happily, "How sweet the bells ring, now the nuns are dead!" And he goes cheerfully on to his next project, that of poisoning all the monks in a neighboring monastery. The joy and love he feels in his activity will probably seem ill-conceived to most of us.

Excessive pity, even for a worthy cause, can quite incapacitate one for a normal life: the morning papers could keep a pity-prone man in futile tears the whole day long. Aristotle thought an overabundance of emotion so harmful to the psyche that he defended Greek tragedy as a necessary release from pity and fear.

Healthy emotion is object-directed; sentimentality is subject-directed. Objectless emotion is often found among the insane, who can be seized by unmotivated fear, anger, melancholy, or conceit. A useful distinction is sometimes made between emotion and what we might (just for now) call "feeling"—as when we feel cold or hot or hungry. When we feel cold, the feeling as such has no object: *we* feel cold, and what we are conscious of is *we as feeling*. We might think of sentimentality as the tendency to treat an emotion as if it were a "feeling." The sentimentalist is less concerned with the object of his emotion than with the fact that he himself is feeling it. He is also saying, in effect: "Look how tender I am! How sensitive to beauty! How capable of deep emotions! How rich in sympathy!" Since he may feel that his unusual sensitivity is unappreciated, he may easily fall into self-pity.

To experience any emotion is exciting—we never feel so alive as when we are emotionally aroused. So we are tempted to fake our emotions, to build them up deliberately into more than they are. In order to sustain such fake passion, we have to create or falsify its object. In this respect, Sartre's view of emotion as magical behavior seems all the more true of excessive or sentimental emotion. The sentimentalist hallucinates, turns the world into a warm nest in which he can coddle his own snug feelings. He sees only so much of reality as confirms him in his enjoyment of the more tender and tearful emotions. He likes things that are cute and quaint and tiny; he can, indeed, miniaturize even the strongest and noblest objects until they become of a size to merit his pity and his tears.

Writers of sentimental poetry like to play on our stock responses—those built-in automatic reactions we have to many things we think dear and familiar: childhood; barefoot boys; home, sweet home; the old porch swing; the old oaken bucket; old rocking chairs; dust-covered toys; motherhood; the fidelity of dogs. It was no doubt the sentimentalist's doting views on children and dogs that led W. C. Fields, a lifelong crusader against sentimentality in life and art, to overreact with his famous pronouncement, somewhat rephrased: "Nobody who hates dogs and little children can be all bad."

The innocent happiness of childhood is particularly dear to the sentimentalist. He chooses not to know (at least in his rosy moods) about unhappy childhoods—like that of W. B. Yeats, who said, "Indeed I remember little of childhood but its pain." Any parent knows that children, lovable as they are, can be exasperating, simply because they are little individuals who want what they want. A parent of young children, coming home tired after a hard day at the office, is not likely to find his little ones in the pose described by William Cullen Bryant:

> And some to happy homes repair,
> Where children, pressing cheek to cheek,
> With mute caresses shall declare
> The tenderness they cannot speak.

"Papa's Letter" is the kind of sentimental falsification that shows up in anthologies of "best-loved poems." It plays shamelessly on a number of stock responses.

PAPA'S LETTER

I was sitting in my study,
  Writing letters when I heard
"Please, dear mama, Mary told me
  Mama mustn't be disturbed.

"But I's tired of the kitty;
  Want some ozzer fing to do.
Writing letters, is 'ou, mama?
  Tan't I wite a letter too?"

"Not now, darling, mama's busy;
  Run and play with kitty, now." 10
"No, no, mama, me wite letter;
  Tan, if 'ou will show me how."

I would paint my darling's portrait
  As his sweet eyes searched my face.
Hair of gold and eyes of azure,
  Form of childish, witching grace.

But the eager face was clouded,
  As I slowly shook my head,
Till I said: "I'll make a letter
  Of you, darling boy, instead." 20

So I parted back the tresses
  From his forehead high and white,
And a stamp in sport I pasted
  'Mid its waves of golden light.

Then I said, "Now, little letter,
Go away and bear good news."
And I smiled as down the staircase
Clattered loud the little shoes.

. . .

Down the street the baby hastened
Till he reached the office door. 30
"I'se a letter, Mr. Postman;
Is there room for any more?

'Cause dis' letter's doin' to papa,
Papa lives with God, 'ou know,
Mama sent me for a letter,
Do 'ou fink 'at I tan go?"

But the clerk in wonder answered,
"Not today, my little man."
"Den I'll find annozzer office,
'Cause I must go if I tan." 40

. . .

Suddenly the crowd was parted,
People fled to left, to right,
As a pair of maddened horses
At the moment dashed in sight.

No one saw the baby figure—
No one saw the golden hair,
Till a voice of frightened sweetness
Rang out on the autumn air.

'Twas too late—a moment only
Stood the beauteous vision there, 50
Then the little face lay lifeless
Covered o'er with golden hair.

Rev'rently they raised my darling,
Brushed away the curls of gold,
Saw the stamp upon the forehead
Growing now so icy cold.

Not a mark the face disfigured,
Showing where the hoof had trod;
But the little life was ended—
"Papa's letter" was with God. 60

Anonymous (nineteenth century)

There are kind and sensitive people who would read this poem with guffaws of derision—not out of sadism, but simply because they find it unbelievable. They feel they are being had, that this tear-jerker is exploiting some of our deepest emotions in a contrived and cynical way, is using us as calculatingly as advertisers try to do. (Who ever saw in a beer ad anyone surly, pugnacious, or unshaven, although such beer drinkers exist?)

For an extreme contrast, suppose we look at one of the best poems about the death of a child.

BELLS FOR JOHN WHITESIDE'S DAUGHTER

There was such speed in her little body,
And such lightness in her footfall,
It is no wonder her brown study
Astonishes us all.

Her wars were bruited in our high window.
We looked among orchard trees and beyond
Where she took arms against her shadow,
Or harried unto the pond

The lazy geese, like a snow cloud
Dripping their snow on the green grass, 10
Tricking and stopping, sleepy and proud,
Who cried in goose, Alas,

For the tireless heart within the little
Lady with rod that made them rise
From their noon apple-dreams and scuttle
Goose-fashion under the skies!

But now go the bells, and we are ready,
In one house we are sternly stopped
To say we are vexed at her brown study,
Lying so primly propped. 20

John Crowe Ransom

This is a real little girl. No doubt lovable—but still, in her vitality, a vexation to those around. No escape from that little voice! No peace for the creatures on the farm! She dies, but there is nothing melodramatic about her death—no touching deathbed scenes. Nor is her "angelic beauty" described as she lies there "primly propped." There are no professions of anguish or despair or of heavenly hope from the relatives. We know, without being told, that here is a sorrow too deep for words, and that what we are confronted with is one of the mysteries of our existence.

Here, for comparison, are two other baby poems, one sentimental and one not.

ÉTUDE RÉALISTE (I)

A baby's feet, like sea-shells pink,
  Might tempt, should heaven see meet,
An angel's lips to kiss, we think,
  A baby's feet.

---

[3] **brown study:** *deep absorption, day dreaming* [5] **bruited:** *sounded*

Like rose-hued sea-flowers toward the heat
  They stretch and spread and wink
Their ten soft buds that part and meet.

No flower-bells that expand and shrink
  Gleam half so heavenly sweet
As shine on life's untrodden brink   10
  A baby's feet.

Algernon Charles Swinburne (1837–1909)

A SONG FOR THE MIDDLE OF THE NIGHT

By way of explaining to my son the following curse by Eustace Deschamps: "Happy is he who has no children; for babies bring nothing but crying and stench."

Now first of all he means the night
  You beat the crib and cried
And brought me spinning out of bed
  To powder your backside.
I rolled your buttocks over
  And I could not complain:
Legs up, la la, legs down, la, la,
  Back to sleep again.

Now second of all he means the day
  You dabbled out of doors   10
And dragged a dead cat Billy-be-damned
  Across the kitchen floors.
I rolled your buttocks over
  And made you sing for pain:
Legs up, la la, legs down, la, la,
  Back to sleep again.

But third of all my father once
  Laid me across his knee
And solved the trouble when he beat
  The yowling out of me.   20
He rocked me on his shoulder
  When razor straps were vain:
Legs up, la la, legs down, la la,
  Back to sleep again.

So roll upon your belly, boy,
  And bother being cursed.
You turn the household upside down,
  But you are not the first.
Deschamps the poet blubbered too,
  For all his fool disdain: 30
Legs up, la la, legs down, la la,
  Back to sleep again.

James Wright (b. 1927)

The sentimental poet has such devotion to the saintly mother at whose knee he learned to prattle that he professes to see her virtues in all old ladies.

OLD LADIES

In every old lady I chance to meet
  Whoever, wherever she be,
From her snow-crowned head to her patient feet
  My own brave mother I see.

In every old lady whose patient eyes
  Are deeps of a fathomless sea,
So patient and tender and kind and wise
  My mother looks out at me.

In every old lady in silent prayer
  To God on her bended knee, 10
I vision my own mother kneeling there
  Praying a prayer for me.

In every old lady I bend above,
  Asleep in death's mystery,
I whisper, "Please carry my lone heart's love
  To my angel mother for me."

In every old lady I meet each day,
  The humble, or lofty and fine,
I see an angel stand, guarding the way,
  Somebody's mother and mine. 20

Will Allen Dromgoole (1860–1934)

It may be sweet of the poet to feel that way. But she must also be somewhat nearsighted or undiscriminating. We all know marvelous old ladies—brave, witty, beautiful. But are we really honoring their exceptional qualities by asserting that *all* old ladies are equally wonderful? Lady Macbeth, had she lived, might not have turned out so well. Nor did the mother in the old ballad "Edward, Edward," who, after apparently goading her son into murder, was told by him that she deserved "the curse of hell." But we need not turn to literature—we can easily find old ladies—at the races, on barstools—we might hesitate to compare our mothers to. John Crowe Ransom—again—gives us a frankly unsentimental view.

BLUE GIRLS

Twirling your blue skirts, travelling the sward
Under the towers of your seminary,
Go listen to your teachers old and contrary
Without believing a word.

Tie the white fillets then about your hair
And think no more of what will come to pass

Than bluebirds that go walking on the grass
And chattering on the air.

Practise your beauty, blue girls, before it fail;
And I will cry with my loud lips and publish 10
Beauty which all our power shall never establish,
It is so frail.

For I could tell you a story which is true;
I know a lady with a terrible tongue,
Blear eyes fallen from blue,
All her perfections tarnished—yet it is not long
Since she was lovelier than any of you.

John Crowe Ransom

What comes through in this poem of mixed emotions, this "story which is true," is more than dislike of the "terrible tongue" and the faded eyes. The poet remembers, with something like admiration and love, a lady once lovelier than any of the beautiful and careless young girls before him.

The sentimentalist tends to overvalue the companionship of an animal, since its response to him is less critical than that of a human being and, therefore, more flattering. He can feel its moist, unfocused eyes adoring him. All the better if the animal has a sad fate, which, by encouraging his own pity and self-pity, permits him to drop a gentle tear. We think of the "trembling maid, of her own gentle voice afraid" in Thomas Moore's "Lalla Rookh":

Oh! ever thus from childhood's hour,
I've seen my fondest hopes decay;
I never loved a tree or flower,
But 'twas the first to fade away.
I never nursed a dear gazelle,
To glad me with its soft black eye,
But when it came to know me well,
And love me, it was sure to die!

Such sentimentality arouses not only disbelief but derision in sensible readers. Few lines in English have been more honored with parody, which taunts our self-pitying little gazelle-nurser with such lines as those of James Payn:

I've never had a piece of toast
Particularly long and wide,
But fell upon the sanded floor,
And always on the buttered side.

Even cat lovers may feel that Rod McKuen goes overboard in his love for his cat Sloopy. For years, the poet tells us, it had been Rod and Sloopy "against the world." Then one day Rod did not come home. A day later he came running through the snow, "screaming *Sloopy Sloopy*," only to find her gone!

I was a madman
to have stayed away
  one minute more
than the appointed hour.

Sloopy, he reflects, is now a bitter cat, and

I'm bitter too
and not a free man any more . . . .

Looking back
perhaps she's been
the only human thing
that ever gave back love to me.

For contrast, here is May Swenson seeing a snowfall through the eyes of a cat.

CAT & THE WEATHER

Cat takes a look at the weather:
snow;
puts a paw on the sill;
his perch is piled, is a pillow.

Shape of his pad appears:
will it dig? No,
not like sand,
like his fur almost.

But licked, not liked:
too cold. 10
Insects are flying, fainting down.
He'll try

to bat one against the pane.
They have no body and no buzz,
and now his feet are wet;
it's a puzzle.

Shakes each leg,
then shakes his skin
to get the white flies off;
looks for his tail, 20

tells it to come on in
by the radiator.
World's turned queer
somehow: all white,

no smell. Well, here
inside it's still familiar.
He'll go to sleep until
it puts itself right.

May Swenson

Leonardo da Vinci, "*Studies of Cats*"

Emotions are to be evaluated with reference to their object. It is precisely such an evaluation that William Stafford is concerned to make in his poem about an unborn fawn: should one risk human lives in a probably vain effort to save the fawn?

TRAVELING THROUGH THE DARK

Traveling through the dark I found a deer
dead on the edge of the Wilson River road.
It is usually best to roll them into the canyon:
that road is narrow; to swerve might make more dead.

By glow of the tail-light I stumbled back of the car
and stood by the heap, a doe, a recent killing;
she had stiffened already, almost cold.
I dragged her off; she was large in the belly.

My fingers touching her side brought me the reason—
her side was warm; her fawn lay there waiting, 10
alive, still, never to be born.
Beside that mountain road I hesitated.

The car aimed ahead its lowered parking lights;
under the hood purred the steady engine.
I stood in the glare of the warm exhaust turning red;
around our group I could hear the wilderness listen.

I thought hard for us all—my only swerving—,
then pushed her over the edge into the river.

William Stafford (b. 1914)

Flowers, like other pretty things in nature, lend themselves to sentimental treatment. A page from *How to Know the Wild Flowers* (1900) shows three ways of describing the corpse plant. Miss Higginson's sonnet associates the flower with objects she thinks poetic—religion and virginity, for example. The writer of the prose paragraph is more realistic. He points out that the flower has a tendency "to decompose and turn black when handled."

INDIAN-PIPE. CORPSE-PLANT. GHOST-FLOWER.

Monotropa uniflora. Heath Family.

A low fleshy herb from three to eight inches high; without green foliage; of a wax-like appearance; with colorless bracts in the place of leaves. *Flower.*—White or pinkish; single; terminal; nodding. *Calyx*—Of two to four bract-like scales. *Corolla.*—Of four or five wedge-shaped petals. *Stamens.*—Eight or ten; with yellow anthers. *Pistil.*—One, with a disk-like, four or five-rayed stigma.

"In shining groups, each stem a pearly ray,
Weird flecks of light within the shadowed wood,
They dwell aloof, a spotless sisterhood.

No Angelus, except the wild bird's lay,
Awakes these forest nuns; yet, night and day,
Their heads are bent, as if in prayerful mood.
A touch will mar their snow, and tempests rude
Defile; but in the mist fresh blossoms stray
From spirit-gardens, just beyond our ken.
Each year we seek their virgin haunts, to look 10
Upon new loveliness, and watch again
Their shy devotions near the singing brook;
Then, mingling in the dizzy stir of men,
Forget the vows made in that cloistered nook."*

The effect of a cluster of these nodding, wax-like flowers in the deep woods of summer is singularly fairy-like. They spring from a ball of matted rootlets, and are parasitic, drawing their nourishment from decaying vegetable matter. In fruit the plant erects itself and loses its striking resemblance to a pipe. Its clammy touch, and its disposition to decompose and turn black when handled, has earned it the name of corpse-plant. It was used by the Indians as an eye-lotion, and is still believed by some to possess healing properties.

** Mary Thacher Higginson (nineteenth century)*

One protection against sentimentality is a sense of humor—which means a sense of proportion. Although Theodore Roethke's attitude toward his geranium is less pious than Miss Higginson's toward the corpse plant, he seems to have more concern and affection for his plant than she has for hers.

THE GERANIUM

When I put her out, once, by the garbage pail,
She looked so limp and bedraggled,
So foolish and trusting, like a sick poodle,
Or a wizened aster in late September,
I brought her back in again
For a new routine
Vitamins, water, and whatever
Sustenance seemed sensible
At the time: she'd lived
So long on gin, bobbie pins, half-smoked cigars, dead beer, 10
Her shriveled petals falling
On the faded carpet, the stale
Steak grease stuck to her fuzzy leaves.
(Dried-out, she creaked like a tulip.)

The things she endured!—
The dumb dames shrieking half the night
Or the two of us, alone, both seedy,
Me breathing booze at her,
She leaning out of her pot toward the window.

Near the end, she seemed almost to hear me— 20

And that was scary—
So when that snuffling cretin of a maid
Threw her, pot and all, into the trash-can,
I said nothing.

But I sacked the presumptuous hag the next week,
I was that lonely.

Theodore Roethke (1908–1963)

Sentimental poetry demands that we feel without thinking. If one is handsome and attractive, aglow with youth, does it matter if he commits a few crimes here and there—or even as many as one can commit in a "thousand nights"? Not to Laurence Hope, who has not only a confused sense of justice but a naïve idea of how juries behave.

YOUTH

I am not sure if I knew the truth
  What his case or crime might be,
I only know that he pleaded Youth,
  A beautiful, golden plea!

Youth, with its sunlit, passionate eyes,
  Its roseate velvet skin—
A plea to cancel a thousand lies,
  Or a thousand nights of sin.

The men who judged him were old and grey,
  Their eyes and their senses dim, 10
He brought the light of a warm Spring day
  To the Court-house bare and grim.

Could he plead guilty in a lovelier way?
His judges acquitted him.

Laurence Hope (1865–1904)

Robert W. Service goes a step further in "The Outlaw." One may commit hideous crimes one's whole life long, even murdering infants, but if, as this excerpt points out, he gets a humble dog to lick his feet he will be on the road to salvation.

The golden trumpets blew a blast
That echoed in the crypts of Hell,
For there was Judgment to be passed,
And lips were hushed and silence fell.
The man was mute; he made no stir,
Erect before the Judgment Seat . . .
When all at once a mongrel cur
Crept out and cowered and licked his feet.

It licked his feet with whining cry.
Come Heav'n, come Hell, what did it care? 10

It leapt, it tried to catch his eye;
Its master, yea, its God was there.
Then, as a thrill of wonder sped
Through throngs of shining seraphim,
The Judge of All looked down and said:
"Lo! here is ONE who pleads for him . . . .

Exercises and Diversions

A. The philosopher Jean Paul Sartre sees emotion as the process by which we escape, when frustrated by reality, into a make-believe world. For example, a man who gets the worst of it in an argument escapes from the world of logic (where he cannot win) to the world of fury (where he can win). His face reddens, his muscles swell, he jumps to his feet with a threatening "Oh yeah? Maybe you'd like a punch in the nose!" Or a rejected man sulks in a corner, his eyes dull so he cannot see the real world, his muscles lax so he cannot cope with it. He escapes into a despair that says the world is not worthwhile anyway. For Sartre, emotion is symbolic activity, magical behavior—a way of transforming what we cannot deal with.

1. Can you find poems in this chapter in which someone uses emotion as an escape from a reality he cannot face?
2. Can you recall poems in earlier chapters in which emotion was used in this way?
3. As opposed to Sartre, the physician-writer Gustav Eckstein holds, in *The Body Has a Head*, that "without emotion there is nothing that could be called mind. Clarification of thought depends on it." What poems have we read in which emotion seems to stimulate thought rather than distort it?
4. Do you feel that although Sartre's theory may not fit all emotions, it does fit sentimental ones, which are a kind of magical behavior aimed at transforming reality? Cite examples.

B. Sentimentality, which gives free access to unearned emotions, is at home in the popular arts—the movies, TV, best-selling fiction, advertising—which show us not the world as it is but the world as magically transformed to what we would like it to be.

YES, THE AGENCY CAN HANDLE THAT

You recommend that the motive, in Chapter 8, should be changed from ambition to
a desire, on the heroine's part, for doing good; yes, that can be done.
Installment 9 could be more optimistic, as you point out, and it will not be hard to
add a heartbreak to the class reunion in Chapter 10.
Script 11 may have, as you say, too much political intrigue of the sordid type;
perhaps a diamond-in-the-rough approach would take care of this. And 12 has a
reference to war that, as you suggest, had better be removed; yes.
This brings us to the holidays, that coincide with our prison sequence. With the
convicts' Christmas supper, if you approve, we can go to town.

Yes, this should not be difficult. It can be done. Why not? 10

And script 600 brings us to the millennium, with all the fiends of hell singing Bach
chorales.

And in 601 we explore the Valleys of the Moon (why not?), finding in each of them
fresh Fountains of Youth.

And there is no mortal ill that cannot be cured by a little money, or lots of love, or
by a friendly smile; no.
And few human hopes go unrealized; no.
And the rain does not ever, anywhere, fall upon corroded monuments and the
graves of the forgotten dead.

Kenneth Fearing

1. The "agency" is preparing a series of programs for mass presentation. Is it true that the revisions they are willing to make are all in the direction of sentimental treatment of the material?
2. Do you think the poem has the same speaker—an agency executive—throughout? Or does the poet himself begin to cut in with his own voice? If so, where?
3. What is the basis of the irony we get toward the close? Why does the irony become stronger as it becomes more concrete?
4. Is the poem essentially an attack on sentimental taste? On what grounds does the poet seem to think of sentimentality as a kind of falsehood?
5. "Yes, this should not be difficult" (l. 14). Is it true that the sentimental treatment of a theme is easier than the emotionally honest treatment?
6. Write a poem or a paragraph about "the convicts' Christmas supper," the kind of writing that would "go to town" as an agency-pleaser.

C. The typical Japanese haiku gives "simple descriptions of actual scenes and events" that suggest emotions. (It can be difficult for non-Japanese readers, for whom the objects mentioned may have non-Japanese connotations.) What emotions do these four haiku suggest to you?

So the spring has come?
There's a nameless little hill
In the morning mist. *Bashō (1644–1694)*

Sandy shore: and why
Do they make a fire beneath
The midsummer moon? *Shiki (1867–1902)*

On a withered branch
Look where a crow settles down.
Autumn nightfall too. *Bashō*

Neither earth nor sky;
Nothing left, only the snow
Falling fast oh fast.
Hashin (nineteenth century)

D. What objects do you think you yourself tend to be sentimental about? Let yourself write a frankly sentimental poem or prose paragraph about such an object.
Now rewrite it so that, while still heartfelt, it has no traces of sentimentality.

III the words

9

Machine for Magic the fresh usual words

Up to now we have been considering how the senses give us—and the poet—the images that are a picture of our world, and how these images affect us with desire or aversion or any of the other emotions.

When we have given examples, however, we have had to anticipate still another element of poetry: the *words* through which the image and emotion are expressed.

In the mind of the poet and his reader, image, emotion, and word all interact together. And they interact with other elements we have not yet come to, such as sound and rhythm and the shape of sentences. Neither the poem nor the poet's mind is compartmentalized as neatly as a table of contents would seem to indicate. But in trying to arrive at an understanding of any complicated object, the best we can do is take it part by part. In medical school, for example, the student listens to lectures on various parts of the body as if they were separate, though he is well aware that separately they cannot live. Nor is he likely to object to his professors because they divide and classify.

The fact that we are moving on now to the role of words in poetry does not mean that we can put imagery and emotion behind us, as if we had "finished" them. What we have said about the two ought to be kept in mind and retested as we contemplate what is almost the only way we have of sharing them: the spoken word.

Poetry consists not so much in saying memorable things as in saying things memorably. The interplay of image and emotion is not yet poetry; without the word it would remain forever silent, unshared, locked in the core of the individual. The poet's job is to make out of words a machine that will transmit what is in his mind to the mind of others—a machine so finely built that those others will admire it at least as much for its own beauty as for the message it transmits.

To some, "machine" may seem too unpoetic a metaphor. And yet it was the poet William Carlos Williams who called a poem "a small (or large) machine made out of words." He was echoing what the poet Paul Valéry had already said more than once: "A poem is really a kind of machine for producing the poetic state of mind by means of words."

When poets are constructing one of their magic-machines, they are not so much *saying* something as *making* something out of words, just as a sculptor is making something out of stone, a painter something out of shapes and colors, a composer something out of sounds.

Much of our nonpoetic speech aims at communicating information. We say, "Jacksonville is five miles away," or "The room will cost ten dollars a night." It does not matter what words we use provided the message is clear; we may forget the exact words once they have served their purpose. But the poet cares *how* he says what he says. He cares about the sound and length of words, their suggestions, their rhythm when put together. He wants to say something not only right for the occasion, but something that will keep forever. He is getting back, in short, to language as a kind of magic. In childhood, words have magic power. "For the child," says Piaget, "the name is still closely bound up with the thing." Primitive people share the child's feeling—words are so much what they mean that some men have a secret name they tell no one, believing that if an enemy learned it he would have power over them. Eskimos believe that a man consists of three parts: his body, his soul, and his name.

The poem "Moon, Sun, Sleep, Birds, Live" of Kenneth Patchen (*1911–1972*), on the opposite page, is like a working model of a poem, cut away to give us a vivid glimpse of the moving parts.

It might be hard to state the "meaning" of this page of poetry, in which the words of the title, dramatized by typography, stand out in a field of seven little poems. Around this composition is a frame of about a hundred words, some related by association of ideas. The page, capable of being read in many ways, seems a meditation on existence and language, on words as expressing the basic realities of our lives. It is also a lesson in the language of poetry. The vocabulary it uses is taken from the best words available to the poet—what Joseph Conrad called the "fresh usual words" and André Breton "les mots sans rides," the unwrinkled words. All have endured, as alive today as in Shakespeare's time. They are still the words we use for many of our deepest experiences. A large number come to us as sense impressions: "rain," "wind," "light," "cold," etc. Some directly express emotions; many more name objects that have long been charged with emotion: "flame," "knife," "garden," "morning," etc. All are rich in **connotation,** the suggestions that words accumulate in addition to their **denotation,** or dictionary meaning.

The vitality of Patchen's vocabulary is clear if we contrast his page with a page of words that are dead or close to dying, words we would not be likely to use if we had anything urgent or passionate to say.

rain wind light cold cold dark late stem gate bar flame knife garden blue

noise morning son loud art alive net tiger storm lily job tear maker shove

mirror
coast
deer
frog
tunnel
grave
noose
supper
beauty
fear
heights
garden
taste
climb
will
look
wing
valley
rule
name
knock
angel
shadow
terror
quest

Moon

SUN

I am the music you make

the blue wings of the ocean

the crying of the black swan

SLEEP

I am the friend

of your childhood

Birds

It is in my heart to wish you

no sorrow

no pain

no betrayal

for I am the will of your last being

the shudder of the breaking open

of terrible gates

O thou art good

and wise

and kindling

a new fire

I am the cave and the light

the watch God keeps

when His children go mad

LIVE

I am the death you seek

the life you are afraid

to know

behold this eye of blood!

work
star
good
soul
book
lift
world
body
stone
town
weave
center
break
afraid
skill
thing
laugh
grow
three
keep
force
other
charm
soar
fence

power rise tree knowledge innocence fall hand thorn get father chain spool

law peace turtle grass snow prayer life black deep first tie hit see eye

One cannot insist that a poet will never use any of these; sometimes he has his reasons for trying to revive a dead word, or even for laying it forth in state. But a poem with a high percentage of such verbiage has little chance of coming to life. The deadest words are the merely "poetic" ones, words once alive but now embalmed long since. Some readers, seeing them only in poetry of the past and thinking of them as uncontaminated by daily handling, may believe them especially worthy of the poet's attention. But devotion to such words or phrases as those below is a kind of necrophilia.

"Poetic Diction and Cliché"

opalescent proffered beauteous waning haunting witchery
ethereal lightsome behest wrought sought supernal sunder
sever besmirch benison ope sup smite darkling thrice
rhapsodic wend illume boon waft tranced pageantry array
mart lave rive clime crystal pattern filigree silhouette
arabesque furled mute enmeshed cacophony sere symmetry
linger frail etched mystic morsel abode aureole endowed
design rhythm (of life, etc.) chaste (moonlight, etc.)
symphony (of life, of the city, etc.) tracery (of branches, etc.) happy haunts
endearing grace eyes' tender light fierce beauty sadly yearn
one brief space teeming life life's evening sunset glow silvery laugh
unison divine first faint blush of dawn swaying in the breeze
wee fleeting touch radiant smile willing hands heavy laden
wondrous tales beauty's elixir light and gay friends of yesteryear
long-cherished dreams piny grove 'neath the starlit canopy
the kiss of the breeze kindly deeds broken dreams peacefully sleeping
mute orchestras of spring murmured hymn cannot fathom
thousands cheered memories of lost days cadenced words of pure delight
snow-capped peaks dew-kissed flowers allotted span golden deeds
star-jeweled sky earth's pageantries rippling stream bitter tears
mystic mingling numbered days softly pervades seething humanity
rhapsodic balm would that I could falls in benediction the young wind
harborward sighing winds timeless flight the thrill of nature's lyre
ancient days loved familiar things the verdant earth in glad array
dream-fraught musings amorous troubadours the days of wine and roses
haunting mood brooding quietude solemn majesty muted rage
soul aglow naked trees mountains towering high quick suspicion
feathered songsters choiring in the blue untethered sails

A number of these expressions have become **clichés.** A "cliché" was originally a printing term for a single piece of type with words so often used together that it was handy to have them in one piece. Clichés have caught on because when first used they were apt and striking: "sadder but wiser," "tired but happy," "strong as an ox." The first man to compare the cheeks of a girl to a rose, said Dali, was obviously a poet; the first to repeat it was possibly an idiot.

Most revolutions in poetry aim at getting back to a more natural language. "The *norm* for a poet's language," said T. S. Eliot, "is the way his contemporaries talk." Pound has insisted on this norm again and again. "Good god! isn't there one of them that can write natural speech without copying clichés . . . ?"

The greatness of Robert Frost lies partly in that he was one of the few who brought poetry back to natural speech. One early poem, however, has about every fault that "poetic diction" can have, and is sentimental as well. Yet it has a couple of lines—one line in particular—that the young Frost recognized as prophetically good. The first third of the poem, "My Butterfly," reads:

> Thine emulous fond flowers are dead, too,
> And the daft sun-assaulter, he
> That frighted thee so oft, is fled or dead:
> Save only me
> (Nor is it sad to thee!)—
> Save only me
> There is none left to mourn thee in the fields.
>
> The gray grass is scarce dappled with the snow;
> Its two banks have not shut upon the river;
> But it is long ago— 10
> It seems forever—
> Since first I saw thee glance,
> With all thy dazzling other ones,
> In airy dalliance,
> Precipitate in love,
> Tossed, tangled, whirled and whirled above,
> Like a limp rose-wreath in a fairy dance . . . .

Amid much faded literary diction, the good line stands out in all its plainness:

> Its two banks have not shut upon the river.

The metaphor—ice like closing doors—is only implied. The plainest words are used—"shut," for example, instead of the more genteel "closed." A young person who liked his poetry "poetic" about 1890 might have written:

> King Winter hath not clanged
> His crystal portals o'er the finny chamber.

And typical readers might have thought, "How poetic!" But Frost knew better.

Once, when he went outside after a difficult or boring day, he felt a little tingle of pleasure at the way a crow powdered him with falling snow as it stirred. He wrote:

DUST OF SNOW

The way a crow
Shook down on me
The dust of snow
From a hemlock tree

Has given my heart
A change of mood
And saved some part
Of a day I had rued.

Robert Frost

This is no more than a small poem about a small experience, like those so dear to writers of haiku. Although every word is fitted into a rhythm and about one out of four has a rhyming sound, all fall easily into their natural place. The feeling, communicated more through the little dance of rhythm and rhyme than through what is said, would have gone flat if Frost had merely annotated the experience:

The way that a crow
shook down right on me
some snow, rather like dust,
from a high hemlock bough
has given my heart
a different feeling about things,
and partly saved
a day I felt had been wasted.

For some, this constitutes "writing a poem"—just putting it down any old way. Frost made his statement memorable by giving it breath and lilt. A less direct poet might have felt such plain language was inadequate for such an experience; he might have inflated it with preachments and poetic diction:

PULVEROUS SILVER ESSENCE!

How dear the ways of Nature! Lo, yon crow
Precipitated earthward, even on me,
A pulverous silver essence, dust of snow,
White benefactions of a hemlock tree;

Bequeathing (legacy unto my heart!)
Transfigurations of an erstwhile mood,
Redeeming a jeweled modicum, wee part
Of one diurnal unit I had rued.

Many readers would consider our dressed-up version more poetic than Frost's unassuming sentence. Other readers, more cerebral, might prefer it this way:

WITTGENSTEIN AND THE CROW

Event
as instanced in
"the progress of phenomena":
Item: the avian
disbursal of elate frigidities
from a species Old Pop Longfellow saluted
as second in his paradigm of murmurers.
Which same
affords me *möglichkeit*
of shifting psyche-gears:
thereby reclaiming data stamped KAPUT. 10

It seems unlikely that either version would fix itself in the memory quite as successfully as Frost's original.

Some of the best poems are made up of very simple words:

all, along, any, ashore, back, bar, cannot, comes, day, deep, ever, far, glass, ground, gull, hull, keep, land, like, long, look, more, one, pass, people, raising, reflects, sand, sea, ship, standing, takes, truth, turn, vary, water, watch, way, wetter, when, wherever.

Not a rare word here, not a "poetic" one. And yet out of these words, plus a couple of *the*'s and *a*'s, Frost made a poem (about "the response of mankind to the empty immensity of the universe") that Lionel Trilling said he often thinks "the most perfect poem of our time."

NEITHER OUT FAR NOR IN DEEP

The people along the sand
All turn and look one way.
They turn their back on the land.
They look at the sea all day.

As long as it takes to pass
A ship keeps raising its hull;
The wetter ground like glass
Reflects a standing gull.

The land may vary more;
But wherever the truth may be— 10
The water comes ashore,
And the people look at the sea.

They cannot look out far.
They cannot look in deep.
But when was that ever a bar
To any watch they keep?

Robert Frost

Emily Dickinson is another who can get eye-opening effects, make us do the double take that fixes our attention, by putting ordinary words in new contexts. What could one make of a list of words like this?—

acre, alone, attended, barefoot, boggy, bone, boy, breathing, closes, comb, cool, cordiality, corn, divides, feel, feet, fellow, floor, further, gone, grass, know, likes, may, met, more, narrow, nature, never, noon, notice, occasionally, once, opens, passed, people, rides, secure, seen, several, shaft, spotted, stooping, sudden, sun, then, thought, tighter, too, transport, unbraiding, when, whiplash, with, without, wrinkled, zero

One could make—if he were Emily Dickinson—one of the best poems ever written about one of God's creatures.

A NARROW FELLOW IN THE GRASS

A narrow Fellow in the Grass
Occasionally rides—
You may have met Him—did you not
His notice sudden is—

The Grass divides as with a Comb—
A spotted shaft is seen—
And then it closes at your feet
And opens further on—

He likes a Boggy Acre
A Floor too cool for Corn— 10
Yet when a Boy, and Barefoot—
I more than once at Noon
Have passed, I thought, a Whip lash
Unbraiding in the Sun
When stooping to secure it
It wrinkled, and was gone—

Several of Nature's People
I know, and they know me—
I feel for them a transport
Of cordiality— 20

But never met this Fellow
Attended, or alone
Without a tighter breathing
And Zero at the Bone—

Emily Dickinson

A more conventional poet might have shuddered, at the close, with

I gasp, and icy chills go
Up and down my spine!

But look at Emily Dickinson's last two lines!

Many of the words in the two lists above have one syllable. English, unlike Spanish or Italian, uses monosyllables for many of the basic realities: day, night, birth, death, boy, girl, love, hate, youth, age, etc. Concentrations of monosyllables can give powerful lines, as in Shakespeare's "There would have been a time for such a word." They can be forceful too played off against the longer Latinate words that English is rich in:

> Will all great Neptune's ocean wash this blood
> Clean from my hand? No, this my hand will rather
> The multitudinous seas incarnadine,
> Making the green, one red.

There are exceptions—here as elsewhere—to almost everything we are saying. The bigger, rarer word may be the effective one:

> Sometimes these *cogitations* still amaze
> The troubled midnight and the noon's repose.
>
> *T. S. Eliot*

> Some brat has chalked the word "screw"
> at the edge of my drive, and doodled
> around it *unequivocal hieroglyphics.*
>
> *Keith Waldrop*

Eliot uses "cogitations" with a kind of self-mockery: his speaker is not only a thinker, he is that more deliberate thing, a cogitator, and therefore all the more amazed to confront emotional realities. "Unequivocal hieroglyphics" is telling because of the very discrepancy between the level of the language and the crude reality it refers to.

We accept an occasional rare word from a writer who, through the overall naturalness of his diction, has won our confidence. Such a writer, we concede, is using the language so expertly that he must know what he is doing in taking liberties with it.

MOON LANDING

It's natural the Boys should whoop it up for
so huge a phallic triumph, an adventure
  it would not have occurred to women
  to think worth while, made possible only

because we like huddling in gangs and knowing
the exact time: yes, our sex may in fairness
  hurrah the deed, although the motives
  that primed it were somewhat less than *menschlich.*

A grand gesture. But what does it period?
What does it osse? We were always adroiter 10
  with objects than lives, and more facile
  at courage than kindness: from the moment

the first flint was flaked, this landing was merely
a matter of time. But our selves, like Adam's,

---

[8] **menschlich:** *human, humane (German)*

[9] **period:** *conclude (obsolete)*

[10] **osse:** *signify, portend (obsolete)*

still don't fit us exactly, modern
only in this—our lack of decorum.

Homer's heroes were certainly no braver
than our Trio, but more fortunate: Hector
was excused the insult of having
his valor covered by television. 20

Worth *going* to see? I can well believe it.
Worth *seeing?* Mneh! I once rode through a desert
and was not charmed: give me a watered
lively garden, remote from blatherers

about the New, the von Brauns and their ilk, where
on August mornings I can count the morning
glories, where to die has a meaning,
and no engine can shift my perspective.

Unsmudged, thank God, my Moon still queens the Heavens
as She ebbs and fulls, a Presence to glop at, 30
Her Old Man, made of grit not protein,
still visits my Austrian several

with His old detachment, and the old warnings
still have power to scare me: Hybris comes to
an ugly finish, Irreverence
is a greater oaf than Superstition.

Our apparatniks will continue making
the usual squalid mess called History:
all we can pray for is that artists,
chefs and saints may still appear to blithe it. 40

W. H. Auden

Enough of Auden's diction is colloquial, even slangy, for us to know that he is not addicted to pomposity. If he likes to indulge a hobby by dredging up an occasional rare specimen from the *Oxford English Dictionary*, he seems to have earned the privilege.

If we believe in the speech, we believe in the speaker. In "Plus Ça Change . . . ," Philip Whalen is dealing with a fantastic situation; yet the speech could not be more realistic. The dialogue seems to be a half-angry domestic spat. The male speaks first; the female, whose speeches are indented, replies.

21–22 **Worth** *going* **. . . Worth** *seeing?*: *Boswell once asked Johnson: "Is not the Giant's-Causeway worth seeing?" Johnson: "Worth seeing? yes; but not worth going to see."*
30 **glop:** *stare (obsolete)*
32 **several:** *private property*
34 **Hybris:** *arrogance, presumption (Greek)*
37 **apparatniks:** *gadgeteers*
40 **blithe:** *gladden, delight (obsolete as a verb)*

"PLUS ÇA CHANGE . . ."

What are you doing?

I am coldly calculating.

I didn't ask for a characterization.
Tell me what we're going to do.

That's what I'm coldly calculating.

You had better say "plotting" or "scheming"
You never could calculate without a machine.

Then I'm brooding. Presently
A plot will hatch.

Who are you trying to kid? 10

Be nice.

(SILENCE)

Listen. Whatever we do from here on out
Let's for God's sake not look at each other
Keep our eyes shut and the lights turned off—
We won't mind touching if we don't have to see.

I'll ignore those preposterous feathers.

Say what you please, we brought it all on ourselves
But nobody's going out of his way to look.

Who'd recognize us now? 20

We'll just pretend we're used to it.
(Watch out with that goddamned tail!)
Pull the shades down. Turn off the lights.
Shut your eyes.

(SILENCE)

There is no satisfactory explanation.
You can talk until you're blue

Just how much bluer can I get?

Well, save breath you need to cool

Will you please shove the cuttlebone a little closer? 30

All right, until the perfumes of Arabia

Grow cold. Ah! Sunflower seeds!

Will you listen, please? I'm trying to make
A rational suggestion. Do you mind?

Certainly not. Just what *shall* we tell the children?

Philip Whalen (b. 1923)

About halfway through the poem, we discover that both speakers ("There is no satisfactory explanation") have been turned into birds, blue in color—possibly lovebirds? Both are rather literary; they make the kind of bookish allusions that modern poets have learned from Pound and Eliot.

The title of Whalen's poem is from the nineteenth-century French journalist Alphonse Karr: "Plus ça change, plus c'est la même chose" ("The more things change, the more they remain the same"). Here it seems to be telling something about the human condition, now changed to the bird condition. In world literature, a great many lovers have wished they were birds, as Yeats does in his early "The White Birds":

> I would that we were, my beloved, white birds on the
> foam of the sea!

A commonsense explanation of Whalen's uncommon-sense poem might be that the poet is debunking this romantic cliché. The lovers, if turned into birds, would not only find themselves involved in the same old bickering, but would have new problems as well.

When the bird-woman says, in her first remark, that she is trying to figure out the situation, the bird-man deliberately misunderstands her. In her next remark, there are puns on "brooding" and "hatch," which the bird-man picks up with his "trying to *kid*." "Save breath" is the proverbial "Save your breath to cool your broth." This reminds the bird-woman of food—of bird food, naturally. The following exchange garbles two quotations. Lady Macbeth, during her sleepwalking scene, says, "All the perfumes of Arabia will not sweeten this little hand." Bayard Taylor's "Bedouin Song" has an Arabian lover professing fidelity

> *Till the sun grows cold,*
> *And the stars are old . . . .*

With "Ah! Sunflower seeds!" the female notices more bird food; she continues the allusion game by remembering Blake's "Ah Sun-flower! weary of time . . . ." (p. 282).

Whalen's poem is having fun with language—something which poems have been doing for many centuries. Here are some older verses that have long had a strange fascination.

THERE WAS A MAN OF DOUBLE DEED

There was a man of double deed
Sowed his garden full of seed.
When the seed began to grow,
'Twas like a garden full of snow;
When the snow began to melt,
'Twas like a ship without a belt;
When the ship began to sail,
'Twas like a bird without a tail;

---

[6] **belt:** *band of metal plates*

When the bird began to fly,
'Twas like an eagle in the sky; 10
When the sky began to roar,
'Twas like a lion at the door;
When the door began to crack,
'Twas like a stick across my back;
When my back began to smart,
'Twas like a penknife in my heart;
When my heart began to bleed,
'Twas death and death and death indeed.

Anonymous (date unknown)

Robert Frost, W. H. Auden, Philip Whalen, and the writer of the anonymous rhyme are not much alike as poets. And yet, in the poems we have seen, they have one thing in common: they use the structure and cadence of English speech so that we feel that what we are hearing, even under the strangest of circumstances, is a voice we believe in.

Exercises and Diversions

A. 1. When García Lorca's speaker (p. 42) says he would like to trade his horse, saddle, and knife for a house, mirror, and blanket, he is not thinking of the *denotation* or dictionary meaning of the words ("**horse:** a large, solid-hoofed, herbivorous quadruped, *Equus caballus* . . .") but of the *connotation* or cluster of associations each has. The horse connotes an outdoor life of wandering, adventure, and peril; the saddle connotes homelessness, discomfort, and hardship; the knife, passion and violence. The objects for which he would like to trade connote safety, comfort, and settled domesticity. The words in Patchen's poem (p. 147) are rich in connotation. "Rain," in the upper-left-hand corner, suggests coolness, fertility, flowers, freshness, renewal, purity, snugness by the fire; but it also connotes chilliness, discomfort, loneliness, gloom, deprivation (as in "to save for a rainy day"). What association clusters go along with each of these words: "gate," "fence," "flame," "snow," "garden," "coast," "lily," "thorn," "mirror," "shadow," "star," "stone"?

2. Do any other words in Patchen's poem strike you as being especially strong in connotation?

3. Does it seem to you that such words—or what they stand for—could be symbols of what they connote? Is "rain," for example, a fertility symbol?

B. Each of the following lists gives the words out of which a poem we have already read was constructed.

a. art, bed, crimson, dark, destroy, flies, found, howling, invisible, joy, life, love, night, rose, secret, sick, storm, warm

b. afternoon, bed, changed, cleanliness, curtains, down, flowers, glass, immaculate, key, late, lavender, lying, pitcher, smell, sunshine, tray, tumbler, turned, white, window, yellow

c. alive, asked, bank, black, board, clay, close, coffin, crew, dead, down, funeral, hear, idiots, living, new, no, oak, pray, pressing, rave, rend, round, sick, stand, steep, talk, teeth, walking, white

d. angel, baby, brink, buds, expand, feet, flower-bells, gleam, heat, heaven, heavenly, life, lips, meet (adjective), part, pink, rose-hued, shine, shrink, soft, spread, stretch, sweet, tempt, ten, think, sea-flowers, sea-shells, untrodden, wink

1. How do the words used in each list support the points we have been making about the theoretically best vocabulary for poetry?
2. Are most of the words in each list simple? Concrete thing-words? Evocative of emotion?
3. Which lists would you guess offer the most promising material for a poem?
4. Do you recognize any of the poems?

C. Adrian Henri, the English poet, painter, and musician, sees hope for the cliché, which he calls "a living piece of language that has gone dead through overwork. . . . At any time it can be energized or revitalized, often by . . . putting it in an alien context, contradicting its apparent meaning." As an example he cites Roger McGough's revitalization of "to have a familiar ring":

Your finger sadly
Has a familiar ring about it.

1. Could you revitalize any of the following by using them in a new and unexpected way: "happy haunts," "sunset glow," "swaying in the breeze," "silvery laugh," "radiant smile," "seething humanity," "naked trees," "pearly teeth"?
2. Why does an expression like "familiar ring" lend itself more easily to revival than one like "endearing grace"?

D. 1. Is the line that Frost especially liked in "My Butterfly" good only because it is plain and simple? If so, could we improve the first lines of his poem by rewriting them as follows?

All the flowers are dead.
And that daffy bird that scared you is gone too.
Nobody left but yours truly
(Not that you care)
To feel sorry for you here.

2. Would the lines of Shakespeare on page 153 be improved if rewritten as below?

Is there enough water anywhere to get my hand clean?
No, instead it would make the oceans turn red instead of green.

3. Besides plainness and simplicity, what else is required of the language of poetry?

E. 1. In "The Shield of Achilles" (p. 110), monosyllables and polysyllables tend to occur in clusters. Do they seem to have any affinity for certain kinds of material?

2. Is there a similar correlation in "The Purse-Seine" (p. 23)?
3. Is it significant that there is such an unrelieved concentration of monosyllables in "The Mill" (p. 90)? How are adjectives used in this poem? Does there seem to be a connection between the high percentage of monosyllables and the scarcity of adjectives?

F. 1. Recall that Eliot said that "the *norm* for a poet's language is the way his contemporaries talk," and that Pound was in favor of "natural speech." What would they probably think of the diction in this poem?

IN COOL, GREEN HAUNTS

A sweet, deep sense of mystery filled the wood.
  A star, like that which woke o'er Bethlehem,
  Shone on the still pool's brow for diadem—
  The first to fall of summer's multitude!
In cool, green haunts, where, haply, Robin Hood
  Ranged royally, of old, with all his train,
  A hushed expectance, such as augurs rain,
  Enthralled me and possessed me where I stood.

Then came the wind, with low word as he went;
  The quick wren, swift repeating what he said; 10
  A chattering chipmunk lured me on and led
Where scented brakes 'neath some wee burden bent:—
  One look—'twas this those wild things yearned to say:
  "A little brown-eyed fawn was born today!"

Mahlon Leonard Fisher (twentieth century)

2. Some would consider this sonnet sentimental. Does the kind of diction used contribute to the possibly sentimental effect?
3. This kind of language is sometimes called "sonnet diction." How would you characterize it?
4. Could this poem be saved if rewritten in the natural speech of your contemporaries? Try to write such a version.

Less is More lean language, fat language

10

One quality of memorable speech is concentration: much in little. Of a mother punishing her child with such ineffectual fury that the child himself feels sorry for her weakness, John Ciardi writes:

She beat so hard it hurt me not to hurt.

To describe how daughters drift away from their mothers:

And still they grew away because they grew.

To describe the long period over which a widow received insurance payments:

Two mailmen died before his mail stopped coming.

The beauty of conciseness is like that of the globe or sphere (in many cultures a symbol of spiritual perfection)—both cover the greatest volume with the minimum surface area.

The poetry of primitive peoples tends to be concentrated. A South Australian poem about a falling star (thought of as alarming) has only four words:

kandanga daruarungu manangga gilbanga.

It means, literally: "star—falling—at night—go away!" A sophisticated technique: the line is richly rhymed; in not mentioning the emotion the star arouses, it works by suggestion. The Imagists, around 1912, were in agreement with an ancient poetic principle when they insisted on using "absolutely no word that does not contribute to the presentation." This is an ideal that most poetry aspires to.

BREAK, BREAK, BREAK

Break, break, break,
  On thy cold gray stones, O Sea!
And I would that my tongue could utter
  The thoughts that arise in me.

O well for the fisherman's boy,
  That he shouts with his sister at play!
O well for the sailor lad,
  That he sings in his boat on the bay!

And the stately ships go on
  To their haven under the hill; 10
But O for the touch of a vanish'd hand,
  And the sound of a voice that is still!

Break, break, break,
  At the foot of thy crags, O Sea!
But the tender grace of a day that is dead
  Will never come back to me.

Alfred, Lord Tennyson

We appreciate the leanness of this lament for bygone days if we contrast it with another which has a high fat content. "Retrospection," an anonymous poem of the late nineteenth century, begins:

When we see our dreamships slipping
  From the verge of youth's green slope—
Loosening from the transient moorings
  At the golden shore of hope—
Vanishing, like airy bubbles,
  On the rough, tried sea of care,
Then the soul grows sick with longing
  That is almost wild despair.

Far behind lies sunny childhood—
  Fields of flowers our feet have trod 10
When our vision-bounded Eden
  Held no mystery but God;
When in dreams we spoke with angels,
  When awake, with brooks and birds,
Reading in the breeze and sunshine
  Love's unspoken, tender words.

When the stars were lighted candles
  Shining through God's floor of blue,
And the moon was but a window
  For the angels to look through 20

And so on for more than four stanzas.

An often quoted remark of Ezra Pound reminds us that poetry should be as well written as prose. Some of the material in the rest of this chapter may seem to refer not just to poetry but to writing in general. And indeed it does: though good writing will not guarantee a good poem, bad writing will guarantee a bad one.

Some parts of speech are more necessary than others. Nouns and verbs are the most important, the most existential—nouns referring to the forms that being can take, verbs to their activity. Adjectives and adverbs are hangers-on with little independent existence of their own. Used weakly, they are decorative rather than structural, and hence attractive to the apprentice writer, who needs surface decoration to cover up the architectural flaws. Humpty Dumpty, in telling Alice about words, says, "They've a temper some of them; particularly verbs, they're the proudest—adjectives you can do anything with, but not verbs. . . ." In his writings on style, Pound constantly warns against adjectives. His friend Wyndham Lewis gave advice all young writers ought to consider: "Take out all the adjectives."

Nothing so weakens a poem as to have the nouns "chaperoned" (as Pound said) by adjectives, or the verbs by adverbs.

> Mild western wind, when will thou softly blow,
> The small rain down can delicately rain?
> Sweet Christ, that my blushing love were in my arms,
> And my blissful self in my downy bed again.

Adjective fanciers are surprised at how many poems are almost without their favorite part of speech. In the poems that follow, we might notice how few adjectives there are, of what kind they are, and for what occasions they seem to be saved.

ALONG THE FIELD AS WE CAME BY

Along the field as we came by
A year ago, my love and I,
The aspen over stile and stone
Was talking to itself alone.
'Oh who are these that kiss and pass?
A country lover and his lass;
Two lovers looking to be wed;
And time shall put them both to bed,
But she shall lie with earth above,
And he beside another love.' 10

And sure enough beneath the tree
There walks another love with me,
And overhead the aspen heaves
Its rainy-sounding silver leaves;
And I spell nothing in their stir,
But now perhaps they speak to her,
And plain for her to understand
They talk about a time at hand
When I shall sleep with clover clad,
And she beside another lad. 20

A. E. Housman (1859–1936)

---

3 **stile:** *steps over a wall or fence*

One can imagine these lines bedizened with modifiers:

Along the fragrant summer fields as gaily we came by,
One oh-so-happy year ago, my beauteous love and I,
The trembling aspen over stile and over rugged stone
Was softly talking, softly, to its brooding self alone:
"Oh who are these impassioned ones that warmly kiss and pass?
A sturdy country lover and his rosy-beaming lass.
Two young and happy lovers looking sweetly to be wed;
And brutal time shall cruelly put them separately to bed.
The much-lamented girl shall lie with dank old earth above;
And he lie pleasantly beside another buxom love.

The airman in a poem of Yeats uses hardly an adjective in explaining why he took part in World War I. (As an Irishman, he could not hate the Germans or love the English; his impulse to enlist came from an existential love of adventure.)

AN IRISH AIRMAN FORESEES HIS DEATH

I know that I shall meet my fate
Somewhere among the clouds above;
Those that I fight I do not hate,
Those that I guard I do not love;
My country is Kiltartan Cross,
My countrymen Kiltartan's poor,
No likely end could bring them loss
Or leave them happier than before.
Nor law, nor duty bade me fight,
Nor public men, nor cheering crowds, 10
A lonely impulse of delight
Drove to this tumult in the clouds;
I balanced all, brought all to mind,
The years to come seemed waste of breath,
A waste of breath the years behind
In balance with this life, this death.

W. B. Yeats

Hopkins uses hardly any in his poem about the sorrow of a child as she watches the leaves fall. (She is really grieving, the poet tells her, over the fact of mortality—as Homer did when he said that the generations of men were like the generations of leaves.)

SPRING AND FALL:
to a young child

Márgarét, áre you gríeving
Over Goldengrove unleaving?
Leáves, líke the things of man, you
With your fresh thoughts care for, can you?
Ah! ás the heart grows older

It will come to such sights colder
By and by, nor spare a sigh
Though worlds of wanwood leafmeal lie;
And yet you *will* weep and know why.
Now no matter, child, the name: 10
Sórrow's sprígs áre the same.
Nor mouth had, no nor mind, expressed
What heart heard of, ghost guessed:
It ís the blight man was born for,
It is Margaret you mourn for.

Gerard Manley Hopkins (1844–1889)

"Wanwood" is a word made up for woods that have lost their color; "leafmeal" is analogous to "piecemeal"—that is, leaf by leaf.

What we have been saying about modifiers is a caution, not a rule. Adjectives and adverbs tend to run to fat, to be sagging appendages on the bone and muscle of poetry. But just as we need some fat for the health and contour of the body, so we need some adjectives in poetry: for precision, for luxuriance, sometimes even for a needed sense of muchness.

The most useless adjectives duplicate the meaning of their noun, or express a quality implied by it. We have no need of them in such expressions as: "celestial stars," "fragrant flowers," "vernal spring," "deep abyss," "empty chasm," "cold winter sun," "flaming pyre," "fair beauty," "soft whispers," "sweet perfume," "loud strife," "bleak waste," "stimulating wine," "dark forebodings," "nobly enshrined." If the nouns did not have their usual qualities—if the stars were *infernal*, or the spring *chilly*, or the strife *quiet*—the fact might be interesting enough to deserve an adjective.

Adjective-prone writers tend to favor such hyphenated expressions as "the day-tired town" or "her life-glad form" or "age-forgotten songs." Some hyphenated expressions are natural: "the spring-fed lake," "thick-wooded acres," "the air-cooled theater," "salt-caked tugs." But new ones made up only for poetic effect call attention to themselves as unnatural intruders. They can also be imprecise. Does "She entered the wood, deer-cautious" mean she was cautious as a deer, or cautious because there were deer around? With such expressions as the following, one suspects the writer has made a self-conscious effort to lift natural English to a more "poetic" level: "brook-gladdened meadows," "hate-lashed storms," "terror-tinged yearning," "chimneys sulphur-flamed," "fruit-ripe with child," "God-proceeding rays," "the salmon-feeding bear."

There are writers, it is true, who openly profess their affection for adjectives. Denise Levertov likes to accumulate them in groups of threes:

. . . I wake up laughing, tell you:
"I was writing an
ad for gold—gold cups,
gold porridge-bowls—*Gold*

beautiful, durable—while I mused
for a third adjective . . . .

This may be a joke, but even wide awake this poet sometimes piles up three or more adjectives:

. . . our own histories,
a brutal dream drenched with our lives,
intemperate, open, illusory . . . .

The mountains through the shadowy
flickering of our propellors, steady,
melancholy, relaxed, indifferent . . . .

Three adjectives together tend to drag, but Milton uses that very drag expressively in describing how his rather coy Eve yields to Adam with "sweet, reluctant, amorous delay. . . ." Richard Wilbur can keep three adjectives in sharp focus, as in his lines about a doomed turkey just before Thanksgiving:

The pale-blue bony head
Set on its shepherd's crook
Like a saint's death-mask, turns a vague, superb,
And timeless look . . . .

A writer careful about adjectives and adverbs, keeping them in reserve for special effects, can make them vigorous and vivid.

A pale horse,
Mane of flowery dust . . . . *Yvor Winters*

The autumn night receives us, hoarse with rain . . . .
Louise Bogan

The freighter, gay with rust . . . . *Randall Jarrell*

You lay still, brilliant with illness, behind glass . . . .
Thomas Kinsella

The old farmer, his scarlet face
Apologetic with whiskey . . . . *James Wright*

Sometimes surprising effects can result from transferring a modifier from the noun it really belongs with to an associated noun. We often use such transfers in ordinary speech—as when we say we had a "noisy evening," even though it was the *we*, not the evening, that was noisy. We speak of "giddy heights," of a "shivery horror movie," of "dishonest money." Sir Philip Sidney said he did not "aspire to Caesar's bleeding fame." Contemporary poets are still transferring adjectives:

And all throughout a Breughel matinee
Those buxom waltzes ran . . . . *James Merrill*

Kenneth Patchen transfers his adverbs, from *some*where, in

The sleigh tinkled snowily down the street . . . .

. . . chickens
Squatting sunfully on every roof . . . .

This seems a form of the metonymy discussed in Chapter Four. A detail is shifted from one part of a cluster of associations to another part.

Humpty Dumpty may have found verbs the hardest words of all, but writers have coped with them. (John Berryman says of Hemingway, who prided himself on coping, "He verbed for forty years. . . .") Here are some interesting verbs performing:

A little wind investigates the page . . . . *Stanley J. Kunitz*

The river talks all through the night, proving
its gravel . . . . *William Stafford*

. . . Leaves discuss the wind . . . . *Cid Corman*

Scolding your pipe against a tree . . . . *Marcia Masters*

Pigs blister the hillside. *Robert Dana*

The Hammond Organ lubricates the air . . . .
Miller Williams

Such vivid verbs are often compressed metaphors: pigs look like round pink blisters, pigs *are* blisters, etc.

John Donne even made passionate use of prepositions (or adverbs?) in a love poem:

License my roving hands and let them go
Behind, before, above, between, below . . . .

Poets, like all writers, achieve concentration by packing double meanings into single words. When Galway Kinnell writes

. . . suddenly
an alderfly glitters past, declining
to die . . . .

his word *declining* can mean (1) the insect is sinking as it flies; (2) is sinking toward death; (3) is refusing to die; (4) is running through the forms of "to die"—"I die," "you die," "he dies," etc. This kind of double talk—these puns—which poets are fond of, is not confined to poetry. We often see slogans like:

DRIVE AS IF YOUR LIFE DEPENDED ON IT.
ARE YOU DYING FOR A CIGARETTE?

Today we think of puns as the kind of humor more likely to evoke groans than laughter. But puns were taken more seriously in earlier times. When John Donne put his future in jeopardy by marrying Sir George More's underage daughter without the father's consent, someone—probably not Donne himself—composed a one-liner:

John Donne, Anne Donne, Un-done.

Donne himself was not joking when he wrote, during an illness that might have been fatal, his "A Hymn to God the Father," with its punning:

When Thou hast done, Thou hast not Donne,
For I have more.

(Some think that "more" is a pun on his wife's name.)

Richard Crashaw, in writing an epitaph, even played on the name of the deceased, a procedure we might think in bad taste today:

AN EPITAPH UPON DOCTOR BROOK

A BROOK whose stream so great, so good,
Was loved, was honored as a flood,
Whose banks the Muses dwelt upon
More than their own Helicon,
Here at length hath gladly found
A quiet passage underground;
Meanwhile, his loved banks now dry
The Muses with their tears supply.

Richard Crashaw (1612?–1649)

And yet poets are not above this kind of pun even today. In his poem on the pack rat, Robert Pack lets the possible pun on his name hint that the imagery of the poem may be not without its symbolism.

THE PACK RAT

Collector of lost beads, buttons, bird bones,
Catalogue-maker with an eye for glitter,
Litter lover, entrepreneur of waste—
Bits of snail-shell, chips of jugs, red thread,
Blue thread, tinfoil, teeth; fair-minded thief
(Leaving in my pocket when I slept,
A pine cone and two nuts for the dime you stole);
Reasonable romancer, journeying more
Than half a mile to meet a mate, split-eared
Lover with a bitten tail (your mate mates rough), 10
You last all courtship long, you stick around
When the brood comes, unlike most other rats;
Payer of prices, busy with no dreams,
But brain enough to get along; moderate
Music maker with moderate powers, thumping
The drum of frightened ground with both hind feet
Or scraping dry leaves till the still woods chirp;
Simple screamer seized by the owl's descent,
One scream and one regret, just one; fellow,
Forebear, survivor, have I lost my way? 20

Robert Pack (b. 1929)

Some puns play on different meanings of the same word, as in George Starbuck's

The world has a glass center.
I saw the sign for it.
TOLEDO, GLASS CENTER OF THE WORLD.

Others play on different words that sound alike.

ON HIS BOOKS

When I am dead, I hope it may be said,
"His sins were scarlet, but his books were red."

Hilaire Belloc (1870–1953)

Besides storing his words with multiple meanings, the writer can give them more charge, more mass, by making full use of their connotations—the suggestions and associations they bring along with them in addition to their dictionary meaning. They can, like people, be interesting because of their background, because of where they have been and the company they have kept in the past.

When the Normans came over from France in 1066, the language of the people was Old English (or Anglo-Saxon), which gave us many of the words for down-to-earth realities. French became the language of the court; words of French ancestry are redolent of courtliness, chivalry, romance. For centuries Latin was the language of the church and of scholarship; words patently from the Latin can still suggest erudition or pedantry. In ordinary speech we do not separate these three components, but a high concentration of any one can make itself felt as unusual. In "The Wanderer," W. H. Auden makes use of Old English derivatives, some few of them odd enough to call for the dictionary. Such words, as opposed to the more cultivated French and Latin ones, evoke a rugged and heroic life in a primitive northern setting. Auden's poem is about the archetypal figure of the seeker, the adventurer, the pioneer who leaves his home, his establishment, to fare forth into new territory.

THE WANDERER

Doom is dark and deeper than any sea-dingle.
Upon what man it fall
In spring, day-wishing flowers appearing,
Avalanche sliding, white snow from rock-face,
That he should leave his house,
No cloud-soft hand can hold him, restraint by women;
But ever that man goes
Through place-keepers, through forest trees,
A stranger to strangers over undried sea,
Houses for fishes, suffocating water, 10
Or lonely on fell as chat,
By pot-holed becks

---

1 **dingle:** *deep cleft or hollow*
11 **fell:** *hill, ridge*
chat: *a kind of bird*
12 **becks:** *brooks*

A bird stone-haunting, an unquiet bird.
There head falls forward, fatigued at evening,
And dreams of home,
Waving from window, spread of welcome,
Kissing of wife under single sheet;
But waking sees
Bird-flocks nameless to him, through doorway voices
Of new men making another love. 20

Save him from hostile capture,
From sudden tiger's leap at corner;
Protect his house,
His anxious house where days are counted
From thunderbolt protect,
From gradual ruin spreading like a stain;
Converting number from vague to certain,
Bring joy, bring day of his returning,
Lucky with day approaching, with leaning dawn.

W. H. Auden

The first eighteen words are from the Old English; not until we come to "flower" do we have a word that derives, through Old French, from the Latin. We can see how different the poem would sound if we Latinized it:

Fate is more obscure and profound than any ocean-valley . . .

The vocabulary keeps us in an Old-English world until we reach

Save him from hostile capture,

which is pure Latin-French. So is

Converting number from vague to certain,

and words like "sudden," "protect," "anxious," "gradual." As the wanderer returns home, he returns to a more genteel vocabulary.

THE WINDHOVER:
To Christ our Lord

I caught this morning morning's minion, king-
dom of daylight's dauphin, dapple-dawn-drawn Falcon, in his riding
Of the rolling level underneath him steady air, and striding
High there, how he rung upon the rein of a wimpling wing
In his ecstasy! then off, off forth on swing,
As a skate's heel sweeps smooth on a bow-bend: the hurl and gliding
Rebuffed the big wind. My heart in hiding
Stirred for a bird,—the achieve of, the mastery of the thing!

Brute beauty and valour and act, oh, air, pride, plume, here
Buckle! AND the fire that breaks from thee then, a billion 10

---

[1] **minion:** *darling* [4] **wimpling:** *rippling, hiding in folds*

Times told lovelier, more dangerous, O my chevalier!

No wonder of it: shéer plód makes plough down sillion[12]
Shine, and blue-bleak embers, ah my dear,
Fall, gall themselves, and gash gold-vermilion.

Gerard Manley Hopkins

Gerard Manley Hopkins, though a professor of Latin and Greek, favored native English words. In "The Windhover" there are almost no words whose Latin ancestry would be obvious. The vocabulary is basically Old English, but what is unusual is the large number of words, all crucial to the meaning, that suggest a French world of chivalry, adventure, and even romance: "minion," "dauphin," "falcon," "achieve," "mastery," "beauty," "valour," "buckle," "billion," "dangerous," "chevalier," "sillion," "vermilion." That the language has so French a cast is appropriate: the poet, seeing a kind of knightly adventurousness in the daring falcon, thinks of Christ, his chevalier or supreme knight-figure.

The eighteenth century was particularly fond of a sonorous Latinate vocabulary, as in these lines from Samuel Johnson's "The Vanity of Human Wishes":

Let *Observation* with *extensive* view,
Survey mankind from China to Peru....

Delusive Fortune hears the *incessant* call,
They mount, they shine, *evaporate,* and fall....

The form *distorted justifies* the fall,
And *detestation* rids the *indignant* wall....

Even when such words are the natural ones for their meaning, an accumulation can sound learned or pompous.

人
man

木
tree

日
sun

Ezra Pound believed the ideograms that stand for words in Chinese to be pictograms, which look so much like the objects they denote that a sensitive observer "could read a certain amount of Chinese writing without ANY STUDY." Among the examples he gives are the three at the left, which, simple as they are, seem rather shaky support for his views. When we are told that the first means *man* or *person,* we can see that, yes, it is two-legged. But we might just as well have guessed that it meant *tent* or *mountain peak* or *arrowhead* or anything sharp. Only a minority of Chinese characters are actually pictograms; and very few even of these bear a recognizable resemblance to the object.

But sometimes words come to us with a halo of ghostly images: apparitions from the underworld of etymology. When one remembers

[12] **sillion:** *furrow (French,* sillon*)*

that "deliberate" has to do with weights and balances, the word becomes a pictogram: one sees the weighted mechanisms shifting as the bridge begins to rise in Richard Wilbur's:

> Deliberately the drawbridge starts to rise....

We become more sensitive to ordinary words by realizing how haunted they are. Merely turning the pages of a dictionary will stir up quite a few ghosts. "Alarm" is more exciting when we realize it is a cry, "To arms!" ("All' arme!" in Italian). An ordinary "derrick" becomes a grislier part of the industrial landscape if we remember that it was named after a certain Derrick, a famous London hangman. "Nonchalant" means *not heating up.* "Curfew" has a setting when we know it comes from two Old French words we would now spell *couvre-feu* or *cover the fire*—put it out for the night. A curfew for teen-agers picks up interesting symbolic overtones if we think of it as meaning "time to put the fires out." "Dexterity" refers to the right hand, most people's best hand; "sinister" refers to the left, or unlucky, side: to speak of a magician, or a ball handler, as having "sinister dexterity" gives us a curious punning oxymoron. Many words become like pictograms in the light of their history. This is one more way in which the poet can concentrate meanings.

Exercises and Diversions

A. Evaluate the worth of each adjective in the following quotations:

1. Whate'er false shows of short and slippery good
   Mix the mad sons of men in mutual blood. . . . *Richard Crashaw*

2. Poor world, said I, what wilt thou do
      To entertain this starry Stranger?
   Is this the best thou couldst bestow,
      A cold and not too cleanly manger?
   Contend, ye powers of heaven and earth,
      To fit a bed for this huge birth. *Richard Crashaw*

3. . . . the argillaceous clays, the zircon and sapphire. . . . *Edith Sitwell*

4. I stood in the glassy sun of September
   Noonday. . . . *Brewster Ghiselin*

5. ["The Hemorrhage"]
      The people made a ring
      Around the man in the park . . .
      Exhibitor of the dark
      Abominable rose. . . . *Stanley J. Kunitz*

6. The responsible sound of the lawnmower. . . . *William Stafford*

7.   . . . barefoot gulls
      designing the sand. . . . *William Stafford*

8. [Of a beggar]

   How much money would erase him in a dream,
   his lids inflamed, his bare feet biblical
   with sores? . . . The bay across the street
   is affluent with sun. . . . *Richard Hugo*

B. In the following quotations, identify the various practices discussed in this chapter. Evaluate the success of each.

1. Mellifluous as bees, these brittle men
   droning of Honeyed Homer give me hives. . . . *George Starbuck*

2. And the ox, with sleek hide, and with low-swimming head;
   And the sheep, little-kneed, with a quick-dipping nod;
   And a girl, with her head carried on in a proud
   Gait of walking, as smooth as an air-swimming cloud. *William Barnes*

3. From what I've seen tacked up, you can't draw water.
   Your plan is "going into art"? Oh, daughter,
   What would you learn? How man bends at the knee?
   Better bone up on such anatomy
   At first hand. . . . *X. J. Kennedy*

4. [Of a deer]
   We do not discern those eyes
     Watching in the snow . . .
   We do not discern those eyes
     Wondering, aglow,
     Fourfooted, tiptoe. . . . *Thomas Hardy*

5.
   . . . change is never sent
   Like a valentine, but waits, a plot of earth,
   A green conspiracy. . . . *James Merrill*

C. What kind of pictures haunt these words from their etymological past? (Consult a good dictionary.)

fool, generous, companion, lunacy, planet, maudlin, tawdry, sabotage, pandemonium, tangerine, bungalow, chivalrous, cavalier, bedlam, gargoyle, focus, exaggerate, disaster, dilapidated, carnivore, carnival, carnation, carnage, carnal

D. 1. Contrast the use of adjectives in Karl Shapiro's "A Cut Flower" (p. 61) with that in his "Girls Working in Banks" (p. 51). Why the difference?

2. Examine the use of adjectives preceding their nouns in "The Woodspurge" (p. 118), "Love, 20¢ the First Quarter Mile" (p. 74), and "Spoils" (p. 98). Why is the use of adjectives so very different in "Leda and the Swan" (p. 62)? Could any of the adjectives there be omitted without loss?

3. In Jarrell's "The Knight, Death, and the Devil" (p. 174) which is based on Dürer's engraving, there are many hyphenated modifiers. Do they seem to work here? Is there anything, for example, in the texture of the engraving itself to which they correspond?

Albrecht Dürer, "*The Knight, Death, and the Devil*"

THE KNIGHT, DEATH, AND THE DEVIL

Cowhorn-crowned, shockheaded, cornshuck-bearded,
Death is a scarecrow—his death's-head a teetotum
That tilts up toward man confidentially
But trimmed with adders; ringlet-maned, rope-bridled,
The mare he rides crops herbs beside a skull.
He holds up, warning, the crossed cones of time:
Here, narrowing into now, the Past and Future
Are quicksand.
A hoofed pikeman trots behind.
His pike's claw-hammer mocks—in duplicate, inverted— 10
The pocked, ribbed, soaring crescent of his horn.
A scapegoat aged into a steer; boar-snouted;
His great limp ears stuck sidelong out in air;
A dewlap bunched at his breast; a ram's-horn wound
Beneath each ear; a spur licked up and out
From the hide of his forehead; bat-winged, but in bone;
His eye a ring inside a ring inside a ring
That leers up, joyless, vile, in meek obscenity—
This is the devil. Flesh to flesh, he bleats
The herd back to the pit of being. 20

In fluted mail; upon his lance the bush
Of that old fox; a sheep-dog bounding at his stirrup,
In its eyes the cast of faithfulness (our help,
Our foolish help); his dun war-horse pacing
Beneath in strength, in ceremonious magnificence;
His castle—some man's castle—set on every crag:
So, companioned so, the knight moves through this world.
The fiend moos in amity, Death mouths, reminding:
He listens in assurance, has no glance
To spare for them, but looks past steadily 30
At—at—
a man's look completes itself.

The death of his own flesh, set up outside him;
The flesh of his own soul, set up outside him—
Death and the devil, what are these to him?
His being accuses him—and yet his face is firm
In resolution, in absolute persistence;
The folds of smiling do for steadiness;
The face is its own fate—*a man does what he must*—
And the body underneath it says: *I am*. 40

Randall Jarrell (1914–1965)

E. Write a descriptive poem (of, say, a dozen lines, in any rhythm) about a familiar object, or anything of interest to you. Do not use a single adjective until the last line, and then try to use, effectively, a series of three.

IV the sounds

Gold in the Ore 11 the sounds of english

This chapter may look as if it were about some such abstraction as acoustical theory. It is actually about the way we use our bodies—instruments of flesh and bone—to produce the sounds we call voice: the sounds of poetry and all our human speech. We can realize how sensitive the mouth is and what care the brain takes of it if we contemplate a "homunculus" (see p. 178)—a representation of the way man would look if the proportions of his body corresponded to the brain area devoted to each part. More brain-space is needed for the mouth than for all the rest of the body except the hands.

We can think of words as having not only a mind—their meaning—but also a body—the structure of sound in which their meaning lives. Most poets, who are not Platonic about language, care as much for the body of their words as for the mind. The sound of poetry, what Robert Frost called "the gold in the ore," is what we turn to now.

A poem comes to us first as speech, on sound waves that register as barometric changes against the drums and gauges of the ear, an apparatus so sensitive it takes notice if the pressure against it varies by one part in ten billion. "A breath of the mouth becomes a picture of the world," said Herder, ". . . everything that man has ever thought and willed . . . depends on a moving breath of air."

We hear poems even when we seem to be taking them silently from the page. Tiny wires attached to the speech areas of the throat have picked up electrical currents—evidence that the muscles were being stimulated during silent reading. The body participates sympathetically with what it experiences. Colors affect us physically:

Experiments in which individuals are required to contemplate psychologically pure-red for varying lengths of time have shown that this color has a

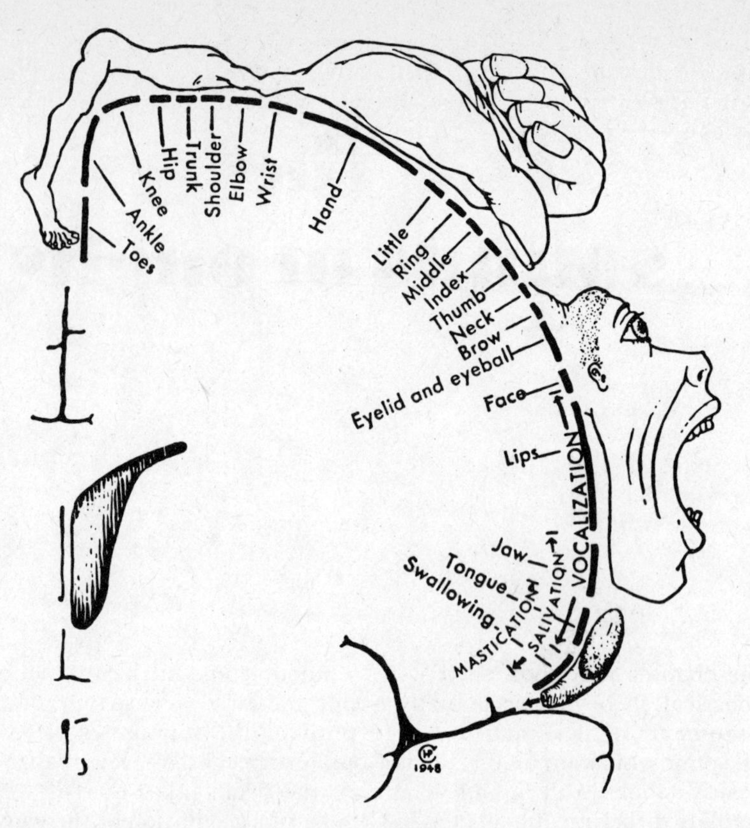

decidedly stimulating effect on the nervous system—blood pressure increases, respiration rate and heartbeat both speed up. . . . Similar exposure to psychologically pure-blue on the other hand has the reverse effect—blood pressure falls, heartbeat and breathing both slow down.

Images of sound must affect us no less profoundly, since as very young children we were more at home in the world of sound (which we had

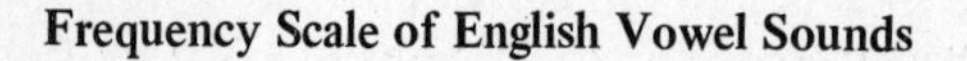

Frequency Scale of English Vowel Sounds

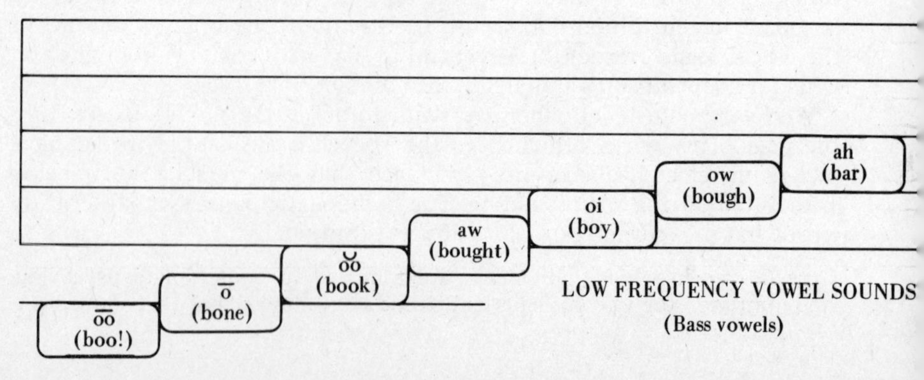

known even before birth) than in the world of sight. The rest of this chapter will be about the physical nature of speech. This is not theoretical material to be merely read; these are physical facts to be acted out physically—to be felt and tried in the mouth as we read.

Vowels

Our speech sounds are conventionally divided into vowels and consonants. With vowels the airflow from the lungs is not impeded. If we pronounce *a e i o u,* we can feel that we are nowhere obstructing the breath but only, by raising our tongue, rounding our lips, etc., reshaping the instrument it flows through. How we manage so complicated a process would astound us if we thought about it.

Our feats of hearing are equally incredible. We follow as many as twenty distinct sounds a second; we notice sounds that fade into nothingness in a few thousandths of a second; and we do so while turning this complicated acoustic input into electrochemical nerve impulses that the brain can process. The most complicated sound patterns a poet ever uses are as nothing compared to the patterns we handle habitually.

Vowels are in a way like musical notes, so that we can set up a vowel scale (rather like a musical scale) based on the frequencies that the sounds have in themselves. Sound, as we know, travels in waves. Since it travels at constant speed, the shorter the waves, the more per second—the higher, that is, the frequency of the sound. Shortwave sounds are high-frequency sounds, shrill sounds, like the *ee* of "whee!" The longer the waves, the fewer per second, and the slower and deeper the sound seems to be. (We know that if a 78 rpm record is slowed down to the 33⅓ speed, the sound will get slower and deeper.) The *oo* of "moon" is a low-frequency sound.

A difficulty we run into in making up a vowel scale is that vowels are not notes but chords made up of tones and overtones from the resonating system of throat, mouth, and head. Some of our fifteen

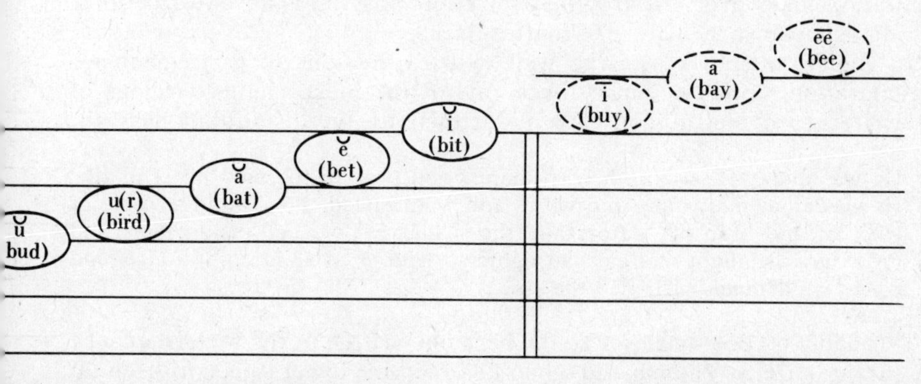

MIDDLE FREQUENCY VOWEL SOUNDS
(Tenor Vowels)

HIGH FREQUENCY VOWEL SOUNDS
(Alto Vowels)

sounds, the diphthongs, are two chords sounded in sequence. The *i* sound of "good-by" is a run-together *áh-ee.* Several other sounds are also vowels in motion—"glides" from one sound into another. Our scale, though it would not provide a basis for laboratory experiment, is on the whole accurate for American speech, and it serves well enough for the reading of poetry.

The upness and downness of vowel sounds affect us physically in different ways. The *ee* sound, at the top of the scale, comes in a pattern of waves that could be diagramed like this:

in contrast to the *oo* sound at the bottom:

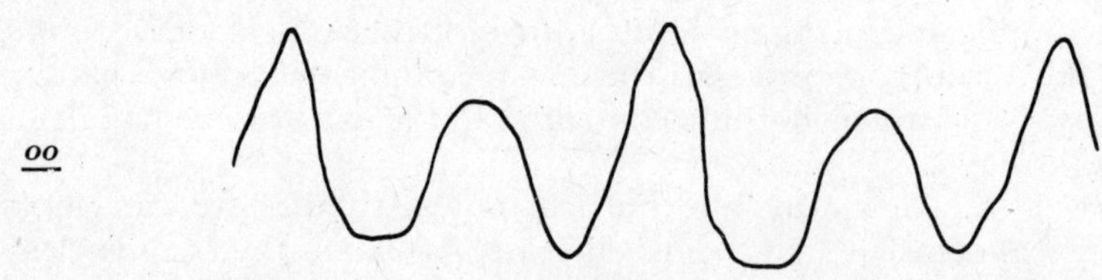

The high-frequency *ee* is busier, gives the ear more to process. Its greater activity suggests greater vitality, speed, excitement than the slower moving, more sluggish waves of the *oo.*

Few categories in our experience are richer in emotional suggestion than upness and downness. We associate being "up" or "high" with an increase of vitality, being "down" or "low" with a lessening of it. Our heart "sinks" when we feel grief, the physical effect of which Darwin describes as follows: "The muscles [become] flaccid; the eyelids droop; the head hangs on the contracted chest; the lips, cheeks, and lower jaw all sink downward from their own weight." The last phrase explains why downness is bad: when we give up or lose strength, gravitation takes over. All growth, aspiration, striving is an upward thing, almost against the nature of matter itself.

High-frequency vowels go well with expressions of excitement, exhilaration, vivacity. James Joyce, one of the most sound-conscious of writers, provides a good example of their use in an exultant passage:

> He was alone. He was unheeded, happy and near to the wild heart of life. He was alone and young and wilful and wildhearted, alone amid a waste of wild air and brackish waters and the seaharvest of shells and tangle and veiled grey sunlight and gayclad lightclad figures, of children and girls and voices childish and girlish in the air....

Probably no poet has ever so deliberately written in the high-frequency range as Dylan Thomas did when he urged his dying father to keep up his courage to the end.

DO NOT GO GENTLE INTO THAT GOOD NIGHT

Do not go gentle into that good night,
Old age should burn and rave at close of day;
Rage, rage against the dying of the light.

Though wise men at their end know dark is right,
Because their words had forked no lightning they
Do not go gentle into that good night.

Good men, the last wave by, crying how bright
Their frail deeds might have danced in a green bay,
Rage, rage against the dying of the light.

Wild men who caught and sang the sun in flight, 10
And learn, too late, they grieved it on its way,
Do not go gentle into that good night.

Grave men, near death, who see with blinding sight
Blind eyes could blaze like meteors and be gay,
Rage, rage against the dying of the light.

And you, my father, there on the sad height,
Curse, bless, me now with your fierce tears, I pray.
Do not go gentle into that good night.
Rage, rage against the dying of the light.

Dylan Thomas

The rhyming sounds, throughout, are ī ("night") and ā ("day"). With these are many high, bright ē's ("deed"). The effect is not only in the high-frequency vowels themselves, but in the fact that they occur about twice as often here as they do in the normal run of English speech. The unlooked-for percentage must come as a shock of excitement, an aural pick-me-up, to the sensitive, if largely subconscious, mechanisms of the brain.

A more somber poem gives a very different concentration of sound:

ONCE BY THE PACIFIC

The shattered water made a misty din.
Great waves looked over others coming in,
And thought of doing something to the shore
That water never did to land before.
The clouds were low and hairy in the skies,
Like locks blown forward in the gleam of eyes.
You could not tell, and yet it looked as if
The shore was lucky in being backed by cliff,
The cliff in being backed by continent;
It looked as if a night of dark intent 10
Was coming, and not only a night, an age.
Someone had better be prepared for rage.
There would be more than ocean-water broken
Before God's last *Put out the Light* was spoken.

Robert Frost

A scary poem. Something in the universe, it implies, is threatening our existence; things are going to get worse before they get better. The vowel sounds gravitate toward the lower, darker notes: there are more than twice as many *aw*'s, *oo*'s, and *o*'s as we are used to hearing in spoken English.

The larger an object is and the more volume it has, the more slowly it is likely to vibrate. The long strings in a piano give us the deep tones; a double bass can go lower than a violin. Avalanches and stormy seas have deeper reverberations than hailstones on the roof—not merely louder. The larger object produces a low-frequency sound.

Since low notes are related to largeness, they also evoke what is powerful or awesome or ominous or gloomy. We think of them as *dark* notes, perhaps because our experience of caverns and other reverberating hollows is associated with the dark. (The voice of the great singer Caruso was said to "darken" as over the years it changed from tenor to baritone.)

Vowels have their characteristic resonance from the shape and size of the cavities in which they resound—that is, from the way in which we make use of the resonating chambers of mouth and head. The larger the hollow in which a vowel sound vibrates, the deeper the sound and the more clearly our nerves and muscles tell us that *we ourselves* are embodying largeness, hollowness, darkness, etc. If we could see—which heaven forbid!—a cross section of the head of a person pronouncing *"Ee,"* it would look rather like the lefthand figure below. The front part of the tongue has been raised to permit only a narrow stream of air to pass through. Such a high front vowel, tensely produced, can suggest not only speed, brightness, and vitality but also littleness, as in "needle" or "teeny-weeny." It *is* a littleness, and we are doing a kind of charade of littleness by squeezing our mouth to the narrowest opening that permits any sound at all.

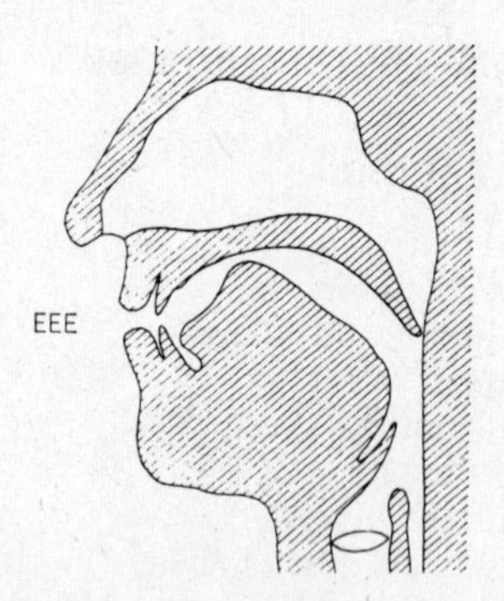

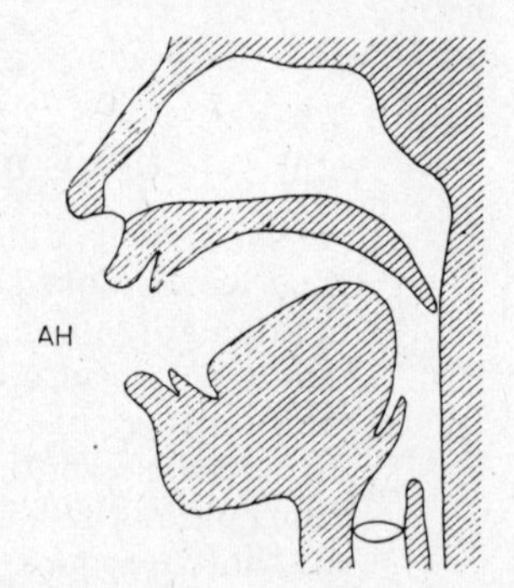

A person producing an *ah* sound (righthand figure, above) has to make his mouth a noticeably larger resonating chamber: has to make a sensitive part of his body, very close to the brain, a more sonorous cavern for the deeper, more solemn, more awesome sound. Not only do the sounds we produce have certain qualities, but our bodies, in producing them, are trying to be *like* those very qualities.

Sounds also affect us through the memories they arouse of what we have heard in life. The 10 billion neurons of the brain have almost infinite interconnections. Hearing certain sounds cannot fail to remind us of surf or thunder or the hiss of a snake or the whine of the winter wind through telephone wires on the prairie. Or of feet echoing in an empty street at night, the scream of brakes, the siren of a firetruck. Sounds like these can be deeply emotional, bringing, as we have learned, their messages of life and death.

For many reasons, then, the sounds of human speech are charged with emotional potential. Poets have always felt this. When Shelley begins his "Ode to a Skylark" with a line that features the four highest-frequency vowels, he sets the poem in the key of these vowels:

> Hail to thee, blithe spirit!

When Frost uses almost all of the bass vowels in the first two lines of "An Old Man's Winter Night," his introductory chords prepare us to expect the worst:

> All out-of-doors looked darkly in at him
> Through the thin frost, almost in separate stars....

Once we have uttered a sound, we take pleasure in repeating it. We find repetition in magic spells, in solemn oaths, in orations, in ads, as well as in the speech noises a baby makes for its own pleasure. When a sound is clearly struck in a poem, it tends to attract similar sounds. At the beginning of Gary Snyder's "Oil," many of the sounds that we hear can be heard again within the next few syllables:

> soft rainsqualls on the swells
> south of the Bonins, late at night. Light
> from the empty mess-hall
> throws back bulky shadows
> of winch and fairlead
> over the slanting fantail where I stand....

Repetition of a vowel sound ("soft"/"squalls"; "rain"/"late") is known as **assonance.**

Each of the fifteen vowel sounds of our scale has its own character or tone color. Skillful writers and sensitive readers are aware of the differences, just as one is aware of the differences between the tones of a flute, a violin, and a bassoon. But since poets for the most part work with the language as it is, and since words that combine a desired sound and an appropriate meaning are not always available, the use of expressive sound in poetry is not to be expected as a regular thing. The most we can say is that a poet is sensitive to the sounds he is making and uses them expressively when he sees the opportunity. The benefit that most of us, as readers, derive from meditating at least briefly on the quality of individual sounds is that we come to participate more completely, more physically, in the experience of the poem. The remarks that follow—we repeat—should be tested in the mouth.

A writer or reader who wanted to master the keyboard of sound could concentrate on each of the fifteen vowel sounds in turn, noticing what happens in his mouth when he pronounces it, listening to its quality and deciding on its emotional possibilities, thinking of words in which it seems especially expressive, and watching for it to turn up in the poetry he is reading. He would not be surprised to discover that, just as such symbols as "earth" and "sea" have room at the same time for opposite connotations, so one sound can be appropriate for opposite emotions—the shrill *i* of "strike" can serve for either exultation or despair. Sounding this diphthong, he would feel how it originates as an *ah* in the lax back region of the throat but climbs instantly into the vibrant *ee* region. He could feel it move in his mouth. He might guess that since more energy goes into its production than into that of a pure vowel, it has more energy to convey. He might well decide that it is the most dynamic of the high-frequency vowels, that it strikes the ear more forcibly than the others, has more audibility. He might come upon Sylvia Plath using it almost brutally for its cutting power in

> Christ! they are panes of ice,
> A vice of knives....

or upon James Tate dramatizing its shrillness in

> ... sirens malign
> the sky....

or upon Coleridge using its brightness and sparkle in

> Or if the secret ministry of frost
> Shall hang them up in silent icicles,
> Quietly shining to the quiet moon.

One could work through all the vowel sounds in this way—though we do not have the time or space to do so here. Suppose we pick out only a few for examination.

Even the dullest vowel sound has its individuality. The little *i* (of "bit") has been a favorite with writers trying to depict things that are brisk, quick, little, slim, glittery. Plato thought it especially apt for showing movement. Many would feel that "skinny-dipping" sounds more like what it means than "nude bathing" does. The effect is in the thin, glittery vowels. "Shivery hickory" sounds right for a baseball bat. Robert Fitzgerald uses it in his well-known baseball poem (p. 298), which has other quick-moving *i*-sequences as well:

> ... the baseman
> Gathers a grounder in fat green grass,
> Picks it stinging and clipped as wit
> Into the leather: a swinging step
> Wings it deadeye down to first....

It is easy to find other examples of expressive *i*'s:

> Slim pickerel glint
> in the water.... *Donald Hall*

near the winter river with silt like silver....
William Stafford

[a bird] flits nimble-winged in thickets....
Sylvia Plath

The short ŭ sound, *u* or *uh,* has a definite but disreputable personality. It has been called the "shudder vowel"—the *uh* or *ugh* we make when feeling horror or disgust. Pronouncing it is like clearing the throat or ejecting something from the mouth. The slang word "upchuck" (for *vomit*) has the appropriate sound. (Slang is frequently more sound conscious than standard English.) An investigation of hundreds of monosyllables has shown that the ŭ of "mud" has generally undesirable connotations. One scholar has listed many *uh* words that express dislike, disgust, or scorn: "blunder," "bungle," "clumsy," "humdrum," "slum," "slush," "muck," "muddle," "slut." We could all think of others: "dump," "crummy," "sludge," "chump," "bunk," "punk," "runt," "pus," "muss," "fuzz," "puffy," "repugnant."

Man saying "Ugh!"

When we sort of push a grunt up, with tongue, cheek, and lips left slack, what comes out is an *"Uh."* We use it as the hesitation sound, when we don't, uh, quite know what to say. Some of the better-known obscenities exploit its ŭgliness.

Any observations we make about sound and sense will have MANY exceptions. These in no way disprove the expressiveness of sound; they merely show that in some words that particular element is inert or subordinate to other considerations. We can all think of pleasant *uh* words: "young love," "summer," "cuddle," "comfort," "slumber," "lullaby," "yummy."

E. E. Cummings has combined the pleasant-unpleasant associations of ŭ and its slushy sound in his poem about the "mud-luscious," "puddle-wonderful" world of childhood.

CHANSONS INNOCENTES, I

in Just-
spring when the world is mud-
luscious the little
lame balloonman

whistles far and wee

and eddieandbill come
running from marbles and

piracies and it's
spring

when the world is puddle-wonderful 10

the queer
old balloonman whistles
far and wee
and bettyandisbel come dancing

from hop-scotch and jump-rope and
it's
spring
and
    the

        goat-footed 20

balloonMan whistles
far
and
wee

E. E. Cummings (1894–1962)

The seven low-frequency vowel sounds, resonated from the back of the mouth, owe their deeper tone to the larger volume of air set in motion. They are more mouth-filling because they have more mouth to fill. To many, *aw* will seem the most powerful of the vowel sounds, a hollow reverberation from far back in the throat, rougher, grander, larger than the even lower-frequency *oh* and *oo* sounds. Some find the word "God" more impressive when they drop the vowel a couple of notes and pronounce it "Gawd." Milton's "Lycidas" (p. 228) opens impressively with a string of three stressed *aw*'s:

Yet once more, O ye laurels, and once more . . . .

There are a half-dozen in the opening lines of *Paradise Lost*:

. . . that forbidden tree, whose mortal taste
Brought death into the world, and all our woe,
With loss of Eden, till one greater man
Restore us . . . .

One of Yeats' most sonorous lines is built on *aw*:

That dolphin-torn, that gong-tormented sea.

The vowel sound of lowest frequency is the *oo* of "moon." Because the lips are more rounded than for *oh* and the tongue a bit higher, *oo* picks up a flutelike quality from the narrower aperture. It sounds smoother, less hollow than the other deep tones. Helped by *b* and *m* it can indeed go "boo!" or "boom!" But since one of its formants, or constituent sounds, is the same as for the much higher *ee*, and since *oo* is articulated high in the mouth, it can also have an eerie crooning quality. Better than any description is the range of emotions for which Sylvia Plath uses it in the love-hate poem, all cooing and hooting, she wrote to the Teutonic "daddy" she felt had abandoned her by dying in her childhood. Of its eighty lines, over half end in *oo,* with such stanzas as:

> I have always been scared of *you,*
> With your Luftwaffe, your gobbledygoo.
> And your neat moustache
> And your Aryan eye, bright blue.
> Panzer-man, panzer-man, O You— . . . .
>
> Bit my pretty red heart in two.
> I was ten when they buried you.
> At twenty I tried to die
> And get back, back, back to you.
> I thought even the bones would do . . . .

Consonants

Vowels are produced by an unimpeded flow of breath. Consonants are produced by interference that sets up an audible turbulence or cuts off the airflow completely. It might seem that the fewer consonants we use, the more musical our speech would be. But consonant power is one of the glories of English. Hawaiian, by contrast, has a high percentage of vowels and cannot pronounce two consonants together—"Merry Christmas" comes out "Mele Kalikimaka." Hawaiian may seem "prettier" than English, but its effect has been called childlike and effeminate. It is the consonants that give shape and energy to our speech.

Like vowels, consonants have their distinctive characters, which are felt more emphatically in repetition. Such repetition at the beginning of words or syllables is called **alliteration.**

The most vowellike of the consonants are *w* and *y. W* is double *U*—an *oo* sound. When we read "Western Wind," we begin *"oo-estern oo-ind, hoo-en oo-ill* . . . ," with the *oo*'s gliding so rapidly into the following vowel that we are hardly aware of their *oo*ness at all. Vowellike *w*'s alliterate very smoothly.

> O sylvan Wye! thou wanderer through the woods . . . .
>
> *William Wordsworth*

> O wild west wind, thou breath of autumn's being . . . .
>
> *Percy Bysshe Shelley*

> It is a red bird that seeks out his choir
> Among the choirs of wind and wet and wing . . . .
>
> *Wallace Stevens*

It may be that the two *w*'s account for the popularity of the western wind among poets. The east wind seems to have had no such luck:

> When the wind is in the east,
> 'Tis neither good for man nor beast . . . .

Nor good for alliteration.

In the opinion of many, the common American *r* is more vowel than consonant. Except for custom, "bird" could just as well be spelled "brd." But since it has a dark throaty quality—especially when combined with a guttural like *g*—we use it to represent the growl or *grrrr* of an animal or angry man. Ben Jonson was not the first to call it the dog's letter. François Villon put his French *r* (then rolled) to amusing use when he wrote a ballade (p. 368) to a lady he was angry at; for twenty-eight lines his rhymes, all ending in *r*, snarl and snap at her.

The *r* and *l* are both called *liquid sounds*. They seem to flow on or around the tongue instead of being clicked or popped or hissed forth. Probably *l* would win a popularity contest for the prettiest vowel sound. Lord Byron makes fun of the overuse of soft *l*'s:

> When amatory poets sing their loves
> In liquid lines mellifluously bland . . . .

He would probably not have objected to the less conspicuous *l*'s with which Yeats' old woman wonders:

> What lively lad most pleasured me
> Of all that with me lay?

Ben Jonson said *l* was called a liquid because "it melteth in the sounding." More down-to-earth theorists have noticed that the sound seems to be formed low in the mouth, near the surface of the tongue and the inner surface of the lower teeth, which are more bathed in saliva than other parts of the mouth. Saliva-bathed or not, *l* does go well with liquidity:

> And on a sudden, lo! the level lake
> And the long glories of the winter moon.
>
> *Alfred, Lord Tennyson*

> I hear lake water lapping with low sounds
> by the shore . . . . *William Butler Yeats*

> . . . large-lobed ladies laughing in brook water . . . .
>
> *A. R. Ammons*

The *m, n,* and *ng* sounds are known as *nasals*. The airflow is diverted into the nasal passages to vibrate there. We can feel the change in our mouth by sounding the three in sequence: "bam," "ban," "bang."

We use an *m* sound—sometimes conventionalized as "yum!"—for warm appreciation. Probably no other consonant is so expressive by itself. In reply to "Do you like my dress?" a perfectly intelligible answer would be "Mmmmmmmm!" The sound is prolonged, not broken off; is internal (behind closed lips) and hence warm and cherished; is associated with the affectionate and sensitive lips, which bring the human child the first pleasure it knows—food and the warm presence of its mother. It has been noticed that *m* occurs in the word for "mother" in many languages, presumably because this is the sound happy babies make. Because it is about the only sound we can make with closed lips, we hum it when engaged in such pleasurable activities as eating something or kissing someone.

The sound of *n* is somewhat higher in tone, more a whine than a hum. It is smaller and sharper than an *m*; it seems to pick up a bony hardness from being sounded near the roof of the mouth. We might think of mosquitoes as going *"Nnnnnn,"* but not *"Mmmmmm."* The suggestion has been made that its through-the-nose quality accounts for its presence in words of negation in many languages: "no," "non," "nicht," etc.

The *ng* sound has a metallic resonance that qualifies it for many sound words: "bang," "boing," "bong," "clang," "ding-dong," "gong," "jangle," "ping," "ring," etc. Gary Snyder uses it for both of the sounds he mentions in his poem on page 7: the "ringing tire iron" and the "whang of a saw."

The seven sounds we have so far discussed have been called semi-vowels; they would probably be thought of as the most musical of the consonants.

The sounds known as *fricatives* are produced by audible friction over something that interferes with the airflow from the lungs. They include: *h*; *f*, *v*; *th* ("thing"), *dh* ("that"); *s*, *z*; *sh*, *zh* ("pleasure"). The *h* is only a roughness in the breath, the rasp of air through the vocal cords as they get in place for the vowel that follows.

In *f* and *v*, turbulence is heard as the air passes between the lower lip and the upper teeth. Both sounds are pleasantly soft, probably a writer's favorite fricatives.

> Snow falling and night falling fast, oh, fast
> In a field I looked into going past .... *Robert Frost*

Coleridge may have the record with six *f*'s in two lines, followed quickly by a seventh:

> The fair breeze blew, the white foam flew,
> The furrow followed free;
> We were the first that ever burst
> Into that silent sea.

When the breath hisses between tongue and teeth, the result is an *s* sound. Jonson spoke of it with mixed feelings: "a most easy and gentle letter, and softly hisseth against the teeth ... it is called the serpent's letter." Ancient critics looked down on it as "more suited to a brute beast than to a rational being." Tennyson tried to get rid of *s*'s; he called it "kicking the geese out of the boat." Robert Graves says his deathbed advice will be: "The art of poetry consists in knowing exactly how to manipulate the letter S." Graves finds Shelley particularly crude in his handling of *s* sounds, as in these lines from "Ode to the West Wind":

> Thou on whose stream, mid the steep sky's commotion,
> Loose clouds like earth's decaying leaves are shed ....
>
> ... when to outstrip thy skiey speed
> Scarce seemed a vision ....

Sometimes a writer makes his lines hiss on purpose. One famous example is the conspiratorial whisper of Macbeth:

> ... if the assassination
> Could trammel up the consequence and catch,
> With his surcease, success ....

Many of the sounds we have been considering can change their character in the company of other sounds. The *sn* and *st* might be taken as typical.

Woman saying "Sn— !"

Of the words that start with *sn*, only a few are pleasant: "snow," "snuggle," "snug," etc. Most are unpleasant: "snag," "snare," "snake," "sneak," "snide," "snitch," "snob," "snoop," "snub," etc. One large group of *sn* words has to do with the nose: "sneeze," "sniff," "snuffle," "snivel," "snoot," "snore," "snort," "snout," "snuff," "sneer," etc. Darwin thought that "sneer" and "snarl" were related, and that both were produced by muscular contractions like those of a snarling dog, with lip drawn back to expose the threatening canine tooth.

Many words beginning with *st* mean things that "stand steady" or are "stable" or "stabilized"; or that support something, like "staff," "stake," "stem," "stilt," "stirrup," "strut," "stud"; or that are somehow strong, like "stern," "stiff," "strict," "stubborn," "sturdy," "stag," "steed"; or that show energetic action, like "stalk," "stamp," "storm," "stun."

> And she who seemed eaten by cankering care
> In statuesque sturdiness stalks .... *Thomas Hardy*

A. E. Housman almost builds a poem around seventeen *st*'s as his statue urges a drooping youth to stand strong.

LOITERING WITH A VACANT EYE

Loitering with a vacant eye
Along the Grecian gallery,
And brooding on my heavy ill,
I met a statue standing still.
Still in marble stone stood he,
And stedfastly he looked at me.
'Well met,' I thought the look would say,
'We both were fashioned far away;
We neither knew, when we were young,
These Londoners we live among.' 10

Still he stood and eyed me hard,
An earnest and a grave regard:
'What, lad, drooping with your lot?
I too would be where I am not.

I too survey that endless line
Of men whose thoughts are not as mine.
Years, ere you stood up from rest,
On my neck the collar prest;
Years, when you lay down your ill,
I shall stand and bear it still. 20
Courage, lad, 'tis not for long:
Stand, quit you like stone, be strong.'
So I thought his look would say;
And light on me my trouble lay,
And I stept out in flesh and bone
Manful like the man of stone.

A. E. Housman

Robert Graves, often a skeptic in these matters, commends the muscular *str* words as being like what they mean: "strain," "strength," "strangle," "struggle," "strike," "strive," etc.

Sh, sounded farther back in the mouth, is less sharp but has more body than *s*. We use it, as a kind of "white noise," to overpower other sounds when we say, "Shhhh!" or "Hush!"—whereas "Sssss!" is to get attention or express disapproval.

The final group of consonants—*p, b*; *t, d*; *k, g*—called *stops* (or *plosives* or *explosives*), are more drastic. They cut off the air for a moment, let pressure build up behind the barrier of lips or tongue, then release it with a tiny explosion. With *p* and *b*, the most forceful of the consonant sounds, it is the lips that block and explode the air. Repetitions of *p* call instant attention to themselves by sounding like the "Peter Piper picked . . ." tongue twister. Carolyn Kizer packs several into one line for sarcasm:

You can wait for the menopause, and catch up on your reading.
So primp, preen, prink, pluck and prize your flesh,
All posturings! All ravishment! All sensibility!

The *b* can be almost as obstreperous. When Shakespeare wants to make fun of excessive alliteration (consonant repetition), *b* is the letter he chooses for his ridicule:

Whereat, with blade, with bloody blameful blade,
He bravely broached his boiling bloody breast . . . .

Sylvia Plath uses *p* and *b* for the texture of rocky soil:

What flinty pebbles the ploughblade upturns . . . .

Other contemporaries have used these stops for abrupt physical motion:

The lobbed ball plops, then dribbles in the cup . . . .
Robert Lowell

Plop, plop. The lobster toppled in the pot . . . .
John Berryman

Browning put the exuberance of *b* to good use in describing the buxom abundance of a woman's body:

> Was a lady such a lady, cheeks so round and lips so red,—
> On her neck the small face buoyant, like a bell-flower on its bed,
> O'er the breast's superb abundance where a man might base his head?

A *p* (and a *b* almost as well) can express rejection by holding back the air and then violently expelling it, as in "Pooh!" or "Bunk!" Comic strips use the spit sound "*Ptui!*" for disgust. (The classical Greek word for "spit" was almost the same—*ptuo*.) Such words originate, it seems, in the natural mouth movements of the act of spitting. When we pronounce *p* or *sp*, the muscles of the mouth mimic disgust—which means that, if disgust happens to be what we feel, we can throw ourselves more completely, with more body English, into what we are saying.

When we pronounce *t* or *d*, the air is stopped by the tongue tip, which is clicked against the ridge behind the teeth. The effect is neater, trimmer than with the more explosive *p* and *b*; clocks and watches show a sense of fitness in saying "ticktock" instead of "bing bang."

When we pronounce *k* or *g* (a hard *g*, as in "guttural," not as in "gesture"), the airflow is stopped farther back toward the throat by the bunched-up back of the tongue. Particularly when reinforced with *r* or the deeper vowels, these give us the most throaty sound available—as in "choke," "crow," "gag," "gargle."

> Crows crowd croaking overhead . . . . *John Clare*

> . . . blue-bleak embers . . .
> fall, gall themselves, and gash gold-vermilion.
> *Gerard Manley Hopkins*

Alliteration is as old as language. Babies alliterate before they can speak a sentence: "da-da," "bye-bye." We all know what alliteration can do for a slogan or catch phrase. Political sloganeers revel in it. Alliterative phrases have entwined themselves into the language we use every day. One could find hundreds of examples like "house and home," "rack and ruin," "spick and span," "rough and ready," "a dime a dozen," "in the fourth and final quarter." Driving into Tennessee from the north, one passes a restaurant–gas station called "Tank 'n' Tummy," among fireworks dealers known as "Goofy Goober," "Lonely Luke," "Crazy Charley," and—with assonance—"Loco Joe." Somebody believes in sound values!

Alliteration can, like any useful thing, be vulgarized by overuse. Politicians and ad-men are probably the most flagrant offenders. But poets have also been at fault. Edmund Spenser, coming on the line

> For lofty love doth loathe a lowly eye . . .

objected to this "playing with the letter." Good alliteration, however, is much more than a literary gewgaw. It can create a bond of identity between words, hinting that if they have a sound in common, perhaps they have something more.

Their treasure is their only trust . . . .
Sir Edward Dyer

So all their praises are but prophecies
Of this our time, all you prefiguring . . .
William Shakespeare

Of man's first disobedience, and the fruit
Of that forbidden tree . . . . *John Milton*

It can also represent, by its muchness of sound, any kind of muchness:

Great England's glory and the world's wide wonder . . .
Edmund Spenser

Fish, flesh and fowl, commend all summer long
Whatever is begotten, born, and dies . . . .
William Butler Yeats

Mao's own mountain of murderd men,
the alliteration of ems like Viet Nam's
burnd villages . . . . *Robert Duncan*

Or weary repetition:

The plowman homeward plods his weary way . . . .
Thomas Gray

It may link words together by sound only to contrast their meaning:

O in all place and shape and kind
Beyond all thought and thinking,
The graceful with the gross combined,
The stately with the stinking . . . .
Arthur Hugh Clough

It may be a mark of abundant energy:

To leap large lengths of miles when thou art gone . . . .
William Shakespeare

Clinging alliteration can stand for clinging things:

Nor cast one longing lingering look behind . . .
Thomas Gray

And though it loved in misery
Close and cling so tight,
There's not a bird of day that dare
Extinguish that delight. *William Butler Yeats*

. . . the stale
steak grease stuck to her fuzzy leaves . . . .
Theodore Roethke

In writing about the bewildering death of a little girl (p. 131), John Crowe Ransom uses stiff alliteration for two kinds of immobility:

In one house we are sternly stopped
To say we are vexed at her brown study,
Lying so primly propped.

Assonance can serve the same purposes as alliteration, though often more subtly.

Exercises and Diversions

A. About such matters as we have been discussing in this chapter, the Roman critic Quintilian once wrote: "Studies of this kind harm only those who stick in them, not those who pass through them." Explore the implications of his remark, particularly in regard to our treatment of sound.

B. 1. If you *whisper* the words "June," "Joan," "John," "Jan," "Jen," "Gin," "Jane," "Jean," in that order, you should be able to feel how the vowel sounds move progressively up the scale. *Whisper* them in reverse order, and they descend. See if you can manage the contrary; that is, whisper from "June" to "Jean" so that you make the sounds go down the scale, and from "Jean" to "June" so that they go up.

2. What do you notice about the use of sound in Vliet's "Games, Hard Press and Bruise . . ." (p. 8)?
3. What do you notice about the use of sound in Pound's "Alba" (p. 15)?
4. Shakespeare's "Sonnet 129" (p. 116) was referred to earlier as a poem of disgust or revulsion. The poem is full of expressively ugly sounds. Point them out.

C. In each of the following quotations, some sound effect is conspicuous. Decide, with each, if it is too conspicuous. Or are the sounds appropriate and expressive?

1. Oh for that night! When I in Him
Might live invisible and dim. — *Henry Vaughan*

2. I saw, alas! some dread event impend. . . . — *Alexander Pope*

3. A vacant sameness grays the sky. . . . — *Thomas Hardy*

4. The mother looked him up and down,
And laughed—a scant laugh with a rattle. — *Edwin Arlington Robinson*

5. Here in this good green scene above the sea. . . . — *John Ciardi*

6. Tossed
by the muscular sea,
we are lost,
and glad to be lost
in troughs of rough
love. — *May Swenson*

7. . . . A rook's wet wing
Cuffed abruptly upward through the drizzle. — *Thomas Kinsella*

8. . . . salt flats,
Gas tanks, factory stacks, that landscape. . . . — *Sylvia Plath*

9. While the cock . . .
. . . to the stack, or the barn door,
Stoutly struts his dames before. . . . — *John Milton*

10. Gr-r-r—there go, my heart's abhorrence!
Water your damned flower-pots, do! *Robert Browning*

11. From the sails the dew did drip. . . . *Samuel Taylor Coleridge*

12. On Jordan's banks the Arab's camels stray. . . . *George Gordon, Lord Byron*

13. Up many and many a marvellous shrine
Whose wreathèd friezes intertwine
The viol, the violet, and the vine. . . . *Edgar Allan Poe*

14. For me, the firefly's quick, electric stroke
Ticks tediously the time of one more year. . . . *Wallace Stevens*

15. my father moved through dooms of love
through sames of am through haves of give. . . . *E. E. Cummings*

16. The other cut through the thicket, the thorns and vines. . . . *Lisel Mueller*

17. Till I see her glittering eye
Has taken this thought exactly
As the toad's tongue takes a fly. . . . *Howard Nemerov*

18. Shallows slosh over rocks with a washing sound. . . . *Gray Burr*

19. The window showed a willow in the west,
But windy dry. No folly weeping there. *James Wright*

D. 1. In 1655 Milton wrote one of his greatest sonnets to protest an atrocity of the time, the slaughter in the mountains of over 1,000 members of the Vaudois by the Duke of Savoy. How is sound used expressively? (Notice that sounds at the end of lines are especially prominent—even more so when they happen to rhyme.)

ON THE LATE MASSACRE IN PIEDMONT

Avenge, O Lord, thy slaughtered saints, whose bones
Lie scattered on the Alpine mountains cold,
Even them who kept thy truth so pure of old
When all our fathers worshiped stocks and stones
Forget not: in thy book record their groans
Who were thy sheep and in their ancient fold
Slain by the bloody Piedmontese that rolled
Mother with infant down the rocks. Their moans
The vales redoubled to the hills, and they
To Heaven. Their martyred blood and ashes sow 10
O'er all th' Italian fields where still doth sway
The triple tyrant: that from these may grow
A hundredfold, who having learnt thy way
Early may fly the Babylonian woe.

John Milton (1608–1674)

E. 1. Think of ten other common alliterating phrases like "might and main," "friend or foe," etc.

2. We discussed words beginning with *sn* and *st*. Do you find any pattern in words beginning with *bl* and *br*? (Recall words you know, like "blare" and "brisk," or skim a dictionary.) The following little poem seems to mean

that without the dark side of life we would not properly value the bright side. Is the sound appropriate?

LOVE AND DEATH

And yet a kiss (like blubber) 'd blur and slip,
Without the assuring skull beneath the lip.

F. Write a short poem or paragraph on an "up" theme, using many high-frequency vowels. Do the same with a "down" theme, using many low-frequency vowels.

(You might also enjoy reversing the process to see what happens: write on an "up" theme using "down" vowels, etc.)

Working with Gold 12 the devices of sound

Language as Mimicry

Poetry used to be magic. Far away and long ago, among people simpler than most of us, poetic formulas, perhaps in rhyme or some other form of sound-play, were thought to bring rain or put a curse on an enemy or charm someone into loving. In all such spells, as we recall from fairy tales, the sound was as important as the sense. Origen, the third-century theologian from Egypt who wrote in Greek, mentions certain charms found useful in ridding one's house of devils; he cautions, however, that they will not work in translation. Not because devils are poor linguists, but because the power of the formula lay in the sound itself. The aspects of language we will be concerned with in this chapter may seem more a matter of magic than of science.

Some 15,000 years ago, when the glaciers of the last Ice Age drove our ancestors into cave openings near the Mediterranean, reindeer, natives of the Arctic tundra, roamed freely over what are now the resort areas of the Riviera. Earth dwellers had been human for hundreds of thousands of years before the Ice Age, but early man comes before us with particular vividness when we see the cave drawings he made in those centuries. They exist for us in a soundless world. "Many of the painted caves are really very terrifying places; the silence is intense, broken only occasionally by a distant boom when a drop of water falls from the roof into some silent pool below."[1] But the artist did not live in a world of silence. Ice and gravel crackled underfoot, thunder roared and reechoed, animals made the same cries and growls that, if extant, they make today.

[1] M. Burkitt, *The Old Stone Age* (New York: New York University Press, 1956), p. 216.

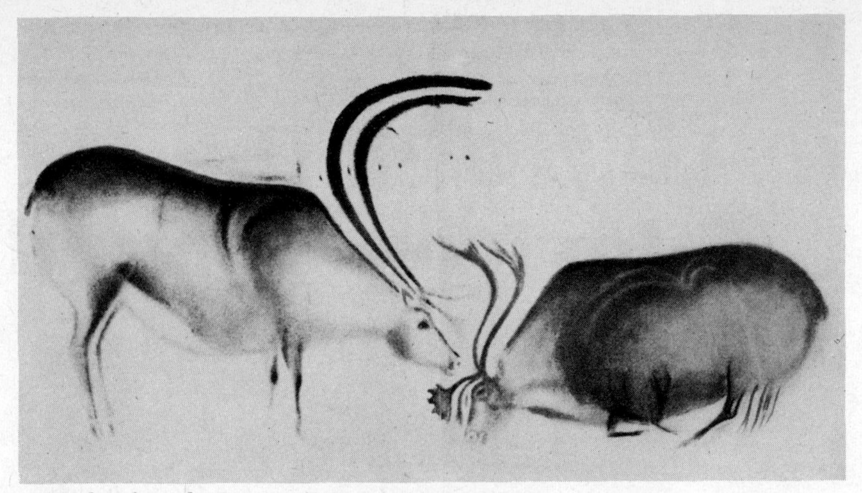

Reindeer from the Caverns of Font-de-Gaume, France

The men who did these sensitive drawings must have used their built-in sound systems to imitate animals or the sounds of nature. Many an early man, crouched by his fire near the cave mouth and listening to thunder reverberating among the rocks, must have amused or frightened himself and his companions by making thunder sounds deep in his throat—probably bursting into wild, delighted laughter at his success or lack of it. Likely enough man's earliest words for thunder would be thunder sounds—as "thunder" itself seems to be.

When our cave man let rumbling sounds roll around in his throat, he was beginning to use what we call **onomatopoeia.** The Greek word means *name making,* as if something in nature made its own name by sounds associated with it—as a dog does for a child when it seems to say "bowwow." These verbal mimicries are as deeply rooted in human nature as the desire to draw is. We know that children find them expressive: Not only the "choo-choo" and "ticktock," they learn from others, but also the words they originate themselves, like the "ffttt" one little boy made up as a name for soda water or the "pooh" one little girl called a match, from the sound made in blowing it out. Onomatopoetic words occur in primitive languages all over the world. Comic strips rely heavily on them. One had this sound track for a fight sequence: "KAK . . . BTAK . . . FTAK . . . BUTOOP . . . YAGGHHHH . . . KAPOWK . . . FOOM . . . SZAK . . . BOK . . . THWIK . . . THAK . . . BRUP . . . KLIP!" "Thump," "thud," and other such words may have originated as *btak* or *foom* sounds long ago. Dictionaries show many words described as "of imitative origin"—"giggle," "gargle," "whizz," "bang," "pop," "sizzle," etc. A dictionary of American slang gives a long list of more recent inventions, such as "beep," "bebop," "boing," "burp," "clunk," "ding-a-ling," "plunk," "putt-putt," "smooch," "yackety-yak."

If our caveman of 15,000 years ago did rumble his thunder sounds, he was doing no more than men had done long before him and would be doing long afterward. John Keats made thunder sounds in his way:

> A shout from the whole multitude arose,
> That lingered in the air like dying rolls
> Of abrupt thunder, when Ionian shoals
> Of dolphins bob their noses through the brine....

Six deep *oh* sounds, the dull *u*'s of "abrupt thunder," and perhaps the *ah*'s of "dolphins bob."

Another cave painting shows men or long-haired girls climbing a high tree to rob a swarm of wild bees of its honey. The bees are swirling around the extended arms of one of the figures. The bee-robbers would surely have talked of their experience, and talking of it would surely have made sounds like *mmmmmmmmmmm* or *uuuuzzzz* or *buzzzz* to describe the angry bees. If so, they would have been doing what Tennyson did thousands of years later in his

> The moan of doves in immemorial elms,
> And murmuring of innumerable bees....

Some are skeptical of onomatopoeia because, although dogs, cats, falling objects, thunder, etc., make the same sounds all over the world, speakers of different languages have different words to represent the sounds. We may think we hear "bowwow" when a dog barks. But a Spaniard hears "¡guau! ¡guau!"; a Frenchman, "ouâ-ouâ"; a German, "waŭwau"; a Swede, "vov-vov." Hawaiian dogs bark in vowels: "aoaoao." Russian dogs go "ГАВ, ГАВ." Ancient Greek dogs said, "*βάυ, βάυ*." If human beings cannot even agree on how a dog barks, some may feel, what good is onomatopoeia?

But these dog sounds do have something in common. One can hardly imagine a language in which barking would be represented by "twee-twee" or "sisszizz." The barks are unlike because different languages have different ways of putting sounds together. A French dog would not say "bowwow" because French uses a *w* only in foreign words. Why should French dogs bark like foreigners in their own country?

Such sound words are produced by the limited resources of our vocal equipment, which pretends, not very successfully, to be something else. And which has to produce a word that can be written down. But how can we *spell* the way a dog barks? Or spell the sound of the rain or the rush of wind in the trees or any of the nonhuman sounds? Our onomatopoetic words are like imitations done in another medium —as when Prokofiev, in *Peter and the Wolf,* uses different musical instruments to represent human and animal noises. The sound of a clarinet is not really like that of a cat nor an oboe like that of a duck nor three French horns like that of a wolf. "Sizzle" is a good onomatopoetic word, yet we could stand in the kitchen and say "sizzle" until we were blue in the face and no one would really think bacon was cooking.

Most sound words are expressive only *after* we know their meaning —the sound alone communicates little. Tennyson's line about the bees has been facetiously rewritten as

The murdering of innumerable beeves

to cast suspicion on sound effects. But the *m* sounds, relevant to the humming of bees, have now lost all meaning: no one would claim that they relate well to murder or to cattle (unless the latter were mooing at the time). Since onomatopoeia, like other sound effects we have considered, can only reinforce or dramatize a meaning we already know is there, its utility is very limited. One seldom finds a poem constructed as wholly for sound effects as the following two are. Both are deliberately noisy. (The spelling in the blacksmith poem, written about 1450, is somewhat modernized.)

SWART-SMEKED SMITHES

Swart-smeked smithes smattered with smoke
Drive me to death with din of their dints!
Such noise on nights ne heard men never.
What knavene cry & clattering of knocks!
The cammede kongons cryen after "Coal! Coal!"
And blowen their bellows that all their brain bursts.
"Huff! puff!" sayeth that one; "Haff! paff!" that other.
They spitten & sprawlen & spellen many spells;
They gnawen & gnashen, they groan together,
And holden them hot with their hard hammers. 10
Of a bull-hide been their barm-fells;
Their shanks been shackled for the fire-flinders.
Heavy hammers they have that hard been handled;
Stark strokes they stricken on a steeled stock;
Luss, buss! Lass, dass! rowten by row.

---

[1] **swart-smeked:** *smoked black*
smattered: *grimy*
[2] **dints:** *blows*
[3] **ne heard men never:** *men never heard*
[4] **knavene cry:** *workmen's cry*
[5] **cammede kongons:** *Tolkien, the author of the famous Hobbit stories, thinks the first word means either* snub-nosed *or* crooked. *The second means something like* changeling. *A phrase like* ugly bastards *would probably be truer to the tone of the original.*
[8] **spellen many spells:** *tell many stories*
[11] **barm-fells:** *leather aprons*
[12] **shackled:** *protected with shinguards*
fire-flinders: *fiery sparks*
[14] **steeled stock:** *steel anvil*
[15] **rowten by row:** [*they*] *crash in turn*

Such doleful a dreme the devil it to-drive!
The master longeth a little & lasheth a less,
Twineth them twain & toucheth a treble.
Tick, tack! Hick, hack! Ticket, tacket! Tick, tack!
Luss, buss! Luss, dass! Such life they leaden! 20
All clothe-mares, Christ give them sorrow!
May no man for burn-waters on night have his rest!

Anonymous (c. 1450)

PLAYER PIANO

My stick fingers click with a snicker
And, chuckling, they knuckle the keys;
Light-footed, my steel feelers flicker
And pluck from these keys melodies.

My paper can caper; abandon
Is broadcast by dint of my din,
And no man or band has a hand in
The tones I turn on from within.

At times I'm a jumble of rumbles,
At others I'm light like the moon, 10
But never my numb plunker fumbles,
Misstrums me, or tries a new tune.

John Updike (b. 1932)

In onomatopoeia, the sound of a word is supposed to imitate a sound associated with its meaning. Suppose we are dealing not with sound at all, but with some other category of experience. Are words then in any way like what they mean? Children think they are. A five-year-old, in Colorado for the first time, was heard to exclaim, "Those are mountains, daddy? There ought to be a bigger word for *those!*" So do poets. Alexander Pope was thinking like the child when he wrote:

I'd call them mountains, but can't call them so,
For fear to wrong them with a name too low . . . .

In an ideal language, many believe, sound and sense would be in perfect accord. Humpty Dumpty was thinking along these lines when he asked Alice what her name meant.

"*Must* a name mean something?" Alice asked doubtfully.

"Of course it must," Humpty Dumpty said with a short laugh, "my name

---

16 **such doleful a dreme:** *so dreadful a racket*
to-drive: *drive away*
17-18 **The master longeth . . . a treble:** *It is not completely clear what noisy operation the master smith is performing. Perhaps it means that he beats a little piece till it is longer, pounds a smaller one, twists the two together, and strikes a shrill note.*
21 **clothe-mares:** *horse-dressers, men who make armor for horses.*
22 **burn-waters:** *blacksmiths (because their hot iron steams in water)*

means the shape I am—and a good handsome shape it is, too. With a name like yours, you might be any shape, almost."

Humpty Dumpty's idea of the meaningfulness of names is at least as old as the second chapter of Genesis: ". . . the Lord God formed every beast of the field, and every fowl of the air; and brought them unto Adam to see what he would call them: and whatsoever Adam called every living creature, that was the name thereof." Biblical scholars point out that for the Hebrews names were thought of as symbols, magic keys to the nature, character, or role of the bearer. John Hollander's poem "Adam's Task" is about Adam giving appropriate names to the strange beasts:

> Thou, paw-paw-paw; thou, glurd; thou, spotted
>   Glurd; thou, whitestap, lurching through
> The high-grown brush; thou, pliant-footed,
>   Implex; thou, awagabu . . . .

One would have to see these fabulous animals to judge the appropriateness of the names. A "glurd" might glow, like Blake's tiger (though in a sort of a blur), as it glides. An "awagabu" sounds waggy and sinuous—perhaps a bit like the "ongologo," a word certain primitive tribes use for the centipede. An "ongologo" would have to have a lot of something.

Plato, in his *Cratylus*, may be the first philosopher to have discussed an ideal language based on sound. In the dialogue, Socrates (who is sometimes joking) entertains the notion that words should not be merely arbitrary or conventional, but natural as well—something in their being should correspond to the nature of what they denote. The letter *r* belongs in words of motion because (in the trilled *r*) there is more activity in the mouth than for any other sound. *L* is for looseness or fluidity, since the tongue seems to slip in pronouncing it. But the heavier *g* in front of *l* will slow it down and make it sticky—as in our word "glue." If we could use such likenesses, says Socrates, "this would be the most perfect state of language."

Such a language might be ideal, and it would certainly be fun to use. But Plato knew that a language like that had never existed and probably never would, since there are only certain categories of objects, qualities, or experiences that can be matched up with certain sounds. Some sounds may be *harder, faster, larger, stickier* than other sounds, but how can they be more *possible,* more *true,* or more *virtuous*?

In everyday life, the sound of a word is not of much immediate importance. No one would refuse to cry "Fire!" or "Help!" because he felt the word had an inappropriate combination of vowels and consonants.

But a good writer, the critic Herbert Read believes, will pick and choose among the existing words for those that "by some subtle combination of vowel and consonant suggest by a seeming appropriateness the quality or kind of object named." Beyond simple onomatopoeia, he finds two subtly appropriate classes of words: those in which movement of lips, tongue, and cheek, together with suggestive sound, simulate the action described—as in "blare," "flare," "brittle," "whistle," "creep," "scrabble," "puddle," "shiver," "fiddle," "sling," "globe"—and those in which sounds are not imitative, but suggestive musical equivalents—as in "swoon," "mood," "sheen," "horror," "smudge," "jelly."

We can figure out the "magic" of most of these. "Blare" and "flare" have a big, loose lip movement. "Brittle" breaks in two in the middle. "Sling" hisses—*sssss*—and then lets go suddenly—*llll-ING!* "Mood" is a deep-inside sound. "Horror" catches in the throat. Even some very ordinary words strike us as having a physical rightness about them. The word "match" moved a classical scholar to exclaim, "How admirably it catches the scrape of sulphurated stick on emery!" Jespersen likes the word "roll," as in *rolling along.* It is a word one can keep rolling around in one's mouth; *r, o,* and *l* can all be sounded as long as one wants or has breath for. Whereas the Russian word for "roll" (*katat'* or *katit'*) sounds like something bumping along on square wheels. "Level" is a word like its meaning, sounding the same forward or backward and ending as levelly as it began. "Uneven," however, has that little bump of an accent sticking up in the middle. One well-known maker of jams and jellies has shown that it knows people are sensitive to sound suggestion by turning its own rather ugly name to account. "With a name like Smucker's," say the labels, "it has to be good."

Not many of us take the sound of words as seriously as the hero of Peter De Vries' novel *Witch's Milk* did. With a poet's instinct, he felt that all the words having to do with sex in English had a wrong and ugly sound. So he proceeded to create a wholly new sexual vocabulary.

He said that the English vocabulary for sex was hopeless, very nearly all down the line. There were only the coarse words on the one hand, and, on the other, the bookish ones, hardly less embarrassing. There was nothing in between, nothing really and honestly usable for two people. But he not only talked about it; he did something about it. He applied himself to filling this need by revamping the entire erotic vocabulary.

For every organ or act for which a foul or a stilted word was the only existing alternative, he tried to think of a suitable one, from the phonetic and other standpoints. He kept a notebook of his creations, tirelessly changing, resubstituting, polishing and perfecting, till his scholarship yielded at last a finished dictionary, and they had a whole new glossary for "thrunkling," as the act was now called. The word was deliberately devised to convey implications of muffled intimate uproar, of drunken bedded ecstasies, and so much more. It packed a host of related concepts such as throbbing, rumpling, tumbling, grunting, humping, pumping, and Christ knew what all. Even spelunking, with its Freudian overtones of darkly penetrated mammalian caverns, was embedded in it (though not always with the speaker's awareness, of course, and possibly not even Pete's, except on a subliminal level which was the important one). Poe had not put more painstaking and systematic thought into what combination of syllables would best communicate melancholy, before deciding on Ulalume for that.

When the lexicon was finished, he showed it to her with an air of long, exhausted inquiry, like one showing you a thesis that must be his life's work. She read it through with nods and murmurs of approval. "Very good," she said. "Some of these are marvellous. So expressive. So onomatopoeic."

"Vut?"
"They combine sense with sound."

His devotion to the sound of words and his loving endeavors to purify the dialect of the tribe are a very good account of the poet at work.

What we are dealing with is a form of synesthesia (p. 63) that tries to provide an equivalent in sound for appearance, smell, taste, touch, and movement. Such "sound images" occur in primitive languages all over the world. Most of us know that there are analogies between the senses, and that the imagination likes to play with them. Very hot curry, for example, tastes more like a bright color—yellow or red—than like a pastel gray or lavender. Anyone sensuously alive feels these correspondences. Saint Augustine, among other things a professor of rhetoric, was well aware of synesthesia as a source of vocal appropriateness. After speaking of sound-words used to denote actual sounds, he says, "But since there are things which have no sound, for these the analogy of touch comes into play: if they touch the sense smoothly or roughly, smoothness or roughness of touch is heard in the letters. . . ."

The reason why the poet likes to unite sound and sense should be clear from all we have been saying about poetry, which speaks not merely for the brain but for the whole human being, body and mind. When sound goes along with sense, the meaning of a poem becomes *physicalized.* It resists the authoritarianism of the intellect, which claims the right to force a meaning on any combination of sounds, regardless of their nature. Appropriate sound invites the body to participate in the being of a poem, just as the poet's body participated in its creation.

A Reason for Rhyme?

When we say "neither rhyme nor reason," we imply that rhyme lies outside the domain of reason. In a way it does, though we can see some of the reasons for its appeal. If in the pages that follow we seem to be devoting inordinate attention to it, we are doing so because it can stand for those other "magical" devices of sound that poets use to keep their language from being too purely rational.

Although for about a generation now rhyme has been out of favor with many of the poets (but not with the song writers and folksingers), we are beginning to see signs of a resurgence of interest in what has been a feature of English poetry for most of the eight centuries it has existed.

Poetry, of course, does not *have* to rhyme. Many of the poems we have read are without rhyme and live quite happily that way. All we are doing in this section is investigating what rhyme has to contribute when it is present. The inquiry may not be as simple as it seems. One modern authority finds rhyme to be the most mysterious of all sound patterns. With it we are back once more in the world of magic and unreason.

When Lord Byron writes,

> There's not a sea the passenger e'er pukes in
> Turns up more dangerous breakers than the Euxine

his lines are vitalized by the rhyme. The effect is gone if we read:

> There's not a sea the passenger e'er pukes in
> Turns up more dangerous breakers than the Black Sea.

The ingenuity and impudence of linking by sound the folksy "pukes in" with the classical name for the Black Sea are what give these lines their electric tingle. This is the way good rhyme likes to work. It likes to spark a current of thought or emotion between two poles.

Rhyme is by no means the special property of poets. Expressions like "fair and square," "rough and tough," "moaning and groaning," and such reduplicating ones as "willy-nilly," "shilly-shally," "hocus-pocus" show how it has worked itself into the fabric of the language. As fast as slang changes, it still retains its fondness for rhyme. One decade says, "See you later, alligator"; another says "super-duper" or "slick chick." When a tall basketball player is named Wilt, he naturally becomes Wilt the Stilt. Furry Lewis, the blues composer, says:

> The time when you get a blues . . . you have to go all over it again until you rhyme it. It got to be rhymed up if you call yourself being with the blues. If it ain't rhymed up it don't sound good to me or nobody else.

Arlo Guthrie gives up logic for rhyme when he sings:

> I don't want a pickle,
> Just want to ride on my motorsickle . . . .

The origin of rhyme is mysterious. So is the reason for its great appeal. One of the most mysterious things about it, as Paul Valéry observed, is the rage it inspires in those who fail to see its function.

Probably the commonest objection to rhyme is that it prevents the poet from saying what he wants to say—which (defenders of rhyme would retort) is like the hurdler complaining that the hurdles get in his way. In any field, power shows itself in the ease with which obstacles are overcome.

Another objection is that rhyme is associated with so much bad poetry that it is no longer fit to associate with good poetry. It is certainly true that much bad poetry is in rhyme. Bad rhyming can be boring, can give us "the sure returns of still expected rhyme"—like the "June"/"moon" and the "breeze"/"trees" that Pope objected to:

> Where'er you find the cooling western breeze,
> In the next line it whispers through the trees . . . .

There are other expected rhymes: "breath" can only bring up "death"; "mountains" are fond of "fountains"; "anguish" means that someone is bound to "languish"; and "kiss" leads to "bliss" so inevitably that Byron could make fun of the pair:

> "Kiss" rhymes to "bliss" in fact as well as verse—
> I wish it never led to something worse....

Rhyme is made up of a sameness plus a difference. The sameness, the fixed element, is an accented vowel sound, like the *oh* in "poet," "know it," "show it." Any sounds coming after the accented vowel must be identical: "form"/"storm"; "bonnet"/"sonnet"; "tenderly"/"slenderly." The difference, the variable, is in what comes before: "form"/"storm," etc.

Rhyme, by no means peculiar to English, seems to be an almost universal phenomenon. It is found in the poetry of many primitive peoples. Chances are it goes back, long before written records, to the very beginnings of verse. One does not have to be an expert in African languages to recognize it in a song of the Gabon Pygmies:

> Msore i nia n'fare,
> Msore i nia n'sare.

Nor does one have to know Swahili to recognize the rhyme in four consecutive lines ending with *jehazi, ngazi, wazi, mjakazi.* Rhyme occurs in Chinese verse from the earliest times; one authority deplores that most translations give us no inkling of this. Long before the time of the medieval monks in England, rhyme flourished in Ireland and Wales. Irish missionaries may have brought it to the continent. Or perhaps it came from Arabia, whose culture may have given the Provençal poets of the twelfth century their interest in elaborate rhyming, of which Ezra Pound gives some idea in his adaptation of a little Provençal poem:

ALBA

When the nightingale to his mate
Sings day-long and night late
My love and I keep state
In bower,
In flower,
'Till the watchman on the tower
Cry:
"Up! Thou rascal, Rise,
I see the white
Light
And the night
Flies."

Ezra Pound

Rhyme was so important in old Persian poetry that the quatrains of Omar Khayyám (p. 262) were arranged according to rhyming sounds. It is so built into the syntax of Greek and Latin (in which the endings of nouns, adjectives, and verbs make up a constant chiming) that there was no need to seek additional rhyme for the end of lines. This is true also of Japanese, in which all words end with a vowel or an *n*, so that it is almost impossible to find a haiku without rhyming words.

Many reasons have been given for the appeal of rhyme. One of the oldest is that we like to see any stunt skillfully performed: we like to watch acrobats and tightrope walkers and jugglers. Good rhyming is a feat of skill with words.

A second reason is based on a psychological tendency that we feel even more clearly in music. It has been called "the law of return," which holds that it is better to return to any starting point than not to return—a law which operates in both primitive melodies of two or three notes and in complex orchestral music. Prominent sounds arouse in us the expectation of hearing them again. We wait with a kind of subconscious tension or anxiety for our expectation to be satisfied and the tension resolved. Ogden Nash plays on this sense of expectation in a special way; we know that when one of his rhymes is about to come up it may be an outrageous one, and we wait for it with the kind of pleasure-pain with which we see an upheld tray of glassware tipping and about to crash to the floor.

VERY LIKE A WHALE

One thing that literature would be greatly the better for
Would be a more restricted employment by authors of simile and metaphor.
Authors of all races, be they Greeks, Romans, Teutons or Celts,
Can't seem just to say that anything is the thing it is but have to go out of
their way to say that it is like something else.
What does it mean when we are told
That the Assyrian came down like a wolf on the fold?
In the first place, George Gordon Byron had had enough experience
To know that it probably wasn't just one Assyrian, it was a lot of 10
Assyrians.
However, as too many arguments are apt to induce apoplexy and thus hinder
longevity,
We'll let it pass as one Assyrian for the sake of brevity.
Now then, this particular Assyrian, the one whose cohorts were gleaming in
purple and gold,
Just what does the poet mean when he says he came down like a wolf on
the fold?
In heaven and earth more than is dreamed of in our philosophy
there are a great many things, 20
But I don't imagine that among them there is a wolf with purple
and gold cohorts or purple and gold anythings.
No, no, Lord Byron, before I'll believe that this Assyrian was actually like a
wolf I must have some kind of proof;
Did he run on all fours and did he have a hairy tail and a big red mouth and
big white teeth and did he say Woof woof woof?
Frankly I think it very unlikely, and all you were entitled to say, at the very
most,
Was that the Assyrian cohorts came down like a lot of Assyrian
cohorts about to destroy the Hebrew host. 30

But that wasn't fancy enough for Lord Byron, oh dear me no, he had to invent a lot of figures of speech and then interpolate them.
With the result that whenever you mention Old Testament soldiers to people they say Oh yes, they're the ones that a lot of wolves dressed up in gold and purple ate them.
That's the kind of thing that's being done all the time by poets, from Homer to Tennyson;
They're always comparing ladies to lilies and veal to venison,
And they always say things like that the snow is a white blanket after a winter storm. **40**
Oh it is, is it, all right then, you sleep under a six-inch blanket of snow and I'll sleep under a half-inch blanket of unpoetical blanket material and we'll see which one keeps warm,
And after that maybe you'll begin to comprehend dimly
What I mean by too much metaphor and simile.

Ogden Nash (1902–1971)

A third reason is our experience of physical reality, in which we are accustomed to corresponding pairs—left and right, up and down, far and near, etc. Something like mirror-image rhyme has been found in Browning's "Meeting at Night." In each six-line stanza the rhyme scheme begins with an *a b c* and then reverses itself with a *c b a*, forming the pattern *a b c c b a*—perhaps (as a scientist has suggested) to represent the ebb and flow of sea waves. (Rhyme schemes are indicated by letters, with one letter standing for each rhyming sound. In *a b c c b a*, the first and sixth lines rhyme, the second and fifth, and the third and fourth.)

MEETING AT NIGHT

I

The gray sea and the long black land;
And the yellow half-moon large and low;
And the startled little waves that leap
In fiery ringlets from their sleep,
As I gain the cove with pushing prow,
And quench its speed i' the slushy sand.

II

Then a mile of warm sea-scented beach;
Three fields to cross till a farm appears;
A tap at the pane, the quick sharp scratch
And blue spurt of a lighted match, **10**
And a voice less loud, thro' its joys and fears,
Than the two hearts beating each to each!

Robert Browning (1812–1889)

The supreme experience of bilateral symmetry is the human body, with its almost perfect correspondence of right and left. When we

A DEFENSE OF RHYME
A
A
A
B
B
C
C
D
D
E
E

walk, our two sides swing forward not only in rhythm but in something very like rhyme—ankle rhymes with ankle, knee with knee, hip with hip, wrist with wrist, shoulder with shoulder. The best defense of the naturalness of rhyme is the sight of any healthy man or woman walking down the street—*a b a b*—rhyme in motion.

A fourth theory of the nature of rhyme is even more physical. According to Goethe, words rhyming are words making love, words snuggling, in as close a union as possible, almost fusing but—*vive la différence*—still a little different, just as the two sexes are different.

In Act II of the second part of *Faust* we are shown a magical meeting between Faust and Helen of Troy. Helen, brought up on classical Greek verse, is astonished to hear speech in rhyme, which to her ear sounds "strange and friendly":

> One sound, it seems, fits snugly with another.
> And when a word is nestled in our ear,
> Another comes beside it with caresses . . . .

Faust explains to her that it is easy enough to speak in rhyme if one has a passionate heart. Then he and Helen break into a little love duet in which Helen completes the sentences of Faust with a rhyme of her own.

For a poem that lends some support to Goethe's theory because it does have snuggled or entwined rhyme, we could look at a well-known lyric about lovers. It is saying that lovers no longer have a *meum* and a *tuum*, a "mine" and a "yours"; they have a *nostrum*, an "ours." *Nostrum* also means *a remedy*, like one a drugstore might describe as *our* specialty.

THE THIEVES

Lovers in the act dispense
With such meum-tuum sense
As might warningly reveal
What they must not pick or steal,
And their nostrum is to say:
'I and you are both away.'

After, when they disentwine
You from me and yours from mine,
Neither can be certain who
Was that I whose mine was you. 10
To the act again they go
More completely not to know.

Theft is theft and raid is raid
Though reciprocally made.
Lovers, the conclusion is
Doubled sighs and jealousies
In a single heart that grieves
For lost honour among thieves.

Robert Graves

We can feel how expressive the hugging rhymes are if we try some lines without them:

> After, when they disentwine
> You from me and mine from yours,
> Neither can be certain which
> Was that I whose mine was you.
> To the act again they turn
> More completely not to know.

A fifth explanation is based on what some consider a disadvantage—rhyme interferes with the rational processes of thought by obliging us to say other things than we originally had in mind. But are rational processes so important? In many of us, even in poets, they can be dull and predictable. An interruption, a few detours and unexpected turns, might make a trip with them less routine. The necessity of finding a rhyme may jolt the mind out of its ruts, force it to turn wildly across the fields in some more exhilarating direction. Force it out of the world of reason into the world of mystery, magic, and imagination, in which relationships between sounds may be as exciting as a Great Idea. Prospecting for rhymes is very like the surrealist process as André Breton describes it: "To compare two objects, as remote from one another in character as possible, or by any other method put them together in a sudden and striking fashion, this remains the highest task to which poetry can aspire. . . ." A fondness for healthy rhyme suggests that one feels that everything in the universe is related, even though it may take some probing and zigzagging to track down the connections. It is surprising that the intellectual Hegel defended rhyme by saying that without such devices words become "mentalized"—we forget they have a body and use them only as tools to communicate.

By permission of John Hart and Field Enterprises, Inc.

A sixth reason for rhyme is in the way it can intensify a word by amplifying its sound. When John Clare, in "The Parish," wanted to show us a pretentious ignoramus, he might have written:

> Young Farmer Bigg, of this same flimsy sort,
> Wise among fools, and with the wise an ass . . . .

"Ass," the key word, is not especially resonant here. But Clare wrote:

> Young Farmer Bigg, of this same flimsy class,
> Wise among fools, and with the wise an ass . . . .

And then we really hear the word.

A seventh reason for rhyme is in its structural possibilities. It can even serve as a scaffolding for poetry not yet built. Some of Shelley's manuscripts show that he left certain lines blank except for the rhyme, which furnished not only necessary sounds but key ideas. One can see how it works as a kind of structural blueprint, below, in a complicated stanza like that of Donne's "The Canonization," in which the speaker is telling others to do whatever they want as long as they do not interfere with his love.

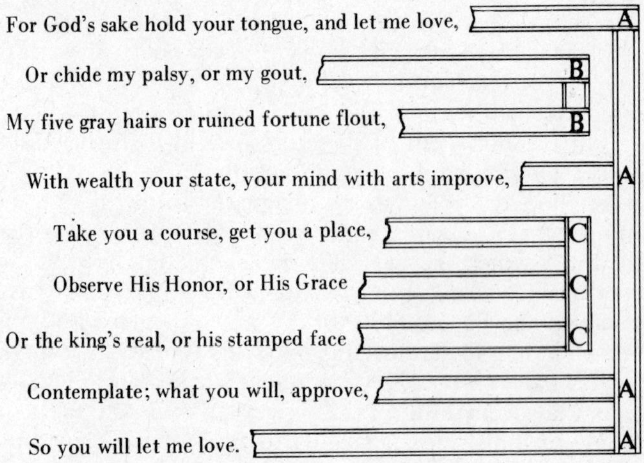

For God's sake hold your tongue, and let me love, A
Or chide my palsy, or my gout, B
My five gray hairs or ruined fortune flout, B
With wealth your state, your mind with arts improve, A
Take you a course, get you a place, C
Observe His Honor, or His Grace C
Or the king's real, or his stamped face C
Contemplate; what you will, approve, A
So you will let me love. A

One can also set up a rhyme scheme to see how successfully one can resist it—by treating it as an opponent rather than as a teammate. This wrestling match with rhyme, which is now on top, now underneath, is visible in Browning's "My Last Duchess," in which an art-loving and self-centered Renaissance duke tells, very casually, how he had to get rid of a wife whose innocent friendliness toward others made it seem as if she was not giving him, the noble duke, her full attention. The poem is in rhyming couplets, yet many of the rhymes are hurried over as if not there because the syntax will not permit us to pause.

MY LAST DUCHESS
Ferrara

That's my last Duchess painted on the wall,
Looking as if she were alive. I call
That piece a wonder, now: Frà Pandolf's hands
Worked busily a day, and there she stands.
Will't please you sit and look at her? I said
"Frà Pandolf" by design, for never read
Strangers like you that pictured countenance,
The depth and passion of its earnest glance,
But to myself they turned (since none puts by
The curtain I have drawn for you, but I) 10
And seemed as they would ask me, if they durst,

How such a glance came there; so, not the first
Are you to turn and ask thus. Sir, 'twas not
Her husband's presence only, called that spot
Of joy into the Duchess' cheek: perhaps
Frà Pandolf chanced to say "Her mantle laps
Over my lady's wrist too much," or "Paint
Must never hope to reproduce the faint
Half-flush that dies along her throat:" such stuff
Was courtesy, she thought, and cause enough 20
For calling up that spot of joy. She had
A heart—how shall I say?—too soon made glad,
Too easily impressed; she liked whate'er
She looked on, and her looks went everywhere.
Sir, 'twas all one! My favor at her breast,
The dropping of the daylight in the West,
The bough of cherries some officious fool
Broke in the orchard for her, the white mule
She rode with round the terrace—all and each
Would draw from her alike the approving speech, 30
Or blush, at least. She thanked men,—good! but thanked
Somehow—I know not how—as if she ranked
My gift of a nine-hundred-years-old name
With anybody's gift. Who'd stoop to blame
This sort of trifling? Even had you skill
In speech—(which I have not)—to make your will
Quite clear to such an one, and say, "Just this
Or that in you disgusts me; here you miss,
Or there exceed the mark"—and if she let
Herself be lessoned so, nor plainly set 40
Her wits to yours, forsooth, and made excuse,
—E'en then would be some stooping; and I choose
Never to stoop. Oh sir, she smiled, no doubt,
Whene'er I passed her; but who passed without
Much the same smile? This grew; I gave commands;
Then all smiles stopped together. There she stands
As if alive. Will't please you rise? We'll meet
The company below, then. I repeat,
The Count your master's known munificence
Is ample warrant that no just pretence 50
Of mine for dowry will be disallowed;
Though his fair daughter's self, as I avowed
At starting, is my object. Nay, we'll go
Together down, sir. Notice Neptune, though,
Taming a sea-horse, thought a rarity,
Which Claus of Innsbruck cast in bronze for me!

Robert Browning

In "Musée des Beaux Arts," Auden makes rhyme almost inconspicuous by having, in lines of uneven length, rhyming words the sense will not let us pause after. Some are far apart.

Pieter Brueghel the Elder, "*Landscape with the Fall of Icarus*"

MUSÉE DES BEAUX ARTS

About suffering they were never wrong,
The Old Masters: how well they understood
Its human position; how it takes place
While someone else is eating or opening a window or just walking dully along;
How, when the aged are reverently, passionately waiting
For the miraculous birth, there always must be
Children who did not specially want it to happen, skating
On a pond at the edge of the wood:
They never forgot
That even the dreadful martyrdom must run its course 10
Anyhow in a corner, some untidy spot
Where the dogs go on with their doggy life and the torturer's horse
Scratches its innocent behind on a tree.

In Brueghel's *Icarus,* for instance: how everything turns away
Quite leisurely from the disaster; the ploughman may
Have heard the splash, the forsaken cry,
But for him it was not an important failure; the sun shone
As it had to on the white legs disappearing into the green
Water; and the expensive delicate ship that must have seen
Something amazing, a boy falling out of the sky, 20
Had somewhere to get to and sailed calmly on.

W. H. Auden

But perhaps the eighth and final reason for the use of rhyme is the best of all: people find it fun. Poetry has been seen as the supreme example of the play spirit in man. "The hitting of the mark by rhyme" is part of the game—as in the many target games we like to play. There have always been reformers, of course, who disapprove of fun, especially when they think they have something serious to say.

The rhyme we have been talking about and giving examples of is called *end rhyme*. Rhymes within the line, *internal rhymes*, are also common.

> Once upon a midnight dreary, while I pondered weak and weary....

Sometimes rhymes placed irregularly or jostled together can give effects of perplexity or confusion. There is a feeling of lostness, of going in circles, in this passage from T. S. Eliot's "Ash Wednesday":

> Where shall the word be found, where will the word
> Resound? Not here, there is not enough silence
> Not on the sea or on the islands, not
> On the mainland, in the desert or the rain land,
> For those who walk in darkness
> Both in the day time and in the night time
> The right time and the right place are not here
> No place of grace for those who avoid the face
> No time to rejoice for those who walk among noise and deny the voice....

Yeats' jostling rhymes express a more physical confusion:

> He stumbled, tumbled, fumbled to and fro....

Ron Loewinsohn uses the device for the uproar in a baseball park:

> Their cheers, their jeers, fall on deaf ears....

Marianne Moore uses internal rhyme as a structural principle in her "A Carriage from Sweden" (p. 52). We notice easily enough the end rhymes in lines 2 and 3 of each stanza. But one could probably read the poem for years and not notice that in the first line of every stanza the third syllable rhymes with the last one—"there"/"air," "may"/ "away," "resined"/"wind," etc.—or that in the last line of every stanza the first syllable rhymes with the eighth (in one stanza, the ninth)— "*some*thing"/"*home*," "*in*tegrity"/"*vein*," "*A*dolphus"/"de*cay*," etc.

What we call rhyme in Marianne Moore does not always fit the definition given some pages back. "*Some*thing" and "*home*," "*in*tegrity" and "*vein*" do not have the same vowel sound; "some" calls for "hum," not "home"; "in" calls for "vin," not "vein." This kind of "imperfect rhyme"—also called "off-rhyme," "slant rhyme," "oblique rhyme," "near rhyme," "half rhyme"—has been deliberately employed by some earlier poets and many modern ones.

Emily Dickinson uses it so often that it becomes characteristic. Her earliest work shows she could rhyme perfectly when she wanted to, but for some reason she became fond of the little dissonance of off-rhyme. Instead of rhymes like "June"/"moon" she prefers "June"/ "men," "June"/"mean," or "June"/"moan." She often has rhymes like "port"/"chart," "affair"/"more," or "wheel"/"mill." She seems to feel that a vowel can rhyme with any other vowel: "know"/"withdrew," "dough"/"sky," "sky"/"tree."

No poet has called attention to the expressive value of off-rhyme more movingly than Wilfred Owen in his poems of World War I. Owen wrote in both full rhyme and off-rhyme. The use of off-rhyme in itself does not guarantee a better or more original or even more "modern" poem, but it does offer a different kind of music.

ANTHEM FOR DOOMED YOUTH

What passing-bells for these who die as cattle?
  Only the monstrous anger of the guns.
  Only the stuttering rifles' rapid rattle
Can patter out their hasty orisons.
No mockeries now for them; no prayers nor bells,
  Nor any voice of mourning save the choirs,—
The shrill, demented choirs of wailing shells;
  And bugles calling for them from sad shires.

What candles may be held to speed them all?
  Not in the hands of boys, but in their eyes 10
Shall shine the holy glimmers of good-byes.
  The pallor of girls' brows shall be their pall;
Their flowers the tenderness of patient minds,
And each slow dusk a drawing-down of blinds.

Wilfred Owen (1893–1918)

ARMS AND THE BOY

Let the boy try along this bayonet-blade
How cold steel is, and keen with hunger of blood;
Blue with all malice, like a madman's flash;
And thinly drawn with famishing for flesh.

Lend him to stroke these blind, blunt bullet-leads
Which long to nuzzle in the hearts of lads,
Or give him cartridges of fine zinc teeth,
Sharp with the sharpness of grief and death.

For his teeth seem for laughing round an apple.
There lurk no claws behind his fingers supple; 10
And God will grow no talons at his heels,
Nor antlers through the thickness of his curls.

Wilfred Owen

The second poem is all off-rhyme. But there is something special about the first three pairs: the vowel sounds change while the consonants before and after remain the same, so that we have a framing of "bl-d," "fl-sh," and "l-ds" with different vowel sounds in the middle. This pattern is known as **consonance.** In "Arms and the Boy," most of the rhyming pairs drop to a deeper vowel sound in the second word—an effect like that of a flatted "blue note" in music. Off-rhymes are like discords; they suggest that something is irregular and disturbed, has somehow failed or fallen short. They have been popular with many poets of our century, who feel that a discordant medium is appropriate for a discordant age.

When James Wright composed his "rhyme be damned" poem "of flat defeat in a flat voice," off-rhyme gave him the blue notes he needed.

SPEAK

To speak in a flat voice
Is all that I can do.
I have gone every place
Asking for you.
Wondering where to turn
And how the search would end
And the last streetlight spin
Above me blind.

Then I returned rebuffed
And saw under the sun 10
The race not to the swift
Nor the battle won.
Liston dives in the tank,
Lord, in Lewiston, Maine,
And Ernie Doty's drunk
In hell again.

And Jenny, oh my Jenny
Whom I love, rhyme be damned,
Has broken her spare beauty
In a whorehouse old. 20
She left her new baby
In a bus-station can,
And sprightly danced away
Through Jacksontown.

Which is a place I know,
One where I got picked up
A few shrunk years ago
By a good cop.
Believe it, Lord, or not.
Don't ask me who he was. 30
I speak of flat defeat
In a flat voice.

I have gone forward with
Some, a few lonely some.
They have fallen to death.
I die with them.
Lord, I have loved Thy cursed,
The beauty of Thy house:
Come down. Come down. Why dost
Thou hide thy face? 40

James Wright

Exercises and Diversions

A. 1. Say the following words over slowly to yourself, feeling them in the mouth. In which ones does the sound seem to go well with the sense? Can you always say why?

Slump, murmur, spoon, fork, encumber, cucumber, curt, fife, bassoon, abrupt, cluster, sullen, moody, potrzebie, lackadaisical, brisk, brusque, languid, robust, keen, dull, smooth, rough, woofer, tweeter, hiccup, glee, glum, glimmer, glow, flip, flop, fluff, drip, droop, creak, croak, glut, gulp, gobble, cantankerous, gleam, gloom, flabbergast, lollipop, gorge, oily, shudder, pomp, tinsel.

2. Could the meaning of any be reversed (where possible) without loss of expressiveness? Could "slump," for example, just as well mean *to straighten up*, "murmur" mean *to howl*?
3. List a dozen or so other words that seem to you to be like their meaning.
4. List a dozen or so that seem to be conspicuously unlike their meaning.

B. Think about the relationship between sound and sense in the following quotations. What do you conclude about each?

1. They err that would bring style so basely under:
The lofty language of the law was thunder. — *Thomas Randolph*

2. The luscious clusters of the vine
Upon my mouth do crush their wine. . . . — *Andrew Marvell*

3. Dear, damned, distracting town, farewell! — *Alexander Pope*

4. Oh what a tangled web we weave,
When first we practice to deceive! — *Sir Walter Scott*

5. The billows whiten and the deep seas heave. . . . — *Arthur Hugh Clough*

6. How many dawns, chill from his rippling rest,
The seagull's wings shall dip and pivot him,
Shedding white rings of tumult, building high
Over the chained bay waters Liberty . . . — *Hart Crane*

7. More beautiful and soft than any moth
With burring furred antennae feeling its huge path
Through dusk, the air liner with shut-off engines
Glides over suburbs. . . . — *Stephen Spender*

8. The soft cat, clawless, padded with Persian fluff,
A muff-puff lodged in the armchair all day eyeless. . . . — *Brewster Ghiselin*

9. Bolstered by bifocal
Tinted glass
And a transistor-batteried plastic
Flesh-colored hearing aid. . . . — *Hollis Summers*

10. The crows, a hoarse cone in the wind. . . . — *George Garrett*

11. I scrape char off a board with a dull knife. — *Peter Davison*

12. The trees
say *Wesson. Mazola*
replies a frog. — *James Schuyler*

C. Describe the type of rhyme and the role it plays in each of the following quotations.

1. From which to part it maketh my heart as cold as any stone,
   For in my mind of all mankind I love but you alone.
   Anonymous, "The Nut Brown Maid"

2. Why should we rise, because 'tis light?
   Did we lie down, because 'twas night? *John Donne*

3. ["On Mr. Milton's *Paradise Lost*"]
   Well mightest thou scorn thy readers to allure
   With tinkling rhyme, of thy own sense secure . . .
   I too transported by the mode offend,
   And where I meant to *praise* thee, must *commend.* *Andrew Marvell*

4. But temperate birth dealt forth, and so discreet-
   ly that it makes the meat more sweet. . . . *Robert Herrick*

5. But—Oh! ye lords of ladies intellectual,
   Inform us truly, have they not hen-peck'd you all? *Lord Byron*

6. But what black Boreas wrecked her? he
   Came equipped, deadly electric. . . . *Gerard Manley Hopkins*

7. Yet shall your ragged moor receive
   The incomparable pomp of eve. . . . *Robert Louis Stevenson*

8. And now a gusty shower wraps
   The grimy scraps
   Of withered leaves about your feet. . . . *T. S. Eliot*

9. O Heart: this is a dream I had, or not a dream.
   Lovingly, lovingly, I wept, but my tears did not rhyme. *Stanley J. Kunitz*

10. And in those evenings when the lovely moon
    Shone through the smiling woods of deepest June. . . . *Edith Sitwell*

11. . . . the Hesperides' thick-leaved trees—
    And they were lovely as the evening breeze. *Edith Sitwell*

12. Up spoke the man in the moon:
    "What does the moan mean?
    The plane was part of the plan.
    Why gnaw the bone of a boon?" *James Merrill*

13. What's in the pool? A fish.
    Swishing away all day.
    Wavery, isn't he though?
    Throw him a bit of your cheese.
    These are the days that fish
    Wish they could sing in a tree. . . . *Tracy Eilers*

14. Even is come; and from the dark Park, hark,
    The signal of the setting sun—one gun!
    And six is sounding from the chime, prime time
    To go and see the Drury Lane Dane slain. . . . *Thomas Hood*

D. How is rhyme used in these two poems?

NEW HAMPSHIRE

Children's voices in the orchard
Between the blossom- and the fruit-time:
Golden head, crimson head,
Between the green tip and the root.
Black wing, brown wing, hover over;
Twenty years and the spring is over;
To-day grieves, to-morrow grieves,
Cover me over, light-in-leaves;
Golden head, black wing,
Cling, swing,
Spring, sing,
Swing up into the apple tree.

T. S. Eliot

UNDER BEN BULBEN, VI

Under bare Ben Bulben's head
In Drumcliff churchyard Yeats is laid.
An ancestor was rector there
Long years ago, a church stands near,
By the road an ancient cross.
No marble, no conventional phrase;
On limestone quarried near the spot
By his command these words are cut:

Cast a cold eye
On life, on death.
Horseman, pass by!

W. B. Yeats

E. Examine the use of rhyme in the following poems, noticing especially the rhyme scheme, the use of perfect rhyme and off-rhyme, the expressiveness of the rhyme.

1. "The End of the Weekend," p. 16.
2. "The Hand that Signed the Paper," p. 115.
3. "The Woodspurge," p. 118.
4. "Bells for John Whiteside's Daughter," p. 131.
5. "Travelling through the Dark," p. 137.
6. "A Narrow Fellow in the Grass," p. 152.

F. Test the eight theories of rhyme given in this chapter by keeping them in mind, one by one, as you read rhymed poetry. Which, if any, seem especially valid to you? Which, if any, seem especially foolish or far-fetched? Do you have a theory of your own?

G. Make up a poem in which the lines end with these words in this order: quiet, kiss, riot, abyss, trees, June, peas, prune, crystal, bar, pistol, guitar, brooded, concluded. Find possible connections between the words, so that your poem tells a logical story. Since we have not yet discussed rhythm, use any rhythm you want to, free or not. But if you do happen to use a line that has five beats (as in "I'd *re*ally *like* to *have* a *lit*tle *qui*et") you will have written a sonnet (like Shakespeare's!).

The Taste of Sound 13

a rasher of poems

How sound can determine the very structure of a poem is clear from the Russian text of Andrei Voznesensky's "I Am Goya," which is about the horrors of conflict as imagined through the eyes of the Spanish painter whose "The Disasters of War" is a terrifying series of brutal battlefield events. Starting with the sound of "Goya," which has the same hollow guttural as our word "gore," Voznesensky builds his poem around other *gaw* words: *nagoye, ya gore, ya golos, goda, ya golod, ya gorlo, goloi* (the *g* words mean *naked, grief, voice, year, hunger, throat, bare*).[1]

I AM GOYA

I am Goya
of the bare field, by the enemy's beak gouged
till the craters of my eyes gape
I am grief

I am the tongue
of war, the embers of cities
on the snows of the year 1941
I am hunger

I am the gullet
of a woman hanged whose body like a bell 10
tolled over a blank square
I am Goya

[1] The poem has been recorded in Russian: "The Voices of Yevtushenko and Voznesensky." Monitor, MR 113.

O grapes of wrath!
I have hurled westward
the ashes of the uninvited guest!
and hammered stars into the unforgetting sky—like nails
I am Goya

Andrei Voznesensky (b. 1933)
(Translated by Stanley Kunitz)

The Russian original is high in what is called bond density, the number of sound ties that hold the structure together. Poets differ in their concern for it. There is much less bond density in T. S. Eliot's

If all time is eternally present
All time is unredeemable.
What might have been is an abstraction....

than in Gerard Manley Hopkins'

Thou mastering me
God! giver of breath and bread;
World's strand, sway of the sea;
Lord of living and dead....

in which almost every word is bonded by sound to another word. Unless the bonding is done skillfully, results can be unpleasant.

When we say that language is euphonious or has euphony we mean that it is pleasant to the ear. But we probably also mean that we pronounce it so easily that there is a pleasure in the physical movements, as there is in any muscular activity we perform with ease. (A French poet-critic has written a book of more than 500 pages on the "muscular pleasure" of poetry.) Eurhythmics is the art of moving our body in harmony with music or the spoken word; euphony might be thought of as oral eurhythmics. Its opposite is cacophony, the harsh or inharmonious use of language—harsh to listen to because harsh to pronounce. We cannot, as we say, get our tongue around it. Robert Frost has talked about this:

One of the things that I notice with myself is that I can't make certain word sounds go together, sometimes—they won't *say*. This has got something to do with the way one vowel runs into another, the way one syllable runs into another... the mouth and throat are like this... certain sounds are here and you can't go right from this one to that one....

Sometimes poets deliberately write rough lines to give a sense of physical effort, as Pope did:

When Ajax strives some rock's vast weight to throw,
The line too labors, and the words move slow....

Our tongue muscles have as much trouble with the *xstr, s/s, ksv,* and *t/t* of the first line as Ajax had with his rock. Byron wrote some stick-in-the-gullet lines in *Don Juan*:

Bombs, drums, guns, bastions, batteries, bayonets, bullets,—
Hard words, which stick in the soft Muses' gullets.

Robert Lowell aims at muscularity in lines our tongue has to wrestle with:

. . . who will dance
The mast-lashed master of Leviathans
Up from that field . . . .

In "The Haystack in the Floods," William Morris has lines that invite the participation of our facial muscles:

. . . A wicked smile
Wrinkled her face, her lips grew thin,
A long way out she thrust her chin:
"You know that I should strangle you
While you were sleeping, or bite through
Your throat, by God's help . . . ."

Such effects are more muscular than musical.

Even though we have found that it is possible to arrange vowels in a kind of scale, the relationships between them are not like those between musical notes. We can sing *do mi so do* and feel a pleasurable harmony in the intervals. There is no such pleasure in saying *o͞o ah ă ee*. The tones do get higher but the intervals are not related. We sometimes get a general sense of vowels ascending, as in Shakespeare's

Like to the lark at break of day arising
From sullen earth, sings hymns at heaven's gate . . . .

or in Robert Graves'

O love, be fed with apples while you may . . . .

Or we may feel the vowels dropping, as in Whitman's

When lilacs last in the dooryard bloom'd . . . .

or Emily Dickinson's

The thunder gossiped low . . . .

The simplest way to make a sound ring out is to repeat it immediately, as Shakespeare does in phrases like "brave day" or "time's scythe." Or to repeat it after an unstressed syllable, as he does in "ragged hand" or "mortal war." Emily Dickinson liked this simple figure—"stumbling buzz," "satin cash." So did Sylvia Plath—"gristly-bristled," "cuddly mother." Such linked repetitions of sound turn up everywhere in poetry:

This fabulous shadow only the sea keeps. *Hart Crane*

and bats with baby faces in the violet light . . . .
T. S. Eliot

Often we find two sounds interlocked, as in Shakespeare's "that in black ink." Or elsewhere:

> Under the glassy, cool, translucent wave ....
>
> *John Milton*

> ... brown hair over the mouth blown .... *T. S. Eliot*

Or we find one pair of sounds bracketing another, as in Shakespeare's "outlive this powerful."

> And chaste Diana haunts the forest shade ....
>
> *Alexander Pope*

> In which sad light a carvēd dolphin swam ....
>
> *T. S. Eliot*

These three simple arrangements—linked, interlocked, bracketed—can be used to build up more involved combinations:

> Many lost sighs long I spent .... *Thomas Campion*

> And still she slept an azure-lidded sleep ....
>
> *John Keats*

These are examples of vowels in patterns. Consonants can be patterned in the same ways:

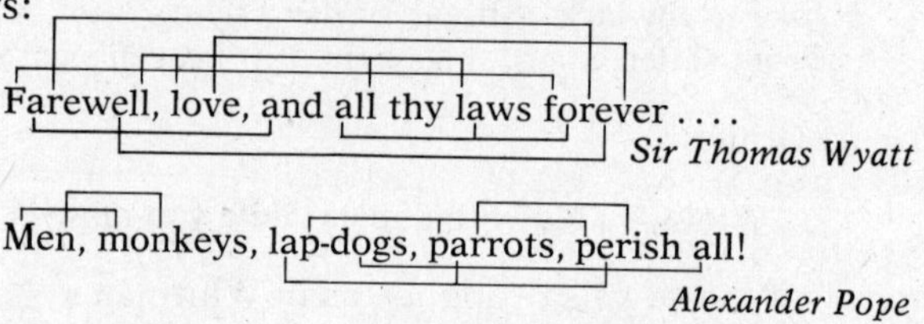

These little figures of repetition are not used systematically. All the poet does is repeat sounds when he feels the repetition would be pleasant or meaningful. If his repetitions happen to fall into a pattern, well and good.

Most poets, we find, care very much about such sound effects and work hard at them. A friend of Keats tells us that one of the poet's "favorite topics ... was the principle of melody in verse ... particularly in the management of open and close vowels" ("height"/"hit," "load"/"lid," etc.). Keats' theory, "worked out by himself ... was, that the vowels should be so managed as not to clash one with another so as to mar the melody,—and yet that they should be interchanged, like differing notes of music to prevent monotony."

Keats also believed that certain sounds are more or less appropriate for certain feelings, and can be all the more expressive if skillfully repeated. The first stanza of the "Ode to a Nightingale" is a good example:

My heart aches, and a drowsy numbness pains
My sense, as though of hemlock I had drunk,
Or emptied some dull opiate to the drains
One minute past, and Lethe-wards had sunk:
'Tis not through envy of thy happy lot,
But being too happy in thine happiness,—
That thou, light-wingèd Dryad of the trees,
In some melodious plot
Of beechen green, and shadows numberless,
Singest of summer in full-throated ease.

In the first line, dark, dull vowel sounds ("heart," "drowsy," "numbness") are contrasted with shriller ones ("aches," "pains"). We have heard the high *a*'s used before, as in Joyce, for effects of gaiety. But the intensity that recommended them to Joyce also qualifies them to express keen feelings of another sort. (Certain kinds of pleasure and pain are close together; the instinctive cries that go with each can hardly be told apart.) The same sound can be used to intensify the expression of exactly opposite feelings. An *ooo!* or a sharply indrawn breath can mean either ecstasy or anguish.

All the sounds of line 1 are repeated in the stanza, but none so much as the dull *u* of "numbness," which recurs in "drunk," "some," "dull," "one," "sunk." The next sequence to notice is the short *e* followed by a nasal—"sense," "hemlock," "emptied," "envy." The repetition of this unexciting little vowel is monotonous, like the numbness that Keats, for all his "aches" and "pains," says he is feeling. These *en*'s and *em*'s are vitalized by the brighter vowel in the "beechen green" of line 9. Rather gloomy vowels set the tone for the first few lines of the stanza, but the song of the nightingale (which Keats thinks of as a Dryad, or tree goddess) brings in a run of excited vowels such as we have not heard before: "light-wingèd Dryad of the trees." The four prominent syllables even make up a little tune or figure at the top of the vowel scale. The keen *ee* sound becomes even clearer in "beechen green." The last line is tonally interesting: the prominent syllables slide down the scale to the throaty *oh*, only to rise to the very top in a final *ee* that echoes the other happy *ee* sounds.

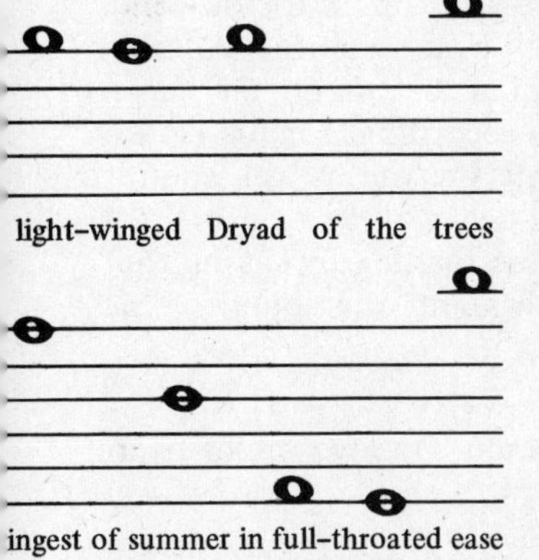

An early poem of Yeats —which owed something to his reading of *Walden*—is said to have "set the professors agog by the arrangements of the vowel sounds."

THE LAKE ISLE OF INNISFREE

I will arise and go now, and go to Innisfree,
And a small cabin build there, of clay and wattles made:

[2] **wattles:** *interwoven sticks or branches*

Nine bean-rows will I have there, a hive for the honeybee,
And live alone in the bee-loud glade.

And I shall have some peace there, for peace comes dropping slow,
Dropping from the veils of the morning to where the cricket sings;
There midnight's all a glimmer, and noon a purple glow,
And evening full of the linnet's wings.

I will arise and go now, for always night and day
I hear lake water lapping with low sounds by the shore; 10
While I stand on the roadway, or on the pavements grey,
I hear it in the deep heart's core.

W. B. Yeats

All we find is what has been standard practice among sound-conscious poets—a pleasant variety of vowels that lets us range freely over the scale (as in the *ī, i, oh, ow,* and *ee* of the first line); certain clearly felt repetitions amid the variety (as in "clay"/"made," "nine"/"hive"); uses of vowel and consonant sounds that are right for their meaning (as the three little *i*'s of "cricket sings" and "linnet's wings"); and perhaps an occasional progression up or down the scale, as in the descending *ee ŭ ah oh* of "peace comes dropping slow" and the similar *ee ah aw* of "deep heart's core." In recordings made later, Yeats himself dwelt on the vowel sounds almost the way a singer would; he explained the strangeness of his reading by saying that he cared very much about the sound of his lines.

There are many pretty effects in this short poem. One we might overlook is in

I hear lake water lapping with low sounds by the shore . . .

Thirteen vowel sounds, eleven of them different. The sound of the water is always changing and yet is always the same too, as the continued *l*'s are hinting.

Sometimes the music of a single good line can carry through a poem. One of Byron's most famous lyrics opens with a series of six almost identical *oh* sounds, whose rich melancholy is reechoed at the end. The sound is so compelling that we probably overlook the weakness of the second stanza, with its clumsy diction and imagery, and let sound carry the poem into its immortality.

SO WE'LL GO NO MORE A-ROVING

So we'll go no more a-roving
  So late into the night,
Though the heart be still as loving,
  And the moon be still as bright.

For the sword outwears its sheath,
  And the soul wears out the breast,
And the heart must pause to breathe,
  And love itself have rest.

Though the night was made for loving,
  And the day returns too soon, 10
Yet we'll go no more a-roving
  By the light of the moon.

George Gordon, Lord Byron (1788–1824)

Robert Penn Warren has spoken about the enjoyment we feel in participating physically in the experience of a poem: "... a pleasure, just the way the muscles get into play. In your whole vocal apparatus. ... It's just a wonderful workout, a sense of kinetic involvement in the lines. This release, this muscular play ... just the physical pleasure of a well-turned line is something. ..."

The rest of this chapter will be given over to just such workouts. The poems coming up are meant to be savored, meant to be given a careful gourmet reading, with particular notice of how they feel in the mouth.

The poem that aroused Warren's gymnastic sensibilities is Milton's "Lycidas." Edward King, a Cambridge acquaintance of Milton's, was drowned while on his way to visit his family in Ireland. King had written some poetry himself; he was planning to become a clergyman. Milton thought about himself: he too was a young student with plans and ambitions. Were they indeed worth the effort and sacrifice if life could be ended by a sudden mindless accident? He thought about the church of his time, which seemed in need of such young men as the one it had just lost. Milton dreamed of heaping his friend's body with all the flowers of the countryside, which themselves would grieve for the dead young man—but he was too tough and level-headed to go along with such poetic fancies, which he knew were a "false surmise" (l. 153). The body itself had not been recovered. It was tossing somewhere in the hundreds of miles of wild ocean between the Hebrides and the far-off coast of Spain.

Milton has put some readers off by writing his poem in the form of a pastoral elegy: he imagines that he and his friends are song-loving shepherds in an idyllic culture. The use of such imagery was an old form of make-believe—it had its conventional rules just as games have theirs. What, after all, is more artificial in the world of nature than a tennis court or a golf course? And yet they offer us better scope for certain natural activities than natural terrain would. And so, for some, do such conventions as those of the pastoral. Milton chose to play the game that way, with an ancient form of "let's pretend" that no doubt represents man's desire for a simple life in significant rapport with his environment. He knew poets had been playing that game for at least 2,000 years. He takes the name "Lycidas" from earlier works of that type; he refers to places in Sicily and Italy because they are associated with Theocritus and Vergil, who wrote the best pastoral poetry of antiquity. But he also deliberately breaks with their kind of poetry by making his indignant attack on the corruption of the church, by referring to his own literary status and ambitions, and by admitting not only Apollo and Jove into his poetic world but also—and far more significantly—the founder of Christianity, who triumphantly walked the waves that had engulfed a young Christian. (An **elegy** is a lament for the dead, or a meditation on the thoughts that death arouses.)

LYCIDAS

In this monody the author bewails a learned friend, unfortunately drowned in his passage from Chester on the Irish Seas, 1637. And by occasion foretells the ruin of our corrupted clergy, then in their height.

Yet once more, O ye laurels, and once more,
Ye myrtles brown, with ivy never sere,
I come to pluck your berries harsh and crude,
And with forced fingers rude
Shatter your leaves before the mellowing year.
Bitter constraint and sad occasion dear
Compels me to disturb your season due;
For Lycidas is dead, dead ere his prime,
Young Lycidas, and hath not left his peer.
Who would not sing for Lycidas? he knew 10
Himself to sing, and build the lofty rhyme.
He must not float upon his watery bier
Unwept, and welter to the parching wind,
Without the meed of some melodious tear.
  Begin then, sisters of the sacred well
That from beneath the seat of Jove doth spring;
Begin, and somewhat loudly sweep the string.
Hence with denial vain and coy excuse;
So may some gentle muse
With lucky words favour my destined urn, 20
And as he passes turn,
And bid fair peace be to my sable shroud.
  For we were nursed upon the self-same hill,

---

monody: *originally, an ode sung by one person; a lament*
1–2 **laurels . . . myrtles . . . ivy:** *three kinds of evergreen foliage symbolizing poetry*
2 **sere:** *dry, withered*
3 **crude:** *not yet ripe*
6 **dear:** *heartfelt, grievous*
14 **meed:** *gift*
15 **sisters:** *the Muses*

Fed the same flock, by fountain, shade, and rill;
Together both, ere the high lawns appeared
Under the opening eyelids of the morn,
We drove a-field, and both together heard
What time the gray-fly winds her sultry horn,
Battening our flocks with the fresh dews of night,
Oft till the star that rose at evening, bright, 30
Toward heaven's descent had sloped his westering wheel.
Meanwhile the rural ditties were not mute,
Tempered to the oaten flute;
Rough satyrs danced, and fauns with cloven heel
From the glad sound would not be absent long;
And old Damœtas loved to hear our song.
But O the heavy change, now thou art gone,
Now thou art gone, and never must return!
Thee, shepherd, thee the woods and desert caves,
With wild thyme and the gadding vine o'ergrown, 40
And all their echoes, mourn.
The willows and the hazel copses green
Shall now no more be seen,
Fanning their joyous leaves to thy soft lays.
As killing as the canker to the rose,
Or taint-worm to the weanling herds that graze,
Or frost to flowers, that their gay wardrobe wear,
When first the white-thorn blows;
Such, Lycidas, thy loss to shepherd's ear.
Where were ye, nymphs, when the remorseless deep 50
Closed o'er the head of your loved Lycidas?
For neither were ye playing on the steep
Where your old bards, the famous druids, lie,
Nor on the shaggy top of Mona high,
Nor yet where Deva spreads her wizard stream.
Ay me, I fondly dream!
Had ye been there—for what could that have done?
What could the muse herself that Orpheus bore,
The muse herself, for her enchanting son,
Whom universal nature did lament, 60
When by the rout that made the hideous roar

---

[28] **gray-fly:** *name of several insects, some beetlelike*
[29] **battening:** *feeding, fattening*
[33] **oaten:** *made of an oat straw*
[36] **Damœtas:** *unidentified (an elderly professor?)*
[45] **canker:** *destructive bug or caterpillar*
[46] **taint-worm:** *intestinal worm that infests young cattle*
weanling: *newly weaned*
[53] **druids:** *an order of ancient Celtic priest-poet-magicians*
[54] **Mona:** *the island of Anglesey, off the northern coast of Wales*
[55] **Deva:** *the river Dee, thought to have prophetic powers, which flows through Chester and empties into the Irish Sea*
[56] **fondly:** *foolishly*
[58] **Orpheus:** *legendary Greek poet and musician, son of the muse Calliope, torn to pieces by angered Thracian women. His head—still singing—was swept down the river Hebrus (in Thrace) and across the Aegean to the island of Lesbos.*

His gory visage down the stream was sent,
Down the swift Hebrus to the Lesbian shore?
  Alas! what boots it with uncessant care
To tend the homely, slighted, shepherd's trade,
And strictly meditate the thankless muse?
Were it not better done, as others use,
To sport with Amaryllis in the shade,
Or with the tangles of Neæra's hair?
Fame is the spur that the clear spirit doth raise 70
(That last infirmity of noble mind)
To scorn delights and live laborious days;
But the fair guerdon when we hope to find,
And think to burst out into sudden blaze,
Comes the blind fury with the abhorrèd shears,
And slits the thin-spun life. "But not the praise,"
Phœbus replied, and touched my trembling ears:
"Fame is no plant that grows on mortal soil
Nor in the glistering foil
Set off to the world, nor in broad rumour lies; 80
But lives and spreads aloft by those pure eyes
And perfect witness of all-judging Jove;
As he pronounces lastly on each deed,
Of so much fame in heaven expect thy meed."
  O fountain Arethuse, and thou honoured flood,
Smooth-sliding Mincius, crowned with vocal reeds,
That strain I heard was of a higher mood:
But now my oat proceeds,
And listens to the herald of the sea,
That came in Neptune's plea. 90
He asked the waves, and asked the felon winds,
What hard mishap hath doomed this gentle swain?
And questioned every gust of rugged wings
That blows from off each beakèd promontory:
They knew not of his story;
And sage Hippotades their answer brings,

---

[64] **what boots it:** *what good does it do*
[65] **shepherd's trade:** *poetry, in this pastoral world*
[67] **use:** *habitually do*
[68-69] **Amaryllis . . . Neæra:** *girls' names, borrowed from classical poetry*
[73] **guerdon:** *reward*
[75] **fury:** *death—of the three fates, the one that cuts the thread of our life*
[77] **Phœbus:** *Apollo, god of beauty, poetry, etc. His touching or pulling the ear is a gesture of reproof.*
[79] **foil:** *gold or silver leaf placed to increase the brightness of precious stones*
[85] **Arethuse:** *a spring in Sicily, symbolic here of Sicilian pastoral poetry*
[86] **Mincius:** *Italian river near Vergil's birthplace, symbolic here of Italian pastoral poetry*
[88] **oat:** *see line 33*
[89] **herald of the sea:** *the sea god Triton*
[96] **Hippotades:** *Aeolus, god of the winds*

That not a blast was from his dungeon strayed;
The air was calm, and on the level brine
Sleek Panope with all her sisters played.
It was that fatal and perfidious bark, 100
Built in the eclipse, and rigged with curses dark,
That sunk so low that sacred head of thine.
Next Camus, reverend sire, went footing slow,
His mantle hairy, and his bonnet sedge,
Inwrought with figures dim, and on the edge
Like to that sanguine flower inscribed with woe.
"Ah! who hath reft," quoth he, "my dearest pledge?"
Last came, and last did go,
The pilot of the Galilean lake;
Two massy keys he bore of metals twain 110
(The golden opes, the iron shuts amain).
He shook his mitred locks, and stern bespake:
"How well could I have spared for thee, young swain,
Enow of such as, for their bellies' sake,
Creep and intrude and climb into the fold!
Of other care they little reckoning make
Than how to scramble at the shearers' feast,
And shove away the worthy bidden guest.
Blind mouths! that scarce themselves know how to hold
A sheep-hook, or have learnt aught else the least 120
That to the faithful herdman's art belongs!
What recks it them? What need they? They are sped;
And when they list, their lean and flashy songs
Grate on their scrannel pipes of wretched straw;
The hungry sheep look up, and are not fed,
But swoln with wind and the rank mist they draw,
Rot inwardly, and foul contagion spread;
Besides what the grim wolf with privy paw
Daily devours apace, and nothing said.

---

99 **Panope:** *a sea nymph*
103 **Camus:** *the river Cam, representing Cambridge University*
104 **hairy:** *with the fur trimming of an academic gown (?)*
sedge: *a water plant with a flag-like flower*
106 **flower:** *the hyacinth, the design on whose petals was thought to be the Greek word* Alas!
109 **pilot:** *probably Saint Peter with the keys of heaven and a bishop's cap (miter)*
111 **amain:** *with force*
114 **enow:** *enough*
119 **blind mouths:** *a concentrated way of saying that bad clergymen are all greedy mouths and fail to see what they should see*
120 **a sheep-hook:** *a symbol of the pastor's life, perhaps a bishop's staff*
121 **herdman:** *pastor, clergyman*
122 **What recks it them?:** *What do they care?*
they are sped: *they have prospered*
123 **list:** *want to*
124 **scrannel:** *thin, scratchy*
straw: *cf. l. 33*
128 **wolf:** *apparently the Catholics, in their attempt to make converts*

But that two-handed engine at the door 130
Stands ready to smite once, and smite no more."
Return, Alpheus; the dread voice is past
That shrunk thy streams; return, Sicilian muse,
And call the vales, and bid them hither cast
Their bells and flowrets of a thousand hues.
Ye valleys low, where the mild whispers use
Of shades and wanton winds and gushing brooks,
On whose fresh lap the swart star sparely looks,
Throw hither all your quaint enamelled eyes,
That on the green turf suck the honeyed showers, 140
And purple all the ground with vernal flowers.
Bring the rathe primrose that forsaken dies,
The tufted crow-toe, and pale jessamine,
The white pink, and the pansy freaked with jet,
The glowing violet,
The musk-rose, and the well-attired woodbine,
With cowslips wan that hang the pensive head,
And every flower that sad embroidery wears;
Bid amaranthus all his beauty shed,
And daffodillies fill their cups with tears, 150
To strew the laureate hearse where Lycid lies.
For so to interpose a little ease,
Let our frail thoughts dally with false surmise,
Ay me! whilst thee the shores and sounding seas
Wash far away, where'er thy bones are hurled,
Whether beyond the stormy Hebrides,
Where thou perhaps under the whelming tide
Visit'st the bottom of the monstrous world;
Or whether thou, to our moist vows denied,
Sleep'st by the fable of Bellerus old, 160

---

[130] **two-handed engine:** *Many guesses have been made about this ominous and mysterious object, among them a two-handed sword belonging to God or Saint Michael; the two houses of Parliament; Puritan zeal; the approaching civil war; the combined forces of England and Scotland; etc. The fact that it cannot be identified with certainty makes it the more frightening.*

[132] **Alpheus:** *a Greek river whose waters were thought to flow unmixed through the sea to rise in the "fountain Arethuse" of line 85*

[136] **use:** *are frequent*

[138] **swart star:** *Sirius, the Dog star, associated with the hot weather that burns or tans, makes swart*

[142] **rathe:** *early*

[143] **crow-toe:** *wild hyacinth*

[144] **freaked:** *streaked whimsically (freakishly). Milton made up the word.*

[146] **woodbine:** *honeysuckle*

[149] **amaranthus:** *an imaginary flower thought never to fade*

[151] **laureate:** *crowned with laurel*

[153] **false surmise:** *the notion that the body of Lycidas is available, and the flowers have any real concern for him*

[156] **Hebrides:** *islands off the western coast of Scotland*

[160] **Bellerus:** *a fabulous figure apparently invented by Milton, named for Bellerium, or Land's End in Cornwall*

Where the great vision of the guarded mount
Looks toward Namancos and Bayona's hold;
Look homeward, angel, now, and melt with ruth;
And O ye dolphins, waft the hapless youth.
  Weep no more, woeful shepherds, weep no more,
For Lycidas, your sorrow, is not dead,
Sunk though he be beneath the watery floor;
So sinks the day-star in the ocean bed,
And yet anon repairs his drooping head,
And tricks his beams, and with new-spangled ore 170
Flames in the forehead of the morning sky:
So Lycidas sunk low, but mounted high,
Through the dear might of him that walked the waves,
Where, other groves and other streams along,
With nectar pure his oozy locks he laves,
And hears the unexpressive nuptial song,
In the blest kingdoms meek of joy and love.
There entertain him all the saints above,
In solemn troops and sweet societies,
That sing, and singing in their glory move, 180
And wipe the tears for ever from his eyes.
Now, Lycidas, the shepherds weep no more;
Henceforth thou art the genius of the shore,
In thy large recompense, and shalt be good
To all that wander in that perilous flood.
  Thus sang the uncouth swain to the oaks and rills,
While the still morn went out with sandals gray;
He touched the tender stops of various quills,
With eager thought warbling his Doric lay:
And now the sun had stretched out all the hills, 190
And now was dropt into the western bay.
At last he rose, and twitched his mantle blue:
To-morrow to fresh woods and pastures new.

John Milton

The power of Milton's music makes itself felt in the first line with the three resonant *or* sounds, echoing within a few lines in "forced"

---

161 **great vision:** *Saint Michael, who was said to appear on the mountain in Cornwall named for him*
162 **Namancos and Bayona:** *place names of an old region and a city in northwest Spain, about 500 miles south of the guarded mount, across the Atlantic*
163 **angel:** *Saint Michael*
ruth: *pity*
164 **dolphins:** *probably an allusion to the early Greek poet Arion, saved from drowning by a dolphin. There are other legends of dolphin rescues.*
168 **day-star:** *sun*
170 **tricks:** *trims*
173 **him:** *Christ*
176 **unexpressive:** *inexpressible*
183 **genius:** *protective local deity*
186 **uncouth:** *unknown, obscure*
188 **stops . . . quills:** *finger-holes . . . pipes*
189 **Doric:** *Much Greek pastoral poetry was in the Doric dialect.*

and "before," and recurring in key passages later, most impressively in the six lines beginning with line 58: "Orpheus," "bore," "roar," "gory," "shore." Together, *aw* and *r* make up what must be the strongest combination of vowel and consonant in English. The virile *r*, which we are told Milton pronounced "very hard," seems to be a favorite sound of his—there are eighteen in the first five lines of "Lycidas." This is typical of the music of the poem, which is strong and resonant more often than conventionally melodious. Lowell calls the brusque third line "a very great line in its context . . . largely through sound." The sound itself is "harsh and crude," a roughness in the mouth that is pleasantly chunky to munch on. Many of the most memorable lines are equally rough-textured—really a "workout."

How sound attracts sound could be illustrated in almost every line:

> What time the gray-fly winds . . . .
>
> Toward heaven's descent had sloped his westering wheel . . . .
>
> He must not float upon his watery bier
> Unwept, and welter to the parching wind,
> Without the meed of some melodious tear . . . .
>
> To scorn delights, and live laborious days . . . .
>
> . . . what the grim wolf with privy paw
> Daily devours apace . . . .

A contemporary elegy by a young poet is very different in tone. But the poem seems to have been written with full awareness of what the sounds are doing. Bond density is high. Simple as the language is, prominent sounds are much likelier to be repeated than in talk we hear around us. The deep and solemn *aw,* which occurs three times in the first line of "Lycidas," occurs three times in Taylor's first line too. As in "Lycidas," it becomes a tonal motif in this poem—it is used more than four times as often as we normally expect to hear it. The deep *oh* is used nearly twice as often. There are also more of the three high-frequency sounds than is usual, so that both extremes of the vowel scale are drawn on for their intensities. And yet the poem reads so simply and naturally that we are not *consciously* aware that anything unusual is going on.

THE DEATH OF LESTER BROWN, HOUSE PAINTER

He'd seen his blood before, called forth
by fishhooks, knives, wrenches, and it flashed
in the sun like the river. But something went wrong.
Between the hyacinths on the lake, the quiet
bees in the orange grove, the white house he
lived in, somewhere
between these, the flashing blood
went dark. He started falling
asleep at work and driving through
red-lights. And the doctors 10

had a new word for the family to learn,
but had no words
to help him live.

Everyday he asked for his gun, but no one
knew where it was; no one
asked him why he asked. In that first year
we visited often
and although the birds went hungry
for the bread of his hand, the oranges
got picked and the house had only 20
begun to fall apart.

The doctors gave him only a couple of years,
but they were wrong: five years before it
ended, noiselessly, in a damp side room
where a portable electric-coil heater
had been put—plenty of time
to let his living go and forget
the things he loved, one
by one, until there was nothing
in him. In that second year 30
of his long dying, we came on holidays, ate turkey
and didn't watch when Mrs. Brown
was feeding him. It was the year
of the portable TV and the propped-up feet and blue
terrycloth bathrobe
and all those things were death. Death was in
the mildew on the ceiling and the cracks
between boards and in the rug. It was pale blue
in his thinning arms and face
and hid itself like a red-eyed spider 40
in the dark throat of his fishing trophy.
It was in every word spoken.

You told me last night how he was before,
how, when you were little, he loved you
and took care of you. You were sad
and combed your hair in the mirror.
In the third year he watched his hands
all day, and in the fourth he lay and stared
at his feet. Mrs. Brown, who had known
the strength of his arms and given 50
him three sons and a daughter, turned him in
his bed and washed him with rags. At night
she prayed while the house peeled and the grove
was choking with weeds. In the garage
the tools of his trade deserted him, dried up
or rusted. Then the roof sprang a leak
and had to be patched with tar.

His arteries are too thin
for a needle, the doctors told them.
The year was sucked around the bend 60
of a glass straw and was over. I didn't visit him.

Those who did were not known. They say
that in the last months, he couldn't
close his eyes. Tomorrow we hide him
in earth. Mrs. Brown will be alone then
in the damp sagged boards of the old
house. Maybe, when she cleans, she will find
some thing—a hairbrush with his hair in the bristles,
a fingernail,
and it will be hard to keep on living. 70

Rod Taylor

Exercises and Diversions

A. 1. With euphony and cacophony in mind, read these lines from Shakespeare's "Sonnet 33."

Full many a glorious morning have I seen
Flatter the mountaintops with sovereign eye,
Kissing with golden face the meadows green,
Gilding pale streams with heavenly alchemy;
Anon permit the basest clouds to ride
With ugly rack on his celestial face,
And from the forlorn world his visage hide,
Stealing unseen to west with this disgrace. . . .

Is it physically true that the first four lines are euphonious, the second four cacophonous—or is this an impression foisted on us by the meaning?

2. Make the same experiment with these selections. Is the first really euphonious, or does it merely *seem* so because the subject is pleasant? Does the second merely *seem* cacophonous because the meaning looks difficult? Are euphony and cacophony subjective, or are they really based on the physics of sound?

When dawn woke us, in the small pine-sweet room,
We remembered first that we were not alone.
We opened our eyes and lay in the deep pillows
Seeing the green light through the leaves of mallows,
Hearing the violent sea, unwearied water . . .
The long stillness of spread bubbles breathing. . . .

Brewster Ghiselin

[A parody of Browning]
Ah, how can fear sit and hear as love hears its grief's
heart's cracked grate's screech?
Chance lets the gate sway that opens on hate's way
and shows on shame's beach
Crouched like an imp sly change watch sweet love's
shrimps lie, a toothful in each. . . . *Algernon Charles Swinburne*

3. Try these lines of Sir Philip Sidney in your mouth:

   Sweet kiss, thy sweets I fain would sweetly endite,
   Which even of sweetness sweetest sweetener art. . . .

   One of Sidney's editors explains the repetition of *sw* by the lip movements it requires of us. Are they expressive?

B. Experiments have been made with a form called the *péndeka*, whose fifteen syllables use each of the vowel tones once. Referring back to the vowel scale on pp. 178–179, analyze its use in each of the following.

MOON MISSION

Moon-cold could awe joy's proud star?
Dull earth has sent this
High brave glee!

Ron Baxter (b. 1947)

WINTER: THE ABANDONED NEST

Trees, sway high
This bed that birds loved.
Far-out voice calls, "Look, no moon!"

Ron Baxter

LOVE! LOVE!

Dreams cool. They hold shy looks in awe.
Spread soil and
How her heart hums!

Rhoda McMahon (b. 1952)

LOSS! LOSS!

Love-charms were loud and joy said all!
In brooks,
Ice tolled fey moon-scenes!

Rhoda McMahon

Many readers would feel that these "compositions in the fifteen-tone vowel scale" are failures and leave the reader unmoved. If you agree, what would that show about the relationship between sound and sense in poetry?

C. What sound patterns—linked, interlocked, bracketed—do you find in the following quotations?

1. Leave me, O Love, which reachest but to dust,
   And thou, my mind, aspire to higher things. . . . *Sir Philip Sidney*

2. To see his active child do deeds of youth. . . . *William Shakespeare*

3. The teeming autumn, big with rich increase. . . . *William Shakespeare*

4. And time that gave doth now his gift confound. . . . *William Shakespeare*

5. Now leaves the trees, and flowers adorn the ground. . . . *Alexander Pope*

6. Rough satyrs dance, and Pan applauds the song:
The nymphs forsaking every cave and spring,
Their early fruit, and milk-white turtles bring. . . . *Alexander Pope*

7. I cannot see what flowers are at my feet. . . . *John Keats*

8. A scattered chapter, livid hieroglyph. . . . *Hart Crane*

9. I walk through the long schoolroom questioning;
A kind old nun in a white hood replies. . . . *W. B. Yeats*

10. . . . cardboard boxes, cigarette ends. . . . *T. S. Eliot*

D. Do the opinions expressed about each of the following quotations seem to you to make sense? Nonsense?

1. And like a sky-lit water stood
The blue-bells in the azured wood. . . . *A. E. Housman*

"The magic effect is produced by repeating the syllable *like* inside the words *sky-lit*, but inverted [*ky-l*] as a reflection is inverted in water."

2. He will watch from dawn to gloom
The lake-reflected sun illume
The yellow sun in the ivy bloom. . . . *Percy Bysshe Shelley*

"The enchantment . . . greatly depends on the fact that the second syllable of *reflected* itself reflects in a weaker form the sound of the word *lake*, as the water reflects in weaker form the sun. . . ."

3. The gorges, opening wide apart, reveal
Troas, and Ilion's column'd citadel. . . . *Alfred, Lord Tennyson*

"Here in the first line the vowels in the second, third, fourth and fifth words, which require a gradually wider opening of the mouth to pronounce them, suggest the gradual opening of the gorge, and the sharp, clear sound of *reveal* brings suddenly before the mind's eye the vision of the divinely built city of Ilion far away on the plain."

E. 1. In the rest of the "Ode to a Nightingale" (p. 11), does Keats use sound as richly as in the first stanza? Pick out another stanza for close analysis.
2. How does Edwin Arlington Robinson use sound expressively in "The Dark Hills"?

THE DARK HILLS

Dark hills at evening in the west,
Where sunset hovers like a sound
Of golden horns that sang to rest
Old bones of warriors under ground,
Far now from all the bannered ways

Where flash the legions of the sun,
You fade—as if the last of days
Were fading, and all wars were done.

Edwin Arlington Robinson

F. 1. How does Milton arrange his rhymes in "Lycidas"? What little figures, such as *a b a b* or *a b b a*, do you find? Are any lines left unrhymed? If so, does there seem to be a reason? Does Milton use off-rhyme?

2. Pick out some lines that seem especially smooth. Some that seem especially rough.

G. Write a mouth poem—one that readers might be expected to take pleasure in "eating."

V the rhythms

14 Waves? Corpuscles? the nature of rhythm

A few years ago thousands of young people met in the gymnasium at Cornell to show their concern over vital issues of the day. But as time went on they became listless. Some started throwing Frisbees, some fell asleep in each other's arms. Then a young Irishman took the platform to plead for contributions: "Spontaneously, without any musical backing," the *New York Times* account goes, "he sang an Irish rebel ballad. The words mattered little but the rhythm caught them. The youths rose and danced. They snake-danced in congas. They did jigs. It went on that way until early morning and it picked up again at noon. 'It's pretty bad,' said an editor of the *Cornell Daily Sun*. 'What does this have to do with politics or peace or any real issue?' "

There are times when rhythm has a stronger hold on us than our most sacred concerns. Through rhythm, an authority on the dance has said, man reunites himself with the ecstasy and terror of a moving universe.

Biologists know of at least a dozen human rhythmical cycles, from that of the heart pulsing 100,000 times a day to that of the alpha waves of the brain pulsing almost ten times as fast. Even before we were born, consciousness may have come to us as an awareness of rhythm—the hammocklike swinging as our mother walked, the intimate beating of her heart and our own matching hers in double time. This first sound we hear is the basis of our sense of rhythm. As a recent writer in *Scientific American* puts it: "From the most primitive tribal drumbeats to the symphonies of Mozart and Beethoven there is a startling similarity to the rhythm of the human heart." Long ago men guessed that the heartbeat might be the source of our speech rhythms as well. The Greek physician Galen quotes an earlier medical writer as saying that the heart's weak-strong diastole and systole, whose sound is described as *lub-DUBB* or *ka-BOOM*, is like the weak-strong iambic foot (as in the word "alive").

> Hunched in the dark beneath his mother's heart,
> The fetus sleeps and listens; dropped into light,
> He seeks to lean his ear against the breast
> Where the known rhythm holds its secret place....
>
> *John Updike*

Some have even held that, since the beat of the accents in most poetry is a little faster than the heartbeat, the rhythm acts as a tonic. In *The Emperor Jones,* Eugene O'Neill assumes such a relationship between external rhythms and the pulse rate:

From the distant hills comes the faint, steady thump of a tom-tom, low and vibrating. It starts at a rate exactly corresponding to normal pulse beat—72 to the minute—and continues at a gradually accelerating rate from this point uninterruptedly to the very end of the play.

We know that excitement, anticipation, emotion can speed up the heart or cause it to spark contractions so close together we get the sensation of a skipped beat. Grief and depression can slow it down. All of these effects have their correlation with the rhythms of poetry.

Walking, too, with our legs and arms swinging in pendulum time, has developed our feeling for rhythms. Goethe composed many of his poems while walking. So, in our own day, did Voznesensky: "I may be walking down a street or in the woods . . . and a rhythm starts inside, maybe connected with my breathing. . . ." The kind of work that man and woman did for countless centuries—sowing, mowing, woodchopping, spinning, rocking the cradle—encouraged rhythmical expressions. Robert Graves believes that our most vigorous rhythms originated in the ringing of hammers on the anvil and the pulling of oars through the sea.

We feel rhythms also in the world outside, with its alternations of day and night, its revolving seasons, its pulsing of waves on the shore, and its swaying of trees in the wind.

No wonder man has been fascinated by the nature of rhythm. Thomas Jefferson, while serving as minister to France, even took time out from his diplomatic duties to write on the science of rhythm in his "Thoughts on English Prosody." Though rhythm is not easy to define, we would probably agree that it is some kind of a pattern of recurrence: something happens with such regularity that we can anticipate its return and move our body in time with it.

The Elizabethan George Puttenham said that the effect of rhythm was "to inveigle and appassionate the mind"—to involve and arouse us. A rhythm that we hear can set up sympathetic reactions—we tap a foot, drum with our fingers, or nod in time to it. Rhythm is contagious. It is also hypnotic. We find it difficult, by the ocean, to count to a hundred waves without feeling our mind drift away into a kind of trance. Rhythm, in taking possession of us, leaves less of our attention for other concerns. The trancelike effect of rhythm—almost psychedelic—explains its connection with magic. The language used in primitive ceremonies all over the world is rhythmical. Its affinity with ecstasy (*being outside oneself*) is well known.

Rhythm has also been thought of as distancing or framing (as in a picture or on a stage) the material it deals with. Its sustained cadence—not exactly what we are used to in actual speech—tells us we are in another world, a make-believe world like that of the theater, in which experience is presented to us without the obligations it involves in real life.

Repetition as Rhythm

One of the simplest forms of rhythm, and one of the most emphatic and passionate, is repetition. Among the most emotional paragraphs in William Faulkner's *Absolom, Absolom!* is the last one, in which Quentin is asked why he hates the South.

"I dont hate it," Quentin said quickly, at once, immediately; "I dont hate it," he said. *I dont hate it,* he thought, panting in the cold air, the iron New England dark; *I dont I dont; I dont hate it! I dont hate it!*

Whenever poetry begins, it seems to begin with repetition—which is a form of *dwelling on* something. The African Bushmen have a song in celebration of the new moon, which is thought to bring rain:

New moon, come out, give water for us,
New moon, thunder down water for us.
New moon, shake down water for us.

Such repetitions are fundamental to primitive poetry, as in this wedding song of the Gabon Pygmies:

SLOWLY, SLOWLY
(African)

Slowly, slowly,
Child, counting your steps,
Go away, go away with tears,
With a large heart, with a weary heart,
Without turning your face,
From the house, from the village,
Where your eyes so gaily
Laughed at every comer.

Counting, counting your steps,
Today you go away. 10
With a large heart, with a weary heart,
Go away, go away below!
Counting, counting your steps,

With a large heart, with a weary heart,
Today you go away.
Keep on your heart
And guard well the flower
Of your mother's garden,
The flower which will say to you:
'I am still loved below!' 20
Keep on your heart
And guard well the flower
In memory for ever.

Counting, counting your steps,
Today you go away,
With a large heart, with a weary heart,
Go away, go away below!
With a large heart, with a weary heart,
Today you go away.

They are no less eloquent today.

COUNTING THE BEATS

You, love, and I,
(He whispers) you and I,
And if no more than only you and I
What care you or I?

Counting the beats,
Counting the slow heart beats,
The bleeding to death of time in slow heart beats,
Wakeful they lie.

Cloudless day,
Night, and a cloudless day, 10
Yet the huge storm will burst upon their heads one day
From a bitter sky.

Where shall we be,
(She whispers) where shall we be,
When death strikes home, O where then shall we be
Who were you and I?

Not there but here,
(He whispers) only here,
As we are, here, together, now and here,
Always you and I. 20

Counting the beats,
Counting the slow heart beats,
The bleeding to death of time in slow heart beats,
Wakeful they lie.

Robert Graves

Wallace Stevens uses repetition when dwelling on the melancholy change that autumn brings.

AUTUMN REFRAIN

The skreak and skritter of evening gone
And grackles gone and sorrows of the sun,
The sorrows of sun, too, gone . . . the moon and moon,
The yellow moon of words about the nightingale
In measureless measures, not a bird for me
But the name of a bird and the name of a nameless air
I have never—shall never hear. And yet beneath
The stillness of everything gone, and being still,
Being and sitting still, something resides,
Some skreaking and skrittering residuum, 10
And grates these evasions of the nightingale
Though I have never—shall never hear that bird.
And the stillness is in the key, all of it is,
The stillness is all in the key of that desolate sound.

Wallace Stevens

Probably no poet has made more systematic use of repetition as a rhythmical principle than Walt Whitman.

LEAVES OF GRASS
[*21*]

I am the poet of the body,
And I am the poet of the soul.

The pleasures of heaven are with me, and the pains of hell are with me,
The first I graft and increase upon myself . . . . the latter I translate into a new tongue.

I am the poet of the woman the same as the man,
And I say it is as great to be a woman as to be a man,
And I say there is nothing greater than the mother of men.

I chant a new chant of dilation or pride,
We have had ducking and deprecating about enough, 10
I show that size is only development.

Have you outstript the rest? Are you the President?
It is a trifle . . . . they will more than arrive there every one, and still pass on.

I am he that walks with the tender and growing night;
I call to the earth and sea half-held by the night.

Press close barebosomed night! Press close magnetic nourishing night!
Night of south winds! Night of the large few stars!
Still nodding night! Mad naked summer night!

Smile O voluptuous coolbreathed earth!
Earth of the slumbering and liquid trees! 20
Earth of departed sunset! Earth of the mountains misty-topt!
Earth of the vitreous pour of the full moon just tinged with blue!
Earth of shine and dark mottling the tide of the river!
Earth of the limpid gray of clouds brighter and clearer for my sake!
Far-swooping elbowed earth! Rich apple-blossomed earth!
Smile, for your lover comes!

Prodigal! you have given me love! .... therefore I to you give love!
O unspeakable passionate love!

Thruster holding me tight and that I hold tight!
We hurt each other as the bridegroom and the bride hurt each other. 30

Walt Whitman

Here are two recent examples of the effectiveness of repetition.

THE .38

I hear the man downstairs slapping the hell out of his stupid wife again
I hear him push and shove her around the overcrowded room
I hear his wife scream and beg for mercy
I hear him tell her there is no mercy
I hear the blows as they land on her beautiful body
I hear glasses and pots and pans falling
I hear her fleeing from the room
I hear them running up the stairs
I hear her outside my door
I hear him coming toward her outside my door 10
I hear her banging on my door
I hear him bang her head on my door
I hear him trying to drag her away from my door
I hear her hands desperate on my doorknob
I hear the blows of her head against my door
I hear him drag her down the stairs
I hear her head bounce from step to step
I hear them again in their room
I hear a loud smack across her face (I guess)
I hear her groan—then 20
I hear the eerie silence
I hear him open the top drawer of his bureau (the .38 lives there)
I hear the fast beat of my heart
I hear the drops of perspiration fall from my brow
I hear him yell I warned you
I hear him say damn you I warned you and now it's too late
I hear the loud report of the thirty eight caliber revolver then
I hear it again and again the Smith and Wesson
I hear the bang bang bang of four death dealing bullets
I hear my heart beat faster and louder—then again 30
I hear the eerie silence

I hear him walk out of their overcrowded room
I hear him walk up the steps
I hear him come toward my door
I hear his hand on the doorknob
I hear the doorknob click
I hear the door slowly open
I hear him step into my room
I hear the click of the thirty eight before the firing pin hits the bullet
I hear the loud blast of the powder exploding in the chamber of the .38 40
I hear the heavy lead nose of the bullet swiftly cutting its way through the
barrel of the .38
I hear it emerge into space from the .38
I hear the bullet of death flying toward my head the .38
I hear it coming faster than sound the .38
I hear it coming closer to my sweaty forehead the .38
I hear its weird whistle the .38
I hear it give off a steamlike noise when it cuts through my sweat the .38
I hear it singe my skin as it enters my head the .38 and
I hear death saying, *Hello, I'm here!* 50

Ted Joans (b. 1928)

BEWARE: DO NOT READ THIS POEM

tonite , thriller was
abt an ol woman, so vain she
surrounded herself w/
many mirrors

it got so bad that finally she
locked herself indoors & her
whole life became the
mirrors

one day the villagers broke
into her house , but she was too 10
swift for them . she disappeared
into a mirror
each tenant who bought the house
after that , lost a loved one to
the ol woman in the mirror :
first a little girl
then a young woman
then the young woman/s husband

the hunger of this poem is legendary
it has taken in many victims 20
back off from this poem
it has drawn in yr feet
back off from this poem
it has drawn in yr legs
back off from this poem
it is a greedy mirror

you are into this poem . from
  the waist down
nobody can hear you can they ?
this poem has had you up to here   30
    belch
this poem aint got no manners
you cant call out frm this poem
relax now & go w/ this poem
move & roll on to this poem
do not resist this poem
this poem has yr eyes
this poem has his head
this poem has his arms
this poem has his fingers   40
this poem has his fingertips

this poem is the reader & the
reader this poem

statistic : the us bureau of missing persons reports
  that in 1968 over 100,000 people disappeared
  leaving no solid clues
    nor trace   only
a space   in the lives of their friends

Ishmael Reed (b. 1938)

These repetitions consist of patterns of word arrangement. Other elements of design can be repeated, so that we have a rhythm like that of a painting. If we "read" Kandinsky's *Lines of Marks,* we find the artist repeating and varying a few simple motifs: the bar, the circle, the triangle, the crescent.

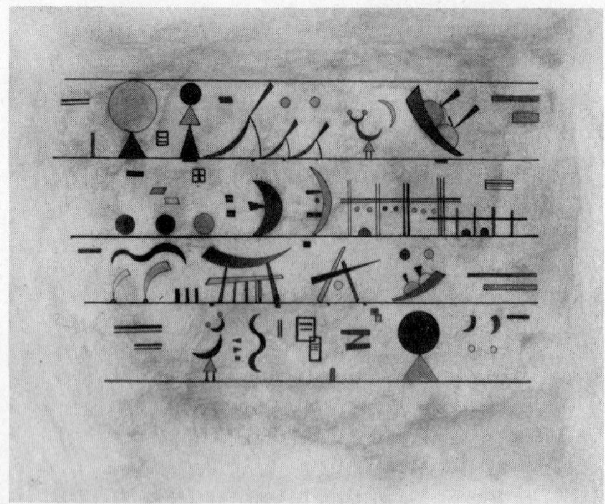

Wassily Kandinsky, *Lines of Marks*

A poem by Dylan Thomas has not only an elaborate rhythmical structure for the ear but also a painterly use of thematic materials.

FERN HILL

Now as I was young and easy under the apple boughs
About the lilting house and happy as the grass was green,
  The night above the dingle starry,
    Time let me hail and climb
  Golden in the heydays of his eyes,
And honoured among wagons I was prince of the apple towns
And once below a time I lordly had the trees and leaves
    Trail with daisies and barley
  Down the rivers of the windfall light.

And as I was green and carefree, famous among the barns 10
About the happy yard and singing as the farm was home,
  In the sun that is young once only,
    Time let me play and be
  Golden in the mercy of his means,
And green and golden I was huntsman and herdsman, the calves
Sang to my horn, the foxes on the hills barked clear and cold,
    And the sabbath rang slowly
  In the pebbles of the holy streams.

All the sun long it was running, it was lovely, the hay
Fields high as the house, the tunes from the chimneys, it was air 20
  And playing, lovely and watery
    And fire green as grass.
  And nightly under the simple stars
As I rode to sleep the owls were bearing the farm away,
All the moon long I heard, blessed among stables, the nightjars
  Flying with the ricks, and the horses
    Flashing into the dark.

And then to awake, and the farm, like a wanderer white
With the dew, come back, the cock on his shoulder: it was all
  Shining, it was Adam and maiden, 30
    The sky gathered again
  And the sun grew round that very day.
So it must have been after the birth of the simple light
In the first, spinning place, the spellbound horses walking warm
  Out of the whinnying green stable
    On to the fields of praise.

And honoured among foxes and pheasants by the gay house
Under the new made clouds and happy as the heart was long,
  In the sun born over and over,
    I ran my heedless ways, 40
  My wishes raced through the house high hay
And nothing I cared, at my sky blue trades, that time allows
In all his tuneful turning so few and such morning songs
  Before the children green and golden
    Follow him out of grace,

---

3 **dingle:** *deep hollow or valley*   25 **nightjars:** *nocturnal birds*

Nothing I cared, in the lamb white days, that time would take me
Up to the swallow thronged loft by the shadow of my hand,
  In the moon that is always rising,
    Nor that riding to sleep
  I should hear him fly with the high fields 50
And wake to the farm forever fled from the childless land.
Oh as I was young and easy in the mercy of his means,
    Time held me green and dying
  Though I sang in my chains like the sea.

Dylan Thomas

The colors green and gold (for grass and sunlight) are used throughout. Five of the six stanzas make mention of singing or music. There are many echoes in syntax or diction: "green and carefree," "green and golden," "green and dying"; "happy as the grass was green," "happy as the heart was long."

The Rhythm of Accent

But what we mean by the rhythm of poetry is more often a rhythm of sound. If we were writing in a language like ancient Greek, in which the length of syllables was prominent, we could make a pattern by alternating long and short ones, as if they were quarter notes and eighth notes. If we were writing in a tonal language like Chinese, we could make a pattern by alternating pitch. But in English, in which accent is more prominent than length or pitch, we generally alternate accented and unaccented syllables.

Most of us have a practical grasp of what a syllable is, perhaps based on the way dictionaries divide up words: mo-lec-u-lar; syn-co-pat-ed; un-pre-ten-tious. We recognize syllables as the little lumps of sound words can be crumbled into—the vowel nucleus with whatever consonants may attach themselves to either side. There may be occasional perplexities. Words like "fire" (fi-er) or "hour" (hou-er) are pronounced sometimes as one syllable, sometimes as two. Other words have a certain play or give: cu-ri-ous or cur-yus; sen-su-al or sench-wul; fa-vor-ite or fav-rite; mur-der-ous or murd-rous.

Some syllables are made more prominent than others by accent—to put it simply, they are uttered with more energy. Nearly all of us (unless tone-deaf) recognize accents when we hear them: what we *imPORT*, we call "IMports"; what we *reJECT*, we call "REjects." In speaking, we tend to alternate accented and unaccented syllables, much as we tend to impose a rhythm on any series of sounds. The language likes to rhythmicize itself. We shift the accent in "reSTORE" to get a better rhythm in "RESTorAtion." Longer words, as Thomas Jefferson noticed, move in rhythm: tubérculósis, enthúsiástically, indústriálizátion. We sometimes shift the usual accent to get a better rhythm: we say "to wálk uphíll," but "an úphill wálk"; we say "goód-nátured," but "a goód-natured mán."

There are, of course, many degrees of accent. We need subtle differences to distinguish, in speaking, between "What's in the road ahead?" and "What's in the road—a head?" Or, to take two of the most hackneyed examples, between "the greenhouse," "the green house," and "the Greene house"; and between "light-housekeeper," "lighthouse keeper," and "light [maybe blonde] housekeeper." Linguistic scientists admit four degrees of stress, though no doubt, for anyone sensitive enough to catch them, there are many in between. But whether there are four or forty, all we need for the rhythms of poetry are *two.* Does a syllable have *more* or *less* mass than the syllables around it? How much more or less is irrelevant. More or less alone can make waves of sound. Like alternations of tension and relief, like the *lub-DUBB* of the heartbeat, like inhaling and exhaling, like Yin and Yang and the antithetical play of existence, rhythm is an interaction between *two* principles, *two* kinds of accent, not among three or more.

The nature of light, as we know, is mysterious. Einstein spent about twenty years trying to understand its schizophrenic behavior. In some ways light acts as if it consisted of waves, in others as if it consisted of particles or corpuscles. It may help to think of the rhythm of poetry as having a similar nature. We can have a wave theory of rhythm or a corpuscular theory.

The writer who is using accents for his rhythm makes sure that they come in waves, as so much energy does in the physical world. What we feel in accentual rhythm is a regular surge of *more* and *less* in the natural flow of the language.

When we go surfing on a rhythm, we take the crests and hollows without particularly analyzing their dynamics. We ride the lines like this:

The CUR few TOLLS the KNELL of PART ing DAY,

very much as we would have pronounced the words anyway, even if we had not been riding the rhythm (which ought to be in the *natural* pronunciation of the words, and not in any artificial singsong we impose on them). We may be content to take these waves of rhythm as they come, as one can be happy merely watching the surf along the shore. But if we really care about waves—as Leonardo da Vinci did, or as Gerard Manley Hopkins did when he stared at them "to unpack the huddling and gnarls of the water and law out the shapes and the sequence of the running"—we would have to immobilize the flux (as with a camera) to see the wave as a surge of rotating particles which themselves move forward hardly at all.

If we could similarly immobilize the waves of the commonest English rhythm (called "iambic"), we would find every unit of trough and crest to be made up of a dip and swell in the accent—of an unstressed syllable and a stressed one, as in "reJOICE," "to LOVE," "at HOME." This unit is called a **foot**, a term that takes us back to the supposed origin of poetry in the dance, when each rhythmic unit was marked by a beat of the dancer's foot.

A NOTE ON SCANSION

If we are to isolate any unit of rhythm-particles for our inspection, we need a set of symbols to stop the action and show what is happening. The process of applying these symbols is what we call **scansion.** Many find it a dreary affair. It seems pedantic and destructive to represent a living line of verse by anything so lifeless as ∪ —|∪—|∪—|∪—|∪—|.

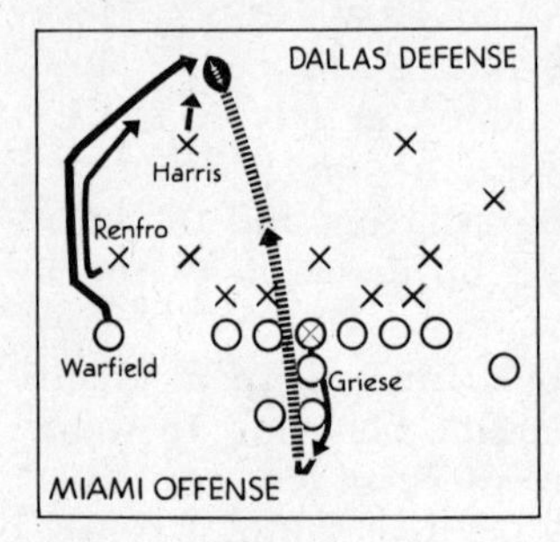

This is certainly not the same thing as a line of poetry. Agreed. But we take for granted the utility of such simplified schemata in many activities. Compared with the color and drama of a football game, the diagram of a play is also dry and pedantic. Yet it is difficult to imagine a professional quarterback looking at the diagram and snarling, "Who needs that kind of stuff? I just want to get out there and play!"

Musical notes are sometimes used with poetry to show how the particles of rhythm are related.

But speech has nothing like so metronomic a regularity. Music is in the world of chronometric time; the metronome, even though the performer may tease and worry it now and then, sets the standard. But the rhythm of poetry exists in the world of psychological time, the kind of time in which, as Romeo says, "Sad hours seem long," or in which happiness, to paraphrase Goethe, can make the day race by on flashing feathers. Time, in the rhythms of poetry, is subjective—as elastic as Dali's famous watch, drooped like a pancake over its tree branch. One could pause for a couple of seconds after a word in poetry ("beech-tree," for example, in the first line of Meredith's poem) and not affect the rhythm in the least. Musical scansion is not of much use to us.

A more modern type of scansion, that of structural linguistics, attempts to show four degrees of stress, four degrees of pitch, and the four kinds of connective pauses between words. But a system that turns a simple line of Yeats into

^{2}∧Spéech + àftĕr + lóng^{2}↗^{3}sílĕncè;^{1}↘^{2}∧ìt + ĭs + ríght^{3}↗ . . .

FISH'S NIGHTSONG

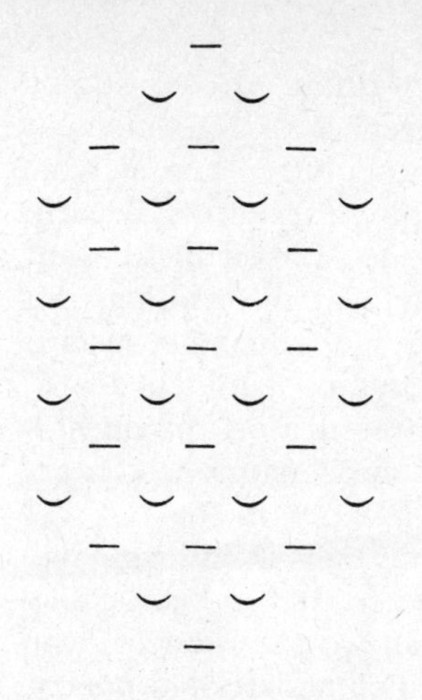

Christian Morgenstern (1871-1914)

is more complex than we need. Readers do not listen that way; poets do not write that way. When Theodore Roethke quotes from a nursery rhyme:

> Hinx, minx, the old witch winks,

he says he feels it as "five stresses [accents] out of a possible six." He does not say he feels it as "three primaries, a secondary, and a tertiary."

All that matters is more or less, and the easiest way to indicate the two is the traditional one—a firm straight line for the accented syllable (—) and a sagging little curve for the slack one (◡), as in the famous "concrete" poem by Christian Morgenstern, in which the symbols stand for silent music as well as for waves and fishes. (Some scanners prefer to tilt the straight line skyward (′) to indicate accent rather than length.)

Sometimes the pattern of accents is clear, as in:

> Thĕ cūr|fĕw tōlls| thĕ knēll| ŏf pārt|ĭng dāy . . . .

Nothing to hesitate over here. If we find ourselves hesitating, the thing to do is to mark the accents we are sure of. There is no doubt about words like "dĕlīght," "rĕmēmbĕr," "āppĕtīte," or (usually) about phrases like "thĕ cāt," "tŏ thĕ stōre," "yŏu wānt tŏ." We generally get enough pieces of the pattern from the known words to complete the rest of it for ourselves by filling it in with matching parts—testing them by means of natural pronunciation to see if they really fit. Once we get into the swing of a rhythm we are pretty sure how it is going to continue. But scansion is not an exact science like mathematics. Stressed and unstressed syllables are not always as instantly identifiable as even and odd numbers are. Occasionally we come across a line that no two of us will scan in exactly the same way; we might even scan the same line differently on different days or in different moods. But we would be in agreement about nearly all syllables. Even when we differ about details, we would probably agree about the basic rhythm.

Iambic Pentameter

The rhythmical line we have been using for our examples is the commonest line in English poetry, the **iambic pentameter.** *Iambic* because for over twenty centuries that has been the name of the trough-and-crest unit (◡—), as in "to dance" or "enjoy." If the word sounds classroomy to us now, we might recall that it originally meant something violent and abusive. In ancient Greece a girl named Iambē personified the obscene songs (in iambics) sung to relieve emotional tension at religious mystery rites. *Pentameter* because there are five of these iambs to a line. Among all people five is the natural unit of counting off (a glance at the hand will show why). The fiveness of the line may have another physiological basis. Since the ratio between a somewhat excited pulse rate and the normal rate of breathing (seventeen breaths a minute) is about five to one, we would not be too far off in thinking of iambic pentameter as a breathful of heartbeats. Recalling this rhythm might even help us save a life. In cardiopulmonary resuscitation—the new technique for keeping alive victims of "sudden death" by mouth-to-mouth breathing and rhythmical pressure on the chest—one breath is given for every five of the chest-compressions which are substitute heartbeats.

Pick up any anthology that covers poetry in English, and you will find that at least two-thirds of it is in this cadence. It has been called the most important meter in the North European world. Chaucer, who got it from the ten- or eleven-syllable line of French and Italian poetry, is given credit for establishing it in English.

HYD, ABSOLON, THY GILTE TRESSES CLERE

Hyd, Absolon, thy giltė tresses clere;
Esther, ley thou thy mekenesse all adoun;
Hyd, Jonathas, all thy frendly manere;
Penelopé and Marcia Catoun,
Mak of youre wifhod no comparisoun;
Hyde ye youre beautés, Isoude and Eleyne:
My lady cometh, that all this may disteyne.

Thy fairė body, lat it nat appere,
Lavine, and thou, Lucresse of Romė toun,
And Polixene, that boghten love so dere, 10
And Cleopatre, with all thy passioun,
Hyde ye your trouthe of love and your renoun;
And thou, Tisbé, that hast of love swich peyne:
My lady cometh, that all this may disteyne.

Hero, Dido, Laudomia, alle ifere,
And Phyllis, hanging for thy Demophoun,
And Canacé, espièd by thy chere,
Ysiphilé, betrayèd with Jasoun,
Maketh of your trouthė neyther boost ne soun,
Nor Ypermystre or Adriane, ye tweyne: 20
My lady cometh, that all this may disteyne.

Geoffrey Chaucer (1340?–1400)

---

[2] **adoun:** *down*
[4] **Marcia Catoun:** *Cato's Marcia*
[5] **wifhod:** *womanhood*
[7] **disteyne:** *bedim, overshadow*
[10] **boghten:** *paid for*
[13] **swich:** *such*
[15] **ifere:** *together*
[17] **espièd by thy chere:** *recognized by your face or expression*
[19] **ne soun:** *nor sound*

Iambics, to be so thoroughly accepted, must have seemed natural—like the way people really talk. Aristotle heard them in the language of everyday Greek. Hopkins commented, "and the same holds for English." Richard Blackmur once said, after listening to recorded poetry in thirty-odd languages, that he could hear the iambic base in all but one.

More iambic pentameters are uttered every day here in America than Shakespeare and all his fellows wrote in a lifetime. When George Starbuck wonders:

> Whaddaya do for action in this place?

he is writing in a cadence we often fall into without knowing it.

> I'd like to introduce a friend of mine.
>
> Please fill 'er up—and better check the oil.
>
> Suppose you take your damn feet off the chair.
>
> Deposit fifty cents for overtime.
>
> Cheeseburger special and a glass of beer.
>
> For rent: one-room apartment near the lake.
>
> You ever been in Albuquerque, hey?
>
> Eleven times eleven comes to what?
>
> I'd like to know exactly what she said.

Leonard Bernstein thinks that iambic pentameter was in on the birth of the blues, out of which jazz and so much modern music was to evolve. The writers of blues lyrics did not use it because it was "classic"; they used it for the same reason that Shakespeare and the Elizabethan dramatists did—it embodies a basic speech pattern.

> I hate to see that evenin' sun go down . . . .
>
> Goin' lay my head right on the railroad track,
> [Be]cause my baby, she won't take me back . . . .
>
> Mr. Crump won't 'low no easy riders here . . . .
>
> The man I love's got low-down ways for true . . . .
>
> Woke up this mornin', blues all round my bed . . . .

VARIATIONS ON IAMBIC

There is no merit (as we will show soon) in mere regularity. We can find perfectly regular iambics, as in the ticktock of Shakespeare's

> When I do count the clock that tells the time . . . .

or in

> Of hand, of foot, of lip, of eye, of brow . . . .

In "Sonnet 66" we have almost eleven consecutive lines (from the "behold" of line 2 through line 12) with only one variation from strict meter—the little stumble that comes in, appropriately enough, with the "tongue-tied" of line 9.

SONNET 66

Tired with all these, for restful death I cry:
As, to behold desert a beggar born,
And needy nothing trimmed in jollity,
And purest faith unhappily forsworn,
And gilded honor shamefully misplaced,
And maiden virtue rudely strumpeted,
And right perfection wrongfully disgraced,
And strength by limping sway disabled,
And art made tongue-tied by authority,
And folly (doctor-like) controlling skill, 10
And simple truth miscalled simplicity,
And captive good attending captain ill.
  Tired with all these, from these would I be gone,
  Save that, to die, I leave my love alone.

William Shakespeare

Nothing so regular is to be found elsewhere in the sonnets, or rarely anywhere in good poetry. But Shakespeare has a reason here for his unvarying rhythm: he is writing about the monotony of injustice in the world, which has its own dreary pattern of recurrence.

If we were tapping our fingers to music and the music suddenly stopped, we could go on tapping without breaking the rhythm, just as we could continue a wavy line, if it ended, with a dotted line of similar waves.

Our expectation of continuing rhythm is so strong that we can even feel an accent where perhaps there is none, as we can feel a tícktock pattern in the undifferentiated ticks of a clock. If we expect an accent on syllables 2, 4, 6, 8, and 10, we are inclined to stress these syllables. When Shakespeare, in "Sonnet 68," complains about such "bastard signs" of beauty as the wearing of wigs from the hair of persons now dead, he writes:

---

2 **desert:** *true merit*
3 **needy nothing:** *a penniless nonentity*
trimmed in jollity: *showily dressed*
6 **strumpeted:** *treated like a harlot*
8 **limping sway:** *defective authority*
11 **simplicity:** *idiocy*

Before the golden tresses of the dead,
The right of sepulchers, were shorn away
To live a second life on second head . . . .

Our projection of the rhythm leads us to expect an accent on "of" (the eighth syllable) in the first line, and on the last syllable of "sepulchers" (the sixth syllable) in the second line. There is no real accent on either; but since we expect to hear one, and since nothing insists we *cannot* hear one, we assume that we do.

But sometimes an apparently misplaced accent is too strong to ignore, and then we have a genuine variation in the rhythm. When Shakespeare begins a line with "To the wide world," we cannot imagine that it should be pronounced, "To THE wide WORLD . . . " or any other way except "To the WIDE WORLD. . . ." Such variations are the life of rhythm. According to what we call the "corpuscular" theory of rhythm, we can stop parts of the moving wave to examine its particles and observe the mechanics of variation. The iambic foot is made up of two particles or syllables, the first having less mass or energy than the second (∪—). But, in place of the normal foot, we find that four options are possible.

The first option is a foot of two syllables, neither of which has an accent, as in the lines from "Sonnet 68" discussed above. This foot is called a **pyrrhic** (∪∪).

When I have seen the hungry ocean gain
Advan|tăge ŏn| the king|dŏm ŏf| the shore . . . .
William Shakespeare

A pyrrhic foot, in giving us *less* than we expect, goes well with anything related to *less*ness—the erosion of the shore, perhaps, in the quotation above; or the sense of a misstep:

While through the window masked with flowers
A lone wasp stag|gĕrs frŏm| the dead . . . .
J. V. Cunningham

The second option is a foot of two syllables, both of which have a positive accent. This is called a **spondee** (— —). We hear it in expressions like "dead beat" (*very tired*), as opposed to "deadbeat" (*one who avoids paying debts*); or in expressions like "dead weight," "dead end," "Dead Sea," as opposed to "deadeye," "deadwood," "deadline," each of which accents the first syllable.

Since the spondee packs as much mass as possible into a two-syllable foot, it can be expressive of any kind of muchness, weightiness, or slowness. Since its very density makes it take longer to pronounce, it can dramatize extent or duration.

Was it the proud |fūll sāil| of his |grēat vērse,|
Bound for the prize of all |tōō prē|cious you . . . ?|
William Shakespeare

Yet once more ere thou hate me, one |fūll kīss . . . .|
A. C. Swinburne

I laid down my |lōng nēt| in the |bīg tīde| . . . .|
Brewster Ghiselin

Clotted spondees have been used for frozen blood:

And though I think this heart's |blo͞od frōze|nōt fāst|
It ran |to͞o smāll| to spare |ōne drōp| for dream|ing . . . .
John Crowe Ransom

Spondees can also slow down the line so that details can be contemplated:

Reign in my thoughts! |fāir hānd!|swe͞et ēye!|rāre vōice!|
Samuel Daniel

The third option reverses the iambic foot from ∪ — to — ∪. "Happy," "token," "over" are examples of this foot (the **trochee**.) Trochees are so common at the beginning of iambic lines that we hardly feel them as variations.

To be or not to be, that is the question.
|Whēthĕr| 'tis nobler in the mind to suffer . . . .

They also fit in easily after a strong pause within the line:

Did heaven look on,
And would not take their part? |Sīnfŭl| Macduff,
They were all struck for thee! |Na͞ught thăt| I am . . . .

But elsewhere, when a trochee substitutes for an iamb, the effect can be like that of strain or abrupt dislocation. A trochee among iambs is out of place, its movement going counter to the tilt of the line. In these examples from Shakespeare a trochee is found roughing the meter, calling attention to some violence in the thought:

With time's injurious hand |crūshed ănd| o'erworn . . . .

|Lēt mĕ|nōt tŏ| the marriage of true minds
Admit impediments . . . .

And in Yeats:

O she had not these ways
When all the wild |sūmmĕr| was in her gaze.

Going along with the meter, we want to read "the WILD sumMER," but cannot. So, with some feeling of strain, we do violence to the meter, which itself is made to rebel as the words recall the girl's rebellious youth.

Perhaps it has taken our ear a few centuries to get used to this mid-line trochee. Even Thomas Jefferson, in so many ways willing to declare his independence, did not easily go along with it. Of the reversed foot in Milton's

To do aught good |nēvĕr| will be our task,

he says, "it has not a good effect." What Jefferson disliked about the irregularity is probably what we like—the shock value of the energetic dislocation. Milton's "never" stands out defiantly against accepted laws of meter, as it would never do if placed tamely after "will."

We can also think of the trochee among iambs as a kind of backspin or underspin or reverse English, as in Allen Tate's

> The going years, |caught in| an after-glow,
> Reverse like balls |englished| upon green baize . . . .

Here the word "englished" is itself englished, its — ◡ spinning against the ◡ —'s of the line.

The fourth option is a foot of three syllables with the accent on the last (◡◡—), as in "disagree," "reproduce," "to the woods." This foot (the **anapest**) adds an extra syllable, as one would do in a series of *de DUM de DUM*'s if he occasionally slipped in a *de de DUM*. Pleasant in itself as a change of pace, it can be expressive in suggesting a burst of speed, something impulsive and capricious, like a skip or little caper interrupting our normal stride. Substitute anapests are common, as in Browning's "Fra Lippo Lippi":

> The world and life's too big to pass |fŏr ă drēam . . . .|

> Scarce had they turned the corner when a titter,
> Likĕ thĕ skīp|pĭng ŏf răb|bĭts bȳ mōōn|light—three slim shapes . . . .

Shakespeare (like most good poets) freely makes use of all possible options, even writing lines in which four of the five feet are non-iambic:

> |Plūck thĕ|kēēn tēēth|frŏm thĕ|fiērce tī|gĕr's jāws . . . .|

> |Lēt mĕ|nōt tŏ|thĕ măr|riăge ŏf|trūē mīnds . . . .|

But he never lets the number of syllables fall short of ten—fall short of five feet of at least two syllables. Iambic pentameter cares about not only accent but also number of syllables—it may add one or two to the ten, but it practically never subtracts. On rare occasions, in what is called a "headless" line, the first syllable is dropped, as in T. S. Eliot's:

> Wipe your hand across your mouth, and laugh.

An extra syllable at the end of the line is so common it is hardly felt as an irregularity:

> To be or not to be, that is |thĕ quēs|tiŏn . . . .|

Much of this chapter has been an account of the structure of iambic pentameter. If one wishes to stop the flow of that rhythm to examine the mechanics of the individual wave, he should now be able to do so.

A pleasant poem for this kind of study is Edward FitzGerald's translation of *The Rubáiyát* (or *Quatrains*) of Omar Khayyám, the twelfth-century Persian poet, mathematician, and astronomer. Rhythmically, the stanzas are easy to follow, since they have a more regular swing than most of the poems we have been reading. And yet in them one can find all of the variations described on the preceding pages.

FROM **THE RUBÁIYÁT OF OMAR KHAYYÁM**[1]

I

Awake! for Morning in the Bowl of Night
Has flung the Stone that puts the Stars to Flight:
  And Lo! the Hunter of the East has caught
The Sultán's Turret in a Noose of Light.

III

And, as the Cock crew, those who stood before
The Tavern shouted—"Open then the Door!
  You know how little while we have to stay,
And, once departed, may return no more."

VII

Come, fill the Cup, and in the Fire of Spring
The Winter Garment of Repentance fling: 10
  The Bird of Time has but a little way
To fly—and Lo! the Bird is on the Wing.

XII c

A Book of Verses underneath the Bough,
A Jug of Wine, a Loaf of Bread—and Thou
  Beside me singing in the Wilderness—
Oh, Wilderness were Paradise enow!

XIII c

Some for the Glories of This World; and some
Sigh for the Prophet's Paradise to come;
  Ah, take the Cash, and let the Credit go,
Nor heed the rumble of a distant Drum! 20

XVIII b

Think, in this batter'd Caravanserai
Whose Portals are alternate Night and Day,
  How Sultán after Sultán with his Pomp
Abode his destined Hour, and went his way.

[1] Stanzas with simple numbers are from the first edition of 1859; those with *b* numbers are from the second edition of 1868; those with *c* from the fifth edition of 1889.

---

21 **Caravanserai:** *inn primarily for caravans*

XXIV b

I sometimes think that never blows so red
The Rose as where some buried Cæsar bled;
  That every Hyacinth the Garden wears
Dropt in her Lap from some once lovely Head.

XIX

And this delightful Herb whose tender Green
Fledges the River's Lip on which we lean— 30
  Ah, lean upon it lightly! for who knows
From what once lovely Lip it springs unseen!

XXIII b

And we, that now make merry in the Room
They left, and Summer dresses in new bloom,
  Ourselves must we beneath the Couch of Earth
Descend—ourselves to make a Couch—for whom?

XXVII c

Myself when young did eagerly frequent
Doctor and Saint, and heard great argument
  About it and about: but evermore
Came out by the same door where in I went. 40

XXXII

There was a Door to which I found no Key:
There was a Veil past which I could not see:
  Some little Talk awhile of ME and THEE
There seem'd—and then no more of THEE and ME.

LXXVI b

The Moving Finger writes; and, having writ,
Moves on: nor all your Piety nor Wit
  Shall lure it back to cancel half a Line,
Nor all your Tears wash out a Word of it.

LXXI

And much as Wine has play'd the Infidel,
And robb'd me of my Robe of Honour—well, 50
  I often wonder what the Vintners buy
One half so precious as the Goods they sell.

LXXII

Alas, that Spring should vanish with the Rose!
That Youth's sweet-scented Manuscript should close!

The Nightingale that in the Branches sang,
Ah, whence, and whither flown again, who knows!

CVIII b

Ah, Love! could you and I with Fate conspire
To grasp this sorry Scheme of Things entire,
  Would not we shatter it to bits—and then
Re-mould it nearer to the Heart's Desire! 60

LXXIV

Ah, Moon of my Delight, who know'st no wane,
The Moon of Heav'n is rising once again:
  How oft hereafter rising shall she look
Through this same Garden after me—in vain!

LXXV

And when Thyself with shining Foot shall pass
Among the Guests Star-scatter'd on the Grass,
  And in thy joyous Errand reach the Spot
Where I made one—turn down an empty Glass!

Omar Khayyám (d. 1123?)
(Translated by Edward FitzGerald)

A more recent use of the Omar Khayyám stanza is in X. J. Kennedy's "B Negative," where it sets up a contrast with Omar's world. It is all very well for Omar to be happy with

A Book of Verses underneath the Bough,
A Jug of Wine, a Loaf of Bread—and Thou . . . .

But what if one is a seedy old man of sixty—even his blood type negative—who has nothing in life but the funny papers to read, a bag of peanuts to share with the pigeons, and no "Thou" at all any more? He does have his cup of soup in the automat and occasionally some cheap wine, and he has his job—picking up after other people in the park. In his despair he has come to understand what motivates "poor loony stranglers," and to think of suicide in a hotel room. This could be a lugubrious poem, but a sense of amusement in the poet and in his speaker saves it from that.

B NEGATIVE
M/60/5 FT 4/W PROT

You know it's April by the falling-off
In coughdrop boxes—fewer people cough—
  By daisies' first white eyeballs in the grass
And every dawn more underthings cast off.

Though plumtrees stretch recovered boughs to us
And doubledecked in green, the downtown bus,
  Love in one season—so your stab-pole tells—
Beds down, and buds, and is deciduous.

Now set down burlap bag. In pigeon talk
The wobbling pigeon flutes on the sidewalk, 10
  Struts on the breeze and clicks leisurely wings
As if the corn he ate grew on a stalk.

So plump he topples where he tries to stand,
He pecks my shoelaces, come to demand
  Another sack, another fifteen cents,
And yet—who else will eat out of my hand?

It used to be that when I laid my head
And body with it down by you in bed
  You did not turn from me nor fall to sleep
But turn to fall between my arms instead 20

And now I lay bifocals down. My feet
Forget the twist that brought me to your street.
  I can't make out your face for steamed-up glass
Nor quite call back your outline on the sheet.

I know how, bent to a movie magazine,
The hobo's head lights up, and from its screen
  Imagined bosoms in slow motion bloom
And no director interrupts the scene:

I used to purchase in the Automat
A cup of soup and fan it with my hat 30
  Until a stern voice from the changebooth crashed
Like nickels: *Gentlemen do not do that.*

Spring has no household, no abiding heat,
Pokes forth no bud from branches of concrete,
  Nothing to touch you, nothing you can touch—
The snow, at least, keeps track of people's feet.

The springer spaniel and the buoyant hare
Seem half at home reclining in mid-air
  But Lord, the times I've leaped the way they do
And looked round for a foothold—in despair. 40

The subway a little cheaper than a room,
I browse the *News*—or so the guards assume—
  And there half-waking, tucked in funny sheets,
I hurtle within my mile-a-minute womb.

Down streets that wake up earlier than wheels
The routed spirit flees on dusty heels
  And in the soft fire of a muscatel
Sits up, puts forth its fingertips, and feels—

Down streets so deep the sun can't vault their walls,
Where one-night wives make periodic calls, 50

Where cat steals stone where rat makes off with child
And lyre and lute lie down under three balls,

Down blocks in sequence, fact by separate fact,
The human integers add and subtract
Till in a cubic room in some hotel
You wake one day to find yourself abstract

And turn a knob and hear a voice: *Insist*
On Jiffy Blades, they're tender to the wrist—
Then static, then a squawk as if your hand
Had shut some human windpipe with a twist. 60

I know how, lurking under trees by dark,
Poor loony stranglers out to make their mark
Reach forth shy hands to touch a woman's hair—
I pick up after them in Central Park.

X. J. Kennedy

Exercises and Diversions

A. What purpose, if any, does repetition serve in the following quotations?

1. But O the heavy change, now thou art gone,
Now thou art gone, and never must return! *John Milton*

2. They all are gone, and thou art gone as well!
Yes, thou art gone! *Matthew Arnold*

3. There was a crooked man, and he walked a crooked mile,
He found a crooked sixpence against a crooked stile;
He bought a crooked cat, which caught a crooked mouse,
And they all lived together in a little crooked house. *Anonymous*

4. This is my play's last scene; here heavens appoint
My pilgrimage's last mile; and my race,
Idly yet quickly run, hath this last pace;
My span's last inch, my minute's latest point. . . . *John Donne*

5. There passed a weary time. Each throat
Was parched, and glazed each eye.
A weary time! a weary time!
How glazed each weary eye. . . . *Samuel Taylor Coleridge*

B. Patterns of repetition are so ancient they have Greek names. When successive units—lines, clauses, sentences—begin with the same (or almost the same) word or words, the pattern is called **anaphora**. When they end with the same words, **epistrophe**. When both patterns are combined, **symploce**. When a unit begins and ends with the same words, **epanalepsis**. When the end of one unit is repeated as the beginning of the next, **anadiplosis**. Find examples of these in the poems of Whitman, Joans, and Reed in this chapter.

C. Each of the following examples of iambic pentameter makes use of one or more of the optional feet. Find and identify them. Beside adding variety to the line, which variations are expressive?

1. [From "Doctor Drink"]
   On a cold night I came through the cold rain
   And false snow to the wind shrill on your pane
   With no hope and no anger and no fear:
   Who are you? and with whom do you sleep here? *J. V. Cunningham*

2. O body swayed to music, O brightening glance,
   How can we know the dancer from the dance? *William Butler Yeats*

3. Tudor indeed is gone and every rose,
   Blood-red, blanch-white that in the sunset glows
   Cries: "Blood, Blood, Blood!" against the gothic stone
   Of England, as the Howard or Boleyn knows. *Ezra Pound*

4. Divinity must live within herself . . .
   Elations when the forest blooms; gusty
   Emotions on wet roads on autumn nights. . . . *Wallace Stevens*

5. Don't the moon look pretty, shinin' through the tree,
   I can see my woman, Lord, but she can't see me. . . . *Anonymous*

6. What is your substance, whereof are you made,
   That millions of strange shadows on you tend? *William Shakespeare*

7. Come, keen iambics, with your badger's feet,
   And badger-like, bite till your teeth do meet. *John Cleveland*

8. The grim eight-foot-high iron-bound serving-man. . . . *John Donne*

9. Bear thine eyes straight, though thy proud heart go wide. . . .
   William Shakespeare

10. And if by noon I have too much of these,
    I have but to turn on my arm, and lo,
    The sun-burned hillside sets my face aglow. . . . *Robert Frost*

11. I know when one is dead, and when one lives. . . . *William Shakespeare*

12. Weeds among weeds, or flowers with flowers gather'd. . . . *William Shakespeare*

13. Cover her face; mine eyes dazzle; she died young. *John Webster*

D. After reading the poems of Omar Khayyám and X. J. Kennedy for pleasure, read them again with your ear alert for metrical variations. Would you agree with the following opinion? "There is more interest, more variety and expressiveness in Kennedy's rhythms than in those of FitzGerald's deliberately narcotic meditation: spondees are used more *physically*, reversed feet (trochees) are more forceful, there are more lively anapests. . . ."

E. 1. Make up a dozen or so iambic pentameters of the kind you might use in conversation, like "This English class has really been a bore" or "You got your tickets for the game tonight?"

2. Compose a dozen or so lines of realistic dialogue in iambic pentameter.

3. Write a few lines of perfectly regular iambic pentameter; then a few that use pyrrhic feet (◡ ◡) for *less*ness; a few that use spondees (— —) for *more*ness or fullness; a few that use trochees (—◡) for abruptness or violence; and a few that use anapests (◡ ◡ —) for speed or impulse.

15 The Dancer and the Dance: the play of rhythms

Meter and Rhythm

In speaking of music, Stravinsky stresses the distinction between meter and rhythm, a distinction that holds also in poetry. In music, meter is what the metronome is doing; rhythm, what the composer or performer actually gives us. In poetry, **meter** (from the Greek word for *measure*) is the basic scheme, the ◡—|◡—|◡—|◡—|◡—, apart from any realization in words—what our mind could continue with if all sound stopped. **Rhythm** (from the Greek word for *flow*) is the way the words of the poem move, sometimes coinciding with the meter and sometimes not. Meter is like the abstract idea of a dance as a choreographer might plan it with no particular performers in mind; rhythm is like a dancer interpreting the dance in his own way.

What we feel in an iambic line is an interplay of two rhythms at once: the meter our mind anticipates, and the rhythm the words have as they are read or spoken. The two are seldom identical. In expecting, in iambic verse, another iambic foot, the mind is right most of the time. When it is not right, it does a double take, and the questionable foot gets more attention than if it were regular.

As we brought out in our discussion of variations in the last chapter, iambic pentameter is monotonous if we think of it merely as meter. Of course: monotony is the only virtue of a metronome. But good poets do not write it as a meter; they use it as a rough gauge for their rhythms. There are as many rhythms based on iambic pentameter as there are individual—really individual—writers. No one would confuse the iambics of Shakespeare with those of Pope or Milton or Tennyson or Yeats or Cummings. Some poets prefer **end-stopped** lines, which have a pause after the tenth syllable; some prefer **run-on** lines, which move on without a pause to the next line. Each poet is likely to handle in his own way the **caesura**—the strong pause that falls toward the middle of many lines.

The individual style is largely a matter of the interplay between meter and rhythm (an interplay that is also called "variation," "tension," "substitution," "counterpoint," etc.). For deviations to be felt at all, there has to be something to deviate from. The offbeats of African music are effective because the sense of a regular beat has been established in the mind of the listener. A musician cannot have offbeats unless he has a metrical beat to be "off." And so in poetry—if the meter is a loose one, the variations will be weak.

The tensions of Beethoven's *Grosse Fuge* are said to have "pushed music to extreme limits, stopped just short of shattering the tonal system." Working with a rigid meter makes it possible for Yeats to get a similar effect in a poem in which his vision of imminent world chaos throws the last line into confusion, beneath the metrical ruins of which there lies, almost buried, the iambic meter.

THE SECOND COMING

Turning and turning in the widening gyre
The falcon cannot hear the falconer;
Things fall apart; the centre cannot hold;
Mere anarchy is loosed upon the world,
The blood-dimmed tide is loosed, and everywhere
The ceremony of innocence is drowned;
The best lack all conviction, while the worst
Are full of passionate intensity.

Surely some revelation is at hand;
Surely the Second Coming is at hand. 10
The Second Coming! Hardly are those words out
When a vast image out of *Spiritus Mundi*
Troubles my sight: somewhere in sands of the desert
A shape with lion body and the head of a man,
A gaze blank and pitiless as the sun,
Is moving its slow thighs, while all about it
Reel shadows of the indignant desert birds.
The darkness drops again; but now I know
That twenty centuries of stony sleep
Were vexed to nightmare by a rocking cradle, 20
And what rough beast, its hour come round at last,
Slouches towards Bethlehem to be born?

W. B. Yeats

---

12 **Spiritus Mundi:** *the "Soul of the World," a kind of storehouse of archetypal memories*

The poem illustrates all of the variations described in the preceding chapter. A pyrrhic foot ("-ing in") makes a gap or hollow in the middle of the first line. The movement of the words before the gap is what is called a "falling rhythm," from accent down to nonaccent—"Tūrnĭng ănd tūrnĭng." The movement after it is a "rising rhythm"—"Ĭn thĕ wīdĕnĭng gȳre." So the two halves of the line strain in opposite directions: things are already falling apart. Spondees are clotted in "Thĕ blōōd-dīmmed tīde" (l. 5); are bulky in "Whĕn ă| vāst īm|ăge" (l. 12); are sluggish in "Ĭs mōv|ĭng ĭts| slōw thīghs" (l. 16). Trochees are abrupt in the "Sūrely̆" that appears in lines 9 and 10; are harsh in "Ă gāze| blānk ănd| pītĭ|lĕss" (l. 15). The anapest spreads out rapidly in "thĕ wīd|ĕnĭng gȳre" (l. 1); it is fast in "Hārd|ly̆ ăre thōse| wōrds ōūt" (l. 11).

These are expressive variations. Not all variations are. Some bring nothing more than a pleasant variety to the verse. As with sound itself, correspondence between expression and meaning is only occasional. When variations are meaningful, they strike with double effect. Some change of speed or mass or energy in the flow of sound dramatizes what is being said.

A much earlier poem of Yeats, "He Remembers Forgotten Beauty," shows how a passionate rhythm can override mathematical meter (which here has four beats instead of the five of pentameter).

> When my arms wrap you round I press
> My heart upon the loveliness
> That has long faded from the world . . . .

While there are wrong ways of scanning these lines ("Whēn my̆| ārms wrăp| yōū rŏund| Ī prĕss . . . ") there is no one right way. Here is one possible way of feeling the stresses:

> Whĕn mȳ|ārms wrāp|yōū rōund|Ĭ prĕss
> My̆ hēart|ŭpŏn|thĕ lōve|lĭnĕss
> Thăt hăs|lōng fād|ĕd frŏm|thĕ wōrld . . . .

One might even stress every syllable in the first line. Instead of the four expected accents, it has anywhere from five to eight. There is much more mass and energy than we expect in this line, fewer of the slacks or sags of unaccented syllables. Metrically, this may be the tightest embrace in poetry. The second line is different, with only two strong accents, one on "heart" and one on the "love-" in "loveliness." ("Upon" itself has an accent, but it is relatively weak as we read this line.) The gap in the middle, between "heart" and "loveliness," is as if the rhythm, in its excitement, had skipped a beat. The definite accents in the third line are on "long," "fad-" (of "faded"), and "world." The spondee "long fad-" is for muchness, for length of time. The slack of "-ed from the" has about as many unaccented syllables as the meter would tolerate between "fad-" and "world," so that what has *faded* is distanced by the rhythm itself.

A poem that illustrates the difference between meter and rhythm is Allen Tate's "The Mediterranean," which the poet composed with that distinction in mind: "The poem is obviously in iambic pentameter, but I made a point of not writing any two lines in the same rhythm."

THE MEDITERRANEAN

Quem das finem, rex magne, dolorum?*

Where we went in the boat was a long bay
A slingshot wide, walled in by towering stone—
Peaked margin of antiquity's delay,
And we went there out of time's monotone:

Where we went in the black hull no light moved
But a gull white-winged along the feckless wave,
The breeze, unseen but fierce as a body loved,
That boat drove onward like a willing slave:

Where we went in the small ship the seaweed
Parted and gave to us the murmuring shore 10
And we made feast and in our secret need
Devoured the very plates Aeneas bore:

Where derelict you see through the low twilight
The green coast that you, thunder-tossed, would win,
Drop sail, and hastening to drink all night
Eat dish and bowl to take that sweet land in!

Where we feasted and caroused on the sandless
Pebbles, affecting our day of piracy,
What prophecy of eaten plates could landless
Wanderers fulfil by the ancient sea? 20

We for that time might taste the famous age
Eternal here yet hidden from our eyes
When lust of power undid its stuffless rage;
They, in a wineskin, bore earth's paradise.

Let us lie down once more by the breathing side
Of Ocean, where our live forefathers sleep
As if the Known Sea still were a month wide—
Atlantis howls but is no longer steep!

What country shall we conquer, what fair land
Unman our conquest and locate our blood? 30
We've cracked the hemispheres with careless hand!
Now, from the Gates of Hercules we flood

Westward, westward till the barbarous brine
Whelms us to the tired land where tasseling corn,

*The Latin epigraph is a slightly changed version of *Aeneid*, I. 241: "What end of sorrows do you give, great king?"

Fat beans, grapes sweeter than muscadine
Rot on the vine: in that land were we born.

Allen Tate (b. 1899)

The imagery, the poet tells us, is "historical and geographical." It was suggested by a deluxe picnic on the Riviera, in just such a cove as Aeneas and his men may have stopped (*Aeneid*, VII. 107 ff.) when they ate the tortillalike flat cakes they had placed their food on, in this way fulfilling a prophecy that they would find their home where hunger would drive them to "eat their tables." The poem contrasts the hardships of the ancient heroes with the comforts of modern man. It goes on to the question of destiny for men and nations and to the way an individual has to find himself and his place in the culture he was born into.

In a poem written in the early 1930s by a college sophomore (later a well-known poet) there is even more freedom within the feet. It is not always easy to isolate the corpuscular units within these free-flowing lines, but there tend to be five accentual crests in each, and the feeling is iambic. The rhythm returns to a regular line (12, 15, 20, etc.) often enough so that we know what the metrical basis is.

EFFORT AT SPEECH BETWEEN TWO PEOPLE

Speak to me. Take my hand. What are you now?
I will tell you all. I will conceal nothing.
When I was three, a little child read a story about a rabbit
who died, in the story, and I crawled under a chair:
a pink rabbit: it was my birthday, and a candle
burnt a sore spot on my finger, and I was told to be happy.

Oh, grow to know me. I am not happy. I will be open:
Now I am thinking of white sails against a sky like music,
like glad horns blowing, and birds tilting, and an arm about me.
There was one I loved, who wanted to live, sailing. 10

Speak to me. Take my hand. What are you now?
When I was nine, I was fruitily sentimental,
fluid: and my widowed aunt played Chopin,
and I bent my head on the painted woodwork, and wept.
I want now to be close to you. I would
link the minutes of my days close, somehow, to your days.

I am not happy. I will be open.
I have liked lamps in evening corners, and quiet poems.
There has been fear in my life. Sometimes I speculate
On what a tragedy his life was, really. 20

Take my hand. Fist my mind in your hand. What are you now?
When I was fourteen, I had dreams of suicide,

---

[35] **muscadine:** *a kind of grape*

and I stood at a steep window, at sunset, hoping toward death:
if the light had not melted clouds and plains to beauty,
if light had not transformed that day, I would have leapt,
I am unhappy. I am lonely. Speak to me.
I will be open. I think he never loved me:
he loved the bright beaches, the little lips of foam
that ride small waves, he loved the veer of gulls:
he said with a gay mouth: I love you. Grow to know me. 30

What are you now? If we could touch one another,
if these our separate entities could come to grips,
clenched like a Chinese puzzle . . . yesterday
I stood in a crowded street that was live with people,
and no one spoke a word, and the morning shone.
Everyone silent, moving. . . . Take my hand. Speak to me.

Muriel Rukeyser (b. 1913)

Line Length

Most of our examples, up to now, have been taken from lines of five feet. But a line may have any number of feet—from one to about eight. In Matthew Arnold's "Dover Beach," somewhat more than half of the lines are pentameter; the rest have from two to four feet. We might feel that a more determined pattern would be inappropriate for this melancholy reverie.

DOVER BEACH

The sea is calm to-night.
The tide is full, the moon lies fair
Upon the straits; on the French coast the light
Gleams and is gone; the cliffs of England stand,
Glimmering and vast, out in the tranquil bay.
Come to the window, sweet is the night-air!
Only, from the long line of spray
Where the sea meets the moon-blanched land,
Listen! you hear the grating roar
Of pebbles which the waves draw back, and fling, 10
At their return, up the high strand,
Begin, and cease, and then again begin,
With tremulous cadence slow, and bring
The eternal note of sadness in.

Sophocles long ago
Heard it on the Ægæan, and it brought
Into his mind the turbid ebb and flow
Of human misery; we
Find also in the sound a thought,
Hearing it by this distant northern sea. 20

The Sea of Faith
Was once, too, at the full, and round earth's shore
Lay like the folds of a bright girdle furled.
But now I only hear
Its melancholy, long, withdrawing roar,
Retreating, to the breath
Of the night-wind, down the vast edges drear
And naked shingles of the world.

Ah, love, let us be true
To one another! for the world, which seems 30
To lie before us like a land of dreams,
So various, so beautiful, so new,
Hath really neither joy, nor love, nor light,
Nor certitude, nor peace, nor help for pain;
And we are here as on a darkling plain
Swept with confused alarms of struggle and flight,
Where ignorant armies clash by night.

Matthew Arnold (1822–1888)

Poems with one foot to the line (**monometer**) are rare. Lines of two feet (**dimeter**) are about as short as is practical.

I TO MY PERILS

I to my perils
Of cheat and charmer
Came clad in armour
By stars benign.
Hope lies to mortals
And most believe her,
But man's deceiver
Was never mine.

The thoughts of others
Were light and fleeting, 10
Of lovers' meeting
Or luck or fame.
Mine were of trouble,
And mine were steady,
So I was ready
When trouble came.

A. E. Housman

Theodore Roethke has written a waltz poem in lines of three feet (**trimeter**).

---

[28] **shingles:** *rocky beaches*

MY PAPA'S WALTZ

The whiskey on your breath
Could make a small boy dizzy;
But I hung on like death:
Such waltzing was not easy.

We romped until the pans
Slid from the kitchen shelf;
My mother's countenance
Could not unfrown itself.

The hand that held my wrist
Was battered on one knuckle; 10
At every step you missed
My right ear scraped a buckle.

You beat time on my head
With a palm caked hard by dirt,
Then waltzed me off to bed
Still clinging to your shirt.

Theodore Roethke

Here is a freer handling of the three-foot unit:

TRIBUTE TO KAFKA FOR SOMEONE TAKEN

The party is going strong.
The doorbell rings. It's
for someone named me.
I'm coming. I take
a last drink, a last
puff on a cigarette,
a last kiss at a girl,
and step into the hall,
bang,
shutting out the laughter. "Is 10
your name you?" "Yes."
"Well come along then."
"See here. See here. See here."

Alan Dugan (b. 1923)

Lines of four feet (**tetrameter**) are the commonest after **pentameter.** Four-stress lines are faster, crisper than five-stress ones—appropriate to the theme of Marvell's best-known poem, which tells us that time is of the essence.

TO HIS COY MISTRESS

Had we but world enough, and time,
This coyness, Lady, were no crime.

---

2 **coyness:** *shyness, reserve, disdain*

We would sit down and think which way
To walk and pass our long love's day.
Thou by the Indian Ganges' side
Shouldst rubies find; I by the tide
Of Humber would complain. I would
Love you ten years before the Flood,
And you should, if you please, refuse
Till the conversion of the Jews. 10
My vegetable love should grow
Vaster than empires, and more slow;
An hundred years should go to praise
Thine eyes and on thy forehead gaze;
Two hundred to adore each breast,
But thirty thousand to the rest;
An age at least to every part,
And the last age should show your heart.
For, Lady, you deserve this state,
Nor would I love at lower rate. 20
But at my back I always hear
Time's winged chariot hurrying near;
And yonder all before us lie
Deserts of vast eternity.
Thy beauty shall no more be found,
Nor, in thy marble vault, shall sound
My echoing song; then worms shall try
That long preserved virginity,
And your quaint honor turn to dust,
And into ashes all my lust: 30
The grave's a fine and private place,
But none, I think, do there embrace.
Now therefore, while the youthful hue
Sits on thy skin like morning dew,
And while thy willing soul transpires
At every pore with instant fires,
Now let us sport us while we may,
And now, like amorous birds of prey,
Rather at once our time devour
Than languish in his slow-chapped power. 40
Let us roll all our strength and all
Our sweetness up into one ball,
And tear our pleasures with rough strife
Thorough the iron gates of life:
Thus, though we cannot make our sun
Stand still, yet we will make him run.

Andrew Marvell (1621–1678)

The six-foot line (**hexameter**) is also known, when iambic, as the Alexandrine (from an Old French poem on Alexander the Great). With

[7] **Humber:** *an English estuary*

[40] **slow-chapped:** *slow-jawed, devouring slowly*

its tendency to break in two in the middle, this line can drag in English:

A needless Alexandrine ends the song,
That like a wounded snake, drags its slow length along. *Alexander Pope*

Yeats uses the long line to dramatize the stretching winter landscape and the vistas of past and future it evokes.

THE COLD HEAVEN

Suddenly I saw the cold and rook-delighting heaven
That seemed as though ice burned and was but the more ice,
And thereupon imagination and heart were driven
So wild that every casual thought of that and this
Vanished, and left but memories, that should be out of season
With the hot blood of youth, of love crossed long ago;
And I took all the blame out of all sense and reason,
Until I cried and trembled and rocked to and fro,
Riddled with light. Ah! when the ghost begins to quicken,
Confusion of the death-bed over, is it sent 10
Out naked on the roads, as the books say, and stricken
By the injustice of the skies for punishment?

W. B. Yeats

Alexandrines also turn up in the lyrics of blues songs:

People have different blues and think they're mighty sad,
But blues about a man the worst I ever had ....

Lines of seven feet (**heptameter**) were popular, as "fourteeners," in the sixteenth century. They also turn up in modern song lyrics:

I want you to tell me, little girl, just where did you
stay last night ...

The seven feet often break up into four and three, the well-known *ballad stanza*, as in "Sir Patrick Spens" or such hymns as John Newton's "Amazing Grace":

Amazing grace, how sweet the sound,
That saved a wretch like me;
I once was lost but now am found,
Was blind but now I see.

Lines of eight feet (**octameter**), though rarer, are found in some well-known poems:

Comrades, leave me here a little, while as yet 'tis early morn:
Leave me here, and when you want me, sound upon the bugle horn ....
Alfred, Lord Tennyson

Once upon a midnight dreary, while I pondered, weak and weary ....
Edgar Allan Poe

---

[1] **rook:** *crow*

Other Rhythms

TROCHEE

According to Robert Frost, there "are virtually but two [rhythms], strict iambic and loose iambic." Nearly all of our examples have been what Frost would call strict iambic, though they have many variations. In much of what he would call free iambic, most readers hear not just a variation, but a different kind of rhythmical unit. Three such units are commonly used.

We have already noticed the trochee (—◡) as an option in the iambic line. It can also constitute a rhythm by itself. The word itself means *rūnnĭng* or *spēēdy̆*. Certain common phrases fall into trochaic patterns: "brēad ănd| būttĕr," "sālt ănd| pēppĕr," "cūp ănd| saūcĕr," "hēad ănd| shōuldĕrs," "rōugh ănd| rēady̆," "hīgh ănd| mīghty̆," "frēe ănd| ēasy̆." Trochaic lines can become monotonous, as they often are in Longfellow's "The Song of Hiawatha":

> Many things Nokomis taught him
> Of the stars that shine in heaven;
> Showed him Ishkoodah, the comet,
> Ishkoodah, with fiery tresses;
> Showed the Death-Dance of the spirits,
> Warriors with their plumes and war-clubs,
> Flaring far away to northward
> In the frosty nights of Winter;
> Showed the broad white road in heaven,
> Pathway of the ghosts, the shadows, **10**
> Running straight across the heavens,
> Crowded with the ghosts, the shadows.

A different trochaic rhythm is Poe's "The Raven." The first two stanzas should be enough to recall the swing of these famous lines:

> Once upon a midnight dreary, while I pondered, weak and weary,
> Over many a quaint and curious volume of forgotten lore—
> While I nodded, nearly napping, suddenly there came a tapping,
> As of some one gently rapping, rapping at my chamber door—
> " 'Tis some visitor," I muttered, "tapping at my chamber door—
> Only this and nothing more."
>
> Ah, distinctly I remember it was in the bleak December;
> And each separate dying ember wrought its ghost upon the floor.
> Eagerly I wished the morrow; —vainly had I sought to borrow
> From my books surcease of sorrow—sorrow for the lost Lenore—
> For the rare and radiant maiden whom the angels name Lenore—
> Nameless *here* for evermore.

The meter is trochaic octameter, with lines 2 and 4 catalectic (*cut short, docked of their final syllable*). Line 6 is tetrameter, also catalectic. If we read the poem naturally, we notice how the individual feet bond together in pairs: "Once upon a | midnight dreary, | while I pondered, weak and weary." Such rhythms, in which two feet together become a unit, are called **dipodic.**

Trochaic and iambic rhythms can seem to turn into each other, as in this early fifteenth-century lyric about Christ and his mother.

I SING OF A MAIDEN

I sing of a maiden
  that is makėless;
king of allė kingės
  to her son sche ches.

He came also stillė
  there his mother was,
as dew in Aprillė
  that falleth on the grass.

He came also stillė
  to his motherės bower   10
as dew in Aprillė
  that falleth on the flower.

He came also stillė
  there his mother lay,
as dew in Aprillė
  that falleth on the spray.

Mother and maiden
  was never none but sche;
well may such a lady
  Goddės mother be.   20

Anonymous (early fifteenth century)

Most of the lines are trochaic, with a final unaccented syllable omitted in the even-numbered lines. But lines 8, 12, 16, and 18 have an iambic swing.

If the first syllable of an iambic tetrameter line is dropped, it will look like this: —◡—◡—◡—. If the last syllable of a trochaic tetrameter line is dropped, it will look—and sound—exactly the same. One knows what name to give each only by the rhythmical context. In themselves they are like such "undecidable figures" as the illustration below. Look at either end, and the figure makes sense; look at both

---

2 **makeless:** *(1) without an equal; (2) without a mate*
4 **to:** *for*
sche ches: *she chose*
5 **also:** *as, just as*
6 **there:** *there where*
10 **bower:** *chamber*
16 **spray:** *little branch with leaves and flowers*

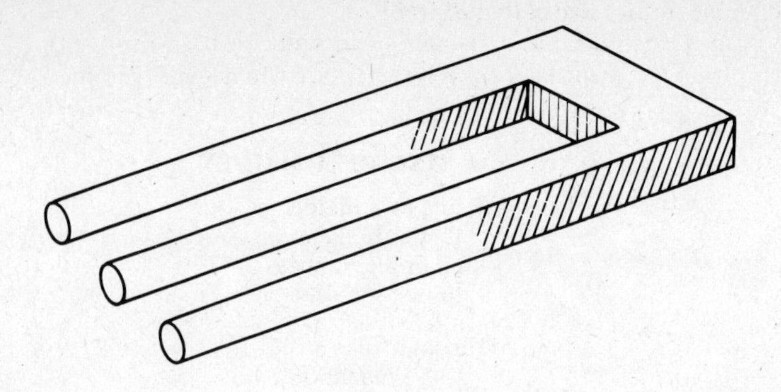

ends, and the figure, like the line of poetry, is undecidable. Fortunately, it is more important to feel the rhythm of a line than to know what to call it.

DACTYL AND ANAPEST

The two basic three-syllable feet are the **dactyl** (—◡◡) and the **anapest** (◡◡—). The first is from the Greek word for "finger." It was so called because in Greek it had a long syllable followed by two short ones, as the finger has a long bone and two shorter ones. In English the dactyl has an accented syllable followed by two unaccented ones, as (twice) in "innocent bystander." Its opposite, with two unaccented syllables followed by an accented one, is called "anapest" from a word that means *knocked back* or *reversed.* We have already mentioned the anapest as an option in iambic verse. Both feet occur in their natural state in English—the dactyl, for example, in a sentence like, "Look at him finish the pint in a gulp or two!"; the anapest in, "For an option on cattle you'd mortgage your house?"

Triple rhythms are busier and faster than double ones; on the other hand, they are lighter, less solid. Triple rhythms are often found in light verse: "Thĕre wās | ă yoŭng lād | y̆ frŏm Dāl | lăs," etc. The distinction between "rising" and "falling" rhythms holds true also for triple feet—anapests rise, dactyls fall.

These are anapests:

THE DESTRUCTION OF SENNACHERIB

The Assyrian came down like the wolf on the fold,
And his cohorts were gleaming in purple and gold;
And the sheen of their spears was like stars on the sea,
When the blue wave rolls nightly on deep Galilee.

Like the leaves of the forest when summer is green,
That host with their banners at sunset were seen:

Michelangelo, Detail from *The Creation*

Like the leaves of the forest when autumn hath blown,
That host on the morrow lay withered and strown.

For the Angel of Death spread his wings on the blast,
And breathed in the face of the foe as he passed; 10
And the eyes of the sleepers waxed deadly and chill,
And their hearts but once heaved—and for ever grew still!

And there lay the steed with his nostril all wide,
But through it there rolled not the breath of his pride;
And the foam of his gasping lay white on the turf,
And cold as the spray of the rock-beating surf.

And there lay the rider distorted and pale,
With the dew on his brow, and the rust on his mail;
And the tents were all silent, the banners alone,
The lances unlifted, the trumpet unblown. 20

And the widows of Ashur are loud in their wail,
And the idols are broke in the temple of Baal;
And the might of the Gentile, unsmote by the sword,
Hath melted like snow in the glance of the Lord!

George Gordon, Lord Byron

In a poem whose symbols yearn for an eternity without the frustrations of this life, William Blake several times changes his simple anapests to a counterbalanced foot like —◡— (**amphimacer**), as in "golden clime," "pined away"—a cross between the anapest and its opposite, a drag of tension and resistance that slows our reading down so that we ponder the images.

AH SUN-FLOWER

Ah Sun-flower! weary of time,
Who countest the steps of the Sun,
Seeking after that sweet golden clime
Where the traveller's journey is done,

Where the Youth pined away with desire,
And the pale Virgin shrouded in snow,
Arise from their graves and aspire
Where my Sun-flower wishes to go.

William Blake

There is more rhythmical variety in the contemporary poem below.

DREAM VARIATIONS

To fling my arms wide
In some place of the sun,
To whirl and to dance
Till the white day is done.
Then rest at cool evening
Beneath a tall tree
While night comes on gently,
  Dark like me—
That is my dream!

To fling my arms wide 10
In the face of the sun,
Dance! Whirl! Whirl!
Till the quick day is done.
Rest at pale evening . . .
A tall, slim tree . . .
Night coming tenderly
  Black like me.

Langston Hughes (1902–1967)

Hughes works musical changes on the anapest by varying it with iambs ("To fling"), with feet like those Blake uses ("day is done," "comes on gent-"), and with units of ⏑ — — ("my arms wide," "in some place"). He also has some syncopated monosyllabic feet ("Thāt| ĭs mў̆ drēam!" and "Blāck| lĭke mē") and a complete reversal of rhythm in "Nīght cŏmĭng| tēndĕrlў̆." But his most musical single variation is the line

Dance! whirl! whirl!

which our ear tries to hear as two feet, since the other lines have two. This makes it like a triplet in music: ♩♩♩ (3) = ♩♩ . Its three beats are to be heard in the time allotted to two.

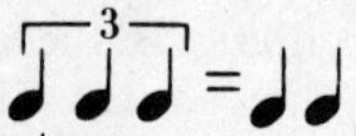

Dactylic rhythms, though rarer in English, are not hard to find.

THE FIRSTLING

Down the soft hillside
The farm girl came frolicking,
Rosy and ribald and
Looking for company.

Quick by a willow she
Stripped for the cooling brook.
Over her bursting breasts
Water meandered.

Soon she lolled ripe for the
Fumble of fingers, the 10
Plunging of pulses, the
Lovely unstringing,

But shortly, unhandled, she
Mounts up the hill again,
Carrying news
To set loose in the village.

How many summers had
Man and boy come to strive
With the nymph naked,
And all been rewarded— 20

All but this firstling, who,
Shirking his trial, lies
Dry-mouthed and still
Beneath the charmed hill?

Peter Davison (b. 1928)

After twenty-two lines of bouncy rhythm we come up against a surprise in the last two lines, which, after the gusto of —◡◡|—◡◡ sink back, frustrated, into a tighter pattern. We will see dactyls less frustrated in Isabella Gardner's "Gimboling" (p. 337).

William Carlos Williams, not normally attracted to formal rhythms, felt the rightness of the lively dactyl to describe the dancers in Breughel's painting *The Kermess.*

THE DANCE

In Breughel's great picture, The Kermess,
the dancers go round, they go round and
around, the squeal and the glare and the
tweedle of bagpipes, a bugle and fiddles
tipping their bellies (round as the thick-
sided glasses whose wash they impound)
their hips and their bellies off balance
to turn them. Kicking and rolling about
the Fair Grounds, swinging their butts, those

shanks must be sound to bear up under such 10
rollicking measures, prance as they dance
in Breughel's great picture, The Kermess.

William Carlos Williams

Rhythms in Conflict

One of the most famous lyrics from an Elizabethan play, a song about the insecurity men feel when they see thousands die during a time of plague, has a rhythmical scheme that is expressively ambiguous: nothing in this world is certain, not even the rhythm that says so.

ADIEU, FAREWELL EARTH'S BLISS

Adieu, farewell earth's bliss!
This world uncertain is:
Fond are life's lustful joys;
Death proves them all but toys.
None from his darts can fly;
I am sick, I must die.
  Lord, have mercy on us.

Rich men, trust not in wealth:
Gold cannot buy you health;
Physic himself must fade. 10
All things to end are made;
The plague full swift goes by.
I am sick, I must die.
  Lord, have mercy on us.

Beauty is but a flower
Which wrinkles will devour;
Brightness falls from the air;
Queens have died young and fair;
Dust hath closed Helen's eye.
I am sick, I must die. 20
  Lord, have mercy on us.

Strength stoops unto the grave;
Worms feed on Hector brave.
Swords may not fight with fate;
Earth still holds ope her gate.
Come, come, the bells do cry.
I am sick, I must die.
  Lord, have mercy on us.

Wit with his wantonness
Tasteth death's bitterness; 30
Hell's executioner
Hath no ears for to hear

What vain art can reply.
I am sick, I must die.
  Lord, have mercy on us.

Haste therefore, each degree,
To welcome destiny:
Heaven is our heritage;
Earth but a player's stage.
Mount we unto the sky! 40
I am sick, I must die.
  Lord, have mercy on us.

Thomas Nashe (1567–1601)

It seems to begin as iambic trimeter, with spondaic substitutions:

Ădīēū,|făre wēll|ēarth's blīss!
Thĭs wōrld|ŭncēr|tăin īs . . .

But soon we come on so many reversals and midline pauses that we begin to read in the swing of

Ī ăm sīck,|Ī mŭst dīe . . .

with two triple feet that vary a good deal and even turn into dactyls (as far from an iamb as one can get):

Wīt wĭth hĭs|wāntŏnnĕss . . .

Hēll's ĕxĕ|cūtiŏnĕr . . .

The most famous lines read as two triple feet:

Brightness falls   from the air;
Queens have died   young and fair;
Dust hath closed   Helen's eye . . .

This is a far more natural pause than any suggested by the original iambs:

Brightness   falls from   the air;
Queens have   died young   and fair;
Dust hath   closed Hel-   en's eye . . .

But when we try to read all of the lines as made up of two triple feet we run into trouble:

Strength stoops un-   to the grave . . .

Earth but a   player's stage . . .

A sense of nervous strain seems inescapable in this tension between meter and rhythm.

Nashe's poem shows a meaningful conflict between rhythms. So does the following twentieth-century poem.

THE LISTENERS

'Is there anybody there?' said the Traveller,
  Knocking on the moonlit door;
And his horse in the silence champed the grasses
  Of the forest's ferny floor:
And a bird flew up out of the turret,
  Above the Traveller's head:
And he smote upon the door again a second time;
  'Is there anybody there?' he said.
But no one descended to the Traveller;
  No head from the leaf-fringed sill 10
Leaned over and looked into his grey eyes,
  Where he stood perplexed and still.
But only a host of phantom listeners
  That dwelt in the lone house then
Stood listening in the quiet of the moonlight
  To that voice from the world of men:
Stood thronging the faint moonbeams on the dark stair,
  That goes down to the empty hall,
Hearkening in an air stirred and shaken
  By the lonely Traveller's call. 20
And he felt in his heart their strangeness,
  Their stillness answering his cry,
While his horse moved, cropping the dark turf,
  'Neath the starred and leafy sky;
For he suddenly smote on the door, even
  Louder, and lifted his head:—
'Tell them I came, and no one answered,
  That I kept my word,' he said.
Never the least stir made the listeners,
  Though every word he spake 30
Fell echoing through the shadowiness of the still house
  From the one man left awake:
Ay, they heard his foot upon the stirrup,
  And the sound of iron on stone,
And how the silence surged softly backward,
  When the plunging hoofs were gone.

Walter de la Mare (1873–1956)

This could be taken as an account of an actual happening. Someone has promised to put in an appearance at a turreted house in the forest; no one answers his knock. But there is something too weird about the situation to be accounted for in such a matter-of-fact way. This must be some kind of symbolic quest or visit or assignation. Perhaps it means that we cannot return to the past or to friends of other years, or that we cannot communicate with the dead, or that there are mysteries in life for which we will find no answer.

There are two levels of reality in the poem: that of the Traveller "from the world of men," on a real horse that *champs* and *crops*; and

TABLE OF FEET

The names of the four important feet are in capitals. The other feet rarely occur except as variations of one of the four. The first four *have* to be variations; none could constitute a rhythm by itself.

Pyrrhic	◡ ◡	of the
Spondee	— —	old loves
Tribrach	◡ ◡ ◡	of a re-
Molossos	— — —	mote lost land
IAMB	◡ —	recalled
TROCHEE	— ◡	all as
ANAPEST	◡ ◡ —	in a dream
DACTYL	— ◡ ◡	mournfully
Bacchius	◡ — —	the closed door
Antibacchius	— — ◡	too rudely
Amphimacer (or cretic)	— ◡ —	overgrown
Amphibrach	◡ — ◡	remembers
Ionic a minore	◡ ◡ — —	and the lost love
Choriamb	— ◡ ◡ —	only recalled
Antispast	◡ — — ◡	in dreams fading
First Paeon	— ◡ ◡ ◡	mournfully as
Second Paeon	◡ — ◡ ◡	as mournfully
Third Paeon	◡ ◡ — ◡	and as mournful-
Fourth Paeon	◡ ◡ ◡ —	ly as the dark

The words used as examples of the nineteen feet themselves constitute the following rather sentimental little poem.

NINETEEN

Of the old loves of a remote lost land,
recalled all as in a dream mournfully.
The closed door too rudely overgrown remembers,
and the lost love only recalled in dreams
fading mournfully as . . . as mournfully . . .
and as mournfully as the dark.

that of the mysterious "others." The unbridgeable gap between the two is dramatized by the schizophrenic meters—the indented, even-numbered lines are of one kind; the odd-numbered lines of another. The even-numbered lines are generally simple: iambic trimeters with anapestic variations. But the odd-numbered lines are from another world of rhythm.

> 'Is there ANybody THERE?' said the TRAVeller . . .
>
> And his HORSE in the SIlence CHAMPED the GRASSes . . .
>
> And he SMOTE upon the DOOR again a SECond TIME . . .

The confusion of some of the long lines comes from the runs of unaccented syllables. Several times there are feet with three or four such syllables:

> Stōōd līs|tĕnĭng ĭn thĕ quī|ĕt ŏf thĕ mōōn|līght . . . .

Or even five.

> Fēll ēch|ŏĭng thrōūgh|thĕ shăd|ŏwĭnĕss ŏf thĕ|stīll hōūse . . . .

In order to feel and enjoy the waves of rhythm in a poem, it is not necessary to be familiar with the terminology, any more than one has to know what "fuel injection" or "universal joint" means if he drives a car. It is reassuring to recall again that Frost said there are only two kinds of rhythm in English, strict iambic and loose iambic. All of the feet listed in the table on page 287, with their sonorous foreign names, will fit into one of these.

Exercises and Diversions

A.

> Out of some subway scuttle, cell or loft
> A bedlamite speeds to thy parapets,
> Tilting there momently, shrill shirt ballooning,
> A jest falls from the speechless caravan.

This stanza, from Hart Crane's "To Brooklyn Bridge," describes how, from some obscure and humble lodging, a deranged man will sometimes rush to the bridge, balance a moment dizzily on the railing, then leap to his death. Show how the interplay between meter and rhythm is expressive in every line (especially lines 2 and 3).

B. Allen Tate says that in writing "The Mediterranean" he "made a point of not writing any two lines in the same rhythm." Chances are there is *one* line that is perfectly regular, with meter and rhythm coinciding.

1. Can you find such a line? Is there only one?
2. Weighing the other lines one by one, determine how rhythm varies from meter. Which variations are expressive?
3. Is it true that no two lines have an identical rhythm?

C.

But knowing now that they would have her speak,
She threw her wet hair backward from her brow,
Her hand close to her mouth touching her cheek,

As though she had had there a shameful blow,
And feeling it shameful to feel ought but shame
All through her heart, yet felt her cheek burned so,

She must a little touch it. . . .

William Morris

Paul Thompson (*The Work of William Morris*) uses the above passage from *The Defense of Guenevere* to show that "odd deviations from the normal iambic beat . . . become masterly devices for creating tension . . . a secondary rhythm drags against the weakened primary meter, so that a purely physical description of Guenevere takes on a sense of sexual shame. . . . The fourth line, clumsy according to conventional metrical standards, is here brilliantly effective. Morris had in fact created a new verse form, like stammering direct speech. . . ."

Do you feel that the "odd deviations" do, indeed, have this effect?

D. **ON THE COUNTESS DOWAGER OF PEMBROKE**

Underneath this sable hearse
Lies the subject of all verse:
Sidney's sister, Pembroke's mother:
Death, ere thou hast slain another,
Fair, and learn'd, and good as she,
Time shall throw a dart at thee.

William Browne (1591–1643)

The meter of this famous little poem, which appears in most anthologies, might appear undecidable, since four of the lines are —◡—◡—◡—, either iambs with the first syllable omitted, or trochees with the last omitted. Winifred Nowottny (*The Language Poets Use*) thinks the poem's brief magnificence comes in part from a change in rhythm. The first three lines are trochaic, except for one reversed foot (can you find it?). But with the word "Death," a reversal of attitude, from mourning to triumph, is accompanied by a reversal of rhythm, to rising iambs—since we cannot reasonably break up the line into

Death, ere   thou hast   slain an-   other . . .

Do you believe this is a sensible analysis of the rhythm?

E. The four-stress lines in Marvell's "To His Coy Mistress" were described as "faster, crisper" than pentameter would have been. Pentameter would sound like this:

Had we but world enough and time, this coy-
ness, lady, were no crime. We would sit down
And think which way to walk and pass our long
Love's day. Thou by the Indian Ganges' side
Shouldst rubies find; I by the tide of Humber. . . .

Is that really slower? What if we doubled the lines? Twice as slow?

Had we but world enough and time, this coyness, lady, were no crime.
We would sit down and think which way to walk and pass our long love's day. . . .

If tetrameters are fast, would dimeters be twice as fast?

Had we but world
Enough and time,
This coyness, lady,
Were no crime.
We would sit down
And think which way
To walk and pass
Our long love's day. . . .

What happens if we read in monometers?

Had we
But world
Enough
And time,
This coyness,
Lady,
Were
No crime. . . .

Does a change in line length change the tempo?

F. Rewrite "The Destruction of Sennacherib" in iambic pentameter.

The foe came down like wolf upon the fold;
His cohorts gleam with purple and with gold. . . .

Or make some equally drastic change in the meter of a famous poem and see what happens.

Or write a poem like "Nineteen" (but probably better), using all the feet in sequence.

16 Different Drummers old rhythms and new

Up to now we have been illustrating only one of the several ways of metering sounds in English. Since it takes into account both the number of syllables and the placing of the accents, it has been called the *syllable-stress* system. But it might just as well, more simply, be thought of as "standard rhythm." Because of the interplay between meter and rhythm—that is, between expectation and actuality—"standard rhythm" produces what we could call, by analogy, something like a stereo effect. In listening to it, we are hearing two voices at once. Other systems have more the nature of monaural sound.

One system counts only accents, disregarding number of syllables. The other counts only number of syllables, disregarding where the accents fall. The first of these, the *strong-stress* (or "Big Bang") system, is the older, going back to the poetic line of Anglo-Saxon times.

Strong-Stress Rhythms

The Old English (or Anglo-Saxon) line is made up of two halves. In each half there are two strongly stressed syllables, as in W. H. Auden's

> There hēad falls fōrward fatīgued at ēvening . . .

Around the two stressed syllables—before them, between them, after them—are their natural clusters of unaccented words or syllables. Since the number of syllables does not matter, there can be a great variety of lengths and patterns—from four syllables, all stressed, to about twenty.

The strong-stressed syllables are emphasized by alliteration, an an-

Piero della Francesca, "*The Resurrection*"

cient feature of Germanic languages. The commonest pattern is to have the first three stresses alliterating (or all beginning with a vowel). Later on, derivatives of strong-stress rhythms have only the four stresses without alliteration, as in the stark little Resurrection poem of the fifteenth century, which recalls the athletic, high-stepping Christ of Piero della Francesca's "Resurrection."

I HAVE LABORED SORE

I have labored sore and suffered death,
and now I rest and draw my breath;
but I shall come and call right soon
heaven and earth and hell to doom;
and then shall know both devil and man,
what I was and what I am.

Anonymous (fifteenth century)

Ezra Pound, in his version of the Anglo-Saxon "The Seafarer," often uses the old pattern:

Nārrow nīghtwatch nīgh the shīp's head . . .
Chīll its chāins are; chāfing sīghs . . . .

As X. J. Kennedy used the Omar Khayyám stanza to contrast two ways of life, so Richard Wilbur has used Old English rhythm in a poem which, by its form alone, points up a contrast between our modern world of plastics and unseasoned wood and an older world of well-made tools and furnishings.

JUNK

Huru Welandes
worc ne geswiceð
monna ænigum
ðara ðe Mimming can
heardne gehealdan.

Waldere[1]

An axe angles
from my neighbor's ashcan;
It is hell's handiwork,
the wood not hickory,

[1] The epigraph, taken from a fragmentary Anglo-Saxon poem, concerns the legendary smith Wayland, and may roughly be translated: "Truly, Wayland's handiwork —the sword Mimming which he made—will never fail any man who knows how to use it bravely." [Wilbur's note]

[4] **doom:** *judgment*

The flow of the grain
not faithfully followed.
The shivered shaft
rises from a shellheap
Of plastic playthings,
paper plates, 10
And the sheer shards
of shattered tumblers
That were not annealed
for the time needful.
At the same curbside,
a cast-off cabinet
Of wavily-warped
unseasoned wood
Waits to be trundled
in the trash-man's truck. 20
Haul them off! Hide them!
The heart winces
For junk and gimcrack,
for jerrybuilt things
And the men who make them
for a little money,
Bartering pride
like the bought boxer
Who pulls his punches,
or the paid-off jockey 30
Who in the home stretch
holds in his horse.
Yet the things themselves
in thoughtless honor
Have kept composure,
like captives who would not
Talk under torture.
Tossed from a tailgate
Where the dump displays
its random dolmens, 40
Its black barrows
and blazing valleys,
They shall waste in the weather
toward what they were.
The sun shall glory
in the glitter of glass-chips,
Foreseeing the salvage
of the prisoned sand,
And the blistering paint
peel off in patches, 50
That the good grain
be discovered again.
Then burnt, bulldozed,
they shall all be buried
To the depth of diamonds,
in the making dark

Where halt Hephaestus
keeps his hammer
And Wayland's work
is worn away. 60

Richard Wilbur

In the first twelve lines, there are eleven different arrangements of accented and unaccented syllables.

W. H. Auden's "The Wanderer" (p. 168) has the feeling of Old English rhythms and often the very pattern:

Doom is dark and deeper than any sea-dingle . . . .

Waving from window, spread of welcome . . . .

In his book-length "The Age of Anxiety," Auden went back to even stricter strong stress:

Ingenious George reached his journey's end
Killed by a cop in a comfort station,
Dan dropped dead at his dinner table,
Mrs. O'Malley with Miss de Young
Wandered away into wild places . . . .

He makes this oldest of English rhythms serve for the jargon of admen:

Definitely different. Has that democratic
Extra elegance. Easy to clean.
Will gladden grand-dad and your girl friend.
Lasts a lifetime. Leaves no odor.
American made. A modern product
Of nerve and know-how with a new thrill . . . .

Auden had to go back very far to find examples of such obstinate alliteration. Even before the time of Chaucer (who did not use it) the line had lost much of its alliteration and had picked up a lilt, learned perhaps from the Latin hymns or the love songs of Provence. In a poem of religious exhortation written about 1275, the alliterative scheme is much modified. Lines 1, 2, 4, and 5 of each stanza show the two halves with two beats in each:

Where beth they   beforen us weren . . . .

But lines 3 and 6 have only three stresses:

and hadden field and wodė . . . .

FROM **UBI SUNT QUI ANTE NOS FUERUNT?**[1]

Where beth they beforen us weren,
houndės ladden and havekes beren,

[1] The title is translated by the first line.

---

[1] **beth:** *are* **havekes beren:** *carried hawks*
[2] **houndės ladden:** *led hunting dogs*

and hadden field and wodė?
The richė levedies in their bower,
that wereden gold in their tressour,
with their brightė rodė?

Eten and drunken and maden them glad;
their life was all with gamen i-lad;
men keneleden them beforen;
they bearen them well swithe high. 10
And in the twinkling of an eye
their soulės weren forloren.

Where is that laughing and that song,
that trailing and that proudė yong,
those havekes and those houndės?
All that joy is went away,
that weal is comen to *weylaway,*
to manyė hardė stoundės. . . .

Anonymous (c. 1275)

The same four-beat and three-beat combination is to be found 650 years later in the poem by John Crowe Ransom on p. 131.

Many of E. E. Cummings' poems—including some of those that seem most modern—come from the older "Where beth they" tradition.

IF EVERYTHING HAPPENS THAT CAN'T BE DONE

if everything happens that can't be done
(and anything's righter
than books
could plan)
the stupidest teacher will almost guess
(with a run
skip
around we go yes)
there's nothing as something as one

one hasn't a why or because or although 10
(and buds know better
than books

---

[4] **levedies:** *ladies*
bower: *chamber*
[5] **tressour:** *ribbons, lace, etc., worn in hair*
[6] **rodė:** *complexion*
[7] **eten:** *they ate*
maden them glad: *had a good time*
[8] **with gamen i-lad:** *spent in having fun*
[10] **well swithe high:** *very proudly indeed*
[12] **forloren:** *lost*
[14] **trailing:** *trailing of dresses*
yong: *going*
[17] **weal:** *happiness, prosperity*
weylaway: *alas!*
[18] **stoundės:** *times*

don't grow)
one's anything old being everything new
(with a what
which
around we come who)
one's everyanything so

so world is a leaf so tree is a bough
(and birds sing sweeter 20
than books
tell how)
so here is away and so your is a my
(with a down
up
around again fly)
forever was never till now

now i love you and you love me
(and books are shuter
than books 30
can be)
and deep in the high that does nothing but fall
(with a shout
each
around we go all)
there's somebody calling who's we

we're anything brighter than even the sun
(we're everything greater
than books
might mean) 40
we're everyanything more than believe
(with a spin
leap
alive we're alive)
we're wonderful one times one

E. E. Cummings

In a work that seems "everything new," Cummings' "anything old" is a rhythm going back at least seven centuries. If we reassemble one of the stanzas Cummings has disguised by his typographical layout, we find four regular strong-stress lines of four beats followed by one of three beats.

if ēverything hāppens   that cān't be dōne
(and ānything's rīghter   than bo͞oks could plān)
the stūpidest tēacher   will ālmost gūess
with a rūn skīp   aro͞und we go yēs
there's nōthing as sōmething as ōne

His lines are symmetrically divided and subdivided: whole line, half line, quarter line, quarter line, whole line, quarter line, quarter line, half line, three-beat line. Though the poem seems all spontaneity, it is worked out with a precision almost mathematical.

Most poets who use the four-beat, strong-stress pattern today use a simplified form of it.

> Summer will rise till the houses fear;
> streets will hear underground streams. . . . *William Stafford*

> I slept under rhododendron
> All night blossoms fell
> Shivering on a sheet of cardboard
> Feet stuck in my pack
> Hands deep in my pockets. . . . *Gary Snyder*

Strong-stress rhythm, based on accent, the most energetic element of speech, serves to communicate physical energy, as in one of the best-known of American baseball poems.

COBB WOULD HAVE CAUGHT IT

In sunburnt parks where Sundays lie,
Or the wide wastes beyond the cities,
Teams in grey deploy through sunlight.

Talk it up, boys, a little practice.

Coming in stubby and fast, the baseman
Gathers a grounder in fat green grass,
Picks it stinging and clipped as wit
Into the leather: a swinging step
Wings it deadeye down to first.
Smack. Oh, attaboy, attyoldboy. 10

Catcher reverses his cap, pulls down
Sweaty casque, and squats in the dust:
Pitcher rubs new ball on his pants,
Chewing, puts a jet behind him;
Nods past batter, taking his time.
Batter settles, tugs at his cap:
A spinning ball: step and swing to it,
Caught like a cheek before it ducks
By shivery hickory: socko, baby:
Cleats dig into dust. Outfielder, 20
On his way, looking over shoulder,
Makes it a triple. A long peg home.

Innings and afternoons. Fly lost in sunset.
Throwing arm gone bad. There's your old
ball game.
Cool reek of the field. Reek of companions.

Robert Fitzgerald (b. 1910)

With the first line of the Robert Hayden poem that follows we know that the arrangement will be a four-beat, strong-stress one—but some lines will come as a rhythmical surprise. ("Juba" is a dance with hand clapping; "conjo" and "juju" are magical objects used in rituals.)

O DAEDALUS, FLY AWAY HOME

Drifting night in the Georgia pines,
coonskin drum and jubilee banjo.
  Pretty Malinda, dance with me.

Night is juba, night is conjo.
  Pretty Malinda, dance with me.

Night is an African juju man
weaving a wish and a weariness together
  to make two wings.

  O fly away home fly away

Do you remember Africa? 10

  O cleave the air fly away home

My gran, he flew back to Africa,
just spread his arms and
  flew away home.

Drifting night in the windy pines;
night is a laughing, night is a longing.
  Pretty Malinda, come to me.

Night is a mourning juju man
weaving a wish and a weariness together
  to make two wings. 20

  O fly away home fly away

Robert Hayden (b. 1913)

"Blackberry Sweet" is really a traditional love lyric, the kind men have written to women at least since the Song of Songs in the Old Testament.

BLACKBERRY SWEET

Black girl black girl
lips as curved as cherries
full as grape bunches
sweet as blackberries

Black girl black girl
when you walk you are
magic as a rising bird
or a falling star

Black girl black girl
what's your spell to make 10
the heart in my breast
jump stop shake

Dudley Randall (b. 1914)

But here the poet is playing off two-beat lines against three-beat lines, the latter becoming the rhythmical equivalent of the former, like triplets in music.

SPRUNG RHYTHM

Strong-stress rhythm is so old that poets keep calling it "new" when they rediscover it. In 1800 Coleridge said that the meter of his "Christabel" seemed irregular because "it was founded on a new principle: namely, that of counting in each line the accents, not the syllables." More influential was the "new prosody" that Gerard Manley Hopkins calls "sprung rhythm." By "sprung" he means *abrupt*, as when one accent directly follows another. We also say a thing is *sprung* when it is forced out of its proper position by its own tension or by that of things pressing against it. Unaccented syllables can be *sprung* out of a line by the pressure of accents around them—as when we say "I'll go" for "I will go." Language itself became *sprung* when final *e*'s ceased to be pronounced in the century after Chaucer.

Hopkins explained that in sprung rhythm "one stress makes a foot," no matter how many unstressed syllables there may be. Some of the stresses he marked in his poems are the kind we dó use in speech, but could not easily guess at from a printed text. Characteristic of sprung rhythm is the way stresses jostle against one another, unbuffered by unaccented syllables in between. In "Spring and Fall" (p. 163), we see this happening. In the thirteenth line, for example, two *had*'s have been sprung out, leaving the accents to clash together.

What héart [had] héard of, ghóst [had] guéssed . . . .

We have now seen examples of the two basic rhythmical systems of English versification: the syllable-stress system and the strong-stress system. Both have given us great poetry. If the syllable-stress system has given us more, it may only be because it has seemed more all-purpose than the bouncy and emphatic strong-stress system.

Some theorists believe that the two are really the same—that iambic pentameter is just the old four-beat strong-stress rhythm. But to most poets the two have a very different feeling.

A WORD ABOUT QUANTITY

A third metrical system tried to impose itself on English around 1580 and for a decade or so thereafter. Classicists wanted to meter English as if it were Greek or Latin—by *length* of syllable rather than by accent.

Although we recognize that some syllables are longer than others—that "home" is longer than "him" and "strength" is longer than "sit"—our ear does not divide syllables into long and short consciously enough for us to feel a pattern in the arrangement. Metering by *quantity*—length of syllable—was a failure in English.

But the study of classical meters did bring some new rhythms into English, once the long and short syllables were replaced by accented and unaccented.

The poem of Sappho, on page 9, transposes her quantitative rhythm into an accentual one. It is not surprising to find Sapphic stanzas[1] in translations of Sappho, but the use to which William Meredith puts them (in a poem which alludes to that of Muriel Rukeyser on p. 272) may come as a jolt. Sapphics to describe a contemporary mugging? Sapphics that say, "God damn it, no!"?

EFFORT AT SPEECH
For Muriel Rukeyser

Climbing the stairway gray with urban midnight,
Cheerful, venial, ruminating pleasure,
Darkness takes me, an arm around my throat and
                    Give me your wallet.

Fearing cowardice more than other terrors,
Angry I wrestle with my unseen partner,
Caught in a ritual not of our own making,
                    panting like spaniels.

Bold with adrenalin, mindless, shaking,
God damn it, no! I rasp at him behind me,   10
Wrenching the leather wallet from his grasp. It
                    breaks like a wishbone,

So that departing (routed by my shouting,
Not by my strength or inadvertent courage)
Half of the papers lending me a name are
                    gone with him nameless.

Only now turning, I see a tall boy running,
Fifteen, sixteen, dressed thinly for the weather.
Reaching the streetlight he turns a brown face briefly
                    phrased like a question.   20

I like a questioner watch him turn the corner
Taking the answer with him, or his half of it.
Loneliness, not a sensible emotion,
                    breathes hard on the stairway.

Walking homeward I fraternize with shadows,
Zig-zagging with them where they flee the streetlights,

[1] Three lines of —∪|—∪|—∪∪|—∪|—∪ and one of —∪∪|—∪.

Asking for trouble, asking for the message
trouble had sent me.

All fall down has been scribbled on the street in
Garbage and excrement: so much for the vision 30
Others taunt me with, my untimely humor,
so much for cheerfulness.

Next time don't wrangle, give the boy the money,
Call across chasms what the world you know is.
Luckless and lied to, how can a child master
human decorum?

Next time a switch-blade, somewhere he is thinking,
I should have killed him and took the lousy wallet.
Reading my cards he feels a surge of anger
blind as my shame. 40

Error from Babel mutters in the places,
Cities apart, where now we word our failures:
Hatred and guilt have left us without language
who might have held discourse.

William Meredith (b. 1919)

A difficulty with such meters in English is their rigidity. We enjoy variations. But a Sapphic line is a Sapphic line, and the writer has almost no freedom to vary accents. Meredith has wisely not tried to apply the template to every line. He is content to give the look and feel of Sapphics. Coming close to a meter (as Meredith does here) is all that one wants in English; a near miss is generally better than a dead-center hit.

Syllabic Meter

A fourth and totally different system—by number of syllables alone, with no regard for accent—is winningly presented by James Tate in his poem about a student in a poetry workshop:

MISS CHO COMPOSES IN THE CAFETERIA

You are so small, I
am not even sure
that you are at all.

To you, I know I
am not here: you are
rapt in writing a

syllabic poem
about gigantic,
gaudy Christmas trees.

You will send it home   10
to China, and they
will worry about

you alone amid
such strange customs. You
count on your tiny

bamboo fingers; one,
two, three—up to five,
and, oh, you have one

syllable too much.
You shake your head in   20
dismay, look back up

to the tree to see
if, perhaps, there might
exist another

word that would describe
the horror of this
towering, tinselled

symbol. And . . . now
you've got it! You jot
it down, jump up, look   30

at me and giggle.

James Tate (b. 1943)

Tate has written his poem exactly as little Miss Cho is writing hers. His, too, is a **syllabic** poem—here, with five syllables to the line. In such poems all that matters, metrically, is the number of syllables, not their accent.

Sylvia Plath has also written a five-syllable poem, but with a difference.

MUSHROOMS

Overnight, very
Whitely, discreetly,
Very quietly

Our toes, our noses
Take hold on the loam.
Acquire the air.

Nobody sees us,
Stops us, betrays us;
The small grains make room.

Soft fists insist on   10
Heaving the needles,
The leafy bedding,

Even the paving.
Our hammers, our rams,
Earless and eyeless,

Perfectly voiceless,
Widen the crannies,
Shoulder through holes. We

Diet on water,
On crumbs of shadow, 20
Bland-mannered, asking

Little or nothing.
So many of us!
So many of us!

We are shelves, we are
Tables, we are meek,
We are edible,

Nudgers and shovers
In spite of ourselves.
Our kind multiplies: 30

We shall by morning
Inherit the earth.
Our foot's in the door.

Sylvia Plath (1932–1963)

Plath treats the line as a line; she likes to pause at the end of a stanza. Tate does not. "Mushrooms" also has another rhythm at work, overriding the syllabic count—alternations of dactyls and trochees, as in the short line of a Sapphic stanza: — ⏑ ⏑ — ⏑. About half of the lines fall into this rhythmic figure ("whitely, discreetly"). Some of the remaining lines reverse the feet ("Very quietly"). We are inveigled, if not appassionated, into the swing of an accentual rhythm, which we hear more compellingly than the syllabic count.

Syllabic poems can have lines of any manageable number of syllables.

ROMP

her
strong
white
legs
are
wet
grass
stained
I
help
her
up

The odd numbers seem more attractive—five and seven are particular favorites. Dave Etter uses only one syllable in "Romp," which could also be imagined in two-syllable lines:

her strong
white legs
are wet
grass stained . . . .

In Thomas' "Fern Hill" (p. 251) the fourth line of every stanza has six syllables:

Time let me hail and climb . . . .

she
grabs
my
neck
rubs
cool
milk
weed
in
my
hot
face
and
I
am
glad
she
chose
to
run

Dave Etter (b. 1928)

The third and fifth lines have nine:

> The night above the dingle starry . . . .

Marianne Moore's "A Carriage from Sweden" (p. 52) has eight syllables in lines 1, 2, 3, and 5 (with two exceptions):

> They say there is a sweeter air
> where it was made, than we have here;
> a Hamlet's castle atmosphere . . . .
> something that makes me feel at home . . . .

Sylvia Plath's "Metaphor," a poem about pregnancy, has nine lines of nine syllables each. In W. H. Auden's "Moon Landing" (p. 153), the third line of each stanza has nine syllables; the fourth line, ten; the first two lines, eleven each. If we count, we find there are no exceptions. In "Fern Hill," lines 1, 2, 6, and 7 of each stanza have fourteen syllables. Two of the twenty-four lines are excessive by one syllable, but only a finger-counter would notice. It seems unlikely that our ear will catch any exact number of syllables above about five, since nothing in our speech has accustomed us to attach any importance to such units.

More elaborate arrangements can be found. Richard Howard's "Private Drive: Memorial for a Childhood Playmate," has ten stanzas in which the lines have syllables numbering 11, 9, 7, 5, 3, and 1, in that order:

> Trying to keep out of the builders' way, we
> trampled the strawberries that grew wild
> and cut our fingers on red
> tiles where the blood might
> not show so
> much.

A series of syllables in itself is hardly a source of excitement or emotion in poetry. A man in a passion may resort to stress rhythms ("You SON of a BITCH!"), but he is not likely to count his syllables. The charm of James Tate's poem owes little to its doling out of five-syllable units. Good syllabic poems are good because of their use of words, or because of their imagery, or because they have an over-rhythm that we feel more strongly than the enumeration of syllables, as in "Mushrooms."

Free Verse, Free Rhythms

When we pass on from syllabics to **free verse**, we probably think of the new poetry that, over sixty years ago, Ezra Pound and some of his friends began to write and theorize about. One of the principles they agreed on, says Pound, was "to compose in the sequence of the musical phrase, not in sequence of a metronome. . . ." Pound meant that instead of writing in preordained meters, one should let his emotion find its own natural rhythm.

THE RETURN

See, they return; ah, see the tentative
    Movements, and the slow feet,
    The trouble in the pace and the uncertain
    Wavering!

See, they return, one, and by one,
With fear, as half-awakened;
As if the snow should hesitate
And murmur in the wind,
                and half turn back;
These were the "Wing'd-with-Awe," 10
                Inviolable.

Gods of the wingèd shoe!
With them the silver hounds,
                sniffing the trace of air!

Haie! Haie!
        These were the swift to harry;
These the keen-scented;
These were the souls of blood.

Slow on the leash,
                pallid the leash-men! 20

Ezra Pound

Here the diffidence of the ghostly figures, once so alive, finds its equivalent in the hesitating cadence, which owes much to the ancient rhythms that Pound knew so well. The rising rhythm of "they return" is immediately reversed, retracted, in the falling rhythm of "see the tentative/movements," which is followed by the dragging "and the slow feet." Lines 3 and 4 are perturbed and unsubstantial with their many short syllables, especially in the two fourth-paeons (◡◡◡—) of "thĕ troū|blĕ ĭn thĕ pāce| ănd thĕ ŭncēr|taĭn . . . ." The rest of the poem is basically iambic, with the usual variations.

Such poems of Pound represent free verse at its best. Perhaps we should say they are in **free rhythm,** reserving the term "free verse" for poems with less sense of rhythm, like these:

A MAN SAID TO THE UNIVERSE

A man said to the universe:
"Sir, I exist!"

"However," replied the universe,
"The fact has not created in me
"A sense of obligation."

Stephen Crane (1871–1900)

"THINK AS I THINK"

"Think as I think," said a man,
"Or you are abominably wicked;
You are a toad."

And after I had thought of it,
I said, "I will, then, be a toad."

Stephen Crane

By "free rhythms" we mean rhythms that have no set line length and no one kind of meter. The feet link together according to their natural affinities, as certain atoms and molecules link together. Rising feet have an affinity for each other; iamb and anapest go easily together, and easily admit a fourth paeon (◡◡◡—). Falling feet have their affinities. Monosyllabic feet, spondees, and pyrrhic feet are neutral and fit in with either kind. All of these feet, as well as the others we have mentioned, are the building blocks of rhythm, just as atoms, molecules, and the rest are the building blocks of matter.

When the English Bible appeared, the English ear became habituated to its cadences—two or three simple groupings, generally parallel, and, as translated, in free rhythms.

> The heavens declare the glory of God; and the firmament
> showeth his handiwork.
> Day unto day uttereth speech, and night unto night showeth
> knowledge.

The most familiar and musical of free rhythms are Walt Whitman's, vigorous as his own zest and confidence, spacious as the American vistas he loved to sing. In his great poem of love and death, we are easily caught up in the surge of his Biblical cadence. The best way to read this poem the first few times is to ride with the rhythm without trying to analyze its nature.

OUT OF THE CRADLE ENDLESSLY ROCKING

Out of the cradle endlessly rocking,
Out of the mocking-bird's throat, the musical shuttle,
Out of the Ninth-month midnight,
Over the sterile sands and the fields beyond, where the child leaving his bed
wander'd alone, bareheaded, barefoot,
Down from the shower'd halo,

[3] **Ninth-month:** *the Quaker name for September*

Up from the mystic play of shadows twining and twisting as if they were alive,
Out from the patches of briers and blackberries,
From the memories of the bird that chanted to me, 10
From your memories sad brother, from the fitful risings and fallings I heard
From under that yellow half-moon late-risen and swollen as if with tears,
From those beginning notes of yearning and love there in the mist,
From the thousand responses of my heart never to cease,
From the myriad thence-arous'd words,
From the word stronger and more delicious than any,
From such as now they start the scene revisiting,
As a flock, twittering, rising, or overhead passing,
Borne hither, ere all eludes me, hurriedly,
A man, yet by these tears a little boy again, 20
Throwing myself on the sand, confronting the waves,
I, chanter of pains and joys, uniter of here and hereafter,
Taking all hints to use them, but swiftly leaping beyond them,
A reminiscence sing.

Once Paumanok,
When the lilac-scent was in the air and Fifth-month grass was growing,
Up this seashore in some briers,
Two feather'd guests from Alabama, two together,
And their nest, and four light-green eggs spotted with brown,
And every day the he-bird to and fro near at hand, 30
And every day the she-bird crouch'd on her nest, silent, with bright eyes,
And every day I, a curious boy, never too close, never disturbing them,
Cautiously peering, absorbing, translating.

Shine! shine! shine!
Pour down your warmth, great sun!
While we bask, we two together.

Two together!
Winds blow south, or winds blow north,
Day come white, or night come black,
Home, or rivers and mountains from home, 40
Singing all time, minding no time,
While we two keep together.

Till of a sudden,
May-be kill'd, unknown to her mate,
One forenoon the she-bird crouch'd not on the nest,
Nor return'd that afternoon, nor the next,
Nor ever appear'd again.

And thenceforward all summer in the sound of the sea,
And at night under the full of the moon in calmer weather,
Over the hoarse surging of the sea, 50
Or flitting from brier to brier by day,
I saw, I heard at intervals the remaining one, the he-bird,
The solitary guest from Alabama.

---

25 **Paumanok:** *the Indian name for Long Island*

Blow! blow! blow!
Blow up sea-winds along Paumanok's shore;
I wait and I wait till you blow my mate to me.

Yes, when the stars glisten'd,
All night long on the prong of a moss-scallop'd stake,
Down almost amid the slapping waves,
Sat the lone singer wonderful causing tears. 60

He call'd on his mate,
He pour'd forth the meanings which I of all men know.

Yes my brother I know,
The rest might not, but I have treasur'd every note,
For more than once dimly down to the beach gliding,
Silent, avoiding the moonbeams, blending myself with the shadows,
Recalling now the obscure shapes, the echoes, the sounds and sights after
their sorts,
The white arms out in the breakers tirelessly tossing,
I, with bare feet, a child, the wind wafting my hair, 70
Listen'd long and long.

Listen'd to keep, to sing, now translating the notes,
Following you my brother.

Soothe! soothe! soothe!
Close on its wave soothes the wave behind,
And again another behind embracing and lapping, every one close,
But my love soothes not me, not me.

Low hangs the moon, it rose late,
It is lagging—O I think it is heavy with love, with love.

O madly the sea pushes upon the land, 80
With love, with love.

O night! do I not see my love fluttering out among the breakers?
What is that little black thing I see there in the white?

Loud! loud! loud!
Loud I call to you, my love!

High and clear I shoot my voice over the waves,
Surely you must know who is here, is here,
You must know who I am, my love.

Low-hanging moon!
What is that dusky spot in your brown yellow? 90
O it is the shape, the shape of my mate!
O moon do not keep her from me any longer.

Land! land! O land!
Whichever way I turn, O I think you could give me my mate back again if
you only would,
For I am almost sure I see her dimly whichever way I look.

O rising stars!
Perhaps the one I want so much will rise, will rise with some of you.

O throat! O trembling throat!
Sound clearer through the atmosphere! 100
Pierce the woods, the earth,
Somewhere listening to catch you must be the one I want.

Shake out carols!
Solitary here, the night's carols!
Carols of lonesome love! death's carols!
Carols under that lagging, yellow, waning moon!
O under that moon where she droops almost down into the sea!
O reckless despairing carols.

But soft! sink low!
Soft! let me just murmur, 110
And do you wait a moment you husky-nois'd sea,
For somewhere I believe I heard my mate responding to me,
So faint, I must be still, be still to listen,
But not altogether still, for then she might not come immediately to me.

Hither my love!
Here I am! here!
With this just-sustain'd note I announce myself to you,
This gentle call is for you my love, for you.

Do not be decoy'd elsewhere,
That is the whistle of the wind, it is not my voice, 120
That is the fluttering, the fluttering of the spray,
Those are the shadows of leaves.

O darkness! O in vain!
O I am very sick and sorrowful.

O brown halo in the sky near the moon, drooping upon the sea!
O troubled reflection in the sea!
O throat! O throbbing heart!
And I singing uselessly, uselessly all the night.

O past! O happy life! O songs of joy!
In the air, in the woods, over fields, 130
Loved! loved! loved! loved! loved!
But my mate no more, no more with me!
We two together no more.

The aria sinking,
All else continuing, the stars shining,
The winds blowing, the notes of the bird continuous echoing,
With angry moans the fierce old mother incessantly moaning,
On the sands of Paumanok's shore gray and rustling,
The yellow half-moon enlarged, sagging down, drooping, the face of the sea
almost touching, 140
The boy ecstatic, with his bare feet the waves, with his hair the atmosphere
dallying,
The love in the heart long pent, now loose, now at last tumultuously
bursting,
The aria's meaning, the ears, the soul, swiftly depositing,

The strange tears down the cheeks coursing,
The colloquy there, the trio, each uttering,
The undertone, the savage old mother incessantly crying,
To the boy's soul's questions sullenly timing, some drown'd secret hissing,
To the outsetting bard. 150

Demon or bird (said the boy's soul,)
Is it indeed toward your mate you sing? or is it really to me?
For I, that was a child, my tongue's use sleeping, now I have heard you,
Now in a moment I know what I am for, I awake,
And already a thousand singers, a thousand songs, clearer, louder and more sorrowful than yours,
A thousand warbling echoes have started to life within me, never to die.

O you singer solitary, singing by yourself, projecting me,
O solitary me listening, never more shall I cease perpetuating you,
Never more shall I escape, never more the reverberations, 160
Never more the cries of unsatisfied love be absent from me,
Never again leave me to be the peaceful child I was before what there in the night,
By the sea under the yellow and sagging moon,
The messenger there arous'd, the fire, the sweet hell within,
The unknown want, the destiny of me.

O give me the clew! (it lurks in the night here somewhere,)
O if I am to have so much, let me have more!

A word then, (for I will conquer it,)
The word final, superior to all, 170
Subtle, sent up—what is it?—I listen;
Are you whispering it, and have been all the time, you sea-waves?
Is that it from your liquid rims and wet sands?

Whereto answering, the sea,
Delaying not, hurrying not,
Whisper'd me through the night, and very plainly before daybreak,
Lisp'd to me the low and delicious word death,
And again death, death, death, death,
Hissing melodious, neither like the bird nor like my arous'd child's heart,
But edging near as privately for me rustling at my feet, 180
Creeping thence steadily up to my ears and laving me softly all over,
Death, death, death, death, death.

Which I do not forget,
But fuse the song of my dusky demon and brother,
That he sang to me in the moonlight on Paumanok's gray beach,
With the thousand responsive songs at random,
My own songs awaked from that hour,
And with them the key, the word up from the waves,
The word of the sweetest song and all songs,
That strong and delicious word which, creeping to my feet, 190

---

151 **demon:** *here and in line 184, a demigod or attendant spirit (more often spelled "daemon" or "daimon")*

(Or like some old crone rocking the cradle, swathed in sweet garments,
bending aside,)
The sea whisper'd me.

Walt Whitman

Often the rhythm comes on waves of parallel syntax—as in the twenty-two-line first sentence or the fourteen-line sentence beginning with line 130. Whitman professed to dislike regularity, and yet his numerous revisions show that he worked for it, changing many lines to bring them into an iambic dance. Though his lines vary greatly in length and are made up of many kinds of feet, almost always the cells of rhythm join in strands according to their natural affinity.

He has both rising lines,

> Whĕn thĕ lī|lăc-scēnt| wăs ĭn thĕ āir| ănd Fīfth-|mōnth
> grāss| wăs grōw|ĭng . . .

and falling ones,

> Ōut ŏf thĕ| crādlĕ| ēndlĕsslў̆| rōckĭng . . .

He has the same foot—or almost the same foot—running through a line:

> Ōut frŏm thĕ| pātchĕs ŏf| brīĕrs ănd| blăckbĕrrĭes . . .

Often we come on a familiar shape in the surf of rhythm—perhaps an iambic pentameter or two:

> Blow up sea-winds along Paumanok's shore;
> I wait and I wait till you blow my mate to me . . .

perhaps hexameters:

> I, chanter of pains and joys, uniter of here and hereafter,
> Taking all hints to use them, but swiftly leaping beyond them . . .

Rhythmical figures are likely to be repeated. The first line has the same figure twice (—⏑⏑—⏑), the Sapphic combination of dactyl and trochee. Sometimes he uses this motif without the final unaccented syllable, so that it becomes the choriambus (—⏑⏑—). Whitman may not have thought in these terms, but he did feel in these rhythms. These two figures, in the first dozen lines, make up nearly the whole texture of the poem.

—⏑⏑—⏑	—⏑⏑—
Out of the cradle	
endlessly rocking	
Out of the mocking-	
musical shuttle	
Out of the Ninth-month	
Over the sterile	
sands and the fields be-	-yond where the child
	leaving his bed
	wander'd alone

bareheaded, barefoot
Down from the shower'd
Up from the mystic
twining and twisting   they were alive
Out from the patches
briers and blackber-

                chanted to me
                memories sad

risings and fallings
under that yellow   -risen and swol-
                yearning and love
                there in the mist
                never to cease

Sound attracts sound, we said, in speaking of alliteration and assonance. And units of rhythm attract similar units. If we find one amphimacer (—◡—), chances are we will find another, and then another:

> Sāt thĕ lōne| sīngĕr wōn|dĕrfŭl| cāusĭng tēars . . .
>
> Whāt ĭs thāt| līttlĕ blăck| thīng Ĭ sēe . . . ?

Little wonder the lines are so musical.

About half a century after Whitman, a rhythm like his turns up in the work of Carl Sandburg:

> I am the prairie, mother of men, waiting,
> They are mine, the threshing crews eating beefsteak,
> the farm boys driving steers to the railroad cattle pens . . .

and, about a century later, in the litanies of Allen Ginsburg:

> Holy the groaning saxophone! Holy the bop apocalypse! Holy
> the jazzbands marijuana hipsters peace & junk & drums!
> Holy the solitudes of skyscrapers and pavements! Holy the
> cafeterias filled with the millions! Holy the mysterious
> rivers of tears under the streets!

The Variable Foot

William Carlos Williams, though he wrote poems in free verse, came to feel it was "not the answer." He rejected its looseness, going so far as to say that "free verse wasn't verse at all," since "all art is orderly." He did believe, however, that the traditional rhythms were no longer appropriate for the American idiom.

Williams found his cue in the work of Einstein. If everything else in our world is relative, why not have a relative or "variable" foot in poetry? The three-line "triadic" stanzas that he evolved were divided according to his "new measure." Williams advises us to count a single beat for each line—which, in his system, is considered a foot.

THE DESCENT

The descent beckons
as the ascent beckoned.
Memory is a kind
of accomplishment,
a sort of renewal
even
an initiation, since the spaces it opens are new places
inhabited by hordes
heretofore unrealized,
of new kinds— 10
since their movements
are toward new objectives
(even though formerly they were abandoned).

No defeat is made up entirely of defeat—since
the world it opens is always a place
formerly
unsuspected. A
world lost,
a world unsuspected,
beckons to new places 20
and no whiteness (lost) is so white as the memory
of whiteness

With evening, love wakens
though its shadows
which are alive by reason
of the sun shining—
grow sleepy now and drop away
from desire

Love without shadows stirs now
beginning to awaken 30
as night
advances.

The descent
made up of despairs
and without accomplishment
realizes a new awakening:
which is a reversal
of despair.
For what we cannot accomplish, what
is denied to love, 40
what we have lost in the anticipation—
a descent follows,
endless and indestructible

William Carlos Williams

In his best poems the lines do move expressively, often doubling back on themselves as if in halting or agonized meditation:

The descent beckons
as the ascent beckoned.
Memory is a kind . . . .

The isolation of some words forces us to ponder their meaning—the implications of "even," for example, in line 6 or "formerly" in line 16. Other lines (17, 21) hurry us urgently ahead.

Though Williams denied that the iamb fits American speech, the very words he used to make his denial are themselves iambic, especially if we change his "is not" to the more American " 's not":

Thĕ ī|ămb's nōt| thĕ nōr|măl mēas|ŭre ŏf| Ămēr|ĭcăn spēech . . .

Whatever he may have said about iambs, he retains many of them in his "new rhythm." A late poem, "Asphodel, That Greeny Flower," begins:

Ŏf ās|phŏdēl,| thăt grēen|y̆ flōw|ĕr,
lĭke ă būt|tĕrcūp
ŭpōn| ĭts brānch|ĭng stēm—
sāve thăt| ĭt's grēen| ănd wōod|ĕn—
Ĭ cōme,| my̆ swēet,|
tŏ sīng| tŏ yōu . . .

Williams mentions with approval Charles Olson's theory of projective verse, in which the poem is a "high-energy construct" that transmits its charge from poet to reader. Poems project themselves forward into an "open field" rather than into the stanzas of a closed form. They move rapidly from perception to perception, unhampered by any commitments to form made in advance.

Olson emphasizes the importance of syllables, "particles of sound," rather than feet. He thinks, too, that not enough attention has been paid to the part that breathing plays in shaping the verse line: "and the line comes (I swear it) from the breath, from the breathing of the man who writes, at the moment that he writes. . . ." In the nineteenth century Oliver Wendell Holmes had accounted for the popular success of *Hiawatha* by reference to the physiology of breathing: "The recital of each line uses up the air of one natural expiration. . . ."

The modern poet is lucky, Olson thinks, in having the typewriter at his disposal, since, with its precise spacing, it can indicate "the breath, the pauses, the suspensions even of syllables." He explains: "If a contemporary poet leaves a space as long as the phrase before it, he means that space to be held, by the breath, an equal length of time. If he suspends a word or syllable at the end of a line . . . he means that time to pass that it takes the eye . . . to pick up the next line. . . ." He makes use of the multiple margin of the typewriter by moving it to the right or left to indicate progress, regress, or return. Spacing becomes one more analogy the poet can use. (Cummings, of course, had done this decades before Olson reduced it to a system.)

These recent developments in visual prosody seem to be working, in one direction, toward the "concrete poetry" we will consider in a later chapter, and, in another direction, toward the freedom of prose. We have already seen some examples of prose poetry. Elizabeth Bishop has written a prose poem, full of ironies, to describe her desk as it might appear to little green men or bug-eyed monsters from another planet.

12 O'CLOCK NEWS

gooseneck lamp

As you all know, tonight is the night of the full moon, half the world over. But here the moon seems to hang motionless in the sky. It gives very little light; it could be dead. Visibility is poor. Nevertheless, we shall try to give you some idea of the lay of the land and the present situation.

typewriter

The escarpment that rises abruptly from the central plain is in heavy shadow, but the elaborate terracing of its southern glacis gleams faintly in the dim light, like fish scales. What endless labor those small, peculiarly shaped terraces represent! And yet, on them the welfare of this 10
tiny principality depends.

pile of mss.

A slight landslide occurred in the northwest about an hour ago. The exposed soil appears to be of poor quality: almost white, calcareous, and shaly. There are believed to have been no casualties.

typed sheet

Almost due north, our aerial reconnaissance reports the discovery of a large rectangular "field," hitherto unknown to us, obviously man-made. It is dark-speckled. An airstrip? A cemetery?

envelopes

In this small, backward country, one of the most back- 20
ward left in the world today, communications are crude and "industrialization" and its products almost nonexistent. Strange to say, however, signboards are on a truly gigantic scale.

ink-bottle

We have also received reports of a mysterious, oddly shaped, black structure, at an undisclosed distance to the east. Its presence was revealed only because its highly polished surface catches such feeble moonlight as prevails. The natural resources of the country being far from com-
pletely known to us, there is the possibility that this may 30
be, or may contain, some powerful and terrifying "secret weapon." On the other hand, given what we *do* know, or have learned from our anthropologists and sociologists about this people, it may well be nothing more than a *numen*, or a great altar recently erected to one of their gods, to which, in their present historical state of superstition and helplessness, they attribute magical powers, and may even regard as a "savior," one last hope of rescue from their grave difficulties.

At last! One of the elusive natives has been spotted! He appears to be—rather, to have been—a unicyclist-courier, who may have met his end by falling from the height of the escarpment because of the deceptive illumination. Alive, he would have been small, but undoubtedly proud and erect, with the thick, bristling black hair typical of the indigenes. 40

typewriter eraser

From our superior vantage point, we can clearly see into a sort of dugout, possibly a shell crater, a "nest" of soldiers. They lie heaped together, wearing the camouflage "battle dress" intended for "winter warfare." They are in hideously contorted positions, all dead. We can make out at least eight bodies. These uniforms were designed to be used in guerrilla warfare on the country's one snow-covered mountain peak. The fact that these poor soldiers are wearing them *here*, on the plain, gives further proof, if proof were necessary, either of the childishness and hopeless impracticality of this inscrutable people, our opponents, or of the sad corruption of their leaders. 50

ashtray

Elizabeth Bishop

Exercises and Diversions

A. How would you describe the rhythm of each of these quotations?

1. No mice in the heath run, no song-birds fly
   For fear of the buzzard that floats in the sky.

   He soars and he hovers, rocking on his wings,
   He scans his wide parish with a sharp eye,
   He catches the trembling of small hidden things,
   He tears them in pieces, dropping them from the sky. . . . *Robert Graves*

2. I'm a riddle in nine syllables,
   An elephant, a ponderous house,
   A melon strolling on two tendrils. . . . *Sylvia Plath*

3. 'Tis the middle of night by the castle clock,
   And the owls have awakened the crowing cock;
   Tu—whit!——Tu—whoo!
   And hark, again! the crowing cock,
   How drowsily it crew. *Samuel Taylor Coleridge*

4. "I have been kissed before," she added, blushing slightly,
   "I have been kissed more than once by Donald my cousin, and others;
   It is the way of lads, and I make up my mind not to mind it. . . .
   Arthur Hugh Clough

5. Thou preparest a table before me in the presence of mine enemies;
   thou anointest my head with oil; my cup runneth over.
   Surely goodness and mercy shall follow me all the days of my life:
   and I will dwell in the house of the Lord for ever. *Psalm 23*

6. A was an archer, who shot at a frog,
B was a butcher, and had a great dog.
C was a captain, all covered with lace,
D was a drunkard, and had a red face.
E was an esquire, with pride on his brow,
F was a farmer, and followed the plough.
G was a gamester, who had but ill-luck,
H was a hunter, and hunted a buck. . . .

Anonymous

B. **IRIS**

a burst of iris so that
come down for
breakfast

we searched through the
rooms for
that

sweetest odor and at
first could not
finds its

source then a blue as 10
of the sea
struck

startling us from among
those trumpeting
petals

William Carlos Williams

Line breaks indicate a pause, however slight (if only while the eye returns to the left-hand margin); stanza breaks indicate a stronger pause. When a reviewer objected that in "Iris" the breaks were arbitrary, eccentric, against the habits of ordinary speech, an admirer of Williams countered that they were expressive and "functional." The break between "its" and "source," for example, dramatizes the poet's halting bewilderment as he looks for the source of the fragrance. Would you agree that Williams' "visual prosody" (the way of indicating rhythm by the spacing on the page) is meaningful? Are his line breaks natural pauses?

C. Is there anything like "sprung rhythm" in Tennyson's "Break, Break, Break" (p. 161) or in Campion's "It Fell on a Summer's Day" (p. 94)?

D. Gary Snyder's "Bubbs Creek Haircut" begins:

High ceilingd and the double mirrors, the
        calendar a splendid alpine scene—scab barber—
in stained white barber gown, alone, sat down, old man
A summer fog gray San Francisco day
I walked right in.   on Howard Street
                haircut a dollar twenty-five.
Just clip it close as it will go.

"now why you want your hair cut back like that."
—well I'm going to the Sierras for a while
Bubbs Creek and on across to upper Kern . . .

Can you find any "crypto-iambs" (hidden iambic pentameters) in these free-looking lines?

E. Write a short poem in strong-stress rhythms on a subject that seems appropriate to their energetic character. Or write a poem in syllabics, of any line length you prefer. Or write a poem that makes use of visual prosody—the resources of the typewriter, for example, as Charles Olson describes them.

VI the mind

The Shape of Thought 17

we go a-sentencing

Up to now we have been dealing with the more physical, or at least non-intellectual, aspects of poetry: sensation, emotion, voice with its sounds and rhythms. All of these, of course, we experience in our consciousness. What the brain does not register might as well not exist for us. Even our sensuality has nothing but mind to reside in.

But there are elements of poetry that seem to have a more intellectual emphasis than those we have looked at. One of these is the way the poet organizes the sentences of his poem. The sentence represents, in greatly simplified form, an act of the mind. In *greatly* simplified form: since the brain has more cells to work with than there are people on this planet, any mental process is almost infinitely complex. The sentence is merely an art-form that tries to give us a few high points of the process.

"To write a poem," said Robert Frost, "is to go a-sentencing." A sentence is the shape words take when they come naturally together; such shapes can be not only expressive but symbolic.

In psychological experiments, people have been asked to draw lines they felt would express certain emotional states. "Beautiful" lines were smoothly curved, continuous, symmetrical. "Ugly" lines were jagged, with mixed angles and curves. In part the correlation between curves and mood is due to the muscular effort demanded of the eye, which moves smoothly or jerkily; in part it is due to our memory of pleasant and unpleasant lines in nature. Sentences affect us in just such a way. The expressiveness of their shape can emphasize what the poem is expressing.

Sentence Length

A poem about the life cycle of the eel (the original is in Italian) has only one long sentence—an incomplete one at that. The effect is to dramatize, in the very thrust of the words, the tireless energy that shows itself in nature. Is not this vitality, the poet asks, like the life force that sparkles so beautifully in the eyes of a woman?

THE EEL

The eel, the
siren of sleety seas, abandoning
the Baltic for our waters,
our estuaries, our
freshets, to lash upcurrent under the brunt
of the flood, sunk deep, from brook to brook and then
trickle to trickle dwindling,
more inner always, always more in the heart
of the rock, thrusting
through ruts of the mud, until, one day, 10
explosion of splendor from the chestnut groves
kindles a flicker in deadwater sumps,
in ditches pitched
from ramparts of the Appennine to Romagna;
eel: torch and whip,
arrow of love on earth,
which nothing but our gorges or bone-dry
gutters of the Pyrenees usher back
to edens of fertility;
green soul that probes 20
for life where only
fevering heat or devastation preys,
spark that says
the whole commences when the whole would seem
charred black, an old stick buried;
brief rainbow, twin
to that within your lashes' dazzle, that
you keep alive, inviolate, among
the sons of men, steeped in your mire—in this
not recognize a sister? 30

Eugenio Montale (b. 1896)

Short sentences, or sentences made up of short elements, may express a nervous discharge of energy, as in the poems of Emily Dickinson. Gwendolyn Brooks uses three-word sentences to express a life of nervous energy recklessly expended.

WE REAL COOL

The Pool Players.
Seven at the Golden Shovel.

We real cool. We
Left school. We

Lurk late. We
Strike straight. We

Sing sin. We
Thin gin. We

Jazz June. We
Die soon.

Gwendolyn Brooks (b. 1917)

Very long sentences or very short ones are the extremes. In between there are many possibilities.

The way in which a poet goes a-sentencing will distinguish his rhythm from that of other poets writing in the same meter. How he paces his sentences, how and where he pauses—things like this make one poet's characteristic tempo different from that of another.

Use of Connectives

The very way the parts of a sentence are held together may be significant. A series of connectives like "and . . . and . . . and" can be childish—or it can be solemnly impressive, as in the first chapter of Genesis.

In the beginning God created the heaven and the earth. And the earth was without form, and void; and darkness was upon the face of the deep. And the Spirit of God moved upon the face of the waters. And God said, "Let there be light": and there was light.

Frost uses many *and*'s for drowsy monotony at the beginning of "Out, Out—," in which a fatal accident happens because people are tired after a long day's work.

"OUT, OUT—"

The buzz saw snarled and rattled in the yard
And made dust and dropped stove-length sticks of wood,
Sweet-scented stuff when the breeze drew across it.
And from there those that lifted eyes could count
Five mountain ranges one behind the other
Under the sunset far into Vermont.
And the saw snarled and rattled, snarled and rattled,
As it ran light, or had to bear a load.
And nothing happened: day was all but done.
Call it a day, I wish they might have said 10
To please the boy by giving him the half hour

"Out, Out—": *The title is from* Macbeth, *V, v:*

Out, out, brief candle!
Life's but a walking shadow. . . .

That a boy counts so much when saved from work.
His sister stood beside them in her apron
To tell them "Supper." At the word, the saw,
As if to prove saws knew what supper meant,
Leaped out at the boy's hand, or seemed to leap—
He must have given the hand. However it was,
Neither refused the meeting. But the hand!
The boy's first outcry was a rueful laugh,
As he swung toward them holding up the hand, 20
Half in appeal, but half as if to keep
The life from spilling. Then the boy saw all—
Since he was old enough to know, big boy
Doing a man's work, though a child at heart—
He saw all spoiled. "Don't let him cut my hand off—
The doctor, when he comes. Don't let him, sister!"
So. But the hand was gone already.
The doctor put him in the dark of ether.
He lay and puffed his lips out with his breath.
And then—the watcher at his pulse took fright. 30
No one believed. They listened at his heart.
Little—less—nothing!—and that ended it.
No more to build on there. And they, since they
Were not the one dead, turned to their affairs.

Robert Frost

When conjunctions are omitted, the tone can be one of abruptness and energy, as in Caesar's famous "I came, I saw, I conquered."

When words that express the logical relationships between clauses are omitted, we have a kind of speech common in primitive languages. "Man hungry. He shoot arrow. Kill deer. He happy." It is found in the song that African Pygmies sing in grieved acceptance of the fact of death.

THE ANIMAL RUNS, IT PASSES, IT DIES
(African)

A. The animal runs, it passes, it dies. And it is the great cold.
B. It is the great cold of the night, it is the dark.
A. The bird flies, it passes, it dies. And it is the great cold.
B. It is the great cold of the night, it is the dark.
A. The fish flees, it passes, it dies. And it is the great cold.
B. It is the great cold of the night, it is the dark.
A. Man eats and sleeps. He dies. And it is the great cold.
B. It is the great cold of the night, it is the dark.
A. There is light in the sky, the eyes are extinguished, the star shines. 10
B. The cold is below, the light is on high.
A. The man has passed, the shade has vanished, the prisoner is free! . . . .

Poetry, caring more for the sensory details than for the logical relationship between them, is especially inclined to use this kind of construction.[1] The author of "Western Wind" never specifies the connection between the wind and the rain and his love. Dreams, too, work purely by means of it; since they have no easy way of indicating relationships like *therefore, because, if, although,* they set objects, persons, or situations meaningfully next to one another. So do some poems.

THE MESSAGE

The door that someone opened wide
The door that someone shut again
The chair where someone came to sit
The cat that someone cuddled there
The fruit that someone bit into
The letter someone read and read
The chair that someone overturned
The door that someone opened wide
The road where someone's running yet
The woods that someone's passing through 10
The river someone's jumping in
The hospital where someone's dead.

Jacques Prévert (b. 1900)

Parallelism

One of the most ancient and powerful ways of organizing a sentence is to give corresponding parts corresponding expression. **Parallelism** is to be found in the poetry of all languages. We recognize it in such Biblical cadences as those of Psalm 19:

> The heavens declare the glory of God; and the
> firmament showeth his handiwork.
> Day unto day uttereth speech, and night unto night
> showeth knowledge . . . .

We recognize it in the characteristic rhythms of Walt Whitman.

I HEAR AMERICA SINGING

I hear America singing, the varied carols I hear,
Those of mechanics, each one singing his as it should be blithe and strong,
The carpenter singing his as he measures his plank or beam,
The mason singing his as he makes ready for work, or leaves off work,
The boatman singing what belongs to him in his boat, the deckhand singing
on the steamboat deck,
The shoemaker singing as he sits on his bench, the hatter singing as he
stands,

[1] It is called **parataxis** or *setting side by side.*

The wood-cutter's song, the ploughboy's on his way in the morning, or at noon intermission or at sundown, 10
The delicious singing of the mother, or of the young wife at work, or of the girl sewing or washing,
Each singing what belongs to him or her and to none else,
The day what belongs to the day—at night the party of young fellows, robust, friendly,
Singing with open mouths their strong melodious songs.

Walt Whitman

Parallelism helps to make even short poems memorable, as in the little eighteenth-century song that both Victoria de los Angeles and Joan Baez have recorded:

Plaisir d'amour ne dure qu'un moment.
Chagrin d'amour dure toute la vie.

Pleasure of love lasts only a moment.
Sorrow of love lasts all life long.

How much less memorable if it read:

Pleasure of love lasts only a moment.
You don't get over it when love goes wrong.

Kenneth Fearing uses parallelism as a rhythmic principle.

Even when your friend, the radio, is still; even
when her dream, the magazine, is finished;
even when his life, the ticker, is silent; even
when their destiny, the boulevard, is bare;
And after that paradise, the dance-hall, is closed;
after that theater, the clinic, is dark....

Parallelism which contrasts words or ideas (often by means of "but" or a word like it) is called **antithesis**; it emphasizes conflicting materials by setting them sharply together. Alexander Pope, like other poets of the rational eighteenth century, likes to strike sparks by clashing the flint of one idea against the steel of another.

Authors are partial to their wit, 'tis true,
But are not critics to their judgment too?

True wit is nature to advantage dressed,
What oft was thought, but ne'er so well expressed.

Sentence Structure

Breaking up the shape of the sentence, some have felt, might enable us to get closer to the complex reality it oversimplifies. Some of the experiments of James Joyce and others have been directed to this end. So have some of the ancient figures of speech, which, as we have seen, are really ways of thinking.

Inversion of the normal word order is one of the most obvious of these. Sometimes writers misplace words because they "need them there" for the rhythm or rhyme; but this is always an ugliness.

Fast to the roof cleave may my tongue
If mindless I of thee be found . . . .

Thomas Campion

. . . Old acquaintances
Seem do we . . . .

Thomas Hardy

Not all inversions are bad. Some we hear in colloquial speech. "But nice he is!" "Raquel Welch she is *not!*" Only our sense of spoken English tells us which inversions come naturally.

We allow Milton his inversion when he says of Satan:

Him the Almighty Power
Hurled headlong flaming from the ethereal sky
With hideous ruin and combustion down
To bottomless perdition . . .

This is upside-down—but so was Satan. When Marvell says of fate:

And therefore her decrees of steel
Us as the distant poles have placed . . . .

we can see that he is dramatizing the world-wide separation of the lovers by isolating "us" in the sentence.

E. E. Cummings uses inversion expressively in his little poem about the glance exchanged between a poisoned mouse and his poisoner.

ME UP AT DOES

Me up at does

out of the floor
quietly Stare

a poisoned mouse

still who alive

is asking What
have i done that

You wouldn't have

E. E. Cummings

Normally we look down on the helpless mouse. In this poem it is the reproachful upward glance of the mouse that is more telling; the words reverse as the electrical charge of the glances does.

Parenthesis also interrupts the conventional order of syntax in the interests of fidelity to thought.

The rabbit with his pink, distinctly, eyes . . . . *John Updike*

I sat by a stream in a
perfect—except for willows—
emptiness . . . .

A. R. Ammons

There are other ways to break up the normal sentence structure in order to follow the working of the mind. We can start a sentence according to one pattern and abruptly abandon it midcourse for another. "Students should be free to read what you want to." "What I'd really like to—how about a long walk?" We all use the device[1] when impulse or a better thought cancels what we were about to say. Peter Viereck's unhappy and ungrammatical lover is entangled in it the moment he says "is" in the first line.

THE LYRICISM OF THE WEAK

I sit here with the wind is in my hair;
I huddle like the sun is in my eyes;
I am (I wished you'd contact me) alone.

A fat lot you'd wear crape if I was dead.
It figures, who I heard there when I phoned you;
It figures, when I came there, who has went.

Dogs laugh at me, folks bark at me since then;
"She is," they say, "no better than she ought to";
I love you irregardless how they talk.

You should of done it (which it is no crime) 10
With me you should of done it, what they say.
I sit here with the wind is in my hair.

Peter Viereck (b. 1916)

Or we can start a sentence and abruptly cut it off, perhaps with the "or else—!" that we know can speak louder than words.[2] "Either you clean up your room, or else—!" Yeats likes to let passion interfere with sentence structure:

Hanrahan rose in frenzy there
And followed up those baying creatures towards—

O towards I have forgotten what—enough!

We have already seen quite a few poems that take liberties with conventional sentence structure. Kenneth Patchen's "Moon, Sun, Sleep, Birds, Live" (p. 147) represents three levels of thought and feeling at the same time. Another of his lyrics is in two interwoven voices, distinguished by two kinds of typography.

[1] **Anacoluthon** *(not following).*
[2] **Aposiopesis** *(falling silent).*

O All down within the Pretty Meadow

how many times, Death
have you done it

The Lovers

to just such golden ones
as these

Toss at Their Wondrous Play

O how many times, Death, have you done it
To just such golden ones as these

Kenneth Patchen

A well-known poem of Archibald MacLeish's has the infinitive "to feel" as its subject, but we look in vain for a predicate. There is none. The fluidity of the syntax is encouraged by an almost total lack of punctuation: the poem moves forward as smoothly and steady as the shadow of night does.

YOU, ANDREW MARVELL

And here face down beneath the sun
And here upon earth's noonward height
To feel the always coming on
The always rising of the night:

To feel creep up the curving east
The earthy chill of dusk and slow
Upon those under lands the vast
And ever climbing shadow grow

And strange at Ecbatan the trees
Take leaf by leaf the evening strange 10
The flooding dark about their knees
The mountains over Persia change

And now at Kermanshah the gate
Dark empty and the withered grass
And through the twilight now the late
Few travelers in the westward pass

And Baghdad darken and the bridge
Across the silent river gone
And through Arabia the edge
Of evening widen and steal on 20

And deepen on Palmyra's street
The wheel rut in the ruined stone
And Lebanon fade out and Crete
High through the clouds and overblown

---

9 **Ecbatan:** *town in ancient Persia*
13 **Kermanshah:** *town in Iran to the west of Ecbatan*
21 **Palmyra:** *ancient town in Syria*

And over Sicily the air
Still flashing with the landward gulls
And loom and slowly disappear
The sails above the shadowy hulls

And Spain go under and the shore
Of Africa the gilded sand 30
And evening vanish and no more
The low pale light across that land

Nor now the long light on the sea:

And here face downward in the sun
To feel how swift how secretly
The shadow of the night comes on . . .

Archibald MacLeish

John Clare, the nineteenth-century poet who spent the last decades of his life in an insane asylum, was indifferent to sentence structure and punctuation in the wild tumble of words in his love song to Mary:

REMEMBER DEAR MARY

Remember dear Mary love cannot deceive
Loves truth cannot vary dear Mary believe
You may hear and believe it believe it and hear
Love could not deceive those features so dear
Believe me dear Mary to press thy soft hand
Is sweeter than riches in houses and Land

Where I pressed thy soft hand at the dewfall o' eve
I felt the sweet tremble that cannot deceive
If love you believe in Belief is my love
As it lived once in Eden ere we fell from above 10
To this heartless this friendless this desolate earth
And kept in first love Immortality's birth

'Tis there we last meet I adore thee and love thee
Theres nothing beneath thee around thee above thee
I feel it and know it I know so and feel
If your love cannot show it mine cannot conceal
But knowing I love I feel and adore
And the more I behold—only loves thee the more

John Clare (1793–1864)

Besides traveling at different paces and in different manners, sentences can also take us through different sectors of the language, or even break into regions not previously explored. The rest of this chapter will present a few samplings of the many kinds of terrain in which the poet can go a-sentencing.

Levels of Language

Language has many levels, from the lowest to the most sublime. Poets avail themselves of an appropriate level—or sometimes get ironic effects by seeking out a deliberately inappropriate one, as Rochester does in his poem about the debauchee whom age and venereal disease have now incapacitated for the seduction, revelry, and rape to which his better years were devoted. Not a lofty theme, but Rochester handles it as if it were—as if the aging rake were a "brave admiral" now in retirement, capable of serving only in an advisory capacity.

THE DISABLED DEBAUCHEE

As some brave admiral, in former war
  Deprived of force, but pressed with courage still,
Two rival fleets appearing from afar,
  Crawls to the top of an adjacent hill,

From whence (with thoughts full of concern) he views
  The wise and daring conduct of the fight,
And each bold action to his mind renews
  His present glory and his past delight;

From his fierce eyes flashes of fire he throws
  As from black clouds when lightning breaks away; 10
Transported, thinks himself amidst the foes,
  And, absent, yet enjoys the bloody day;

So, when my days of impotence approach,
  And I'm by pox or wine's unlucky chance
Forced from the pleasing billows of debauch,
  On the dull shore of lazy temperance,

My pains at least some respite shall afford
  While I behold the battles you maintain,
When fleets of glasses sail about the board,
  From whose broadsides volleys of wit shall rain. 20

Nor let the sight of honorable scars
  Which my too forward valor did procure
Frighten new 'listed soldiers from the wars;
  Past joys have more than paid what I endure.

Should any youth (worth being drunk) prove nice,
  And from his fair inviter meanly shrink,
'Twould please the ghost of my departed vice
  If, at my counsel, he repent and drink.

Or should some cold-complexioned sot forbid,
  With his dull morals, our bold night-alarms, 30
I'll fire his blood by telling what I did,
  When I was strong and able to bear arms.

---

25 **nice:** *over-refined, shy*

I'll tell of whores attacked, their lords at home,
  Bawds' quarters beaten up, and fortress won;
Windows demolished, watches overcome,
  And handsome ills by my contrivance done. . . .

With tales like these I will such thoughts inspire,
  As to important mischief shall incline;
I'll make him long some ancient church to fire,
  And fear no lewdness he's called to by wine. 40

Thus, statesmanlike, I'll saucily impose,
  And, safe from action, valiantly advise;
Sheltered in impotence, urge you to blows,
  And, being good for nothing else, be wise.

John Wilmot, Earl of Rochester (1647–1680)

We are familiar with the language governments use in their press releases. We know that if our side has suffered a humiliating rout, official headlines can make things seem all right with "BRILLIANT STRATEGIC RETREAT CONFUSES FOE!" Robert Graves writes in this mode about the Battle of Marathon (490 B.C.), in which the outnumbered Athenians won a surprising victory over the "barbarians," as they called the Persians. Generally we read the Athenian version, as given by Herodotus: "There fell in the battle of Marathon, on the side of the barbarians, about six thousand and four hundred men; on that of the Athenians, one hundred and ninety-two." Graves imagines how the Persian press releases might have explained the incident at home.

THE PERSIAN VERSION

Truth-loving Persians do not dwell upon
The trivial skirmish fought near Marathon.
As for the Greek theatrical tradition
Which represents that summer's expedition
Not as a mere reconnaissance in force
By three brigades of foot and one of horse
(Their left flank covered by some obsolete
Light craft detached from the main Persian fleet)
But as a grandiose, ill-starred attempt
To conquer Greece—they treat it with contempt; 10
And only incidentally refute
Major Greek claims, by stressing what repute
The Persian monarch and the Persian nation
Won by this salutary demonstration:
Despite a strong defence and adverse weather
All arms combined magnificently together.

Robert Graves

Drawing on the horror movies of the late late shows in his poem about cat people, Edward Field uses a diction that accepts in a matter-of-fact way the melodramatic improbabilities of such films.

CURSE OF THE CAT WOMAN

It sometimes happens
that the woman you meet and fall in love with
is of that strange Transylvanian people
with an affinity for cats.

You take her to a restaurant, say, or a show,
on an ordinary date, being attracted
by the glitter in her slitty eyes and her catlike walk,
and afterwards of course you take her in your arms
and she turns into a black panther
and bites you to death. 10

Or perhaps you are saved in the nick of time
and she is tormented by the knowledge of her tendency:
That she daren't hug a man
unless she wants to risk clawing him up.

This puts you both in a difficult position—
panting lovers who are prevented from touching
not by bars but by circumstance:
You have terrible fights and say cruel things
for having the hots does not give you a sweet temper.

One night you are walking down a dark street 20
and hear the pad-pad of a panther following you,
but when you turn around there are only shadows,
or perhaps one shadow too many.

You approach, calling, "Who's there?"
and it leaps on you.
Luckily you have brought along your sword
and you stab it to death.

And before your eyes it turns into the woman you love,
her breast impaled on your sword,
her mouth dribbling blood saying she loved you 30
but couldn't help her tendency.

So death released her from the curse at last,
and you knew from the angelic smile on her dead face
that in spite of a life the devil owned,
love had won, and heaven pardoned her.

Edward Field (b. 1924)

The language of want ads is put to poignant use by Miller Williams in his lonely love poem.

SALE

Partnership dissolved.
Everything must be sold.
Individually or the set
as follows:

Brain, one standard, cold.
Geared to glossing.
Given to hard replies.
Convolutions convey the illusion
of exceptional depth.
Damaged. 10

think. think of me. but you are not thinking

One pair of eyes. Green. Like new.
Especially good for girls and women walking,
wicker baskets,
paintings by Van Gogh,
red clocks and frogs, chicken snakes and snow.

look at me. but you are not looking at me

One pair of ears, big. Best offer takes.
Tuned to Bach, Hank Williams, bees,
the Book of Job. 20
Shut-off for deans, lieutenants and
salesman talking.

listen. listen please. but you are not listening

Mouth, one wide.
Some teeth missing.
Two and a half languages. Adaptable to pipes
and occasional kissing.
Has been broken but in good repair.
Lies.

tell me. tell me please. why won't you tell me 30

Hands, right and left.
Feet. Neck. Some hair.
Stomach, heart, spleen and
accessory parts.

come. come quickly. there is only a little time

Starts tomorrow
what you've been waiting for
and when it's gone it's gone
so hurry

hurry 40

Miller Williams (b. 1930)

New Words, New Language

Probably the first step toward new ways of sentencing is a reworking of the word itself. New insights, new awarenesses sometimes demand new words; or new words can prove to be new insights. The quotations that follow each use a word we would not find in a dictionary, and yet the meaning is clear.

. . . Over him arches
UNITED STATES OF AMERICA, and, squinched in
Between that and his rump, E PLURIBUS UNUM . . . . *Howard Nemerov*

. . . fields and hedges, the scarlotry of
maple leaves . . . . *A. R. Ammons*

The American from
Minnesota
Speaks Harvardly
of Revolution—
Men of the Mau Mau
Smile
Their fists holding
Bits of
Kenya earth. *Alice Walker*

"Squinched" and "scarlotry" are made up of words we know: the first of "squeeze," "scrunch," "pinch," etc.; the second of "scarlet" and "harlotry." They are like the "portmanteau" words that Lewis Carroll made up so successfully: "chortle" (from "chuckle" and "snort"), "galumph" (from "gallop" and "triumph"). Alice Walker's "Harvardly" we recognize as an ironic invention.

Isabella Gardner, from such words as "gambol," "gamble," "gimlet," "gimbles," etc., constructs a word for love-making:

GIMBOLING

Nimble as dolphins to
dive leap and gimble, sleek, supple
as ripples to slip round each other to
wander and fondle on under and into
the seeking and coupling and swarming of water
compliant as sea-plants to bend with the tide
unfolding and folding to frond and to flower
a winding and twining to melt and to merge
to rock upon billowing founder in surf
and a fathom's down drowning before the sweet waking 10
the floating ashore into sleep and to morning.

Isabella Gardner (b. 1915)

In a poem about Robert Frost, May Swenson, without inventing new words, uses typography to reveal the words that are hidden in other words. Part of it reads:

Lots of trees in the fo
rest but this one's an O
a K that's plan
ted hims elf . . .

His sig nature's on the he art
of his time . . . .

Spelling "forest" as fo/rest emphasizes the "rest" (or peace) in that forest—even for enemies. The "oak" is an O/a K because it is a fine oak, an O.K. oak. Frost, as oak, has not merely planted himself but *plan*ned to plant "hims" (hymns) and is *elf*ish, mischievous. "His sig nature" emphasizes its *natural*ness; his heart is a kind of "he art" or masculine art. In these few lines there are many more such ghostly conjurings.

Not all poets are inclined to break up or invent words. Some, like classic poker players, prefer to stick with the game as it is. On their side would be Frost himself, who stubbornly declares, "We play the words as we find them. We make them do."

John Berryman, in his *Dream Songs*, has devised what often sounds like a new language. He has done this by combining various voices that range from hieratic English in the grand style to dialect and baby talk —a selection from the many tones possible to a psyche split many ways.

4

Filling her compact & delicious body
with chicken páprika, she glanced at me
twice.
Fainting with interest, I hungered back
and only the fact of her husband & four other people
kept me from springing on her

or falling at her little feet and crying
'You are the hottest one for years of night
Henry's dazed eyes
have enjoyed, Brilliance.' I advanced upon (10)
(despairing) my spumoni. —Sir Bones: is stuffed,
de world, wif feeding girls.

—Black hair, complexion Latin, jewelled eyes
downcast . . . The slob beside her feasts . . . What wonders is
she sitting on, over there?
The restaurant buzzes. She might as well be on Mars.
Where did it all go wrong? There ought to be a law against Henry.
—Mr. Bones: there is.

22
of 1826

I am the little man who smokes & smokes.
I am the girl who does know better but.
I am the king of the pool.
I am so wise I had my mouth sewn shut.
I am a government official & a goddamned fool.
I am a lady who takes jokes.

I am the enemy of the mind.
I am the auto salesman and lóve you.
I am a teenage cancer, with a plan.
I am the blackt-out man. (10)

I am the woman powerful as a zoo.
I am two eyes screwed to my set, whose blind—

It is the Fourth of July.
Collect: while the dying man,
forgone by you creator, who forgives,
is gasping 'Thomas Jefferson still lives'
in vain, in vain, in vain.
I am Henry Pussy-cat! My whiskers fly.

John Berryman (1914–1972)

The nonadventure of "4" is typical of the poet's manner. ("Mr. Bones," or "Sir Bones," is the name for the end man in a minstrel show who clacked out castanetlike rhythms on the "bones.") "22" becomes clear if we recall that Thomas Jefferson and John Adams both died on the Fourth of July, 1826. Adams, knowing that death was near, roused himself to say "Thomas Jefferson survives." But Jefferson had died a few hours before Adams did. The twelve characters of the first two stanzas might be seen as typical of the TV-watching public that makes up the nation such men as Jefferson and Adams founded. The poem might have a solemn message: we are unworthy of the heroes who founded our country. But it never takes so indignant or preachy a tone. For all of their basic passion, the voices themselves are colloquial and—in their dark way—amusing.

A poet who goes further in conjuring up a language of his own is E. E. Cummings.

WHERELINGS WHENLINGS

wherelings whenlings
(daughters of ifbut offspring of hopefear
sons of unless and children of almost)
never shall guess the dimension of

him whose
each
foot likes the
here of this earth

whose both
eyes 10
love
this now of the sky

—endlings of isn't
shall never
begin
to begin to

imagine how(only are shall be were
dawn dark rain snow rain
-bow &
a 20

moon
's whis-
per
in sunset

or thrushes toward dusk among whippoorwills or
tree field rock hollyhock forest brook chickadee
mountain. Mountain)
whycoloured worlds of because do

not stand against yes which is built by
forever & sunsmell 30
(sometimes a wonder
of wild roses

sometimes)
with north
over
the barn

E. E. Cummings

Cummings does only one thing that seems new here: he lets any part of speech serve for any other part. Conjunctions can be nouns, adverbs can be adjectives, pronouns can be verbs—anything can be anything. We might think of this as a modern invention, but the practice is so old that the grammarians have not only one word for it but several.

The Old English suffix "-ling" has several meanings. It can mean *having the quality of,* as "darlings" are *dear,* and "hirelings" are *hired.* It can mean *concerned with,* as "worldlings" are concerned with the *world.* It can be a diminutive, as in "gosling" and "suckling." Often it has unfavorable overtones. When Cummings refers to "wherelings" and "whenlings," he means *petty* people, concerned with the local and the temporary instead of the spiritual; wondering "Where am I?" and "When will I . . . ?" instead of living and doing, always conditional, tentative, irresolute. They live in a nonexistent future, vacillating between "hope" and "fear." They will not do things "unless"; they do them only "almost." What people who are really alive care about is not the *where* of this earth but "the here of this earth"; what their eyes love is not the *when* of the sky but "this now of the sky." Unless we really live, really *are,* it can never be said of us that we *were*—it will be as if we had never existed. "Whycoloured worlds" (those of whining *why? why? why?*) can never stand against "yes," which for Cummings means the wholehearted acceptance of life and living.

Transpositions of the parts of speech, as we said, are not new. The Elizabethan Robert Southwell anticipated Cummings when he wrote:

In *was* stands my delight,
In *is* and *shall* my woe,
My horror fastened in the *yea,*
My hope hanged in the *no.*

Cummings' originality is in using the old device in a new way—with systematic intensity.

The following poem is simple once we realize that "anyone," like the medieval Everyman, is a typical human being who marries a typical "noone" (a nobody, as outsiders might think), lives a typical life, dies a typical death, and has a typical hereafter.

ANYONE LIVED IN A PRETTY HOW TOWN

anyone lived in a pretty how town
(with up so floating many bells down)
spring summer autumn winter
he sang his didn't he danced his did.

Women and men(both little and small)
cared for anyone not at all
they sowed their isn't they reaped their same
sun moon stars rain

children guessed(but only a few
and down they forgot as up they grew   10
autumn winter spring summer)
that noone loved him more by more

when by now and tree by leaf
she laughed his joy she cried his grief
bird by snow and stir by still
anyone's any was all to her

someones married their everyones
laughed their cryings and did their dance
(sleep wake hope and then)they
said their nevers they slept their dream   20

stars rain sun moon
(and only the snow can begin to explain
how children are apt to forget to remember
with up so floating many bells down)

one day anyone died i guess
(and noone stooped to kiss his face)
busy folk buried them side by side
little by little and was by was

all by all and deep by deep
and more by more they dream their sleep   30
noone and anyone earth by april
wish by spirit and if by yes.

Women and men(both dong and ding)
summer autumn winter spring
reaped their sowing and went their came
sun moon stars rain

E. E. Cummings

Exercises and Diversions

A. 1. What matters discussed in this chapter are illustrated by the following quotations?

1. getting dressed, in the mirror,
   the bath girl, with a pretty mole and a
   red skirt is watching me. . . . *Gary Snyder*

2. . . . How she loved
   You, me, loved us all, the bird, the cat! *James Merrill*

3. Only, when loosening clothes, you lean
   Out of your window sleepily,
   And with luxurious, lidded mien
   Sniff at the bitter dark—dear she,
   Think somewhat gently of, between
   Love ended and beginning, me. *Stanley J. Kunitz*

4. Looking up from the street,
   geese are the least we can expect
   of a winter sky. *Ron Loewinsohn*

5. Ask of the learn'd the way, the learn'd are blind,
   This bids to serve, and that to shun mankind;
   Some place the bliss in action, some in ease,
   Those call it pleasure, and contentment these;
   Some sunk to beasts, find pleasure end in pain;
   Some swelled to gods, confess ev'n virtue vain;
   Or indolent, to each extreme they fall,
   To trust in everything, or doubt of all. *Alexander Pope*

6. Troops went by the house and down the road and the dust they raised powdered the leaves of the trees. The trunks of the trees too were dusty and the leaves fell early that year and we saw the troops marching along the road and the dust rising and leaves, stirred by the breeze, falling and the soldiers marching and afterwards the road bare and white except for the leaves. *Ernest Hemingway*

7. While I stand on the roadway, or on the pavements grey,
   I hear it in the deep heart's core. *W. B. Yeats*

B. 1. If a poem is written in stanzas (units of the same shape and length), should each stanza be a sentence? If you look back over poems we have read, does it seem that sentences have a tendency to fit the stanza shape, so that stanzas are likely to end with a period? (Cf. "Ode to a Nightingale," p. 11; "Marin-An," p. 16, "Notes for a Movie Script," p. 17.)

2. How could a writer use form expressively by *not* stopping for the stanza break but by overriding it?
3. This happens in "A Carriage from Sweden" (p. 52) and in "Bells for John Whiteside's Daughter" (p. 131). With what effect in each?
4. Go a-sentencing through some of the poems we have read earlier, noticing—for this once at least—the interplay between sentence structure and the demand of the form. Point out some interesting effects.

C. 1. In "Acquainted with the Night" (p. 48), the length of the sentences, in number of lines, is 1, 1, 1, 1, 2, 7, 1. Is this structure related to meaning?

2. In "The End of the Weekend" (p. 16), what is the longest sentence? The shortest? Is the length significant?

3. In the three poems about lovers by Snodgrass (p. 91), Dickey (p. 92), and Thompson (p. 93), the sentence structure is very different. Describe how. Do the differences correspond to differences in mood? Find examples of anacoluthon and aposiopesis. Why would these devices be especially natural in such poems?

D. 1. How many sentences are there in "The Disabled Debauchee"? How does the elaborate structure of the first sentence help establish the tone of the poem?

2. The long "As. . . So . . ." (ll. 1–13) is called an epic or Homeric simile, such as Homer uses to describe the Greeks going into battle:

> As from his post on a hilltop a goatherd sees a cloud driven across the sea by a raging west wind, a cloud which even though far away looks black as pitch as it moves over the waves, bringing with it a furious storm, and the goatherd shudders to see it and hurries his goats into a cave, so the thick ranks of the sturdy Greeks move toward the battle. . . .

Why is the use of such a simile ironic in Rochester's poem?

3. Would a more parallel structure have strengthened the second stanza?

4. Find examples in this poem of a simile within a simile, metaphor, transferred epithets, synecdoche (or metonymy), oxymoron, puns, anacoluthon. Why are such figures of speech especially appropriate here?

5. Examine the adjectives. How many are used ironically?

E. 1. Quite a few expressions in "Curse of the Cat Woman" take on a special tone. How would you describe the tone of "It sometimes happens" (l. 1), "that strange Transylvanian people" (l. 3), "an affinity for cats" (l. 4), "her tendency" (l. 12), "or perhaps one shadow too many" (l. 23), "Luckily you have brought along your sword" (l. 26), "the woman you love" (l. 28), "her breast impaled on" (l. 29)?

2. In a differently handled poem, the last four lines might well be a hopeless tissue of clichés and sentimentality. What saves them here?

F. 1. Write a bad poem—sentimental, cliché-ridden—of about a dozen lines, ending up with the last four lines of Mr. Field's poem.

2. Write a long-sentence poem, a short-sentence poem, or a poem that expressively mixes long and short sentences.

Golden Numbers on nature and form

18

If we leaf through a book of verse we notice immediately that poetry, unlike prose, favors special conformations; it likes to arrange itself in shapes on the page. These shapes in space originally represented shapes in time—shapes to be heard if we were listening to a recitation rather than looking at a book.

In its love for shape, shapeliness, and proportion, poetry is like mathematics.

> . . . Euclid alone
> Has looked on beauty bare. Fortunate they
> Who, though once only and then but far away,
> Have heard her massive sandal set on stone.
>
> *Edna St. Vincent Millay*

Many readers believe that poetry and mathematics are opposed in spirit. Such readers may be repelled by the pages that follow, with their drawings that seem to be straight out of Euclid. But no mathematical background is required—there are no problems to solve. The drawings are only to marvel at. And to be seen as analogies: they are really telling us something about the nature of poetry, and about Nature herself.

To decide in advance that a poem will have seventeen syllables or fourteen lines or that it will be constructed in stanzaic units of this or that size or shape may seem arbitrary and artificial. When a poem begins to germinate in the poet's mind, could it not grow simply and naturally, the way a flower grows, instead of being forced to follow a pattern? This seems a good question—but it shows little knowledge of how flowers do grow. Nature has been working on her flowers for

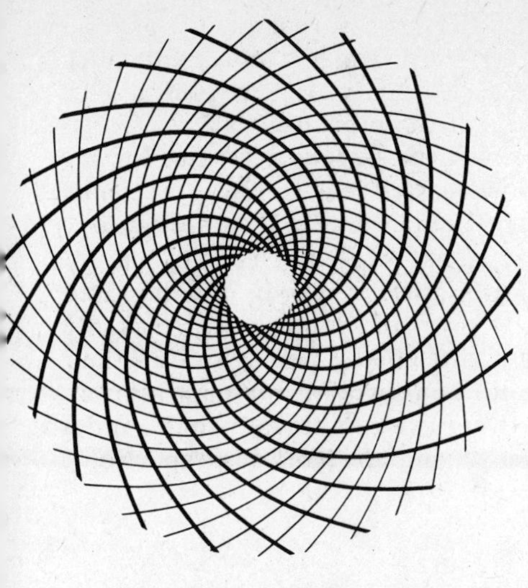

Spiral Pattern in the Sunflower

some millions of years; a close look at them, as at anything in the natural world, will show why Pythagoras said that all things are number, why Plato said that God always geometrizes.

If we take a close look at the head of a sunflower, we see two sets of spirals whirling in opposite directions. The florets that make them up are not of any random number. Typically, there are twenty-one going clockwise and thirty-four going counterclockwise —numbers that a mathematician would come on with a thrill of recognition. They belong to the series of "golden numbers" called the Fibonacci sequence, in which each number is the sum of the two preceding ones: 1, 1, 2, 3, 5, 8, 13, 21, 34, 55, etc. Although the sequence may look like a man-made curiosity, it turns up again and again in nature—in the way rabbits breed, in the generation of bees, in the number and pattern of leaves or petals on certain plants, in the spirals of the sunflower.

A further strangeness about the series is that the ratio between consecutive numbers, after the first few, remains about the same, coming closer and closer to a stabilization in which the smaller number is to the larger as .618 is to 1. This .618 ratio—familiar to the ancient Greeks and to most designers, artists, and architects ever since—is that of the golden section, a way of proportioning dimensions so that the parts (many believe) have the most aesthetically pleasing relationship to each other and to the whole.

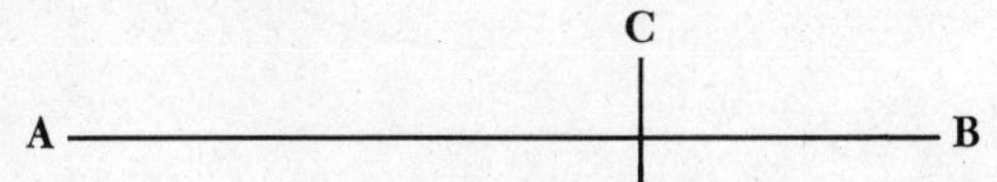

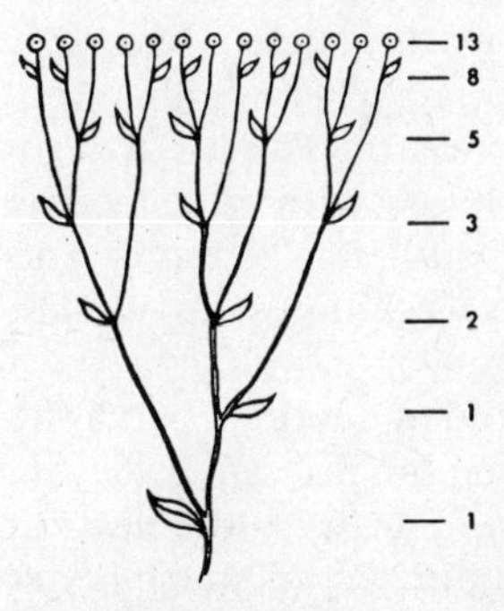

Sneezewort

In this division, the lesser part is to the greater as the greater is to the whole: $CB : AC :: AC : AB$.

It is also a ratio we have perceived, without being aware of it, in many things in nature. The human body, besides having bilateral symmetry, seems to have proportioned itself in accordance with the golden section. The length from the top of the head to the navel and the length from the navel to the toes have the ratio of about .618 to 1. These two divisions are subdivided. The length from navel to knee is to the length from knee to sole as

1 to .618. In reverse order, navel to throat and throat to top of head are related as 1 to .618. The architect Le Corbusier, who has planned buildings on the basis of the golden section, has even devised a scale for designers based on the proportions of the human body.

If bodily proportions might have given the Greeks a feeling for the golden section, geometry would have suggested it with more precision. The mysterious appeal of the ancient pentagram, or "endless knot," one of the most famous of all magic signs, owes much to its play of proportion. This star-shaped figure fairly glitters with its two hundred .618's. *B* cuts both *AC* and *AD* so as to give golden sections. *BE* is .618 of *AB*, etc. The followers of Pythagoras used the pentagram as their secret sign. It stood not only for health and love but for man himself, who was thought to be organized in fives: five senses, four limbs and a head, five fingers (their three bones having the golden proportion).

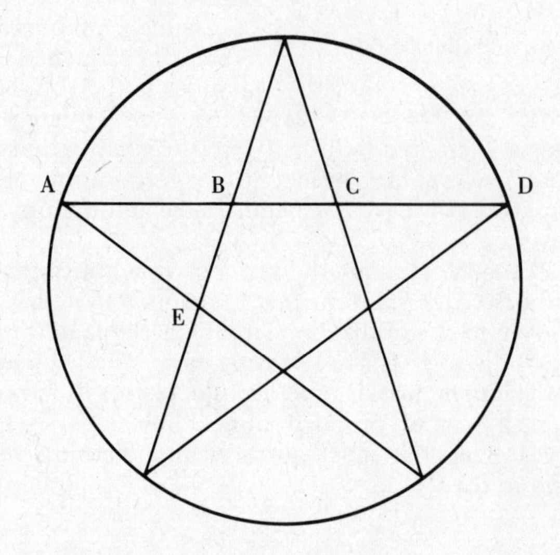

Since the pentagram also stood for the letters in the name "Jesus," it was thought to be an object of fear to hellish spirits. When Mephistopheles finds its *Drudenfuß* or "wizard's foot" drawn on Faust's threshold, it takes some trickery to get by it. Its shape—as with good poems—is its power. In the pentagram—as in good poems—mathematics and magic come together. We are affected by precise relationships we are not aware of.

If we take a line divided according to the golden section, bend the shorter part upward, and then complete the rectangle, we have the golden rectangle with its "divine proportion," which, with the section itself, is supposed to have had an important influence on ancient art and architecture, determining, it may be, the structure of the Parth-

enon, which fits neatly into it. Certainly it made itself felt in the Renaissance and ever since, right down to the architecture of Le Corbusier and the art of Seurat and Mondrian. In 1912 one group of artists even exhibited in Paris as the "Golden Section" painters. It was with them that Marcel Duchamp first showed his *Nude Descending a Staircase.* We can still find it in modern buildings and in many common objects—envelopes, playing cards, magazines. Perhaps we like this rectangle because its proportions correspond with our oval field of vision.

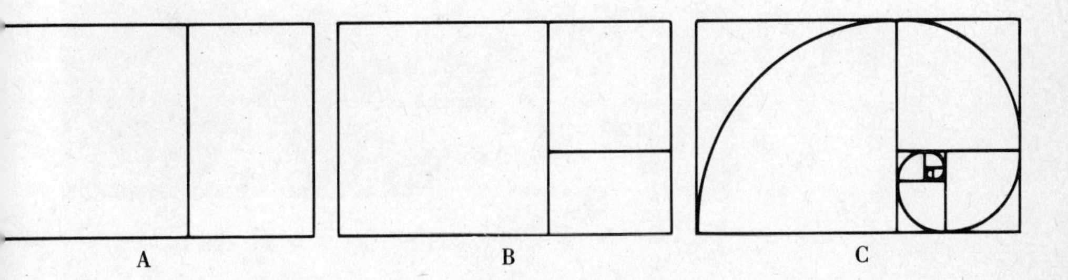

The golden rectangle has been called, with something like Oriental mysteriousness, "the rectangle of the whirling squares." If we divide it by the golden section so that one part is a square, the smaller area will itself be a second golden rectangle within the first (A). If we divide the smaller rectangle in the same way, the same thing will happen—another square, another golden rectangle (B). We can continue in this way, making smaller and smaller squares as we whirl around clockwise. If we then connect, with an evenly curving line, corresponding points of all the squares (C), we will have one of the most beautiful curves in mathematics and one of the most beautiful lines in nature—the logarithmic spiral, whose allure moved an admirer to ask that it be engraved on his tombstone.

This graceful curve, which seems to have been artificially constructed at a drawing board, probably appears most spectacularly in the nautilus seashell, a favorite of collectors. As the creature in the seashell grows, it moves onward, in a spiral, into larger and larger chambers, all of them having the same proportions. Oliver Wendell Holmes found a moral here, which he expressed, by means of a stanza form that itself expands, in "The Chambered Nautilus."

Build thee more stately mansions, O my soul,
  As the swift seasons roll!
Leave thy low-vaulted past!
  Let each new temple, nobler than the last,
Shut thee from heaven with a dome more vast
  Till thou at last art free,
Leaving thine outgrown shell by life's unresting sea.

We find this same curve in the sunflower head and the daisy, in the pine cone and the pineapple, all of which have their opposing spirals in Fibonacci numbers. We find it where the time element of living growth has left its shape on matter—in the curling horns of mountain goats, in the tusks of elephants, in the claws of a cat, the beak of a parrot. It appears in transitory fashion in the coil of an elephant's trunk or a monkey's tail, in a lock of hair falling naturally.

Part of the pleasure man feels in contemplating this spiral may come from his awareness of its continuous proportion, which, in a world of change, gives him the reassurance of what remains similar to itself. Certain well-managed patterns in poetry may have an analogous effect.

Poets cannot hope to work with the geometrical precision of nature. Most trust their own sense of proportion, developed from study, contemplation, and exercise. But Dante does give a mathematical framework to his *Divine Comedy*. And Vergil, Dante's guide, appears to have made an almost unbelievable use of the proportions of the golden section and the Fibonacci numbers (as they were later named).[1] In Book IV of the *Aeneid*, for example, Dido, seeing she is about to be deserted by her lover Aeneas, asks her sister Anna to go and plead with him. This is a passionate moment, but not so passionate that Vergil lets his mathematical composition get out of control. He describes the scene in sections of 5, 8, and 13 lines—all numbers in the basic Fibonacci sequence.

13		8	Look, Anna, all that scurrying on the seashore, Crowds everywhere, sails restless for the wind, The sailors, glad to go, arranging garlands. Well, as I saw this trouble brewing once, So, sister, I'll endure it. Just one thing That you could do in kindness. It was you That liar was polite to, liked to talk with. You knew his ways, and how to manage with him.
13	13	5	Go, dear; go coax a little. Tell His Arrogance I wasn't there at Aulis when those Greeks Swore death to all the Trojans; didn't send Warships to Troy; and didn't kill his father. Why won't he even listen when I speak?
	13	8	Where is he rushing off to? Let him do His love a final favor: wait for friendly Weather and easier sailing. Once he loved me— I don't ask that again; won't block his glorious Future. I only ask: a quiet interval. Time to get used to suffering, used to grief. Pity your sister. Say it's all I'm asking. Say I'll return his favor—with my life.

Anna's visit to Aeneas is described in the section that follows—in exactly thirteen lines. These two passages would prove nothing. But when we are told that over a thousand such correspondences have been found in the *Aeneid*, it does begin to look as if Vergil constructed his episodes like little equations and then related them like larger equations of the same proportions, so that his whole work is a kind of mathematical symphony, as orderly as the music of Bach.

Contrived as this intricacy may seem to be, we can hardly call it artificial. Nature—in the seashell, in the daisy, in a lock of hair—far outdoes our artists with her own use of mathematical symmetry. All that matters, in any art, is that the calculation and effort should not show, that we see the ease and elegance of the achievement but not

[1] George E. Duckworth, *Structural Patterns and Proportions in Vergil's* Aeneid (Ann Arbor: University of Michigan Press, 1962).

the labor that went into it. It is important to realize that imposing a form is not in any way unnatural—Parthenon and nautilus owe their beauty to the same kind of mathematical harmony.

Yeats saw no contradiction between calculated precision and human passion. He once praised Lady Gregory's house as a place in which "passion and precision have been one." He insisted to a friend that "the very essence of genius, of whatever kind, is precision." In "The Statues" he is concerned with the relationship between passion, beauty, and mathematical precision.

THE STATUES

Pythagoras planned it. Why did the people stare?
His numbers, though they moved or seemed to move
In marble or in bronze, lacked character.
But boys and girls, pale from the imagined love
Of solitary beds, knew what they were,
That passion could bring character enough,
And pressed at midnight in some public place
Live lips upon a plummet-measured face.

No! Greater than Pythagoras, for the men
That with a mallet or a chisel modelled these 10
Calculations that look but casual flesh, put down
All Asiatic vague immensities,
And not the banks of oars that swam upon
The many-headed foam at Salamis.
Europe put off that foam when Phidias
Gave women dreams and dreams their looking-glass.

One image crossed the many-headed, sat
Under the tropic shade, grew round and slow,
No Hamlet thin from eating flies, a fat
Dreamer of the Middle Ages. Empty eyeballs knew 20
That knowledge increases unreality, that
Mirror on mirror mirrored is all the show.
When gong and conch declare the hour to bless
Grimalkin crawls to Buddha's emptiness.

When Pearse summoned Cuchulain to his side,
What stalked through the Post Office? What intellect,
What calculation, number, measurement, replied?
We Irish, born into that ancient sect
But thrown upon this filthy modern tide
And by its formless spawning fury wrecked, 30
Climb to our proper dark, that we may trace
The lineaments of a plummet-measured face.

W. B. Yeats

In the first stanza, Pythagoras is given credit for the emphasis on proportion in Greek sculpture, which might seem cold to a cold

...And pressed at midnight in some public place
Live lips upon a plummet-measured face....

Roman copy of the *Diadoumenus* of Polykleitos

beholder. But boys and girls saw their dreams of love embodied in these perfect shapes.

In the second stanza, the spirit of the sculptors, even more than the courage of Greek sailors, is seen as defending the precision of Athenian ideals against the abstractions of Eastern thought. (In 480 B.C. at Salamis, the Greeks defeated the much larger Persian fleet. Phidias was the probable designer of the statuary on the Parthenon.)

In the third stanza, an Eastern Buddha figure, fat and dreamy, out of contact with the physical world and the passionate precision of mathematics, is seen taking over as the Greek spirit declines. ("Gong and conch" suggest an Oriental call to prayer; "Grimalkin" is an old cat or an old woman.)

In the fourth stanza, the Easter Rising of 1916 in Dublin is recalled, when, under the command of Patrick Pearse, Irish nationalist forces seized the Post Office. Cuchulain (Coo-hóo-lin) was a legendary Irish hero whose statue was set up in the Post Office when it was rebuilt after the shelling. Here, Cuchulain (and Pearse) represent "intellect . . . calculation, number, measurement," like that of ancient Athens at its best. These qualities, Yeats believed, were desirable in the formlessness of the modern world.

Yeats would have agreed with one of the conclusions of this section: there is nothing unnatural in man's desire to find form and pattern in his experience. We can hardly keep from doing so. When we look at the starry skies, all we really see are swarms of bright specks. But man has never been content to see that way. He sees hunters and great bears and rocking chairs and dippers. Or he sees figures like lions and scorpions and fish, which he names Leo and Scorpio and Pisces, relating them to long-dead languages. He likes to believe there are connections between these imaginary creatures and the temperament and fate of human beings born under them. Everywhere we like to find forms.

Part of the shapeliness of poems comes from the way certain of their parts correspond. And this is true not only of poems. A popular song some decades back declared, "I met a million-dollar baby in the five-and-ten-cent store." The lover had to meet his girl in *that* store so that "million dollar" could be played off against "five-and-ten-cent." Sing, "I met a million-dollar baby in the local A&P," and the point is gone.

So when Wilfred Owen writes in "Greater Love,"

> Red lips are not so red
> As the stained stones kissed by the English dead . . . .

two crimson things are significantly contrasted.

We can also look for correspondences between the content of a poem and its shape. But the shape of a poem, like its sound, cannot express much apart from the meaning. We might feel a nervous quality in short, fitful, uneven lines, or sustained power in long, even ones, as we might get a sense of crescendo or decrescendo from the shape of stanzas. Blake probably felt that the short lines of his "The Fly" were appropriate. Flies do not go in for long-distance flights.

Little fly,
Thy summer's play
My thoughtless hand
Has brushed away.

Am not I
A fly like thee . . . .

He probably thought that the long lines of his "Holy Thursday" were appropriate for its processional content. His own drawing shows a long line of children across the page, above and below the verses:

'Twas on a Holy Thursday, their innocent faces clean,
The children walking two & two in red & blue & green . . . .

John Donne seems particularly fond of a pyramidal stanza form that dramatizes a crescendo, an excitement mounting to a climax. Lines are shorter toward the beginning of a stanza, longer toward the end, though in no regular progression. Rhymes also tend to amass toward the close. This is the pattern in which he thinks and feels.

THE ANNIVERSARY

All kings and all their favorites,
All glory of honors, beauties, wits,
The sun itself, which makes times as they pass,
Is elder by a year now than it was
When thou and I first one another saw:
All other things to their destruction draw,
Only our love hath no decay;
This, no tomorrow hath nor yesterday;
Running, it never runs from us away,
But truly keeps his first, last, everlasting day. 10

Two graves must hide thine and my corse;
If one might, death were no divorce.
Alas, as well as other princes, we
(Who prince enough in one another be)
Must leave at last in death these eyes and ears,
Oft fed with true oaths and with sweet salt tears;
But souls where nothing dwells but love
(All other thoughts being inmates) then shall prove
This, or a love increasèd there above,
When bodies to their graves, souls from their graves remove. 20

And then we shall be thoroughly blest,
But we no more than all the rest;
Here upon earth we're kings, and none but we
Can be such kings, nor of such subjects be.
Who is so safe as we? where none can do
Treason to us, except one of us two.

---

[11] **corse:** *corpse* [18] **inmates:** *mere tenants*

True and false fears let us refrain;
Let us love nobly, and live, and add again
Years and years unto years, till we attain
To write threescore: this is the second of our reign. 30

John Donne (1572–1631)

There is the same kind of gathering intensity in "The Relic," which begins:

When my grave is broke up again
Some second guest to entertain.
(For graves have learned that womanhead
To be to more than one a bed)
And he that digs it spies
A bracelet of bright hair about the bone,
Will he not let us alone
And think that there a loving couple lies
Who thought that this device might be some way
To make their souls, at the last busy day, 10
Meet at this grave, and make a little stay?

And in "A Valediction: Of Weeping," which begins with the image of a girl's face, at parting, reflected in the man's falling tears:

Let me pour forth
My tears before thy face, whilst I stay here,
For thy face coins them, and thy stamp they bear,
And by this mintage are they something worth,
For thus they be
Pregnant of thee;
Fruits of much grief they are, emblems of more,
When a tear falls, that *thou* fallst which it bore,
So thou and I are nothing then, when on a diverse shore.

Donne's stanza forms, in these three poems, go from less to more. We get just an opposite effect—from more to less—in a poem of Robert Herrick. Again the lineation follows a psychological motive—that of curtailment, littleness, humility. His "A Thanksgiving" begins:

Lord, Thou hast given me a cell
Wherein to dwell;
And little house, whose humble roof
Is weather-proof;
Under the spars of which I lie
Both soft and dry;
Where Thou my chamber for to ward
Hast set a guard
Of harmless thoughts, to watch and keep
Me, while I sleep . . . .

---

[3] **womanhead:** *womanly trait*

The adjectives—"little," "humble"—go with the curtailed form, in which Herrick takes a four-beat line and then cuts it in half. Something like the sadness of deprivation is to be felt in the short last line of the stanza that Keats uses in "La Belle Dame Sans Merci" (p. 116):

> O what can ail thee, knight-at-arms,
>   Alone and palely loitering?
> The sedge has wither'd from the lake,
>   And no birds sing . . . .

In David Wagoner's "The Other Side of the Mountain," a short line has a different effect, that of heels digging in to resist the momentum of the long line:

> To walk downhill you must lean partially backwards,
> Heels digging in,
> While your body gets more help than it can use
> In following directions . . . .

Yeats, in an early poem, dramatizes the poignancy of loss not by using a short line, but by omitting an expected one. The poem starts with a regular quatrain, *a b a b;* then there are three lines of another quatrain; and—just when we expect the fourth line—nothing more.

THE LOVER MOURNS FOR THE LOSS OF LOVE

> Pale brows, still hands and dim hair,
> I had a beautiful friend
> And dreamed that the old despair
> Would end in love in the end:
> She looked in my heart one day
> And saw your image was there;
> She has gone weeping away.

W. B. Yeats

We are left waiting for the line that never comes.

Exercises and Diversions

A. One of the best-known poems of A. E. Housman begins as follows:

> With rue my heart is laden
>   For golden friends I had,
> For many a rose-lipt maiden,
>   And many a lightfoot lad.

His second stanza is one of these two. Can you be fairly sure which is his? And why?

By brooks that murmur softly	By brooks too broad for leaping
The lightfoot boys are laid;	The lightfoot boys are laid;
The rose-lipt girls are sleeping	The rose-lipt girls are sleeping
In many a misty glade.	In fields where roses fade.

B. 1. In "The Statues," check on the rhymes. Why are the final couplets of each stanza likelier to have perfect rhymes than other lines are? Why are there no off-rhymes in the last stanza, though there had been in earlier stanzas?
2. What sounds are repeated in lines 7 and 8? Are they expressive?
3. Do you notice any expressive irregularities (or regularities) in the rhythm?

C. 1. Leafing through sections of the book you have already read, do you notice any stanza shapes that look unusual or interesting? Upon examination, do they prove to be expressive in any way? Merely decorative?
2. In poems you have read, do you recall any "correspondences" like those between "million-dollar baby" and "five-and-ten-cent store" or between red lips and blood-stained stones?

D. This section has been making a case for the naturalness of form. But suppose one lives a chaotic life, or lives in a chaotic age which has little sense of form. Is it then more natural to write formless poetry? Or do you think that the more disorder the artist feels around him, the more obligation he has to create what order he can? Which of the following statements would you agree with?

1. Art had to be confused to express confusion; but perhaps it was truest, so.
Henry Adams

2. [The poetry of primitive people] gives order and harmony to their sudden overmastering emotions and their tumbling thoughts . . . a solid center in what would otherwise be chaos. . . .
C. M. Bowra

3. [Deeply troubled poets, like Thomas Hardy,] tend to use strict forms as a kind of foothold, a fixed point in an uncertain cosmos.
Kenneth Marsden

4. The more [a poet] is conscious of an inner disorder and dread, the more value he will place on tidiness in the work as a *defense*, as if he hoped that through his control of the means of expressing his emotions, the emotions themselves, which he cannot master directly, might be brought to order.
W. H. Auden

E. Write a short critical paper to show whether or not the analogy between fixed forms in nature and fixed forms in poetry is a valid one.

Dealer's Choice the forms of verse 19

Sometimes the shape of verse forms may be expressive, as the spiral of the nautilus expresses the life force that shaped it, or as the snowflake expresses the molecular geometry within. At other times the shape seems arbitrary or accidental—though if a verse form continues to live it must somehow fit the way we feel and think. If the logic of a form eludes us, we might think of it as we think of games. Why *three* strikes in baseball? Why *four* balls? Why the rigidly fixed forms of Olympic events, the 440's and 880's? Without rules, games are impossible. We know what rage a hard-core poker player feels when a slaphappy beginner, given dealer's choice, makes up a fancy variant of his own: free-form poker. Too many wild cards, and the game is meaningless.

This section will consider some of the forms available to the writer. Few poets have written in all of them; some have confined themselves to one or two; most have tried their hands at several. Certain poets, like Thomas Hardy, prefer to make up their own shapes.

Fixed Stanza Forms

Some forms have no fixed number of lines—they run on until they end. **Blank verse**—unrhymed iambic pentameter—is the most familiar. Other forms are arranged in **stanzas,** identical units of groups of lines. The Italian word *stanza* means a *room,* or, more to our purpose, a *place to stop.* (Nonstanzaic divisions, as in blank verse, can be called verse paragraphs.)

We can find poems of just one line.

Nature often prefers to work in fixed forms. The snowflake, after millions of years, is still a hexagonal structure. Yet no two are alike.

EXIT LINE

Love should intend realities: good-bye!

John Ciardi

"Good-bye," said the river, "I'm going downstream."

Howard Nemerov

Two-line poems are more common:

UPON THE DEATH OF SIR ALBERT MORTON'S WIFE

He first deceased; she for a little tried
To live without him, liked it not, and died.

Sir Henry Wotton (1568–1639)

ON READING ALOUD MY EARLY POEMS

This ignorance upon my tongue
Was once the wisdom of the young.

John Williams (b. 1922)

We have seen many poems in **couplets** (units of two lines): Blake's about the tiger (p. 112); Swift's about the morning (p. 78); Marvell's about his mistress (p. 275). The "heroic couplets" of Dryden and Pope were, for a century, the favorite form of poetry.

Three-line units are most simply constructed by having them rhyme *a a a, b b b,* etc.

UPON JULIA'S CLOTHES

Whenas in silks my Julia goes,
Then, then, methinks, how sweetly flows
The liquefaction of her clothes.

Next, when I cast mine eyes and see
That brave vibration each way free,
Oh how that glittering taketh me!

Robert Herrick (1591–1674)

In "Acquainted with the Night" (p. 48), Frost uses the most celebrated of three-line units, **terza rima,** the "triple rhyme" that Dante and others had used. The rhyme scheme is *a b a, b c b, c d c,* etc., with the middle rhyme of each tercet (group of three) becoming the first and third rhyme of the following group. The interconnection of tercets, the way one leads to and sustains the next, gives this form a continuity and momentum such as few others have.

The commonest stanza form in European literature is the **quatrain,** or four-line stanza. Psychologists may account for its popularity by recalling that Jung thought the nucleus of the psyche normally expressed itself in a fourfold structure. Or, as the poet Robert Creeley puts it in an excerpt from "Four":

This number for me
is comfort, a secure
fact of things. The

table stands on
all fours. The dog
walks comfortably,

and two by two
is not an army
but friends who love

one another. Four
is a square,
or peaceful circle,

celebrating return,
reunion,
love's triumph.

Rossetti's "The Woodspurge" (p. 118) is an expressive example of a quatrain in monorhyme (*a a a a*), but this is rare. The commonest quatrain is the ballad stanza, of which we have seen many examples ("Western Wind," p. 5; "Sir Patrick Spens," p. 18; "The Unquiet Grave," p. 127). Lines 1 and 3 are tetrameter; lines 2 and 4 trimeter. Lines 2 and 4 rhyme; lines 1 and 3 are generally unrhymed, as in "Western Wind" and in most of the poems of Emily Dickinson, who, indifferent to metrical experiment, did most of her work in this simplest of stanza forms.

Another well-known quatrain is Tennyson's "In Memoriam" stanza: four tetrameters rhyming *a b b a* in "envelope" fashion—the *a*-rhymes enclose the stanza.

Ring out, wild bells, to the wild sky,
  The flying cloud, the frosty light.
  The year is dying in the night;
Ring out, wild bells, and let him die.

Ring out the old, ring in the new,
  Ring, happy bells, across the snow:
  The year is going, let him go;
Ring out the false, ring in the true.

There are many possible ways of combining rhymes and line lengths in five-line stanzas. No one form is conspicuous. A common practice is to take a standard quatrain and work in an additional rhyming line, as in *a b a b b* or *a b a a b*.

Stanzas of six lines or more are likely to be made up of simpler elements. The "Venus-and-Adonis stanza" (named for Shakespeare's poem) is a quatrain with a couplet added: *a b a b c c*. Dyer uses it in

"The Lowest Trees Have Tops," p. 36. One of the most characteristic is the "Burns stanza" or "Scottish stanza," an *a a a b a b*, in which the *a*'s are tetrameter, the *b*'s dimeter. Robert Burns' "To a Mouse" begins:

Wee, sleeket, cowran, tim'rous beastie,
O, what a panic's in thy breastie!
Thou need na start awa sae hasty,
Wi' bickering brattle!
I wad be laith to rin an' chase thee,
Wi' murd'ring pattle!

I'm truly sorry Man's dominion
Has broken Nature's social union,
An' justifies that ill opinion,
Which makes thee startle, 10
At me, thy poor, earth-born companion,
An' fellow-mortal!

More recent poets often prefer looser arrangements. Robert Lowell's "Skunk Hour" keeps to no fixed scheme in its six-line stanzas about a degenerate New England culture as seen by a speaker whose mind is "not right." What goodness there is seems to belong to the animals, who live according to their nature with assurance and courage.

SKUNK HOUR
(For Elizabeth Bishop)

Nautilus Island's hermit
heiress still lives through winter in her Spartan cottage;
her sheep still graze above the sea.
Her son's a bishop. Her farmer
is first selectman in our village,
she's in her dotage.

Thirsting for
the hierarchic privacy
of Queen Victoria's century,
she buys up all 10
the eyesores facing her shore,
and lets them fall.

The season's ill—
we've lost our summer millionaire,
who seemed to leap from an L. L. Bean
catalogue. His nine-knot yawl
was auctioned off to lobstermen.
A red fox stain covers Blue Hill.

And now our fairy

---

1 **sleeket, cowran:** *glossy, cowering*
3 **na start awa sae:** *not start away so*
4 **wi' bickering brattle:** *with hasty scuttle, hurry-scurry*
5 **wad be laith to rin:** *would be loath to run*
6 **pattle:** *shovel*

decorator brightens his shop for fall; 20
his fishnet's filled with orange cork,
orange, his cobbler's bench and awl;
there is no money in his work,
he'd rather marry.

One dark night,
my Tudor Ford climbed the hill's skull;
I watched for love-cars. Lights turned down,
they lay together, hull to hull,
where the graveyard shelves on the town. . . .
My mind's not right. 30

A car radio bleats,
"Love, O careless Love . . ." I hear
my ill-spirit sob in each blood cell,
as if my hand were at its throat. . . .
I myself am hell;
nobody's here—

only skunks, that search
in the moonlight for a bite to eat.
They march on their soles up Main Street:
white stripes, moonstruck eyes' red fire 40
under the chalk-dry and spar spire
of the Trinitarian Church.

I stand on top
of our back steps and breathe the rich air—
a mother skunk with her column of kittens swills the garbage pail.
She jabs her wedge-head in a cup
of sour cream, drops her ostrich tail,
and will not scare.

Robert Lowell (b. 1917)

Among the seven-line possibilities, **rhyme royal,** an iambic pentameter rhyming *a b a b b c c*, has emerged as especially attractive. We have seen it in Wyatt's "They Flee from Me" (p. 58) and, among modern poems, in the longer stanzas of Auden's "The Shield of Achilles" (p. 110).

The best-known eight-line stanza, an iambic pentameter *a b a b a b c c*, is called **ottava rima** or "eight rhyme." Its most conspicuous success in English is in *Don Juan.* Byron's passion and wit find themselves at home with the elaborate build-up of the triple rhyme, followed by the opportunity for a sudden wisecrack or anticlimax in the concluding couplet.

And Julia's voice was lost, except in sighs,
  Until too late for useful conversation;
The tears were gushing from her gentle eyes,
  I wish, indeed, they had not had occasion;
But who, alas, can love, and then be wise?
  Not that remorse did not oppose temptation:

A little still she strove, and much repented,
And whispering "I will ne'er consent"—consented.

But ottava rima can be used seriously too, as in "The Statues" (p. 350). There are, of course, a great many other ways of building up an eight-line stanza out of simpler elements.

The classic nine-line form is the Spenserian stanza, devised for *The Faerie Queene.* The iambic lines, the first eight of which are pentameter and the last of which is an alexandrine, are richly rhymed: *a b a b b c b c c.* This stanza form was a favorite of the Romantic poets. A stanza from Byron and one from Shelley will show how the form moves through its elaborate pattern, pivoting on the fifth line to begin almost a new movement and closing with the longer, slower line—an effect like the concluding chords of a piece of music.

There is a pleasure in the pathless woods,
There is a rapture on the lonely shore,
There is society, where none intrudes,
By the deep sea, and music in its roar:
I love not man the less, but nature more,
From these our interviews, in which I steal
From all I may be, or have been before,
To mingle with the universe, and feel
What I can ne'er express, yet cannot all conceal.

George Gordon, Lord Byron

He has outsoared the shadow of our night;
Envy and calumny and hate and pain,
And that unrest which men miscall delight,
Can touch him not and torture not again;
From the contagion of the world's slow stain
He is secure, and now can never mourn
A heart grown cold, a head grown gray in vain;
Nor, when the spirit's self has ceased to burn,
With sparkless ashes load an unlamented urn.

Percy Bysshe Shelley

Although today it seems somewhat literary, this stanza form continues to come to life with the right handling. Daryl Hine chooses it for his "Bluebeard's Wife"; Robert Bagg for "The Tandem Ride," a story about Amherst students pedaling off at night in search of a madcap Smithie, who escapes them by diving into a pond with what must be the only bellyflop ever recorded in Spenserian stanzas:

Our cocked ears took the slap
Of a skinspankeroo of a bellyflop . . . .

John Updike has chosen Spenserians for "The Dance of the Solids," which is about the atomic structure of solid-state matter. His scientific terminology is almost a burlesque of Spenser's courtly abstractions.

The *Polymers,* those giant Molecules,
Like Starch and Polyoxymethylene,

Flesh out, as protein serfs and plastic fools,
This Kingdom with Life's Stuff. Our time has seen
The synthesis of Polyisoprene
And many cross-linked Helixes unknown
To *Robert Hooke*; but each primordial Bean
Knew Cellulose by heart. *Nature* alone
Of Collagen and Apatite compounded Bone.

Fixed Forms for Poems

Besides the fixed stanza forms, there are designs for the complete poem. The most famous—and most notorious—is the **sonnet**, which has no rival in popularity. It has been a favorite of some of the best poets—and some of the worst. The name is from the Italian *sonnetto,* which means *little sound* or *little song.* Part of its appeal is in its brevity—a sonnet can easily be read in less than sixty seconds. But, though brief, the sonnet is ingeniously organized, its fourteen iambic-pentameter lines rhyming in various ways. The Italian (or Petrarchan) sonnet is divided into an octave (eight lines) and a sestet (six lines). The 6:8:14 proportions come very close to the 5:8:13 of the Fibonacci numbers and the golden section. People seem to feel, for whatever reason, something satisfying in the proportions. The octave of the Italian sonnet, with its many interrelated symmetries, has a rhyme scheme of *a b b a a b b a.* The sestet combines two or three rhymes in almost any possible way, although final couplets are generally avoided. Common patterns are *c d c d c d* or *c d e c d e.*

Since this type of sonnet needs four rhymes for both *a*'s and *b*'s, it is not an easy form to use in English. Yet poets continue to write Petrarchan sonnets. *Berryman's Sonnets* contains 115 poems in the Petrarchan form. One gives the picture of a girl, "blonde, barefoot, beautiful"—but scarcely the Petrarchan ideal. She drinks too much, likes to lie on the floor listening to music, is willful, can't forbear. The three alliterating adjectives used to describe her are like the girl's willfulness: they are an unrhymed intrusion, a fifteenth line, in a poem otherwise regular.

SIGH AS IT ENDS

Sigh as it ends . . . I keep an eye on your
Amour with Scotch,—too *cher* to consummate;
Faster your disappearing beer than late-
ly mine; your naked passion for the floor;
Your hollow leg; your hanker for one more
Dark as the Sundam Trench; how you dilate
Upon psychotics of this class, collate
Stages, and . . how long since you, well, *forbore.*

Ah, but the high fire sings on to be fed
Whipping our darkness by the lifting sea 10

A while, O darling drinking like a clock.
The tide comes on: spare, Time, from what you spread
Her story,—tilting a frozen Daiquiri,
Blonde, barefoot, beautiful,
  flat on the bare floor rivetted to Bach.

John Berryman

The rhyme scheme of the English (or Shakespearean) sonnet is less demanding: *a b a b, c d c d, e f e f, g g.* Three quatrains and a final couplet. Contemporary poets are still finding new ways of handling it.

SUMMER STORM

In that so sudden summer storm they tried
Each bed, couch, closet, carpet, car-seat, table,
Both river banks, five fields, a mountain side,
Covering as much ground as they were able.

A lady, coming on them in the dark
In a white fixture, wrote to the newspapers
Complaining of the statues in the park.
By Cupid, but they cut some pretty capers!

The envious oxen in still rings would stand
Ruminating. Their sweet incessant plows 10
I think had changed the contours of the land
And made two modest conies move their house.

God rest them well, and firmly shut the door.
Now they are married Nature breathes once more.

Louis Simpson (b. 1923)

A PRIMER OF THE DAILY ROUND

A peels an apple, while B kneels to God,
C telephones to D, who has a hand
On E's knee, F coughs, G turns up the sod
For H's grave, I do not understand
But J is bringing one clay pigeon down
While K brings down a nightstick on L's head,
And M takes mustard, N drives into town,
O goes to bed with P, and Q drops dead,
R lies to S, but happens to be heard
By T, who tells U not to fire V 10
For having to give W the word
That X is now deceiving Y with Z,
  Who happens just now to remember A
  Peeling an apple somewhere far away.

Howard Nemerov

Edmund Spenser, inventor of the Spenserian stanza, devised a matching sonnet form that bears his name. It rhymes *a b a b, b c b c, c d c d, e e.*

SONNET LXXV

One day I wrote her name upon the strand,
  But came the waves and washèd it away;
  Again I wrote it with a second hand,
  But came the tide and made my pains his prey.
"Vain man," said she, "that dost in vain assay
  A mortal thing so to immortalize,
  For I myself shall like to this decay,
  And eke my name be wipèd out likewise."
"Not so," quod I, "let baser things devise
  To die in dust, but you shall live by fame; 10
  My verse your virtues rare shall eternize
  And in the heavens write your glorious name,
Where, whenas death shall all the world subdue,
  Our love shall live, and later life renew."

Edmund Spenser (c. 1552–1599)

Gwendolyn Brooks has written an almost Spenserian wartime sonnet.

THE SONNET-BALLAD

Oh mother, mother, where is happiness?
They took my lover's tallness off to war.
Left me lamenting. Now I cannot guess
What I can use an empty heart-cup for.
He won't be coming back here any more.
Some day the war will end, but, oh, I knew
When he went walking grandly out that door
That my sweet love would have to be untrue.
Would have to be untrue. Would have to court
Coquettish death, whose impudent and strange 10
Possessive arms and beauty (of a sort)
Can make a hard man hesitate—and change.
And he will be the one to stammer, "Yes."
Oh mother, mother, where is happiness?

Gwendolyn Brooks

Quite a few sonnets, like hers, refuse to fit into any class. Some are hybrid—half Italian, half English. Some, like Shelley's "Ozymandias" (p. 110), have original rhyme schemes. Some, still called "sonnets," have more or less than fourteen lines, or more or less than five feet to the line. Hopkins, thinking mathematically, kept the proportions but changed the size in his "curtal" (*curtailed*) sonnet. Instead of the 8:6 ratio he used 6:4½ (or 4 and a fraction):

---

[8] **eke:** *even*   [9] **quod:** *quoth, said*

PIED BEAUTY

Glory be to God for dappled things—
  For skies of couple-color as a brinded cow;
    For rose-moles all in stipple upon trout that swim;
Fresh-firecoal chestnut-falls; finches' wings;
  Landscape plotted and pieced—fold, fallow, and plough;
    And áll trádes, their gear and tackle and trim.

All things counter, original, spare, strange;
  Whatever is fickle, freckled (who knows how?)
    With swift, slow; sweet, sour; adazzle, dim;
He fathers-forth whose beauty is past change: 10
                    Praise him.

Gerard Manley Hopkins

Of the other fixed forms used in English, the oldest and most elaborate is the **sestina.** Invented by a Provençal poet in the twelfth century, the sestina comes as close as any poetic form to the elaborate mathematical patterns in nature. It has six six-line stanzas and a three-line envoy (*short concluding stanza*). The same six words that end the lines in the first stanza return in the other stanzas as line-end words (three of them have to occur midline in the envoy). Their arrangement is different in each stanza, according to a set pattern, which readers sufficiently interested will easily discover in our example.

SESTINA

September rain falls on the house.
In the failing light, the old grandmother
sits in the kitchen with the child
beside the Little Marvel Stove,
reading the jokes from the almanac,
laughing and talking to hide her tears.

She thinks that her equinoctial tears
and the rain that beats on the roof of the house
were both foretold by the almanac,
but only known to a grandmother. 10
The iron kettle sings on the stove.
She cuts some bread and says to the child,

It's time for tea now; but the child
is watching the teakettle's small hard tears
dance like mad on the hot black stove,
the way the rain must dance on the house.
Tidying up, the old grandmother
hangs up the clever almanac

on its string. Birdlike, the almanac
hovers half open above the child, 20
hovers above the old grandmother

and her teacup full of dark brown tears.
She shivers and says she thinks the house
feels chilly, and puts more wood in the stove.

It was to be, says the Marvel Stove.
I know what I know, says the almanac.
With crayons the child draws a rigid house
and a winding pathway. Then the child
puts in a man with buttons like tears
and shows it proudly to the grandmother. 30

But secretly, while the grandmother
busies herself about the stove,
the little moons fall down like tears
from between the pages of the almanac
into the flower bed the child
has carefully placed in the front of the house.

Time to plant tears, says the almanac.
The grandmother sings to the marvellous stove
and the child draws another inscrutable house.

Elizabeth Bishop

Of the forms that have come to us from French poetry, one of the best known is the **ballade** (not to be confused with the English and Scottish ballad).

BALLADE TO HIS MISTRESS

F alse beauty who, although in semblance fair,
R ude art in action, and hast cost me dear,
A s iron harsh, and harder to outwear,
N ame that did spell the end of my career,
C harm that dost mischief, builder of my bier,
O gress who dost thy lover's death require,
Y outh without pity! Womankind, dost hear?
S hould help a man, not drag him in the mire!

M uch better had it been to seek elsewhere
A id and repose, and keep my honour clear, 10
R ather than thus be driven by despair
T o flee in anguish and dishonour drear.
'*H* elp, help!' I cry. 'Ye neighbours all, draw near;
E ach man fetch water for my raging fire!'
Compassion bids that every true compeer
Should help a man, not drag him in the mire.

V anished soon will be thy beauty rare,
I ts blossom will be withered and sere.
I could find cause for laughter, were I there,
L iving and eating still. But nay, 'twere sheer 20
L unacy, for by then I'ld be thy peer,
O ld, ugly as thyself, and sans desire.

N ow drink amain! For drinking and good cheer
Should help a man, not drag him in the mire.

Prince of all lovers, I do scarcely dare
To ask thine aid, lest I provoke thine ire;
But ev'ry honest heart, by God I swear,
Should help a man, not drag him in the mire.

François Villon (1431–1463?)
(English version by Norman Cameron)

The lines all end with an angry *r* sound, as we mentioned on page 188; most begin with the letters of his name or the girl's.

Other forms deriving from Old French poetry look alike and have similar names: *rondel, roundel, rondeau.* They also tend to be bookish—the kind of thing literary folk like to try their hand at instead of doing crossword puzzles, or that young writers attempt once or twice as a stunt. A simpler form of the rondel, the triolet, has given us a well-known anthology piece.

TO A FAT LADY SEEN FROM THE TRAIN

O why do you walk through the fields in gloves,
  Missing so much and so much?
O fat white woman whom nobody loves,
Why do you walk through the fields in gloves,
When the grass is soft as the breast of doves
  And shivering sweet to the touch?
O why do you walk through the fields in gloves,
  Missing so much and so much?

Frances Cornford (1886–1960)

A^1
b
A^2

a
b
A^1

a
b
A^2

a
b
A^1

a
b
A^2

a
b
A^1
A^2

The **villanelle** (a villanella was originally an Italian country song or dance) became a French verse form in the sixteenth century and was taken up by English dilettante poets in the nineteenth. At first it seemed only a literary plaything:

A dainty thing's the villanelle;
It serves its purpose passing well....

But for some reason it has attracted the interest of some of the best poets of our time. A nineteen-line poem, consisting of five tercets followed by a quatrain and having only two rhymes, it repeats the first line (A^1) and the third line (A^2) according to the scheme at the left. It looks as if, with the villanelle, we are back with the complexities of the sunflower. When Dylan Thomas wrote "Do Not Go Gentle into That Good Night" (p. 181), his passionate exhortation to his dying father, he chose this "dainty thing" and made it resonant with love, grief, and indignation—one of the best examples we have of how a poet with enough vitality can breathe life into a form apparently long dead. Robinson, Empson, Auden, and Roethke are others who have used the villanelle for serious purposes.

The shape of poetry in English has also been influenced by Japanese poetry. In Japanese, a syllabic language with little accentual stress, the classical form for over a thousand years has been the **tanka**, a thirty-one-syllable poem whose five lines have 5, 7, 5, 7, 7 syllables. This one is from the tenth century:

Lying here alone,
So lost in thinking of you
I forgot to comb
My tangled tresses—oh for
Your hand caressing them smooth!

Lady Izumi Shikibu (tenth century)

The tanka may have influenced one American invention, the **cinquain,** with its 2, 4, 6, 8, 2 syllables.

CINQUAIN: A WARNING

Just now,
Out of the strange
Still dusk . . . as strange, as still . . .
A white moth flew. Why am I grown
So cold?

Adelaide Crapsey (1878–1914)

As tanka developed, poets began to write them jointly in a series called **renga** (revived by the Mexican poet Octavio Paz and his friends in recent years). One would contribute the first three lines of 5, 7, 5 syllables, another the two lines of 7,7, an so on.

From the first link of renga came the seventeen-syllable **hokku** or **haiku,** popular from the seventeenth century on. In this concentrated, one-breath verse form (we have seen several examples), there is generally a suggestion of season or a "season word" in a tersely described incident or observation that suggests more than it says, stirring a mood by presenting a picture. Often a comparison between two things is implied, as in this one of Bashō's (which rhymes in translation only by accident):

Lightning in the sky!
In the deeper dark is heard
A night-heron's cry.

Bashō

One Japanese-American poet says that haiku thought observes a mathematical proportion like that of the golden section.

Recently American poetry has welcomed the **ghazal,** for centuries the classic lyric form in Arabic, Persian, Turkish, and related languages. The greatest master is the Persian poet Hafiz, a contemporary of Chaucer. Standard themes are love and wine, often symbolizing mystical experience. In shape the ghazal consists of from five to twelve couplets all on the same rhyme. (Contemporary poets have discarded the rhyme.)

GHAZAL XXVI

What will I do with seven billion cubic feet of clouds
in my head? I want to be wise and dispense it for quarters.

All these pushups are making me a muscular fatman. Love would
make me lean and burning. Love. Sorry the elevator's full.

She was zeroed in on by creeps and forgot my meaningful glances
from the door. But then I'm walleyed and wear used capes.

She was built entirely of makeup, greasepaint all the way through
like a billiard ball is a billiard ball beneath its hard skin.

We'll have to leave this place in favor of where the sun
is cold when seen at all, bones rust, it rains all day. 10

The cat is mine and so is the dog. You take the orchard,
house and car and parents. I'm going to Greenland at dawn.

Jim Harrison (b. 1937)

Three fixed forms generally handled as light verse are the **limerick,** the **clerihew,** and the **double dactyl.** The first is so well known that we hardly need an example—which is just as well, since no limerick worth its salt would want to be found in respectable company.

The clerihew, named for E. C(lerihew) Bentley, has two generally mismated couplets with comic rhymes which present the "potted biography" of a famous person.

Sir Isaac Newton
Had no time for rootin' and tootin'.
What did he do instead?
He let apples fall on his head.

The double dactyl was conceived by the poet Anthony Hecht and a classicist friend. Here are two of them, the first untitled:

Higgledy-piggledy
Ludwig van Beethoven
Bored by requests for some
Music to hum,

Finally answered with
Oversimplicity,
"Here's my Fifth Symphony:
Duh, duh, duh, DUM!"

E. William Seaman (b. 1927)

TACT

Patty-cake, patty-cake,
Marcus Antonius,
What do you think of the
African Queen?

Gubernatorial
Duties require my
Presence in Egypt. Ya
Know what I mean?

Paul Pascal (b. 1925)

The form consists of two quatrains, the last lines of each rhyming. All lines except these two have two full dactyls; the rhyming lines have only —◡◡|—. The first line is a sort of nonsense invocation, like "Ibbety-bibbety" or the above. The second line has to be a double-dactyl name: Laurence Olivier, Anna Karenina, etc. Somewhere in the poem, ideally in the sixth line, there has to be a double-dactyl word like "parthenogenesis," "gynecological," "Mediterranean." These are heavy obligations for so light a form, and yet a number of disporting poets have met them triumphantly.

Such unserious poems as these can help us make a serious point about form in poetry. A free-verse limerick is improbable. What happens to the rhyme is part of the fun.

There was a young lady of Tottenham,
Who'd no manners, or else she'd forgotten 'em;
  At tea at the vicar's
  She tore off her knickers,
Because, she explained, she felt 'ot in 'em.

Liberate this into free verse, and we get:

A young lady, a native of Tottenham,
Had no manners, or else they slipped her mind;
  At the vicar's tea
  She tore her knickers off,
Explaining that she found them uncomfortably warm.

The first was at least a limerick and, for some, a passing smile. But the second is a nothing. If we saw it by itself, we might even be puzzled as to its intention. So with the double dactyl about Antony and Cleopatra. If we denude it of its form and leave it as naked meaning we get something like:

"Mark Antony, what do you think of Cleopatra?"
"Well, I have to stay in Egypt anyway, since I'm the governor. Get it?"

Not very funny. Shape is power.

Exercises and Diversions

A. 1. How would you describe the stanza forms or rhyme schemes used in "Rattler, Alert" (p. 20), "Most Like an Arch This Marriage" (p. 28), "The Blindman" (p. 65), "Leaving the Motel" (p. 91), "Playboy" (p. 95), "Blue Girls" (p. 133), "Counting the Beats" (p. 246), and "Sestina" (p. 367)?

2. What form is used in these stanzas? Are there irregularities?

"Courage!" he said, and pointed toward the land,
"This mounting wave will roll us shore-ward soon."
In the afternoon they came unto a land
In which it seemèd always afternoon.
All round the coast the languid air did swoon,
Breathing like one that hath a weary dream.
Full-faced above the valley stood the moon;
And like a downward smoke, the slender stream,
Along the cliff to fall and pause and fall did seem.

Alfred, Lord Tennyson

Meanwhile at the University of Japan
Ko had already begun his studies, which
While making him an educated man
Would also give him as he learned to pitch
And catch—for Ko was more than a mere fan,
But wished as a playing member to do a hitch
With some great team—something to think about
More interesting than merely Safe and Out.

Kenneth Koch

B. 1. Of the six-line stanzas used in the poems listed below, are any two alike? Do some stanza designs seem more successful than others? "The End of the Weekend" (p. 16), "It Fell on a Summer's Day" (p. 94), "A Last Confession" (p. 95), "Dream Songs, 22" (p. 338), "The Thieves" (p. 210), "Ubi Sunt Qui Ante Nos Fuerunt?" (p. 295).

2. Ask yourself the same questions about these eight-line stanzas. "Winter" (p. 71), "The Mill" (p. 90), "Loose Woman" (p. 91), "I to My Perils" (p. 274).

3. How many different five-line stanzas do you notice among the poems read?

C. 1. The sonnets listed below are all irregular in some way. How? "With How Sad Steps, O Moon" (p. 14), "A Soldier" (p. 33), "Leda and the Swan" (p. 62), "Good Ships" (p. 68), "Anthem for Doomed Youth" (p. 216).

2. Milton's "On the Late Massacre in Piedmont" (p. 195) breaks with the Italian sonnet scheme in one small respect, yet the difference makes itself felt so strongly that this is called a "Miltonic sonnet." What is distinct about it?

D. The ballad stanza is also called "common meter" (C.M.), especially when used in hymns. Why is the following stanza form called "short meter" (S.M.)?

"And if I did, what then?
Are you aggrieved therefore?
The sea hath fish for every man,
And what would you have more?"

Thus did my mistress once
Amaze my mind with doubt,
And popped a question for the nonce
To beat my brains about. . . .

George Gascoigne

Why is the following called "long meter" (L.M.)?

[from "Greensleeves"]
Alas, my love! you do me wrong
To cast me off discourteously;

And I have lovèd you so long,
Delighting in your company. . . .

E. Choose from among the following exercises whichever seem most interesting.

1. Write a poem using the letters of your own name (or somebody else's) as first letters of each line.
2. Write a dozen or so lines of terza rima on a theme that exploits its forward movement.
3. Write a stanza of rhyme royal, or ottava rima (perhaps in the manner of Byron), or a Spenserian stanza, or three or four haiku.
4. Would it be harder to write a passable example of a sonnet or a double dactyl? (Write one of each and see.)
5. Would it be unreasonable to expect you to write a villanelle? A sestina?
6. Write two stanzas in two stanza forms which, as far as you know, have never been used before.

A Head on Its Shoulders 20

poetry and common sense

Although complicated ratios and formulas play a part in our sense of proportion, the mathematics that appears openly in poetry is likely to be very simple, like Housman's

> —To think that two and two are four
> And neither five nor three
> The heart of man has long been sore,
> And long 'tis like to be.

Nor is poetry likely to make much use of formal reasoning.

But some poems come close to revealing the bare bones of thought.

TO WOMEN, AS FAR AS I'M CONCERNED

> The feelings I don't have I don't have.
> The feeling I don't have, I won't say I have.
> The feelings you say you have, you don't have.
> The feelings you would like us both to have, we
> neither of us have.
> The feelings people ought to have, they never have.
> If people say they've got feelings, you may be pretty
> sure they haven't got them.
> So if you want either of us to feel anything at all
> you'd better abandon all idea of feelings altogether. 10

D. H. Lawrence

In *Knots,* R. D. Laing comes even closer to being a poet of intellectual analysis.

JILL

I don't respect myself
I can't respect anyone who respects me.
I can only respect someone who does not respect me.

I respect Jack
because he does not respect me

I despise Tom
because he does not despise me

Only a despicable person
can respect someone as despicable as me

I cannot love someone I despise 10

Since I love Jack
I cannot believe he loves me

What proof can he give?

. . .

JILL I'm upset you are upset
JACK I'm not upset
JILL I'm upset that you're not upset that I'm
upset you're upset
JACK I'm upset that you're upset that I'm not
upset that you're upset that I'm upset,
when I'm not. 20

JILL You put me in the wrong
JACK I am not putting you in the wrong
JILL You put me in the wrong for thinking you
put me in the wrong.

JACK Forgive me
JILL No
JACK I'll never forgive you for not forgiving me

R. D. Laing (b. 1927)

These are almost disembodied thoughts, as if we had the speech balloons from a comic strip but no characters beneath them. And no environment—no chairs to sit on, no trees to lounge under, nothing to look at.

In a poem about a sexual misunderstanding between two young people we are shown not only the geometry of human behavior, as in Laing, but that geometry as embodied, as seen through the distorting glass of a young man's embarrassed passion.

THE SUBVERTED FLOWER

She drew back; he was calm:
"It is this that had the power."

And he lashed his open palm
With the tender-headed flower.
He smiled for her to smile,
But she was either blind
Or willfully unkind.
He eyed her for a while
For a woman and a puzzle.
He flicked and flung the flower, 10
And another sort of smile
Caught up like fingertips
The corners of his lips
And cracked his ragged muzzle.
She was standing to the waist
In goldenrod and brake,
Her shining hair displaced.
He stretched her either arm
As if she made it ache
To clasp her—not to harm; 20
As if he could not spare
To touch her neck and hair.
"If this has come to us
And not to me alone——"
So she thought she heard him say;
Though with every word he spoke
His lips were sucked and blown
And the effort made him choke
Like a tiger at a bone.
She had to lean away. 30
She dared not stir a foot,
Lest movement should provoke
The demon of pursuit
That slumbers in a brute.
It was then her mother's call
From inside the garden wall
Made her steal a look of fear
To see if he could hear
And would pounce to end it all
Before her mother came. 40
She looked and saw the shame:
A hand hung like a paw,
An arm worked like a saw
As if to be persuasive,
An ingratiating laugh
That cut the snout in half,
An eye become evasive.
A girl could only see
That a flower had marred a man,
But what she could not see 50
Was that the flower might be
Other than base and fetid:
That the flower had done but part,
And what the flower began
Her own too meager heart

Had terribly completed.
She looked and saw the worst.
And the dog or what it was,
Obeying bestial laws,
A coward save at night, 60
Turned from the place and ran.
She heard him stumble first
And use his hands in flight.
She heard him bark outright.
And oh, for one so young
The bitter words she spit
Like some tenacious bit
That will not leave the tongue.
She plucked her lips for it,
And still the horror clung. 70
Her mother wiped the foam
From her chin, picked up her comb,
And drew her backward home.

Robert Frost

Frost is closer to traditional modes of poetry than Laing is; his young people are more than psyches. They have physical bodies with shining hair and lips and hands; they stand waist-deep in goldenrod and fern; they ache and struggle and are panicked.

We can see how a poet deals with philosophic thought by looking at a poem that wonders whether a man should live for this world or for that afterlife which most religions offer.

SUNDAY MORNING

I

Complacencies of the peignoir, and late
Coffee and oranges in a sunny chair,
And the green freedom of a cockatoo
Upon a rug mingle to dissipate
The holy hush of ancient sacrifice.
She dreams a little, and she feels the dark
Encroachment of that old catastrophe,
As a calm darkens among water-lights.
The pungent oranges and bright, green wings
Seem things in some procession of the dead, 10
Winding across wide water, without sound.
The day is like wide water, without sound,
Stilled for the passing of her dreaming feet
Over the seas, to silent Palestine,
Dominion of the blood and sepulchre.

II

Why should she give her bounty to the dead?
What is divinity if it can come

Only in silent shadows and in dreams?
Shall she not find in comforts of the sun,
In pungent fruit and bright, green wings, or else 20
In any balm or beauty of the earth,
Things to be cherished like the thought of heaven?
Divinity must live within herself:
Passions of rain, or moods in falling snow;
Grievings in loneliness, or unsubdued
Elations when the forest blooms; gusty
Emotions on wet roads on autumn nights;
All pleasures and all pains, remembering
The bough of summer and the winter branch.
These are the measures destined for her soul. 30

III

Jove in the clouds had his inhuman birth.
No mother suckled him, no sweet land gave
Large-mannered motions to his mythy mind.
He moved among us, as a muttering king,
Magnificent, would move among his hinds,
Until our blood, commingling, virginal,
With heaven, brought such requital to desire
The very hinds discerned it, in a star.
Shall our blood fail? Or shall it come to be
The blood of paradise? And shall the earth 40
Seem all of paradise that we shall know?
The sky will be much friendlier then than now,
A part of labor and a part of pain,
And next in glory to enduring love,
Not this dividing and indifferent blue.

IV

She says, "I am content when wakened birds,
Before they fly, test the reality
Of misty fields, by their sweet questionings;
But when the birds are gone, and their warm fields
Return no more, where, then, is paradise?" 50
There is not any haunt of prophecy,
Nor any old chimera of the grave,
Neither the golden underground, nor isle
Melodious, where spirits gat them home,
Nor visionary south, nor cloudy palm
Remote on heaven's hill, that has endured
As April's green endures; or will endure
Like her remembrance of awakened birds,
Or her desire for June and evening, tipped
By the consummation of the swallow's wings. 60

V

She says, "But in contentment I still feel
The need of some imperishable bliss."

Death is the mother of beauty; hence from her,
Alone, shall come fulfilment to our dreams
And our desires. Although she strews the leaves
Of sure obliteration on our paths,
The path sick sorrow took, the many paths
Where triumph rang its brassy phrase, or love
Whispered a little out of tenderness,
She makes the willow shiver in the sun 70
For maidens who were wont to sit and gaze
Upon the grass, relinquished to their feet.
She causes boys to pile new plums and pears
On disregarded plate. The maidens taste
And stray impassioned in the littering leaves.

VI

Is there no change of death in paradise?
Does ripe fruit never fall? Or do the boughs
Hang always heavy in that perfect sky,
Unchanging, yet so like our perishing earth,
With rivers like our own that seek for seas 80
They never find, the same receding shores
That never touch with inarticulate pang?
Why set the pear upon those river-banks
Or spice the shores with odors of the plum?
Alas, that they should wear our colors there,
The silken weavings of our afternoons,
And pick the strings of our insipid lutes!
Death is the mother of beauty, mystical,
Within whose burning bosom we devise
Our earthly mothers waiting, sleeplessly. 90

VII

Supple and turbulent, a ring of men
Shall chant in orgy on a summer morn
Their boisterous devotion to the sun,
Not as a god, but as a god might be,
Naked among them, like a savage source.
Their chant shall be a chant of paradise,
Out of their blood, returning to the sky;
And in their chant shall enter, voice by voice,
The windy lake wherein their lord delights,
The trees, like serafin, and echoing hills, 100
That choir among themselves long afterward.
They shall know well the heavenly fellowship
Of men that perish and of summer morn.
And whence they came and whither they shall go
The dew upon their feet shall manifest.

VIII

She hears, upon that water without sound,
A voice that cries, "The tomb in Palestine

Is not the porch of spirits lingering.
It is the grave of Jesus, where he lay."
We live in an old chaos of the sun, 110
Or old dependency of day and night,
Or island solitude, unsponsored, free,
Of that wide water, inescapable.
Deer walk upon our mountains, and the quail
Whistle about us their spontaneous cries;
Sweet berries ripen in the wilderness;
And, in the isolation of the sky,
At evening, casual flocks of pigeons make
Ambiguous undulations as they sink,
Downward to darkness, on extended wings. 120

Wallace Stevens

"Sunday Morning," a real voice in a real body in a real world, is a vivid example of how poets philosophize. The thoughts of the poem are involved with physical sensations. Philosophical and religious questions come up because the woman is physically happy: she is enjoying her leisure, in comfortable undress, with the taste and fragrance of coffee and oranges, the warmth and gaiety of the sun, the brightly colored bird at liberty on the rug. All of her senses are alive in the first few lines of the poem, which never leaves the sensory world.

In much of this book we have been concerned with what we could call the physiology of poetry. We have stressed, too, that poetry has much in common with primitive or childlike ways of apprehending reality, that it seems more at home with dreams and visions than with syllogisms or statistics. George Santayana, philosopher as well as poet, knew what he was talking about when he said that he was "an ignorant man, almost a poet."

But poetry, related as it is to dream and impulse and mysterious influences from our distant past, certainly has a head on its shoulders. It may even be said to be a matter of common sense. If this statement seems shocking to anyone, in the next section he will find justice done to poetry's invaluable elements of irrationality.

All we mean by common sense is a sense of the way the world is. When we lift a forkful of mashed potatoes toward our face, common sense tells us it goes in our mouth, not in our ear. We can, of course, protest the weary sameness of things by putting it in our ear, though common sense tells us the consequences will be unpleasant. Common sense tells us to move if we are standing in the street and see a four-wheeled, two-ton object hurtling toward us. It tells us not to step outside the window for a breath of air if we are on the fortieth floor. In worlds of fantasy and dream we can disregard it; in the world that is "real" (in that we live or die there), to disregard it is to risk a quick trip to the hospital or worse. In our philosophic moods we may wonder what is "really real," but in the details of our everyday living we have a pretty sound idea.

Ezra Pound, when presented with the notion that intelligence involved "some repressing and silencing of poetry," reacted indignantly: "The intelligence never did anything of the sort." Gary Snyder, in "What You Should Know to Be a Poet," specifies, "Your own six senses, with a watchful and elegant mind."

The function of mind in poetry is worth stressing because there are readers who think the poet works better when he turns his mind off and lets imagination and emotion take over. Imagination and emotion are necessary sources of poetry, but few good poets would agree that they ought to be in charge. "Every true poet is necessarily a first-rate critic," said Paul Valéry. Dylan Thomas insisted that images, regardless of where they come from, "must go through the rational processes of the intellect." Sylvia Plath also thought the mind should be in control —even when dealing with the extremist situations that led to her suicide.

> I think my poems come immediately out of the sensuous and emotional experiences I have, but I must say I *cannot* sympathize with these cries from the heart that are informed by nothing except, you know, a needle or a knife, or whatever it is. I believe one should be able to control and manipulate experiences, even the most terrifying, like madness, like being tortured... and should be able to manipulate these experiences with an informed and intelligent mind....

An even more striking example of intellect controlling poetry when everything else has gone awry is one of the last poems of John Berryman, a poem (as events were to show) that is almost a suicide note.

HE RESIGNS

Age, and the deaths, and the ghosts.
Her having gone away
in spirit from me. Hosts
of regrets come & find me empty.

I don't feel this will change.
I don't want any thing
or person, familiar or strange.
I don't think I will sing

any more just now;
or ever. I must start 10
to sit with a blind brow
above an empty heart.

John Berryman

Unable to keep his life together, the poet keeps his poem more tightly together (*a b a b* in iambic trimeter) than anything he had written in years, instead of simply letting it "flow" from the depths of his agony.

There are readers who consider "poetry" and "common sense" in opposition. Poetry, they think, is some kind of lovely supersense: cloud castles in the airy blue. Most poets, more down to earth than their readers, would agree with Robert Graves that a poem should make prose sense as well as poetic sense. Even ecstatic poetry, thinks Graves, is no exception: a poem cannot make "more than sense" unless it first makes sense.

The painter Miró, for all of his visionary surrealism, believed in keeping in mind his goal of communicating with others. "We Catalans," he said, "believe you must always plant your feet firmly on the ground if you want to be able to jump in the air." Certainly the greatest of the Spanish mystical poets, St. John of the Cross, believed in making sense even when he was talking about experiences beyond any images our minds could hold or any words we could find to express them. Of his "The Dark Night" (p. 49), the Spanish poet Jorge Guillén has written: "We are immediately fascinated by these forms that do not break with the laws of our world." At first this may seem to be low praise. What it means is that the poet shows a reverence and love for the beauty and integrity of the universe.

Few readers are as eagle-eyed as Graves, who can be hard on poetry he thinks deficient in sense. He even finds much to object to in these famous lines:

THE SOLITARY REAPER

Behold her, single in the field,
Yon solitary Highland Lass!
Reaping and singing by herself;
Stop here, or gently pass!
Alone she cuts and binds the grain,
And sings a melancholy strain;
O listen! for the Vale profound
Is overflowing with the sound.

No Nightingale did ever chaunt
More welcome notes to weary bands 10
Of travellers in some shady haunt,
Among Arabian sands:
A voice so thrilling ne'er was heard
In spring-time from the Cuckoo-bird,
Breaking the silence of the seas
Among the farthest Hebrides.

Will no one tell me what she sings?—
Perhaps the plaintive numbers flow
For old, unhappy, far-off things,
And battles long ago: 20
Or is it some more humble lay,
Familiar matter of to-day?
Some natural sorrow, loss, or pain,
That has been, and may be again?

Whate'er the theme, the Maiden sang
As if her song could have no ending;

I saw her singing at her work,
And o'er the sickle bending:—
I listened, motionless and still;
And, as I mounted up the hill, 30
The music in my heart I bore,
Long after it was heard no more.

William Wordsworth

Graves objects that "There are only two figures in sight: Wordsworth and the Highland Lass—yet he cries, 'Behold her!' Do any of you find that reasonable?" If he is talking to himself, why say, "Behold her," when he has already done so, or "O listen!" when he cannot help listening, since the vale is "overflowing with the sound"? Graves also finds the poem wordy. If we were cabling the sense of the first stanza, we could say it in twelve words instead of forty-three:

SOLITARY HIGHLAND LASS REAPING BINDING GRAIN STOP
MELANCHOLY SONG OVERFLOWS PROFOUND VALE

Wordsworth uses four expressions for loneliness: "single," "solitary," "alone," "by herself." Graves also objects to the natural science of the poem: "occasional nightingales . . . penetrate to the more verdurous parts of Arabia Felix, but only as winter migrants, when heavy rains provide them with grubs and caterpillars, and never nest there; consequently they do not *'chaunt.'* " The Hebrides, he says, are far from silent: "The islands enjoy a remarkably temperate climate, because of the Gulf Stream; and the cuckoo's arrival coincides with the equinoctial gales." "Cuckoo-bird" he considers baby talk. He goes on to wonder why Wordsworth asks: "Will no one tell me what she sings?" Who could? he wonders, since no one is present except the poet and the single, solitary girl, all alone and by herself. He concludes by defining a good poem as "one that makes complete sense; and says all it has to say memorably and economically; and has been written for no other than poetic reasons."

Some poems show a more flagrant violation of common sense, which even naïve readers will be startled at. We need no background in highway engineering or the theory of bridge construction to feel that something is wrong in the world of a poem like this one.

BUILDING THE BRIDGE

An old man, going a lone highway,
Came, at the evening, cold and gray,
To a chasm, vast, and deep, and wide,
Through which was flowing a sullen tide.
The old man crossed in the twilight dim;
The sullen stream had no fears for him;
But he turned, when safe on the other side,
And built a bridge to span the tide.

"Old man," said a fellow pilgrim, near,
"You are wasting strength with building here; 10
Your journey will end with the ending day;
You never again must pass this way;
You have crossed the chasm, deep and wide,—
Why build you the bridge at eventide?"

The builder lifted his old gray head:
"Good friend, in the path I have come," he said,
"There followeth after me today
A youth, whose feet must pass this way.
This chasm, that has been naught to me,
To that fair-haired youth may a pitfall be. 20
He, too, must cross in the twilight dim;
Good friend, I am building the bridge for *him*."

Will Allen Dromgoole

Assuming there can be a "lone" highway, traveled only by an old man, a fellow pilgrim, and a fair-haired youth, this one is an example of bad planning: a chasm, vast and deep and wide, has somehow been overlooked by the highway department. We are not told how the old man crossed it, though that is an interesting question. Did he swim, keeping his old gray head above the water? We might wonder, too, why he bothered to cross at all if he was thinking about building a bridge. Why not start building it from the near bank instead of swimming over and then building the bridge back from the far side? Generally the construction of such a bridge requires a little planning and a good supply of heavy materials. It normally takes time, too, especially with just one old man, working in dim light, to drive the pilings and swing the beams into place.

Such a poem breaks violently with the laws of our world. We can see how remote from reality it is by putting it not into one of Mr. Graves' cables, but into journalese.

MAN, 70, BUILDS BRIDGE OVER VAST CHASM

Commuters long accustomed to swimming the deep, cold waters that roll in Vast Chasm, four miles north of town, were agreeably surprised this morning to find a gleaming steel structure spanning the tide.

"Twarn't there last night is all I know," said long-time resident Wilson Finozzle. "Sure is nice not to get soaked in them deep, cold waters, a-coming home with the vittles of an evening. Ain't read a dry newspaper since I was knee-high to a grasshopper."

"It was nothing," said the gray-haired builder, from his cell in the county jail, where he is being held on charges of bridge building without a permit. "I did it for a fair-haired youth. Wouldn't anybody?"

Miss Dromgoole's poem is well intentioned, meant to present us with an edifying example of noble conduct. Nobody would quarrel with her message. But she settles on images so improbable in terms of the world we live in that we are more likely to laugh than to listen seriously. When poetry is working on two levels, that of intended meaning and that of imagery, it has to make sense on *both* levels. One cannot hold back his laughter because "the poet doesn't really mean it that way" or because "it's only a figure of speech." For a poet to claim our indulgence for what he *meant* to say is as futile as for a golfer to demand that his ball be placed where he meant to hit it: unfulfilled intentions count as little in the world of literature as in the world of sports.

When Christ in the *New Testament* (Luke 10) wants to show that one should be kind to others, there is no nonsense about how we ought to build bridges across chasms in the dark. Instead we are given the simple parable of the good Samaritan. We might expect Gerard Manley Hopkins, one of the finest of religious poets and presumably partial to the otherworldly, to be sympathetic to departures from prosaic common sense. But he was not. When, in 1886, he was shown a poem by the young William Butler Yeats, he thought it "a strained and unworkable allegory about a young man and a sphinx on a rock in the sea . . . ," and wanted to ask questions like "How did it get there?" and "What did it eat?" Hopkins explained: "People think such criticisms very prosaic, but common sense is never out of place anywhere, neither on Parnassus nor on Tabor nor on the Mount where our Lord preached . . . parables all taken from real life. . . ."

An affront to our common sense is a reason for **parody.** The parodist feels that some feature of a certain poem is so lacking in balance that he deliberately exaggerates its faults to show their absurdity. The poems of A. E. Housman mention a fair number of love-stricken lads who kill themselves or rush off to death in battle or are hanged for murder. Occasionally the maudlin self-punishment leads to a ridiculous situation, like that in "The True Lover," in which a lad who has cut his throat pays a last call on his love, pleading, "Take me in your arms a space." She does:

> She heard and went and knew not why;
> Her heart to his she laid....

By and by she notices that her lad seems not to be breathing (though he can talk in rather long sentences) and has no heartbeat. There is also an odd salty wetness about him. He explains why:

> "Oh like enough 'tis blood, my dear,
> For when the knife has slit
> The throat across from ear to ear
> 'Twill bleed because of it."

This may bring tears to the susceptible eyes of those whose medical knowledge is limited. Level-headed readers, who refuse to believe what Housman is telling them, are more likely to laugh. Hugh Kingsmill is parodying this aspect of Housman when he writes:

> What, still alive at twenty-two,
> A clean, upstanding chap like you?
> Sure, if your throat 'tis hard to slit,
> Slit your girl's, and swing for it.
>
> Like enough, you won't be glad,
> When they come to hang you, lad:
> But bacon's not the only thing
> That's cured by hanging from a string....

Parody, although it has to be funny to make its point, is a serious literary exercise that amounts to a criticism of some excess or defect in the original. Fundamentally, it is a protest against some violation of common sense.

Exercises and Diversions

A. 1. In "The Subverted Flower," what is meant by the flower symbolism of the first four lines? How is the flower "subverted"?
2. From whose point of view (through whose consciousness) is the situation presented? The boy's? The girl's? The poet's?

B. 1. Is it fair to say that "Sunday Morning" is a dialogue with one speaker represented by the "She said" and words in quotation marks? Who is the other speaker? Is there ever a third?
2. If you summarized in a sentence the meaning of each stanza of "Sunday Morning," would the sentences add up to a logical argument? A logical proof of anything? Does their logical validity affect their poetic validity?

C. In the first of the passages that follow, the Duchess of Newcastle is very sensible in writing about "What Is Liquid." In the second, Marvell is not very sensible in suggesting how one might get a supply of tears for an especially mournful bereavement.

1. All that doth flow we cannot liquid name,
   Or else would fire and water be the same;
   But that is liquid which is moist and wet;
   Fire that property can never get:
   Then 'tis not cold that doth the fire put out,
   But 'tis the wet that makes it die, no doubt.

2. Hastings is dead, and we must find a store
   Of tears untouched, and never wept before.
   Go stand betwixt the morning and the flowers;
   And, ere they fall, arrest the early showers.

Yet most would agree that Marvell's lines are better poetry. Does this show that our discussion has overestimated the importance of common sense in poetry?

D. A poem that uses imagery to make a point ought to make sense on *both* levels —that of the intended meaning and that of the imagery. Are both levels well managed in these poems: "The Tyger" (p. 112), "Traveling through the Dark" (p. 137), "Neither out Far Nor in Deep" (p. 151), "The Eel" (p. 324), "Dover Beach" (p. 273)?

E. Travesty and **burlesque** are akin to parody. The first (related to "transvestite") means that garments are changed—a lofty style, for example, shifted to a vulgar or comic one. Travesty drags something down—we speak of a "travesty of justice." Burlesque (from the Italian *burla, joke*) is less literary or critical than parody. It tries to be funny just for the fun of it.

1. The following verses are a takeoff on what famous poet?
2. Would you classify them as parody, travesty, or burlesque—or a combination of any two or all three?
3. What elements of style of the famous poet have been selected for attention?

I NEVER PLUCKED A BUMBLEBEE

I never plucked—a Bumblebee—
Without I marvelled—"Ouch!"—
Wise Nature—hath such ways to show—
Her children—"Mustn't touch!"

I never chewed—a Beetle up—
Sans pouting—"Icky-poo!"
Did Beetle taste—like "Choc-o-late"—
He were extinctive now.

I never did me—this or that—
Without—I something said.
I put a Pumpkin—on my neck—
And used to call it—"Head"—

Till Robin—cocked his dapper eye—
Impeachment—sir—of me?
As one who—off his rocker flip—
Or fruitcake—nutty be?

F. 1. Do you recall any poems that you read with such disbelief that you found yourself noticing faults with as sharp an eye as Robert Graves'? Write a Gravesian analysis of a poem you find particularly vulnerable.

2. Write a parody (or travesty or burlesque) of any poem or poet that strikes your fancy. (Suggested titles: "Walt Whitman among the Yellow Pages," "The Coy Mistress Replies," "Most Like a Hearse This Marriage," "Gee, You're So Beautiful I Think I'll Chew Another Band-Aid," "anyone lived in a pretty (huh?) town," "The Ruby Yacht of Omar K. Yamm," "The Subverted Stinkweed." Or, better, make up your own.)

The Exquisite Corpse poetry and uncommon sense

21

If we generally look at the world with the eyes of common sense and if, in survival situations, we are obliged to do so, yet there are times when we can disregard it. In our dreams or daydreams all rules are suspended. We hardly need the Dadaists and Surrealists of the twentieth century to tell us what the sensible Horace admitted long ago—on occasion it is fun to act in a crazy way (*dulce est desipere in loco*). And before him the intellectual Greeks, who produced the Parthenon and the works of Phidias, had also allowed for the irrational in human life. Sappho would probably have been the first to admit that she was not behaving sensibly in letting love take over as it did.

We can point to nature as acting like a zany in producing flying fish and the duckbill platypus. If we look through a telescope at spiral nebulae or through a microscope at the cellular structure of our own bodies, what we see is so like surrealist art we can hardly tell one from another. Nature is continually doing things at which our reason boggles—so much so that philosophies of absurdity and meaninglessness have been based on her caprice. As have religions: In "A Masque of Reason," Robert Frost has Jehovah explain to Job:

> But it was of the essence of the trial
> You shouldn't understand it at the time.
> It had to seem unmeaning to have meaning.

Unreason, then, common enough in the universe, has a right to its place in poetry. According to Yeats, who spoke out strongly for the identity of passion and precision and for the mathematical basis of beauty, all great poetry contains an irrational element.

But welcome as occasional unreason may be, our minds are in for a shock when we first come on poems like the following, the first by an Alsatian Dadaist and Surrealist best known for his sculpture and painting, and the second by possibly the best of the French Surrealist poets (one who preferred the sonnet form for his more serious work).

WHAT THE VIOLINS SING IN THEIR BACONFAT BED

the elephant is in love with the millimeter

the snail dreams of lunar defeat
its slippers are pallid and drained
like a gun made of Jell-O that's held by a neodraftee

the eagle has the gestures of an alleged vacuum
his breast is swollen with lightning

the lion sports a mustache that is pure gothic of the flamboyant type
his skin is calm
he laughs like a blot from a bottle of oink

the lobster goes *grrr* like a gooseberry 10
he is wise with the savvy of apples
has the bleeding-heart ways of a plum
he is fiendish in sex like a pumpkin

the cow takes a path that's pathetic
it peters out in a pond of flesh
every hair of this volume weighs volumes

the snake hops with prickety prickling
around about washbowls of love
full of hearts with an arrow in each

the butterfly stuffed is a popover made of papaya 20
papaya popovers grow into papapaya papapovers
papapaya papapovers grow into grandpapapaya grandpapapovers

the nightingale sprinkles on stomachs on hearts on brains on guts
what I mean is on lilies on roses on lilacs on pinks
the flea puts his right leg behind his left ear
his left hand in his right hand
and on his left foot jumps over his right ear

Jean Arp (1888?–1966)

THE DAY IT WAS NIGHT

He flew off to the bottom of the river. The stones of
ebony-wood the iron wires of gold the cross without a
crosspiece.
All nothing.
I hate her with all my love as doesn't everyone.
The deceased was drawing deep breaths of emptiness.
The compass was drawing squares and five-sided triangles.
After which he went downstairs to the attic.
The noon was a splendor of starlight.
The hunter was returning with his game-bag full of fish along 10

the riverbank that was in the middle of the Seine.
An earthworm marks the center of the circle on its circumference.
In silence my eyes talked on at the top of their voice.
Then we were making our way through a deserted lane in a
dense crowd of people.
When the trudging had made us feel rested we had the strength
to sit down then on awaking our eyes popped shut and
dawn poured over us the reservoirs of the night.
The rain dried us off.

Robert Desnos (1900–1945)

To ask what these poems *mean* is a wrong approach. The question is: What do they *do*? They certainly jolt us out of habitual ways of perceiving and thinking. Probably they also amuse us. The writing is very specific—anything but abstract. The "thought" is difficult. But it is not meant to be thought. Instead, it is experience, as dreams are or as the inspection of natural oddities is. If it seems an insult to our ordinary ways of thinking, then the writer would consider it a success. To understand why, we have to know something about the Dadaist and Surrealist philosophy.

The Dadaist movement (the word "Dada" means nothing) came into existence about the middle of the First World War. If man's common sense could lead to the folly of war, the Dadaists felt, perhaps it was time to try another approach—that of "not-sense." They did absurd things in the hope of shocking society into an awareness of the bankruptcy of traditional procedures. They preferred chance to logic as determining a literary work. One of Tristan Tzara's methods of writing a poem was to take a newspaper story, cut out each word with a scissors, drop the words into a hat, pull them out one at a time at random, and paste them up that way.

Surrealism, which took over from Dadaism in 1922, was not just a literary movement; it was a way of life, aimed at startling people out of the old ways. The fun and games were not without a serious purpose—if they were amusing, all the better. Surrealists hoped to promote their revolution by releasing the untapped forces of the unconscious, the marvels of dream, fantasy, hallucination, and chance; they professed to think spontaneity better than effort. "Thought," said Tzara, "is made in the mouth."

One form their spontaneity took was that of automatic writing. In this process, one writes down quickly, without thinking, whatever comes into his head. If the words begin to make sense, he is on the wrong track and should start over. Picasso once spent several months producing page after page of automatic writing that read like this:

A worse scandalmonger had never been known except if the wheedling friend licks the little woolen bitch twisted by the palette of the ash-gray painter dressed in shades of hard-boiled egg and armed with the foam which performs a thousand monkeytricks in his bed when the tomato no longer warms him what does he care if the dew that does not know the winning lottery number which the carnation gives a knock at the mare....

This is probably more fun to write than to read. It was soon found that automatic writing produced almost nothing of interest. For one thing, it was easy to fake. Breton later admitted it had been "a continuous disaster."

Actually, the Surrealists' devotion to spontaneity and absence of control was never complete. They never really meant to repudiate reason—they merely wanted it to go halves with unreason. Most Surrealist art was not at all spontaneous. Tzara spent five years writing and rewriting one of his books. Breton worked for six months on a thirty-word poem, probably setting an all-time record for deliberation. The painter Masson was seen to throw away from sixty to a hundred attempts at an automatic drawing before he got one with the "spontaneous" feeling he wanted.

Although the founders of Surrealism were mostly literary men, it was the painters who had the more resounding success. For every one person who has read the poems of André Breton, thousands have seen the paintings of Dali. We can see what the Surrealists were up to more vividly in their painting than in their literature. René Magritte, too rational to be a regular member of the group, was like them in setting out to defy common sense. In his art he puts things where we least expect to find them, or shows them made out of those materials we least expect.

We see a boot, but the boot is sprouting real toes. A window pane, through which we had been watching the setting sun, shatters; pieces of sun and sky fall to the floor with the jagged glass. We see a house as at midnight—windows lighted, façade glowing in the pallor of a streetlamp—and yet the sky behind the midnight roof and trees is a noon sky. Out of a plain fireplace in a plain room, a little locomotive may come steaming. Every object is painted with perfect fidelity to nature, and yet nature itself is transformed. Magritte has used his eyes and had his wits about him. He knows that before an artist can master the surreal, he had better master the real. Miller Williams has given similar advice to a poet in "Let Me Tell You":

> . . . First notice everything:
> The stain on the wallpaper
> of the vacant house,
> the mothball smell of a
> Greyhound toilet.
> Miss nothing. Memorize it.
> You cannot twist the fact you do not know . . . .

Similar transformations of reality are present in the typical surrealist image—in Breton's "soluble fish" or "white-haired revolver." Such juxtapositions are intended to short-circuit our sanity, to "blow our minds" as a later decade liked to say. No objects are too remote to be coupled—time and distance are annulled. As in collage, one can paste anything next to anything. The Surrealists thought there was something "sublime" in the way the mind could reconcile contraries and find unity in the unlike.

René Magritte, *Time Transfixed*

The Surrealists invented many kinds of word games, and even returned with enthusiasm to the games of their childhood, since this was one more way of flouting the prudential time-is-money world of adults. In their favorite game, the first player would write down a word, fold over the paper so the word could not be seen, pass the folded paper to the next player, who would add a word, fold the paper again, and pass it on. When all had contributed, the composition would be read. The game was called "Cadavre exquis" (*exquisite corpse*) from the first sentence that resulted: "The exquisite corpse shall drink the young wine." Others were: "The winged mist seduces the locked bird" and "The oyster from Senegal will eat the tricolored bread." (Some look suspiciously doctored.) The results of the game—a kind of collage in motion—sound like lines from Surrealist poetry.

The Surrealists not only made up objects in their imagination, they also took a fresh look at ordinary things, particularly the "found objects" that chance presented them with. Duchamp once picked up an ordinary iron bottle-rack, signed his name to it, and declared it art. The group also composed "surrealist objects," of which the most famous were a fur-lined cup, saucer, and spoon.

Surrealism lends itself to schlock confections as easily as any other set of mannerisms does. Not all inversions of experience are necessarily surprising or amusing:

> . . . I run home
> And dip my coffee in bread, and eat some of it . . . .

Nor are all novel figures of speech a revelation:

> . . . You are as arduous as that
> Ashtray . . . .
>
> The sky is an empty keg of purple ketchup . . . .

Some readers may find themselves yawning once the novelty wears off (if there is still any novelty in a technique originated in our grandfathers' time). Frank O'Hara makes lively use of images the Surrealists would have found congenial:

> The stars blink like a hairnet that was dropped
> on a seat and now it is lying in the alley behind
> the theater . . . .
>
> the rain, its tiny pressure
> on your scalp, like ants
> passing the door of a tobacconist . . . .

One of the most skillful users of this sort of imagery is W. S. Merwin, many of whose lines have the authentic looniness:

> I uncover my footprints, I
> Poke them till the eyes open . . . .
>
> I have seen streets where the hands of the beggars
> Are left out at night like shoes in a hotel corridor . . . .

Much contemporary poetry, while not strictly in the Surrealist mode, is reminiscent of its methods and shows its influence. The three poems that follow, if not technically Surrealist, demand the suspension of our usual rationality.

ZEPPELIN

Someone has built a dirigible in my parlor.
What on earth has happened to the boarders?
I go in there sometimes
and tear the fabric off the framework, I shout
"who's responsible for this?"
but nobody answers.
There's nothing underneath
but a wilderness of girders
and a gas bag without any gas.
The dog has taken to living in one of my shoes. 10
Poor thing! His blanket was by the fireplace,
now filled up with the underfin.
When the propellers turn they open the doors,
they scatter papers down the hall to the garden,
sometimes they blow the paper I'm reading into my face.
My first editions are soggy with crankcase oil,
and the batik shawl I brought from ancient Mesopotamia
is soaked in grease.
Up there the pointed cone upon the nose
protrudes through my Matisse. 20
The pilot (at least I suppose he's the pilot)
is balled up on my bed, and when I shake him
he lifts one flap of his aviator's tarboosh to shout
"I didn't do it" and something that sounds like
"metal fatigue." He burrows into my pillow
deeper with his head. I saw a man in a mechanic's uniform
climb up inside this morning. I said
"look here now, this is my living room!"
He only banged with his wrench,
shook his fist at my fractured plaster and shouted 30
"what's important is that in the end it fly!"
I have to admire his singleness of mind.
Why it isn't even a new model. "Gott straff England"
is written across the gondola with lipstick in gothic lettering.
One of these mornings I've got to get out and see my lawyer.
Maybe he will suggest somebody to sue.
In the meantime for my conscience' sake
I need someone authoritative to tell me
what are the principles involved, 40
I mean so I will know if I should
feel resentful or honored.

Andrew Glaze (b. 1920)

---

33 **Gott straff:** *God punish*

THE TUNNEL

A man has been standing
in front of my house
for days. I peek at him
from the living room
window and at night,
unable to sleep,
I shine my flashlight
down on the lawn.
He is always there.

After a while 10
I open the front door
just a crack and order
him out of my yard.
He narrows his eyes
and moans. I slam
the door and dash back
to the kitchen, then up
to the bedroom, then down.

I weep like a schoolgirl
and make obscene gestures 20
through the window. I
write large suicide notes
and place them so he
can read them easily.
I destroy the living
room furniture to prove
I own nothing of value.

When he seems unmoved
I decide to dig a tunnel
to a neighboring yard. 30
I seal the basement off
from the upstairs with
a brick wall. I dig hard
and in no time the tunnel
is done. Leaving my pick
and shovel below,

I come out in front of a house
and stand there too tired to
move or even speak, hoping
someone will help me. 40
I feel I'm being watched
and sometimes I hear
a man's voice,
but nothing is done
and I have been waiting for days.

Mark Strand (b. 1934)

MY GRANDMOTHER'S FUNERAL

At least 100 seabirds attended my grandmother's funeral. And we live over 100 miles from the coast! They flew right into the Episcopal church and stayed for the entire service. No one said anything about them when it was over. We were all sitting around on folding chairs rented from the undertaker and no one said a word about the seabirds! Even the Reverend, who was once a prisoner of the Japanese, and whose eyes were tunneled deep into his head, didn't seem to mind. I watched him when a few of them perched on a special chalice. He didn't budge! It was harder for him, but he knew as well as the rest of us that seabirds are imperturbable, and that they keep away the larger birds, the birds that sit on the coffin, making it almost impossible to carry.....

Thomas Lux (b. 1946)

The last of these is written in a manner that young writers are finding attractive. Nothing in it quite makes sense, yet nothing is impossible. Conventional relevance is mocked by irrelevance. The fact that the reverend was once a prisoner of the Japanese is mentioned, as though it had some bearing on what is happening. It seems to have none.

In many ways surrealist poetry recalls the nonsense verse that has probably existed as long as poetry itself. An anonymous poet of the sixteenth century thought up a series of impossible suppositions—surrealistic details—one might expect to see verified before he could trust a woman.

When sparrows build churches and steeples high,
And wrens carry sacks to the mill,
And curlews carry cloths, horses for to dry,
And sea-mews bring butter to the market to sell,
And wood-doves carry wood-knives thieves to kill,
And griffons to goslings do obedience—
Then put in a woman your trust and confidence.

E. E. Cummings (who had lived in Paris during the early years of Surrealism) sets up a similar series of impossible conditions in "as freedom is a breakfastfood," with lines like

as hatracks into peachtrees grow
or hopes dance best on bald men's hair
and every finger is a toe
and any courage is a fear
—long enough and just so long
will the impure think all things pure
and hornets wail by children stung....

What seem at first to be nonsense poems may sometimes explode into disturbing fragments of sense.

OUR BOG IS DOOD

Our Bog is dood, our Bog is dood,
They lisped in accents mild,

But when I asked them to explain
They grew a little wild.
How do you know your Bog is dood
My darling little child?

We know because we wish it so
That is enough, they cried,
And straight within each infant eye
Stood up the flame of pride, 10
And if you do not think it so
You shall be crucified.

Then tell me, darling little ones,
What's dood, suppose Bog is?
Just what we think, the answer came,
Just what we think it is.
They bowed their heads. Our Bog is ours
And we are wholly his.

But when they raised them up again
They had forgotten me 20
Each one upon each other glared
In pride and misery
For what was dood, and what their Bog
They never could agree.

Oh sweet it was to leave them then,
And sweeter not to sce,
And sweetest of all to walk alone
Beside the encroaching sea,
The sea that soon should drown them all,
That never yet drowned me. 30

Stevie Smith (1902–1971)

Is this a nonsense poem? Or is it a serious poem about the psychology of controversy, religious or political? The word "Bog" does mean *God* in Russian, though why we should invoke a Russian meaning here is not evident to common sense. "Dood" might be baby talk for *good*, or it might mean *dead*, or it might mean nothing. The little ones in the poem, at least, do not agree on its meaning.

A continual source of nonsense or of surrealist revelation is the world of our dreams, daydreams, and fantasies.

The curious fact that many dreams—perhaps most—are in black and white, not in color, is thought to mean that the dreamer is regressing to a primitive stage of human development when we did see in black and white, as some animals still do. In going back so unimaginably far, the dreaming mind falls again into primitive ways of thinking in which reason counts for little. Dream, like myth and fairy tale, prefers emotion, imagery, and symbol to logic and ideas. Every dreamer is a surrealist.

Our waking thoughts have to deal with objects that are hard, sharp, heavy, explosive. A wrong decision can be the end of us. Dreams have no such obligations. We can be run over by dream trains or fall out of dream skyscrapers and be none the worse for it. In dreams we are indestructible. We are free to reassign the properties of matter. Like the surrealist image, anything can become anything else. Time and space lose their power.

Dreams can be poems in themselves. A student in a writing workshop once described a dream that was better than any of her poems. She might well have taken lessons from her unconscious.

I dreamed I was standing somewhere in the middle of a great desert. Off on the horizon I could see some beautiful purple mountains, their peaks bathed in golden light. Suddenly I heard a drumming of hooves, which grew louder and louder. Then I could see the horse coming. As he got near me, I was surprised to see that he had two heads. One head was well shaped and even noble, like a horse in Greek sculpture; its eyes were fixed on the distant mountains. The other head was ugly, misshapen; it had twisted fangs and bloodshot eyes. As the horse ran past me, the noble head did not look in my direction; but the ugly head kept its eyes leeringly on me, twisting around to do so. I fell to my knees and worshipped the two-headed horse.

This is probably a better image than the dreamer could have found consciously for a young girl's view of sex as both idealistic and menacing.

If Coleridge is telling the truth, one classic of English poetry was written in a dream. The poet, who said he was publishing his "Kubla Khan" as a "psychological curiosity" rather than for any "supposed *poetic* merits," tells how he fell asleep in his chair as a result of a pain-relieving drug, just as he was reading how Kublai Khan, the great thirteenth-century Mongolian ruler of China, built his summer palace at Xamdu.

He awakened later with the memory of a two- to three-hundred-line poem in his head, which he immediately began to write down. He had reached line 54 when he was interrupted by "a person on business from Porlock." When he returned to his room he found "to his no small surprise and mortification" that he had forgotten all the rest except for some scattered fragments. The poem as we have it seems to be a spontaneous production of the sleeping mind (which did not, however, create it from nothing). Scholars have traced most of the material of the poem to Coleridge's own reading. Not even the subconscious can dredge up much of interest from a shabbily furnished mind.

KUBLA KHAN

In Xanadu did Kubla Khan
A stately pleasure-dome decree:
Where Alph, the sacred river, ran
Through caverns measureless to man
  Down to a sunless sea.
So twice five miles of fertile ground
With walls and towers were girdled round:

And there were gardens bright with sinuous rills,
Where blossomed many an incense-bearing tree;
And here were forests ancient as the hills, 10
Enfolding sunny spots of greenery.

But oh! that deep romantic chasm which slanted
Down the green hill athwart a cedarn cover!
A savage place! as holy and enchanted
As e'er beneath a waning moon was haunted
By woman wailing for her demon-lover!
And from this chasm, with ceaseless turmoil seething,
As if this earth in fast thick pants were breathing,
A mighty fountain momently was forced:
Amid whose swift half-intermitted burst 20
Huge fragments vaulted like rebounding hail,
Or chaffy grain beneath the thresher's flail:
And 'mid these dancing rocks at once and ever
It flung up momently the sacred river.
Five miles meandering with a mazy motion
Through wood and dale the sacred river ran,
Then reached the caverns measureless to man,
And sank in tumult to a lifeless ocean:
And 'mid this tumult Kubla heard from far
Ancestral voices prophesying war! 30
The shadow of the dome of pleasure
Floated midway on the waves;
Where was heard the mingled measure
From the fountain and the caves.
It was a miracle of rare device,
A sunny pleasure-dome with caves of ice!

A damsel with a dulcimer
In a vision once I saw:
It was an Abyssinian maid,
And on her dulcimer she played, 40
Singing of Mount Abora.
Could I revive within me
Her symphony and song,
To such a deep delight 'twould win me,
That with music loud and long,
I would build that dome in air,
That sunny dome! those caves of ice!
And all who heard should see them there,
And all should cry, Beware! Beware!
His flashing eyes, his floating hair! 50
Weave a circle round him thrice,
And close your eyes with holy dread,
For he on honey-dew hath fed,
And drunk the milk of Paradise.

Samuel Taylor Coleridge (1772–1834)

Unfortunately, the subconscious—like a baseball player who hits one home run in a lifetime career—does not have an impressive record as a writer of finished poems. We have to take Coleridge's word for it that the subconscious finished even this one.

A poem that was not composed in a dream but that looks at the world through a dreamlike haziness, with occasional surrealist images, is one of the gypsy ballads of the Spanish poet García Lorca.

SLEEPWALKERS' BALLAD

Green it's your green I love.
Green of the wind. Green branches.
The ship far out at sea.
The horse above on the mountain.
Shadows dark at her waist,
she's dreaming there on her terrace,
green of her cheek, green hair,
with eyes like chilly silver.
Green it's your green I love.
Under that moon of the gypsies 10
things are looking at her
but she can't return their glances.

Green it's your green I love.
The stars are frost, enormous;
a tuna cloud floats over
nosing off to the dawn.
The fig tree catches a wind
to grate in its emery branches;
the mountain's a wildcat, sly,
bristling its acrid cactus. 20
But—who's on the road? Which way?
She's dreaming there on her terrace,
green of her cheek, green hair,
she dreams of the bitter sea.

"Friend, what I want is to trade
this horse of mine for your house,
this saddle of mine for your mirror,
this knife of mine for your blanket.
Friend, I come bleeding, see,
from the mountain pass of Cabra." 30
"I would if I could, young man;
I'd have taken you up already.
But I'm not myself any longer,
nor my house my home any more."
"Friend, what I want is to die
in a bed of my own—die nicely.
An iron bed, if there is one,
between good linen sheets.
I'm wounded, throat and breast,
from here to here—you see it?" 40
"You've a white shirt on; three hundred
roses across—dark roses.
There's a smell of blood about you;
your sash, all round you, soaked.
But I'm not myself any longer,

nor my house my home any more."
"Then let me go up, though; let me!
at least to the terrace yonder.
Let me go up then, let me!
up to the high green roof. 50
Terrace-rails of the moonlight,
splash of the lapping tank."

So they go up, companions,
up to the high roof-terrace;
a straggle of blood behind them,
behind, a straggle of tears.
Over the roofs, a shimmer
like little tin lamps, and glassy
tambourines by the thousand
slitting the glitter of dawn. 60

Green it's your green I love,
green of the wind, green branches.
They're up there, two companions.
A wind from the distance leaving
its tang on the tongue, strange flavors
of bile, of basil and mint.
"Where is she, friend—that girl
with the bitter heart, your daughter?"
"How often she'd wait and wait,
how often she'd be here waiting, 70
fresh of face, hair black,
here in green of the terrace."

There in her terrace pool
was the gypsy girl, in ripples.
Green of her cheek, green hair,
with eyes like chilly silver.
Icicles from the moon
held her afloat on the water.
Night became intimate then—
enclosed, like a little plaza. 80
Drunken, the Civil Guard
had been banging the door below them.
Green it's your green I love.
Green of the wind. Green branches.
The ship far out at sea.
The horse above on the mountain.

Federico García Lorca (1899–1936)

Since insanity is the supreme form (next to suicide) of the mind's crying out against itself, the Surrealists were interested in the visions of madness—though not as much as we might have expected, possibly because the madder a madman is, the more incoherent he is likely to become. His rantings can be as boring as the sane man's platitudes.

To people of stolid common sense, such poems as those by Arp and Desnos seem "insane." New ideas, new ways of doing things, always look "crazy." This is as true in science as in poetry. One contemporary scientist, speaking of new theories, says, "For any speculation which does not at first glance look crazy, there is no hope."

Because the reactions of poets are likely to be fresh, new, and "different," they sometimes seem crazy to the rest of us. A touch of divine madness, thought Plato, was essential to the poetic gift.

One of the best and strangest poems in English that professes to come from the mind of a madman is "Loving Mad Tom" (or "Tom o' Bedlam's Song"), which first appeared in a manuscript collection of 1615.

The Tom of our poem has been driven out of his mind by love for a girl named Maudlin (or Magdalen), whose name suggests an ex-prostitute. He has been an inmate of Bedlam (the Hospital of St. Mary of Bethlehem), the London lunatic asylum. His treatment there consisted of handcuffs, whippings, and starvation. Now released, he has become a Bedlam beggar—one of the many discharged patients, either still mad or pretending to be, who roamed the country in search of food and money, which they got by begging and threatening. Our Tom declares that when well treated he is generally harmless, though he practices petty thievery when he can and goes hungry when he cannot. He says he is fierce, however—"Tom Rhinoceros!"—when treated harshly. He is also involved in magic and has gaudy hallucinations.

LOVING MAD TOM

From the hag and hungry goblin
  That into rags would rend ye,
The spirit that stands by the naked man
  In the Book of Moons defend ye!
That of your five sound senses
  You never be forsaken,
Nor wander from yourselves with Tom
  Abroad to beg your bacon.

While I do sing, "Any food, any feeding,
  Feeding, drink, or clothing." 10
Come, dame or maid, be not afraid;
  Poor Tom will injure nothing.

Of thirty bare years have I
  Twice twenty been enragèd,
And of forty been three times fifteen
  In durance soundly cagèd.
On the lordly lofts of Bedlam
  With stubble soft and dainty,
Brave bracelets strong, sweet whips ding-dong,
  With wholesome hunger plenty. 20

And now I sing, etc.

---

[4] **Book of Moons:** *an astrological almanac (suggests Robert Graves)*
[14] **enragèd:** *demented*
[17] **Bedlam:** *the Hospital of St. Mary of Bethlehem, a London madhouse*
[18] **stubble:** *rough straw*
[19] **bracelets:** *handcuffs*

With a thought I took for Maudlin,
  And a cruse of cockle pottage,
With a thing thus tall—sky bless you all—
  I fell into this dotage.
I slept not since the Conquest,
  Till then I never wakèd,
Till the roguish boy of love where I lay
  Me found and stripped me naked.

And now I sing, etc.

When I short have shorn my sow's face
  And swigged my horny barrel, 30
In an oaken inn I pound my skin,
  As a suit of gilt apparel.
The moon's my constant mistress,
  And the lowly owl my morrow,
The flaming drake and the nightcrow make
  Me music to my sorrow.

While I do sing, etc.

The palsy plagues my pulses
  When I prig your pigs or pullen,
Your culvers take, or matchless make
  Your chanticleer or sullen. 40
When I want provant, with Humphrey
  I sup, and when benighted,
I repose in Paul's with waking souls
  Yet never am affrighted.

But I do sing, etc.

I know more than Apollo,
  For oft, when he lies sleeping,
I see the stars at bloody wars
  In the wounded welkin weeping,
The moon embrace her shepherd,
  And the queen of love her warrior, 50

---

[21] **Maudlin:** *Magdalen (girl's name)*
[22] **cruse of cockle pottage:** *bowl of shellfish chowder (thought to be an aphrodisiac)*
[23] **sky:** *God*
[27] **boy of love:** *Cupid*
[30] **swigged my horny barrel:** *drunk a rough barrelful (?) Graves reads "snigged my hairy barrel," clipped my hairy torso.*
[31] **In an oaken inn:** *under an oak tree (?); in the stocks (?)*
pound: *impound, enclose*
[35] **drake:** *dragon*
[38] **prig:** *steal*
pullen: *poultry*
[39] **culvers:** *doves*
matchless: *without a mate*
[40] **chanticleer:** *rooster*
sullen: *goose (?),* from *"Solan," a seafowl resembling a goose*
[41] **provant:** *food*
Humphrey: *to dine with Duke Humphrey meant "to go dinnerless."*
[43] **Paul's:** *the churchyard of St. Paul's Cathedral in London*
[48] **welkin:** *heaven*
[49] **shepherd:** *Endymion, with whom the moon was in love*
[50] **queen of love:** *Venus, in love with Mars*

While the first doth horn the star of morn,
And the next the heavenly farrier.

While I do sing, etc.

The Gypsies Snap and Pedro
Are none of Tom's comradoes.
The punk I scorn and the cutpurse sworn
And the roaring boy's bravadoes.
The meek, the white, the gentle
Me handle, touch, and spare not;
But those that cross Tom Rhinoceros
Do what the panther dare not. 60

Although I sing, etc.

With an host of furious fancies
Whereof I am commander,
With a burning spear and a horse of air,
To the wilderness I wander.
By a knight of ghosts and shadows
I summoned am to tourney
Ten leagues beyond the wide world's end—
Methinks it is no journey.

Yet will I sing, etc.

Anonymous (c. 1615)

---

[51] **horn:** *betray by her infidelity*
star of morn: *Phosphorus is thought of here as the husband of the moon.*
[52] **farrier:** *blacksmith. Venus was the wife of Vulcan, god of metal-working.*
[55] **punk:** *prostitute*
[56] **roaring boy:** *boisterous bully*
[57] **white:** *innocent, honest (as in "that's mighty white of you")*

Exercises and Diversions

A. "Kubla Khan" illustrates almost all of the technical points about poetry that we have been discussing.

1. Are there any lines that do not engage one of our senses?
2. Have all the senses been involved by the time the poem ends?
3. Is the vocabulary simple? Does it have a high percentage of "thing-words"?
4. Can you find examples of the functional use of assonance and alliteration?
5. Why did the writer change "Kublai" and "Xamdu" to "Kubla" and "Xanadu" in the poem?
6. How many rhymes can you find on a single sound? How many lines apart can the rhymes be?
7. What two line-lengths are used? Is the shift from one to the other significant? Is there ever a third?
8. Can you find all of the "options" mentioned in our treatment of iambic verse? Are those that you find used expressively?
9. Does the poem, in its own way and as far as it goes, "make sense"? Are there any surrealist details?
10. Do you think it odd that the most celebrated of all dream poems is so craft conscious?

B.

SIMULTANEOUSLY

Simultaneously, five thousand miles apart,
two telephone poles, shaking and roaring
and hissing gas, rose from their emplacements
straight up, leveled off and headed
for each other's land, alerted radar
and ground defense, passed each other
in midair, escorted by worried planes,
and plunged into each other's place,
steaming and silent and standing straight,
sprouting leaves. 10

David Ignatow (b. 1914)

1. Could the Surrealists, if so minded, claim that this poem was influenced by their techniques?
2. What do you think this imagery stands for in terms of the contemporary world?

C. "The exquisite corpse shall drink the young wine." As wild as such lines may be in content, they keep to a traditional sentence structure. Otherwise they would soon become boring gibberish, like "Young drank the exquisite wine corpse." To play this game satisfactorily, one needs something like a plan to show each player what the function of his contribution should be. The following would be a ten-player plan: "The 1. [adjective] 2. [noun] of the 3. [participle in -ing] 4. [noun] 5. [adverb] 6. [transitive verb] the 7. [adjective] 8. [noun] in a 9. [adjective] 10. [noun]." (In one class this gave, "The comfortable tornado of the dreaming eggshell obsessively sifted the quinine cobblestones in a nasty singsong.")

Try filling in a few such plans in class, with no contributor knowing the others' words. Note: for the most striking effects, words have to be concrete and specific.

D. The painter Sophie Taeuber (wife of Jean Arp) describes a dream she once had:

> Last night I dreamt that I was on a beach. . . . I heard the voices of my friends grow fainter and fainter. I was alone, and, while the night fell, my index finger wrote the word "happy" on the sand, as though it had been impelled by an outside force. While tracing the letters, I saw the word sink into the stone. A muffled, whispering noise made me look up. It was a great slab of rock which had broken loose and was poised ominously above me. And the thought flashed into my mind that if it crushed me that very moment, all that would be left of me would be the single word "happy."

Describe a dream of your own in a way that brings out its kinship with poetry.

E. 1. Make up half a dozen or so surrealist images consisting of noun and adjective, like Breton's "soluble fish" or "white-haired revolver."

2. Invent half a dozen or so interesting surrealist objects, like the fur-lined breakfast set.

3. A good deal of surrealist poetry in English looks like these lines from Kenneth Koch's "Irresistible":

> When December fig newtons steer through the enraged
> gas station
> Of lilacs, bringing the crushed tree of doughnuts a
> suitable ornament
> Of laughing bridgework pliable as a kilt in the
> muddiness of this November
> Scene starring from juxtapositioning April languor
> oceans
> Breathless with the touch of Argentina's lilac mouse
> beat in quicksand. . . .

While such lines may be wholly sincere, written out of an inner need of the poet, such verses are easy to fake (as Breton said of automatic writing).

Notice the kind of devices used, and then try a dozen or so lines of your own.

Adam's Curse 22
inspiration and effort

How do poems come into being at all?

Some believe they are produced by a mysterious something called "inspiration." The poet, in this view, is a sort of medium; he has nothing to do but sit there and let himself be played on by celestial fingers.

INSPIRATION

How often have I started out
With no thought in my noddle,
And wandered here and there about,
Where fancy bade me toddle;
Till feeling faunlike in my glee
I've voiced some gay distiches,
Returning joyfully to tea,
A poem in my britches.

A-squatting on a thymy slope
With vast of sky about me, 10
I've scribbled on an envelope
The rhymes the hills would shout me;
The couplets that the trees would call,
The lays the breezes proffered . . .
Oh, no, I didn't *think* at all—
I took what Nature offered.

For that's the way you ought to write—
Without a trace of trouble;
Be super-charged with high delight
And let the words out-bubble; 20
Be voice of vale and wood and stream
Without design or proem:

Then rouse from out a golden dream
To find you've made a poem.

So I'll go forth with mind a blank,
And sea and sky will spell me;
And lolling on a thymy bank
I'll take down what they tell me;
As Mother Nature speaks to me
Her words I'll gaily docket, 30
So I'll come singing home to tea
A poem in my pocket.

Robert W. Service (1874–1958)

Dylan Thomas' account of how he composed is different from Service's. Instead of toddling around out-bubbling, he works—he *labors* at the *exercise* of his *craft* or *art,* which is *sullen* because words, like marble, are resistant material.

IN MY CRAFT OR SULLEN ART

In my craft or sullen art
Exercised in the still night
When only the moon rages
And the lovers lie abed
With all their griefs in their arms,
I labour by singing light
Not for ambition or bread
Or the strut and trade of charms
On the ivory stages
But for the common wages 10
Of their most secret heart.

Not for the proud man apart
From the raging moon I write
On these spindrift pages
Nor for the towering dead
With their nightingales and psalms
But for the lovers, their arms
Round the griefs of the ages,
Who pay no praise or wages
Nor heed my craft or art. 20

Dylan Thomas

A good poem is likely to seem so spontaneous, so easy, so natural, that we can hardly imagine the poet sweating over it—crossing out lines, scrawling in between them, making out lists of rhymes or synonyms. But enough of the poets' scribbled-over manuscripts are extant—under lock and key in rare-book rooms or under glass in museums—for us to know that most poets did indeed find their muse a difficult mistress.

A poem that seems spontaneous may have come into being after a long and painful birth. All that matters is that the finished poem seem spontaneous. Yeats told us with what difficulty his own poems were written:

> . . . A line will take us hours maybe;
> Yet if it does not seem a moment's thought,
> Our stitching and unstitching has been naught.
> . . . It's certain there is no fine thing
> Since Adam's fall but needs much laboring.

This is the paradox—most writers work hard over their lines to make it seem they have not worked at all. When Keats said that unless poetry came "as naturally as the leaves to a tree, it had better not come at all," by "naturally" he cannot have meant *effortlessly,* as his own much worked-over manuscripts demonstrate.

Ideas suddenly and unaccountably flashing into the light of consciousness are inspirations. We get them in any field in which our minds move with knowledge and experience. They are more often foolish than wise, but even when they are promising, we usually have to work out the details. Poets find that words or lines will suddenly be "given" to them, as if flashed on a mental screen. But they then have to work out the continuity that will complete the poem. Without these given lines, these inspirations, not many poems come into being.

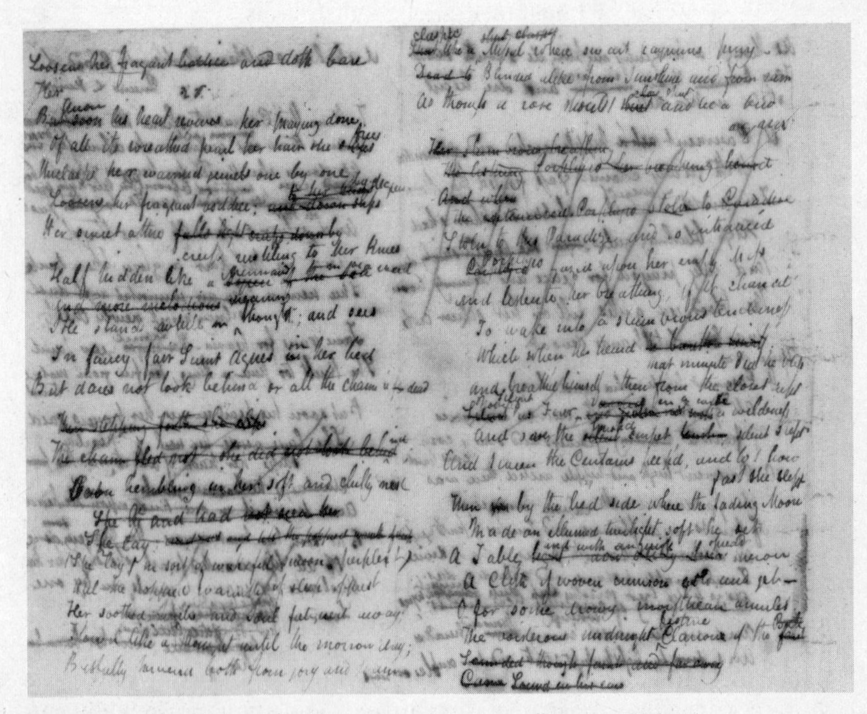

A manuscript of John Keats' "The Eve of St. Agnes," stanzas 24-26

It seems that one cannot *will* to do anything creative, although one can will to bring about conditions favorable to inspiration and can will to work on the inspiration once it comes.

The ratio between inspiration and deliberate effort differs in different artists. Music came easily to Mozart, but not to Beethoven, who had to jot down his ideas, rework them again and again, sometimes completing a theme twenty-five years after the idea for it struck him. His way of composing, compared with Mozart's, was stodgy and plodding, but the music that resulted was no less "inspired." So too with poets. Some work rapidly, some slowly. The number of flashes of inspiration that go into the process may have little to do with the quality of the poem that results.

It should be stressed again that our inspirations are as specialized as our minds are. If our whole bent is toward Romance philology or foot-

ball strategy, we will not come up with inspirations in the field of economic theory. Inspirations follow common-sense rules: we get only the inspirations we are qualified to receive. And unless we have laid the groundwork by conscious effort, there is no inspiration to be hoped for.

Even the members of unspoiled primitive cultures find the writing of poetry difficult. The Eskimo poet Pluvkaq complains that hooking a poem is as difficult as hooking a fish.

I wonder why
My song-to-be that I wish to use,
My song-to-be that I wish to put together,
I wonder why it will not come to me.
At Sioraq it was at a fishing hole in the ice,
I could feel a little trout on the line,
And then it was gone.
I stood jigging.
But why is it so difficult, I wonder?
When summer came and the waters opened, 10
It was then that catching became so hard:
I am not good at hunting.

Pluvkaq (late nineteenth or early twentieth century)

Toujours travailler—always keep on working—was a motto of the sculptor Rodin. The greater the artist (and there are not many exceptions to this), the harder he works. It was Picasso, and not some industrious businessman, who said, "Man invented the alarm clock." A worker in a more popular field, Federico Fellini, told Ray Bradbury that the rumors that he makes up a script as he shoots are "stupid gossip. It's absolutely impossible to improvise. Making a movie is a mathematical operation. It is like sending a missile to the moon. Art is a scientific operation."

"Chance," said Pasteur, "favors the prepared mind." The poet has to condition his mind to produce and handle inspirations. If one has a vocabulary of only a few hundred words, the unconscious has very little to work with. If one has taken little notice of the world around him, his mind will suffer from a poverty of images. If he has not read other poets, he will not know when he is original and when he is not—as if a young physicist, scorning the achievements of the past, were to spend his time reinventing the wheel.

The influence of a well-conditioned conscious mind extends to the unconscious, which continues to work, often more originally and brilliantly, with the patterns we have consciously set up. All the artist's work, before the fact of inspiration, is a way of programing the unconscious along desirable lines.

Malcolm Cowley's description of Hart Crane's writing habits shows that apparently wild bursts of spontaneity were based on months or even years of careful thought.

> There would be a Sunday afternoon party.... Hart would be laughing twice as hard as the rest of us ... he would be drinking twice as much hard cider and contributing more than his share of the crazy metaphors and overblown epithets. Gradually he would fall silent and a little later we would find that he had disappeared....
>
> An hour later ... he would appear in the kitchen or on the croquet court. ... In his hands would be two or three sheets of typewritten manuscript, with words crossed out and new lines scrawled in. "Read that," he would say. "Isn't that the *grrrrea*test poem ever written!" ...
>
> I later discovered that Hart would have been meditating over that particular poem for months or even years, scribbling verses on pieces of paper that he carried in his pockets and meanwhile waiting for the moment of pure inspiration when he could put them all together....
>
> Painfully, perseveringly—and dead sober—Hart would revise his new poem, clarifying its images, correcting its meter and searching through dictionaries and thesauruses for exactly the right word.... Even after the poem had been completed, the manuscript mailed to *Poetry* or the *Dial* and perhaps accepted, he would still have changes to make....[1]

The knowledge of how to make something of our insights is what we call *technique.* In itself it can do little. It would be possible for someone to know everything about the writing of poetry, and yet never manage to write a poem. Technique is only valuable in the service of inspiration or emotion.

Most artists and writers have been passionately concerned with technique, even in what seem to others to be trivial matters. "Trifles,"

[1] From Malcolm Cowley, *Exile's Return* (New York: Viking, 1941), pp. 145–147.

Michelangelo is supposed to have said, "make perfection, and perfection is no trifle." When Frost once digressed into a discussion of some technical point at a reading of his poems, a member of the audience objected: "But Mr. Frost, when you're writing your *beautiful* poems, you can't really be thinking of technical things like that? You can't really like *those*!"

"Like 'em?" Frost growled, "I revel in 'em!"

Dylan Thomas is even more emphatic:

> What I like to do is to treat words as a craftsman does his wood or stone or what-have-you, to hew, carve, mould, coil, polish and plane them into patterns, sequences, sculptures, fugues of sound. . . .
>
> I am a painstaking, conscientious, involved and devious craftsman in words. . . . I use everything and anything to make my poems work and move in the direction I want them to: old tricks, new tricks, puns, portmanteau-words, paradox, allusion, paronomasia, paragram, catachresis, slang, assonantal rhymes, vowel rhymes, sprung rhythm. . . . The inventions and contrivances are all part of the joy that is part of the painful, voluntary work.[2]

Preoccupation with technique can protect a writer against the tyranny of the spontaneous, the zombielike acceptance of absolutely everything—trash and treasure alike—that floats up from the depths of the psyche. It can also encourage the objectivity he needs to judge his own work, a quality not easy to maintain if he lets himself be swept away by the self-indulgence of his own emotions.

After inspiration has struck and has been recorded more or less satisfactorily in a first draft, the poet begins his laborious process of revision. The process is only natural—it assumes that our first thoughts are not always our best ones. In life we often modify the phraseology that first occurred to us—if we have a chance to. We can see how studiously we revise after we have been put down by someone else's clever remark. Perhaps all we can do at the time is mutter something like, "Oh, yeah? Look who's talking!"—not exactly a brilliant comeback. All the way home we may be mulling, "What I *should* have said to that guy was . . . ." As the days go by and we continue to revise, what we should have said gets better and better.

This is exactly what poets are doing when they work over their first thoughts: revision is a what-I-should-have-said process. And even though it relies a great deal on reason and calculation, it can be a very passionate process. Nor is it shutting the door on inspiration. It is merely giving inspiration, which takes its own sweet time, a second chance to strike—and a third, and a fourth, until we feel it is right on target.

Poets, with very few exceptions, take pleasure in the work of revision. The Surrealists revised extensively. D. H. Lawrence said, "It has taken me twenty years to say what I started to say, incoherently, when I was nineteen, in this poem. . . ." E. E. Cummings could exclaim,

[2] From James Scully, *Modern Poets on Modern Poetry* (New York: McGraw-Hill, 1965), pp. 196–197.

rosetree, rosetree
—you're a song to see; whose
every(any)where
opening poems are;
until no small most
miracle is almost

glimpse by wonder
(people of a person)
blossoms the myriad
soul of beatitude
(and from all nothing
gluttons come seething)

each in roguish
(bigger than a wish no)
whom of fragrance
dances a honeydunce;
whirling's a frantic
ego gigantic

out, if stumble
should the brigand, welcome
she'll some another me
(dreamtree; truthtree;
when cannot measure
a now of your treasure)

lovetree! not a
glory you're today but
must(to quite disappear)
three, four, five times declare
dying unfatal—
a heart her each petal

A worksheet of E. E. Cummings—one of the 175 sheets for his nine-stanza "rosetree, rosetree." Numbers to the left of the lines indicate the number of syllables; yet the scansion, in the conventional marks for long and short syllables, shows that the poet was also working with accent. The worksheets also have lists of rhymes, indications of vowel and consonant patterns, and various other charts and graphs. Cummings obviously took tremendous care as he composed his apparently artless poems.

"O sweet spontaneous earth . . . ," but he did not let spontaneity interfere with his own painstaking craftsmanship. Sometimes he wrote one or two hundred versions of a poem before he felt it was right.

Often, lines that look as if they had occurred to the poet in a moment of inspiration turn out to have been revised into their perfection. One example is from Keats' "Ode to a Nightingale":

> The same that oft-times hath
> Charm'd magic casements, opening on the foam
> Of perilous seas, in faery lands forlorn.

The first inspiration was less memorable:

> Charmed the wide casements, opening on the foam
> Of ruthless seas, in faery lands fo'lorn.

Whitman's

> Out of the cradle endlessly rocking

benefited immeasurably from revision. His original inspiration was the toneless

> Out of the rocked cradle . . .

which he varied many ways before he got the simple music he wanted. Whitman, though elsewhere he may have loafed and invited his soul, was a hard worker at his poetry, doing prodigious amounts of revision over the decades.

William Blake is another poet often thought of as inspired, which indeed he claimed to be. "The Authors," he said of his work, "are in Eternity." But an editor familiar with his manuscripts corrects that impression:

> It was Blake's belief . . . that long passages, or even whole poems, were merely transcribed by him from the dictation of spirits. The evidence of extant MSS., however, shows that he himself saw nothing final or absolute in this verbal inspiration, but submitted these writings like any others to such successive changes as at length satisfied his artistic conscience. . . . Blake's meticulous care in composition is everywhere apparent in the poems preserved in rough draft. . . . There we find the first crude version, or single stanza around which his idea was to take shape, followed by alteration on alteration, re-arrangement after re-arrangement, deletions, additions and inversions, until at last the poem as in the case of "The Tiger" attains its perfect form. . . .[3]

Sometimes the poet, in addition to making lesser changes, feels that the whole poem should be reconceived and restructured, as D. H. Lawrence does when he reduces the five stanzas of his early "The Piano" to the three stanzas of "Piano."

[3] From *The Poetical Works of William Blake,* edited by John Sampson (Oxford University Press, 1913).

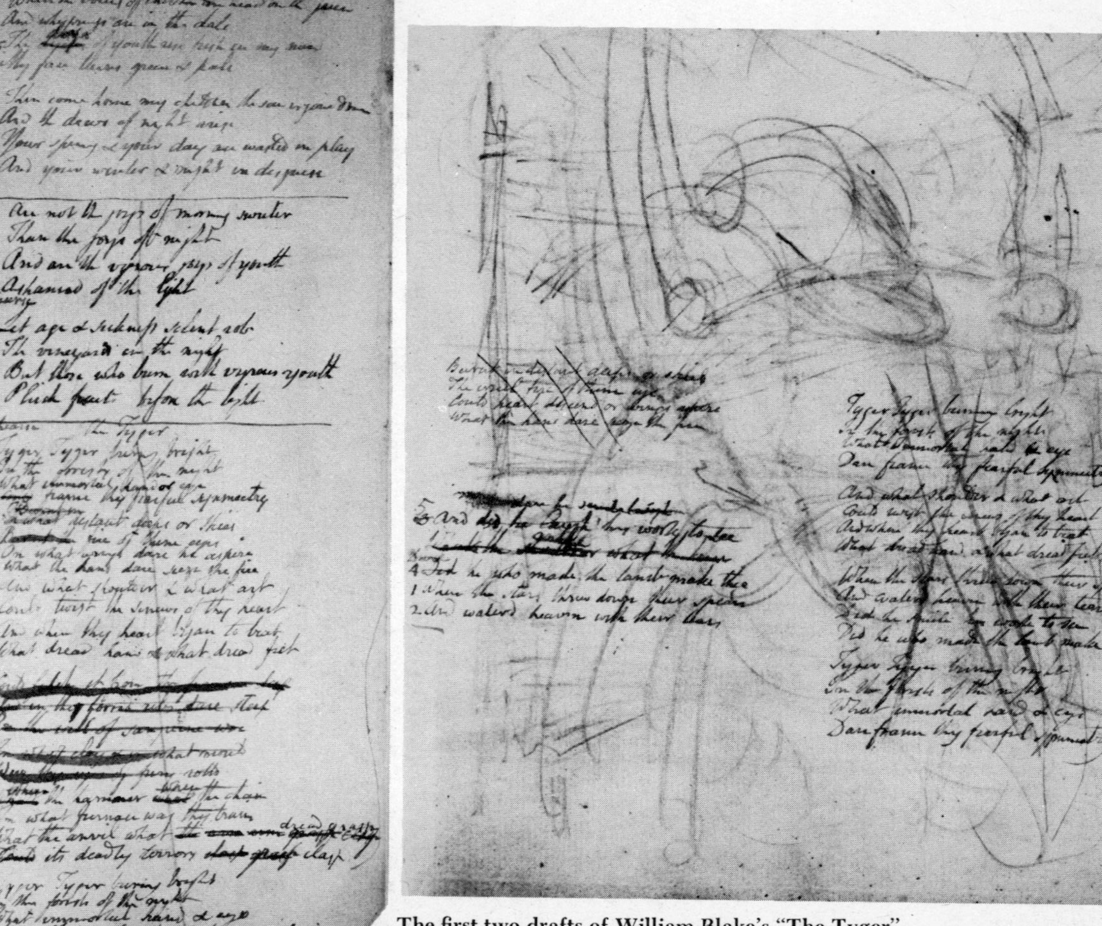

The first two drafts of William Blake's "The Tyger"

THE PIANO

Somewhere beneath that piano's superb sleek black
Must hide my mother's piano, little and brown, with the back
That stood close to the wall, and the front's faded silk both torn,
And the keys with little hollows, that my mother's fingers had worn.

Softly, in the shadows, a woman is singing to me
Quietly, through the years I have crept back to see
A child sitting under the piano, in the boom of the shaking strings
Pressing the little poised feet of the mother who smiles as she sings.

The full throated woman has chosen a winning, living song
And surely the heart that is in me must belong 10
To the old Sunday evenings, when darkness wandered outside
And hymns gleamed on our warm lips, as we watched mother's fingers glide.

Or this is my sister at home in the old front room
Singing love's first surprised gladness, alone in the gloom.
She will start when she sees me, and blushing, spread out her hands
To cover my mouth's raillery, till I'm bound in her shame's heart-spun bands.

A woman is singing me a wild Hungarian air
And her arms, and her bosom, and the whole of her soul is bare,
And the great black piano is clamouring as my mother's never could clamour
And my mother's tunes are devoured of this music's ravaging glamour. 20

D. H. Lawrence

PIANO

Softly, in the dusk, a woman is singing to me;
Taking me back down the vista of years, till I see
A child sitting under the piano, in the boom of the tingling strings
And pressing the small, poised feet of a mother who smiles as she sings.

In spite of myself, the insidious mastery of song
Betrays me back, till the heart of me weeps to belong
To the old Sunday evenings at home, with winter outside
And hymns in the cosy parlour, the tinkling piano our guide.

So now it is vain for the singer to burst into clamour
With the great black piano appassionato. The glamour 10
Of childish days is upon me, my manhood is cast
Down in the flood of remembrance, I weep like a child for the past.

D. H. Lawrence

In the earlier poem the poet, or the character he imagines, is listening to "a wild Hungarian air." The music puts him in mind of a very different kind of music, that of hymns sung at home when he was small enough to sit under the old-fashioned square piano. But the soft music he remembers is swallowed up in the "ravaging glamour" of the wild new music.

In the second version, the childhood memory of music at home is more powerful than the effect of the sexy singer. The poem becomes a lament for the lost innocence of childhood.

If a critical poll were taken, likely enough it would select Yeats as the greatest poet of the twentieth century. No poet ever derived less from inspiration or worked harder at hammering his poems into shape. Yeats found writing an "intense unnatural labor that reduces composition to four or five lines a day." He even said he did much of his work by the critical, rather than the imaginative faculty. We can get some idea of the labor that went into his poetry by looking at the fifth stanza of "Among School Children," which could be summarized as saying: If a mother could see her baby as he will be sixty years later, would all the trouble of his birth seem worthwhile? (Lines 3 and 4 refer to the Platonic notion that the child exists before birth and would like to return to that earlier world unless the memory of it were destroyed by "the drug.")

Yeats' manuscripts show that he started out with a list of possible rhymes for the stanza:

lap	fears	lap
shape	~~tears~~	made
	~~years~~	escape
	~~forth~~ birth	betrayed
	forth	shape
		head

They are obviously not words that just happened to rhyme, as if he were going through the alphabet. The ideas these words stand for are a framework for the way he thought his stanza might develop.

On the two facing pages 420 and 421 we have, on the right-hand page, the clear, simple, and logical lines that finally made up the stanza. The last two lines seem to have come to him easily—or he may have worked hard at them on a manuscript sheet now lost. But the other lines came only after a difficult struggle with alternative versions, printed on the left-hand page (which is mostly a rubble of undistinguished language). Work sheets preliminary to these may well have been lost or destroyed. Yeats may have made many choices in his own head before writing a word down.

Yeats would make further changes as he dictated. He could then go to work on the neatly typed copy, making so many revisions that it would have to be retyped. And so on. If the poem appeared in a magazine, he might further rework it before book publication. Even after the book appeared the revisions continued. Many years after he wrote some of his early poems, he revised them in his later manner—turning "early Yeats" into "late Yeats."

When we see how easily the poem reads (apart from difficulties in the thought) it is hard to remember what must have been the pangs of its birth and the uncertainties of its setting forth.

AMONG SCHOOL CHILDREN

I

I walk through the long schoolroom questioning;
A kind old nun in a white hood replies;
The children learn to cipher and to sing,
To study reading-books and histories,
To cut and sew, be neat in everything
In the best modern way—the children's eyes
In momentary wonder stare upon
A sixty-year-old smiling public man.

II

I dream of a Ledaean body, bent
Above a sinking fire, a tale that she 10
Told of a harsh reproof, or trivial event
That changed some childish day to tragedy—
Told, and it seemed that our two natures blent
Into a sphere from youthful sympathy,
Or else, to alter Plato's parable,
Into the yolk and white of the one shell.

III

And thinking of that fit of grief or rage
I look upon one child or t'other there
And wonder if she stood so at that age—
For even daughters of the swan can share 20
Something of every paddler's heritage—
And had that colour upon cheek or hair,
And thereupon my heart is driven wild:
She stands before me as a living child.

IV

Her present image floats into the mind—
Did Quattrocento finger fashion it
Hollow of cheek as though it drank the wind

---

[9] **Ledaean:** *like that of Leda's daughter, Helen of Troy*
[15] **Plato's parable:** *In a myth that Plato recounts in his* Symposium, *men and women were once united in double bodies, till Zeus, fearing their power, separated them "as you might divide an egg with a hair."*
[19] **she:** *the girl of the "Ledaean body," with whom Yeats had long been in love*
[20] **the swan:** *Zeus in the form of a swan (cf. "Leda and the Swan,"* *p. 62)*
[26] **Quattrocento:** *of the 1400s—the Italian Renaissance*

What mother of a child shrieking the first scream
Of a soul
Of a soul struggling to leave
Degradation of the ———
What mother with a child upon her breast
Shedding there its tears, all the despair
Of the soul betrayed into the flesh
What youthful mother, rocking on her lap

A fretful thing that knows itself betrayed
Still knowing that it is betrayed[?]
Still half remembering that it [is] betrayed
A thing, the ~~oblivious honey has~~ generative honey had betrayed

And struggles with vain clamor to escape
And that shrieks out and struggles to escape
And that must sleep, ~~or~~ shriek struggle to escape

Before its memory and apprehension fade
Before its the memories of its freedom fade
As its drugged memories gleam or fade
As it
As still but half drugged memories decide
As its drugged memories may decide
Where some brief memories or the drug decide
~~As flitting~~ As sudden memories or the drug decide

Would think—[if] it came before her in a vision
Would think—had she ~~foreknown~~ foreknowledge of that shape
Would think her son could she foreknow that shape
Would think her son, ~~could she foreknow~~ did she but see that shape

~~The image~~ What the child would be at sixty years
Her son with sixty winters on his head
With maybe sixty winters on upon his head
With sixty or more winters upon his head
With sixty or more winters on ~~his~~ its head

What youthful mother, a shape upon her lap

Honey of generation had betrayed,

And that must sleep, shriek, struggle to escape

As recollection or the drug decide,

Would think her son, did she but see that shape

With sixty or more winters on its head,

A compensation for the pang of his birth,
Or the uncertainty of his setting forth?

And took a mess of shadows for its meat?
And I though never of Ledaean kind
Had pretty plumage once—enough of that, 30
Better to smile on all that smile, and show
There is a comfortable kind of old scarecrow.

V

What youthful mother, a shape upon her lap
Honey of generation had betrayed,
And that must sleep, shriek, struggle to escape
As recollection or the drug decide,
Would think her son, did she but see that shape
With sixty or more winters on its head,
A compensation for the pang of his birth,
Or the uncertainty of his setting forth? 40

VI

Plato thought nature but a spume that plays
Upon a ghostly paradigm of things;
Solider Aristotle played the taws
Upon the bottom of a king of kings;
World-famous golden-thighed Pythagoras
Fingered upon a fiddle-stick or strings
What a star sang and careless Muses heard:
Old clothes upon old sticks to scare a bird.

VII

Both nuns and mothers worship images,
But those the candles light are not as those 50
That animate a mother's reveries,
But keep a marble or a bronze repose.
And yet they too break hearts—O Presences
That passion, piety or affection knows,
And that all heavenly glory symbolise—
O self-born mockers of man's enterprise:

VIII

Labour is blossoming or dancing where
The body is not bruised to pleasure soul,
Nor beauty born out of its own despair,
Nor blear-eyed wisdom out of midnight oil. 60
O chestnut-tree, great-rooted blossomer,
Are you the leaf, the blossom or the bole?
O body swayed to music, O brightening glance,
How can we know the dancer from the dance?

W. B. Yeats

---

[43] **taws:** *whip. Aristotle was the tutor of Alexander the Great.*

Exercises and Diversions

A. A. E. Housman has this to say about the composition of his "I Hoed and Trenched and Weeded": "Two of the stanzas, I do not say which, came into my head, just as they are printed. . . . A third stanza came with a little coaxing after tea. One more was needed, but it did not come: I had to turn to and compose it myself, and that was a laborious business. I wrote it thirteen times, and it was more than a twelvemonth before I got it right."

Can you guess which two stanzas came easily, which came with a little coaxing, and which came with difficulty?

I HOED AND TRENCHED AND WEEDED

I hoed and trenched and weeded,
  And took the flowers to fair:
I brought them home unheeded;
  The hue was not the wear.

So up and down I sow them
  For lads like me to find,
When I shall lie below them,
  A dead man out of mind.

Some seed the birds devour,
  And some the season mars,
But here and there will flower
  The solitary stars,

And fields will yearly bear them
  As light-leaved spring comes on,
And luckless lads will wear them
  When I am dead and gone.

A. E. Housman

B. 1. In the twenty-five or more years that FitzGerald spent on his five editions of *The Rubáiyát* (p. 262) he tried many of the stanzas several ways. Here are three versions of his original stanza XII. Can you see a progressive improvement?

"How sweet is mortal Sovranty!"—think some:
Others—"How blest the Paradise to come!"
  Ah, take the Cash in hand and waive the Rest;
Oh, the brave Music of a *distant* Drum!

Some for the Glories of This World; and some
Sigh for the Prophet's Paradise to come;
  Ah, take the Cash, and let the promise go,
Nor heed the music of a distant Drum!

Some for the Glories of This World; and some
Sigh for the Prophet's Paradise to come;
  Ah, take the Cash, and let the Credit go,
Nor heed the rumble of a distant Drum!

2. Is there a progressive improvement in the changes made in what was originally stanza LXXIV? (No one holds that *all* revisions are improvements.)

Ah, Moon of my Delight, who know'st no wane,
The Moon of Heav'n is rising once again:
  How oft hereafter rising shall she look
Through this same Garden after me—in vain!

But see! The rising Moon of Heav'n again—
Looks for us, Sweet-heart, through the quivering Plane:
  How oft hereafter rising will she look
Among those leaves—for one of us in vain!

Yon rising Moon that looks for us again—
How oft hereafter will she wax and wane;
  How oft hereafter rising look for us
Through this same Garden—and for *one* in vain!

C. Look closely at the two versions of D. H. Lawrence's poem about the piano, asking yourself such questions as these:

1. Why is the description of the mother's old worn piano omitted in the later version?
2. The nightclub singer is a brilliant figure. Does not the later version suffer by making no mention of her?
3. Why is the original fourth stanza, pleasant in itself, omitted in the later version?
4. Why are "shaking strings" changed to "tingling strings"?
5. Why is "darkness" changed to "winter"?

D. Here is an example of "early Yeats" turned into "late Yeats." In what do the differences chiefly consist? Imagery? Emotion? Diction? Rhythm? Form? Does the meaning change?

THE LAMENTATION OF THE OLD PENSIONER

(*1890 version*)

I had a chair at every hearth,
  When no one turned to see,
With 'Look at that old fellow there,
  And who may he be?'
And therefore do I wander now,
  And the fret lies on me.

The road-side trees keep murmuring.
  Ah, wherefore murmur ye,
As in the old days long gone by,
  Green oak and poplar tree?
The well-known faces are all gone:
  And the fret lies on me.

(*1925 version*)

Although I shelter from the rain
Under a broken tree,
My chair was nearest to the fire
In every company
That talked of love or politics,
Ere Time transfigured me.

Though lads are making pikes again
For some conspiracy,
And crazy rascals rage their fill
At human tyranny, 10
My contemplations are of Time
That has transfigured me.

There's not a woman turns her face
Upon a broken tree,
And yet the beauties that I loved
Are in my memory;
I spit into the face of Time
That has transfigured me.

W. B. Yeats

E. Pick out something you wrote for this class. Along what lines do you think it could be revised? Work at revising it.

postscript

Poems Without Voice 23

concrete and other

The nature of poetry is based on the nature of man, a union of body and mind that work together. Our discussion of poetry has been organized in accordance with our nature. We perceive by images, which stir us to love or hate or other feelings. We express and share those feelings by means of words, with all their sounds and rhythms. The mind, which has been participating in these interests, makes its appraisal and confers a form.

The last section is called a Postscript because it does not follow, as if in order of climax, from the rest of the book. It is about certain techniques which we may think of as new and contemporary—though some of them are very old. They are not by any means what all the centuries of poetry have been leading up to, nor do they necessarily show where it is going. They deserve attention because they are of interest in themselves and because they tell us something about the spirit of our times—but it is important to keep them in perspective. And particularly important not to mistake their novelty for tested worth.

Readers of poetry who feel at home with works ranging from those of Homer to those of T. S. Eliot might be taken aback when they first see a poem like the one at the top of the next page.

The writer (or designer) of what he himself calls a "constellation" is a Swiss founder of a recent poetic movement, or constellation of movements, generally called **concretism.** Although concrete poets differ among themselves in many ways, what they have in common is a concern with the physical appearance of poetry—not primarily with ideas or emotions, not with language as we ordinarily use it, but with the "reduced language" of the word itself as it appears on the page or elsewhere.

WIND

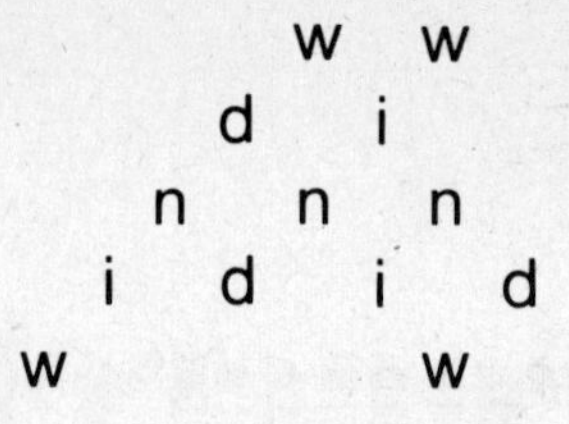

Eugen Gomringer (b. 1924)

Gomringer may not be telling us anything about wind, but he is showing us windiness in action—as far as this can be done by the black and white of letters on a page. We see the wind moving in four directions. Or even more than four. Three times after we have moved through *wi* we are free to veer to either of two *n*'s; after an *n*, we can sometimes almost reverse directions to the *d*—so that a "wind" that started moving southeast can come about and end up by blowing northwest. One could find, if he wished, suggested images in the neat row of *n*'s in the center of the poem. Are they buildings? Square-rigged ships in the wind? Little recurrences of *in* are conspicuous too, as if to remind us that everything we have exists in the wind-world of the poem. We may even find other ghost-words lurking among the letters.

Poets have long been taking an interest in how their work looks on the page. The neat structuring of Thomas Hardy's poems has been attributed to his architectural training. When Whitman's first edition of *Leaves of Grass* was published in 1855, the very appearance of the book demanded attention. Whitman, who was trained as a printer and had worked for some years at that trade, seems to have designed the book himself and to have set some of the type for it. He apparently wanted his page to have the same qualities that the poetry itself had, wanted it to look generous, exuberant, unfenced, far-horizoned. Lengthy as his lines were, most of them could sprawl across the page unconfined. On the original cover of the first edition, "imaged words" were used, words that were themselves little pictures of their meaning —grassy, plantlike, with roots and tubers below, leaves and blossoms above.

For centuries before Whitman, letters of the alphabet had been metamorphosed into trees, flowers, animals, fishes, skeletons, posed human bodies, buildings—almost anything. Victor Hugo is only one of many who meditated on the way letters, so reminiscent of shapes in nature, are like little concrete poems. "Have you noticed how Y is a picturesque letter symbolical of endless things? A tree is a Y; the fork of two roads is a Y; the confluence of two rivers is a Y; the head of a donkey or bullock is a Y; a supplicant raising his arms to the sky is a Y. . . . Letters were first of all signs, and all signs were pictorial images

Title from cover of the 1855 edition of *Leaves of Grass*

before that. Human society, the world, the whole of man is in the alphabet. . . ."

Larger and more complicated images can be made by arranging words or groups of letters. The kind of patience needed to carve the Lord's Prayer on the head of a pin can be used to make a typewritten reproduction of da Vinci's "Last Supper" if one is so minded.

Mr. Hollander's elegant picture-poem (next page) looks experimental, especially to viewers unaware that such poems were done in Greek by Simmias of Rhodes over two thousand years ago. There has probably not been a moment in history in which someone—in India, in China, in Germany—was not patiently working out his picture-poem.

"Machine poetry," especially "typewriter poetry," has been favored by many of the concrete poets. It used to be that poets would invoke their lyres or their lutes when they had something to say. Now it is more likely to be their Olivetti, even when they mean to protest against the increasing mechanization of our culture. The English poet D. J. Enright has protested in a typewriter poem, or peom, of his own:

> The typeriter is crating
> A revlootion in peotry
> Pishing back the frontears
> And apening up fresh feels
> Unherd of by Done or Bleak . . .
>
> TAB e or not TAB e
> i.e. the ?

Instead of "Anyone can do it; you too can be a poet," his sarcastic machine comes out with,

> Anywan can od it
> U 2 can b a
> Tepot

and concludes,

> The trypewiter is cretin
> A revultion in peotry

SWAN AND SHADOW

Dusk
Above the
water hang the
loud
flies
Here
O so
gray
then
What A pale signal will appear
When Soon before its shadow fades
Where Here in this pool of opened eye
In us No Upon us As at the very edges
of where we take shape in the dark air
this object bares its image awakening
ripples of recognition that will
brush darkness up into light
even after this bird this hour both drift by atop the perfect sad instant now
already passing out of sight
toward yet-untroubled reflection
this image bears its object darkening
into memorial shades Scattered bits of
light No of water Or something across
water Breaking up No Being regathered
soon Yet by then a swan will have
gone Yes out of mind into what
vast
pale
hush
of a
place
past
sudden dark as
if a swan
sang

John Hollander (b. 1929)

But Hollander is far more scrupulous than writers of "peotry." For one thing, he has set himself very strict rules: no word division to make the lines come out correctly, no cheating with the typewriter's rigid spaces.

To decide whether Hollander's poem is good as a poem, and not merely as a typographical exploit, we might have to write it out more conventionally, supplying, mostly by guesswork, punctuation that might correspond to the author's intention:

Dusk. Above the water hang the loud flies
Here O so gray, then—
What? A pale signal will appear.
When? Soon, before its shadow fades.
Where? Here in this pool of opened eye . . . .

Such a poem may require as much work on the reader's part as on the writer's.

A much simpler poem that uses typography expressively is this one:

ON APIS THE PRIZEFIGHTER

TO APIS THE BOXER
HIS GRATEFUL OPPONENTS HAVE ERECTED
THIS STATUE
HONORING HIM
WHO NEVER BY ANY CHANCE HURT ONE OF THEM

Lucilius (c. 180–102 B.C.)
(Translated by Dudley Fitts)

The Greek original is not a pattern poem. It was the translator's idea to use the spaced capitals so that they look like both an actual inscription and the pedestal on which it appears.

The Greek word for pattern poetry is *technopaignia,* which means something like *playing around with technique.* There is still an element of play or fun in concrete poetry. But there is also a feeling that we may need this kind of poetry to express the sensibility of the new age of space in which we live. Particularly in France, some kinds of concrete poetry are called "spatialist," in part because they belong to the age of space and in part because they use space, time, structure, and energy in their presentation.

The use of space itself as an expressive element is probably to be credited to Mallarmé, whose "Un coup de dés" (A Throw of the Dice), published in 1897, was republished with the spatial effects he intended in 1914. Mallarmé makes use of typography, white space, and layout in his two-page spreads. The text of his poem, which is about a shipwreck, lurches unevenly from the top of one page to the bottom of the next to give a sense of the ship itself wallowing in heavy seas; white spaces represent the gulf below and the sky above.

In 1914 Guillaume Apollinaire, the French poet of Polish and Italian-Swiss parentage, was at work on his *Calligrammes,* which imitated by designs in typography or handwriting the shapes of objects mentioned —little houses, neckties, watches, hearts, mirrors, automobiles, etc. A poem about rain has the letters streaming down the page instead of going straight across in unrainlike lines. Apollinaire thought of these shapes as leading to "visual lyricism." He thought too of an art form that would be a synthesis of literature, music, and painting.

Any of us could use typography expressively. We could write that we moved v e r y s l o w l y, or moved quickasawink, or jumped o^{ve}r something, or crawled u$_{nde}$r it, or would like to be far away, or felt like SCREAMing. Or we could make our spelling dramatic by writing "addding" or "subtrcting" or di vi ding," or by using such expressive misspellings as "mispelings" or "innacurate" or "warmpth" or "laxadaisical." Or by referring to our date "lassed night" or to something that worries us and will occur "neck's week." Some of these are analogies; some are puns.

E. E. Cummings has occasionally made systematic use of typographical puns and analogies.

(IM)C-A-T(MO)

(im)c-a-t(mo)
b,i;l:e

FallleA
ps!fl
OattumblI

sh?dr
IftwhirlF

(Ul)(lY)
&&&

away wanders:exact 10
ly;as if
not
hing had,ever happ
ene

D

E. E. Cummings

Most of this is visual poetry; there is no use trying to pronounce it. The first two lines show us an immobile cat stretched out, as the word "c-a-t" itself is stretched out by its hyphens. If we were to look at the drowsing cat, we would see it all at once; we would not first see the cat and then its immobility, so that we could say, "The cat is immobile." Cummings breaks up not only the order of words but their integrity by having the "c-a-t" immersed in the middle of "immobile" to show that, in the order of perception, neither comes before the other. The little globes of parentheses at each end of the line even look like a stretched out cat—head at one end, curve of haunch and tail at the other. In line 2, the rest of "immobile" is brought to a stop, made immobile, by the braking action of the punctuation marks, increasing in strength after each letter. Then, from its shelf or sofa, the cat "FallleAps!"—its fall turning immediately into a conscious leap, with the capital *A* showing energy or excitement (as well as a suddenly hunched spine) and the three *lll*'s together showing how smoothly "fall" turns into "leap." Confused flurry or animal noises ("Oo*ps! fl*oor!"?) may be suggested by "ps!fl" as the cat is seen to "flOat" in what could be a tumbling way, so gracefully that it seems to drift as it whirls fully until its feet are beneath it—or perhaps falls "whirlfully," or perhaps both. "(Ul)(lY)" is a four-footed cluster of curves, like the whirling cat. All these things are happening at once; it takes us longer to read the poem than it takes the cat to fall, though Cummings is doing what he can to make things happen as close to all at once as is possible in words. The "&&&" looks like the cat, landed and sitting a moment, shaking itself. Then the poem slows down as the cat casually and langorously strolls away, a kind of gathering speed indicated by punctuation marks now in reverse order, to show acceleration rather than braking. The division of "exactly" and "nothing" stresses the *exact*ness of the one and the negative quality (the *not*) of the other. The four identical, soft *a*-sounds—"exact," "as," "had," and "happ"—are like an echo of the cat's padding off. With the breaking up of the words, they are a guide to the way we pace our reading. The capital letter at the end of the poem, instead of at the beginning, again suggests the simultaneousness of the event: beginning and ending are so close one might confuse them. Since the last lines of the poem are readable, we sound the *D* more crisply ("hap-pen-*duh*!"), with an emphasis of surprise and finality—that's *that*!

Cummings would not have thought of himself as belonging to any "school" of poetry. But his poem, in making use of the look of words and letters on the page, is like that of the concrete poets. The poems that follow are more typical of their work.

Here the letters that spell the word "lilac" are arranged to look like what they mean—a typical "concrete" procedure. Something like an optical illusion in the whirling letters gives a quivering vivacity to the composition, which seems to stir with life as we look at it.

Concrete poetry developed during the early fifties in Switzerland, Brazil, Germany, Sweden, Czechoslovakia, France, Scotland, and elsewhere. This internationalism, attractive to space-age poets, is made easier by the attitude to language the poets share. Concern with the

LILAC

Mary Ellen Solt (b. 1920)

word, with the letter, and even with nonletters does much to break down language barriers that restrict other kinds of poetry.

One does not have to know much German to understand this apple-worm poem, which uses the standard concretist device of drawing a little picture in which the spelled out names of things are like their appearance.

Though Novák is Czechoslovakian, his poem (opposite) is international. The word, meaning *glory* in several languages, is part of a well-known Latin phrase, often set to music, translated as "Glory to God in the highest." No religious allusion need be understood here. The word dramatizes its exultation by the way one of its letters takes off and soars into the upper space of the page. An *O*, looking like the sun or a full moon or perhaps a balloon, is the most appropriate letter to be sent aloft.

In another motion poem, by Mayer, the English word is more graphic than the poet's native *Öl* would have been. By using letters that are perfect circles or straight lines he gives us a very oily poem, all bubbly and dripping. Each letter is used twenty-six times, but nowhere do the letters making up the word "oil" come together. The poem gives us lots of oiliness, but no oil.

The poem on p. 436, active in a different way, is the work of a leading American concretist.

PATTERN POEM WITH AN ELUSIVE INTRUDER

pfelApfelApfelApte
felApfelApfelApfelApfelA
felApfelApfelApfelApfelApfe
ApfelApfelApfelApfelApfelApf
pfelApfelApfelApfelApfelApfel
lApfelApfelApfelApfelApfelApfe
pfelApfelApfelApfelApfelApfelA
ApfelApfelApfelApfelApfelApfe
felApfelApfelApfelApfelApfel
pfelApfelApfelApfelApfelAp
lApfelApfelApfelWurmAp
elApfelApfelApfelApfel
pfelApfelApfelApfel
felApfelApfelA
felApfel

Reinhard Döhl (b. 1934)

O

GL RIA

Ladislav Novák (b. 1925)

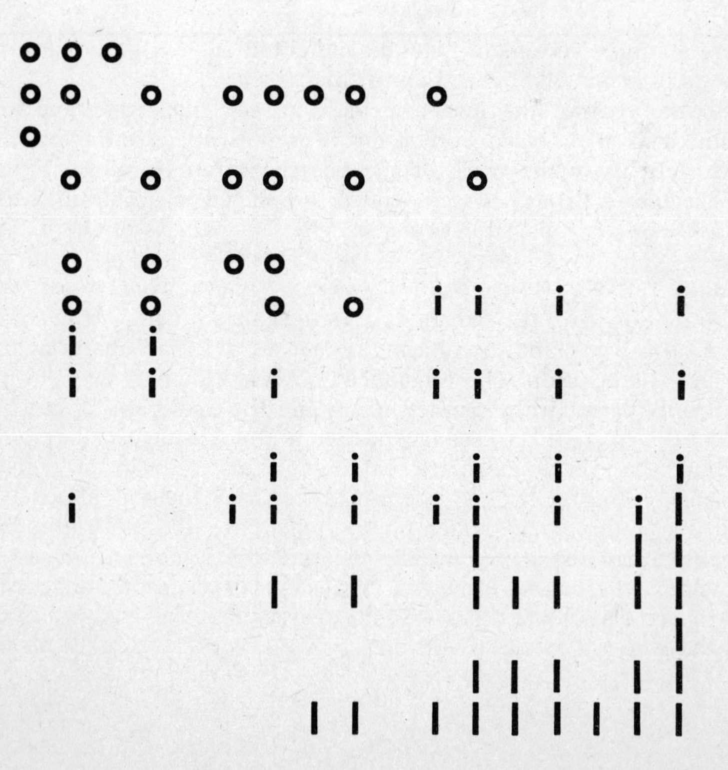

Hansjörg Mayer (b. 1943)

LIKE ATTRACTS LIKE

like attracts like
like attracts like
like attracts like
like attracts like
like attracts like
like attracts like
like attracts like
likeattractslike
likeattractslike
likattraclike
liketraclike
likeralike
likelike

Emmett Williams (b. 1925)

Here a simple statement is made and acted out by the typography. We are *shown* how "like" is drawn to "like."

Spatial poetry, "destined to explore space," likes to escape from the boundaries of the page. Sometimes it even escapes from paper to other materials, as in the work of the Scotsman Ian Hamilton Finlay. His "Fisherman's Cross," a memorial to be placed in a church, was made of *real* concrete, possibly to suggest the ruggedness of the fisherman's life.

With Finlay's "Green Waters" we come back to poetry for the page. Here he has used the names of actual Scottish fishing trawlers rather as an artist working in collage uses pieces of "real" material to make up his composition. The tension in "Green Waters," says the poet, is "not only between the printed poem and the 'real names,' but between it and the conventional sea-lyric which it almost suggests."

Since the pretty names are real, having turned up in the registries of various fishing ports, the poem that includes them is almost what is called a "found poem." Such poems, which are like the "found objects" of the Surrealists, are already existing texts, not meant as poems, which are discovered in news items, menu descriptions, ads, graffiti, or anywhere else. Sometimes the discovered material is simply arranged on the page to look like a poem, as in the *Pop Poems* of Ronald Gross (p. 438).

FISHERMAN'S CROSS

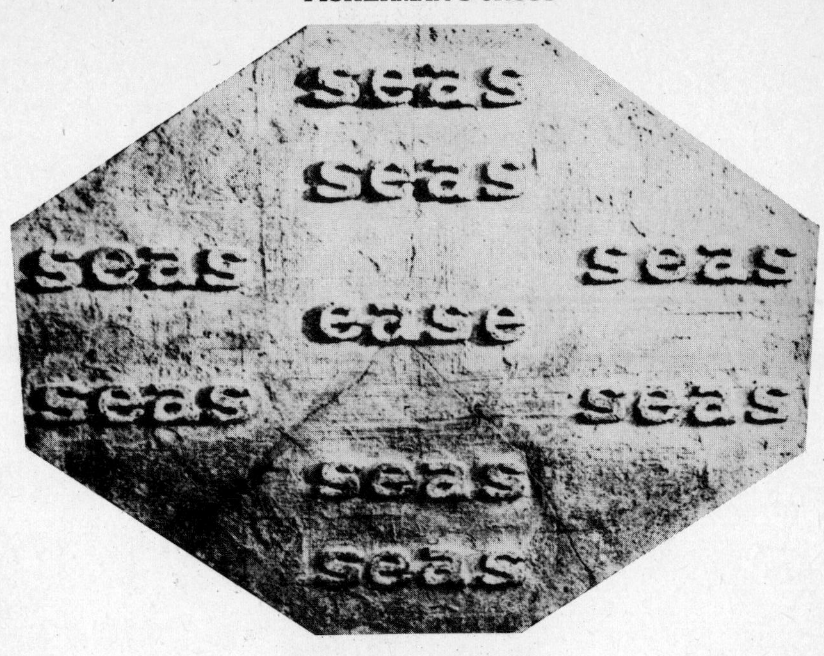

Ian Hamilton Finlay (b. 1925)

GREEN WATERS

Green Waters
Blue Spray
Grayfish

Anna T
Karen B
Netta Croan

Constant Star
Daystar
Starwood

Starlit Waters
Moonlit Waters
Drift

Ian Hamilton Finlay

BARBIE-DOLL GOES TO COLLEGE

Now Barbie's
a co-ed!
Easy-to-assemble
college
includes
Dormitory,
Sweet Shoppe,
Stadium,
Drive-In Movie
and campus scenes, 10
plus exciting
furnishings
and accessories.
All in sturdy,
colorful
chipboard.
Compact, with
convenient
carrying handle.
Folds 20
neatly
away.

Ronald Gross (b. 1935)

Even a reading of the telephone book, with its more than Tolstoyan cast of characters, would probably turn up groups of lines that would read like little poems.

Many of the texts produced by computers programed to write "poetry" seem to be playing at the game of the exquisite corpse:

> Broccoli is often blind . . .
>
> Communism is more porcelain than albino gold . . .
>
> Many whales have broth all day . . .
>
> At lunchtime he looks like bold jelly . . .
>
> It was dirtiest who bleeds behind the piano . . .
>
> Sob suddenly, the bongos are moving . . .

Such lines have the charm of the unexpected, the irrational; we can always imagine a kind of supersense beyond their nonsense. Some artists in various media have been interested in the kind of composition they would call "aleatory" (from the Latin *alea,* which means *dice* or *dice game*). In aleatory composition (which is like the games of the Surrealists) what is done is determined by chance. One might begin "The nightingale . . ." and then open a dictionary at random and take the first verb and noun his eye falls on: "The nightingale melts poverty." Anyone can write aleatory poetry by taking the framework of any sentence, as we described in talking about the exquisite corpse, and filling in the blanks by picking words at random.

A form of concrete poetry not always recognized as such is the poetry reading. Just as a poet like Finlay uses concrete or glass to add expressiveness to the words of the poem, so the poetry reader uses his own personality, his own flesh, voice, costume, "image," and life style to give a resonance to his work which the words alone may not have. The personality can be more impressive than the poem—though this is a distinction hard to keep in mind when we are at a poetry reading. It is hard too for the average listener to know what is poetry and what is show-biz. The English poet-painter-musician Adrian Henri has written action-poems that involve audience as well as poet. For one of these, bags of potato chips are distributed in advance to the audience; the "poem" consists of poet and audience eating the chips together as quickly and noisily as possible. Such happenings help us to keep in perspective the essential frivolity of much that passes for *avant garde* culture. No one can believe that this marks an evolutionary advance—that the laborious triumphs of Shakespeare and Milton and Yeats were only a preparation for the crackling of potato chips in the chomping mouths.

Experiments toward the "total poem" continue. Verses have been printed in ink of several colors, or in scented ink. Some books are accompanied by a little record of the poet's own voice. Recently "a poetry magazine to end poetry magazines" began "publishing" poetry on tape, with bi-monthly twin-cassette issues. Vagn Steen, the Danish poet, has published a book whose title means *Write It Yourself*, in which the pages are all blank.

Some of these experiments are serious, some are jokes and giggles. From most of them we can go back happily to such poems of simple human passion as "Western Wind" on the next page.

If we look at the manuscript of that song-poem, we see that the writer became briefly a concrete poet and had his little joke. The highest and most prominent note in the music is the note over the surprise-word "bed." In the notation of the time it would have looked like this ⊢⊣ . But the writer drew it, hardly by accident, like this ⊢⊣ .

But that is not why we remember the poem. Such effects are like doodlings on the margin of poetry. As Wallace Stevens said of the kind of work that makes use of small letters for capitals, eccentric line-endings, and peculiar punctuation, "These have nothing to do with being alive."

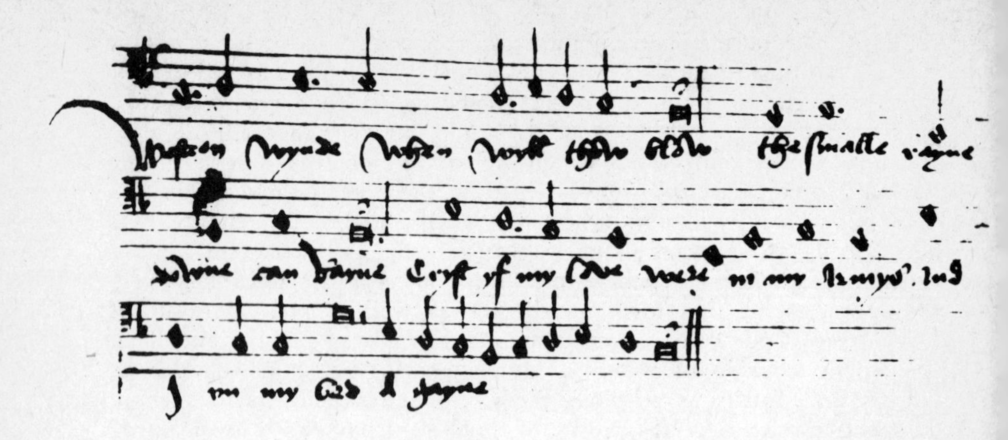

Words and Music of "Western Wind" in the early sixteenth-century manuscript

Exercises and Diversions

A. 1. Concrete poems, according to Eugen Gomringer, should be "as easily understood as signs in airports or traffic signs." Is that true of the concrete poems we have read?

2. Why are we more likely to understand them at a glance than traditional poetry? Is this a proof of their superiority?

3. A good poem, it is often said, is something we can go back to again and again. Probably we even find new meanings as we continue to read it. Does this seem equally true of the concrete poems you have read?

B. Robert Frost's "Dust of Snow" (p. 150) might be turned into a concrete poem of the sort on p. 441.

Using a typewriter or printing by hand, what kind of concrete poem could you make out of one or part of one of the following poems: "Western Wind" (p. 5), "Rattler, Alert" (p. 20), "The Tyger" (p. 112), "The Eel" (p. 324), "Me up at does" (p. 329), "The Dance" (p. 283), "To a Fat Lady Seen from the Train" (p. 369)?

C. 1. What short poem of those we have read do you think would gain in expressiveness if rearranged on the page so as to make use of typography, layout, white space? Try to rewrite it along these lines.

2. Write out Cummings' "(im)c-a-t(mo)" in conventional English. Can you reproduce many of the effects? Is much lost?

D. Do whichever of the following would seem most interesting:

1. Make up your own "concrete" alphabet in which the shape of each letter reminds you of some object.
2. Write a pattern poem which has the shape of the object it is written about.
3. Write a concrete poem that dramatizes action.
4. Find a "found poem" in a newspaper item, an ad, a menu, the telephone book, on a billboard, or anywhere words are used. Will slight changes improve it?
5. Invent a new way of writing an aleatory poem.

w

t
t
T
rrrr T rr   C   o
T
rrr T rrrr   R
T
T
T   S
rrrrrrrrrr T
T rrrrrrrr   n
T
T   o
rrrrrrr T   o
T   o
T
T rrrrrrrrrr   o
T
T rr   o
rrrrr T   o
T   o
T rrrrrrrr   o
rrr T   W
T   !
E E
EEE
E EE   (me) = (ME!)

Index of Poets and Poems

(Page numbers immediately following a poet's name refer to extracts rather than complete poems.)

Index of First Lines

Index of Principal Terms and Topics

Alternate Index of Poems

In this book, poems occur where they do because they are relevant to the topic under discussion. But most poems are equally relevant to many other topics. Ideally, instructors and other readers will do a fair amount of cross-plowing in covering the book. When a new topic comes up, it should be illustrated and tested not only by poems in its chapter, but by poems already familiar from other chapters. New poems should be considered not only in the light of the topic under discussion, but of all the topics handled earlier. With such concepts as *metaphor* or *sound* or *rhythm* in mind, we can look at any poem. Certain combinations, we can see instantly, will have no meaning: there is no point in juxtaposing the concept *sonnet* and the poem "Western Wind."

The Alternative Index provides only suggested readings; there are many other possibilities.

Poems are not like IBM cards being sorted; they may not fall neatly into one proper slot. Nor are the slots themselves fixed and certain. Many terms overlap: what is *metaphor* from one point of view is *symbol* from another; from yet a third it may be *analogy*. A poem may be prevailingly dactylic and yet have lines that in themselves seem anapestic or otherwise "undecidable."

A few chapters are omitted from the index because additional examples are not available or would throw little significant light. Poems considered in the main discussion of a topic or taken up in the exercises are generally not listed under their topic in this index. Poems like "Lycidas" or "Out of the Cradle Endlessly Rocking," which illustrate a great many features of poetry, are not cited.

2. What's It Like? Simile and Metaphor

3. The Broken Coin: The Use of Symbol

4. Ways of Seeing: With Some Figures of Speech

5. Binocular Vision: "Antipoetry," Paradox, Irony

6. With Naked Foot: The Withheld Image

8. True Color and False: Emotion and Sentimentality

10. Less Is More: Lean Language, Fat Language

11. Gold in the Ore: The Sounds of English

12. Working with Gold: The Devices of Sound

14. Waves? Corpuscles? The Nature of Rhythm

15. The Dancer and the Dance: The Play of Rhythms

17. The Shape of Thought: We Go A-Sentencing

19. Dealer's Choice: The Forms of Verse

Couplets

Quatrains

Ottava Rima

21. The Exquisite Corpse: Poetry and Uncommon Sense

Uncommon Sense

23. Poems without Voice: Concrete and Other

ABOUT THE AUTHOR

John Frederick Nims was born in Muskegon, Michigan in 1913. He received his M.A. from the University of Notre Dame and his Ph.D. in Comparative Literature from the University of Chicago. He has taught poetry and workshops in the writing of poetry at Notre Dame, the University of Illinois, the University of Toronto, and Harvard and is presently teaching at the University of Florida. He has also been a Visiting Professor at the universities of Florence and Madrid. Professor Nims is the author of four books of poetry—*The Iron Pastoral, A Fountain in Kentucky, Knowledge of the Evening,* and *Of Flesh and Bone*—which have brought him awards from the National Foundation for the Arts and Humanities and The American Academy of Arts and Letters. His *Knowledge of the Evening* was a National Book Award Nominee. Professor Nims has also published several books of translations, including *Sappho to Valéry: Poems in Translation* and *The Poems of St. John of the Cross.* On the staff of *Poetry* for several years, he spent one year as its Visiting Editor. Professor Nims has also been on the staff of many writers' conferences, including the one at Bread Loaf, Vermont, where he served for over 10 years.